THE GUITAR PICKUP
THE START OF YOUR SOUND HANDBOOK

THE GUITAR PICKUP HANDBOOK
THE START OF YOUR SOUND

Dave Hunter

THE GUITAR PICKUPS HANDBOOK
THE START OF YOUR SOUND

by Dave Hunter

A BACKBEAT BOOK
First edition 2008
Published by Backbeat Books
(an imprint of Hal Leonard Corporation)
19 West 21st Street,
New York, NY 10010, USA
www.backbeatbooks.com

Devised and produced for Backbeat Books by
Outline Press Ltd
2A Union Court, 20-22 Union Road,
London SW4 6JP, England
www.jawbonepress.com

ISBN: 978-0-87930-931-2

Text copyright © Dave Hunter. Volume copyright © 2008 Outline Press Ltd. All rights reserved. No part of this book may be reproduced in any form without written permission, except by a reviewer quoting brief passages in a review. For more information you must contact the publisher.

EDITOR: Robert Webb
DESIGN: Paul Cooper Design

Origination and print by Colorprint (Hong Kong)

08 09 10 11 12   5 4 3 2 1

CONTENTS

6 INTRODUCTION	**110** OTHER GUITAR AND PICKUP MAKERS	**184** MEET THE MAKERS: INTERVIEWS
10 THE DEVELOPMENT OF THE PICKUP	Alembic	Kent Armstrong
	Tom Anderson Guitarworks	Joe Barden
	Kent Armstrong	Larry DiMarzio and Steve Blucher
24 THE ANATOMY OF THE PICKUP	Joe Barden	Seymour Duncan
The Invisible Power	Bare Knuckle	Fender's Mike Eldred
Strings	Burns	Lindy Fralin
Magnet Type and Structure	Carvin	Jason Lollar
Differently Sized and Structured Pickups	Danelectro/Silvertone	
Different Types of Coils	Dearmond	
Measurements and Common Specifications	DiMarzio	**249** Pickup Tone Chart
	Seymour Duncan	**250** CD Notes and Track Listing
	EMG	**252** Index
	Lindy Fralin	**256** Acknowledgements
48 MANUFACTURERS' PROFILES – THE 'BIG FOUR'	G&L	
Rickenbacker	Guild	
Gibson	Harmonic Design	
Fender	TV Jones	
Gretsch	Kinman	
	Lace	
	Bill Lawrence (Wildeusa, Keystone)	
	Jason Lollar	
	PRS	
	Rio Grande	
	J.M. Rolph	
	Van Zandt	

INTRODUCTION

There are a thousand different ways to make a great pickup. Not just 'a pickup', but a *great* pickup. Hell, there's a virtually infinite number of ways of making a functional pickup. But a great pickup, there are still a lot of ways to get that job done. Jason Lollar, TV Jones, Joe Barden, Harry DeArmond, Lindy Fralin, Bill Lawrence, Larry DiMarzio, G&L, the Gibson Custom Shop, Kent Armstrong, Seymour Duncan, Abigail Ybarra at Fender … they all make – or made – them a little differently, sometimes a lot differently, and they all make a range of pickups that represents variations on the form.

As much as each of us, as a player, tends to become enamored, occasionally obsessed, with one particular formulation, tends to feel *this is it* in pickups for us and that nothing else will do, there are many, many ways to put together an outstanding pickup, some of which attack the task from entirely different corners of the playing field.

"Alnico is the 'musical magnet'."
Tell it to Danny Gatton.

"Humbuckers just don't 'twang'."
Tell it to Johnny Hiland.

"Single coils can't rock."
Tell it to Jimi Hendrix.

"P-90s have no finesse."
Tell it to Grant Green.

For every preconception about a pickup's form and function that you're willing to take onboard, there's a hulking contradiction lurking around the corner, just waiting to slap you upside the noggin and to turn your convictions on their head. Yes, there are a lot of ways to get this job done, and it behooves us as musicians to open our minds to any and all approaches that might yield great pickups. It also serves us well to continually remind ourselves that our heads and our hands make the music and, to that end, any competent pickup that offers depth, dynamics, and dimension in the style of music we apply it to will be capable of helping us make great art, provided we get out there and *play it*.

Pickups are where it all starts. Certainly wood, strings, hardware and fingers all interact to produce the note, but the pickup translates it into the signal that makes it electric. With that in mind, there's a Zen-like reaction within the sound chain that every tone-conscious player should consider. Everything is everything – any little change early in the signal chain affects the sound all the way down the line. The beating of that alnico butterfly's wings causes a hurricane of tone at the cone of a speaker many, many yards of wire away. This goes for guitars in general (as well as the effects pedals and amps that follow them), but the theory applies in spades within the humble little pickup itself. The complexity of that interaction between magnet, coil, and metal that produces the electrical signal that allows our guitar tone to travel down a wire and be heard dictates that any little change in the design or construction of a pickup – and I mean *any* – will alter the sound it produces. In many cases these alterations might be slight, sure, but even when miniscule they can often be heard by guitarists who take the time to scrutinize the fine points of their tone. Believe me, different pickups can greatly alter the sound your entire rig makes. But *how* will they alter it? That's a topic that takes some study, if you hope at all to understand it as a musician, as a tone crafter.

Finicky guitarists have always messed with their pickups. The extent to which a pickup is responsible for a guitar's sound didn't begin to enter the collective consciousness of players, however, until the late 1960s, and really took off properly in the 1970s with the first considerable wave of manufacturers of 'hotrodded' after-market pickups. By the late '70s, there seemed to be an accepted wisdom afloat in the universe that declared that electric guitars themselves really were just planks of wood with strings (and a few curves to make them comfortable to play), that it was the pickups that really did all the work, and that you could make them out of just about any type of wood, or anything at all really. Most of us know better by now, but we also know that pickups to make a big, big contribution to the voice of the instrument.

As it happens, with the explosion of small pickup rewinding and custom-building shops of the past ten years or so, it seems the pickup's significance in the sound chain has once again been elevated above that of any other single component, but this does appear to have come about alongside a greater overall awareness of the many other parts of the sonic picture. I mean, as of the early 1990s we already had excellent replacement options in both 'hot' and 'vintage' designs (often with a few variations of each) for everything from Strat pickups to humbuckers, Teles to P-90s, from a range of manufacturers, including DiMarzio, Seymour Duncan, Gibson and Fender themselves, and a few others. Why would makers such as Fralin, Lollar, Rio Grande, TV Jones, Bare Knuckle, Harmonic Design and others have risen to such prominence in recent years if not for a wholesale reassessment of the pickup that resulted in a demand for *more* from the market?

The major growth on the front side of the bell curve that traces the latest boom in pickup makers came in renewed efforts from certain corners to build a better mousetrap – by which I mean, to better capture the 'vintage' pickup. On the heels of that came an awareness that not everyone wants an entirely accurate vintage repro unit, and that a few tweaks to improve midrange response, or to increase output level, or to reduce treble spikes really aren't a bad thing in many cases. Those two directions do largely define the latest wave, though: new pickups that sound like vintage, and new pickups that sound like slightly hotrodded vintage.

In addition, the noiseless single-coil market continues apace, although this doesn't seem to be the forward edge of pickup design that it was around the mid to late '90s. Even so, many new developments do still exhibit a trend toward renewed efforts to capture realistic single-coil tones from hum-canceling designs – as seen in anything from Lindy Fralin's Unbucker to Kinman's AVn series. On the other side of the coin, there has also been a trend for pickups that achieve a traditional, noisy single-coil performance in a route originally intended for a full-sized humbucker, as with Gibson's P-94 or Rio Grande's Bastard. Whatever the next big thing in pickup design, it's clear that players and manufacturers alike are more closely scrutinizing the job performed by this little bundle of wire, magnet, metal and plastic or fiber, and that here in the 21st century the humble pickup is under a more powerful microscope than ever before.

Given the joyous multitude of means of making great electric guitar pickups, most players need a little assistance navigating their way through the options. That's exactly what *The Guitar Pickup Handbook* is here to do. This is a tonal guide, for players, and while I fully intend that anyone interested in the electric guitar will get something from this book, the histories, technical discussions, and specs contained herein are intended to assist you in sliding through the swamp of pickup makes and designs available today and in days gone by, and they don't pretend to go so far as to instruct anyone on how to wind their own pickups, or to provide insight on minutia of the sort that collectors of high-end vintage guitars require to date rare and expensive components. Use this information to better understand the beating electromagnetic heart of your guitar, and to help you craft the tone that's right for you.

Then get out there and play.

THE DEVELOPMENT OF THE PICKUP

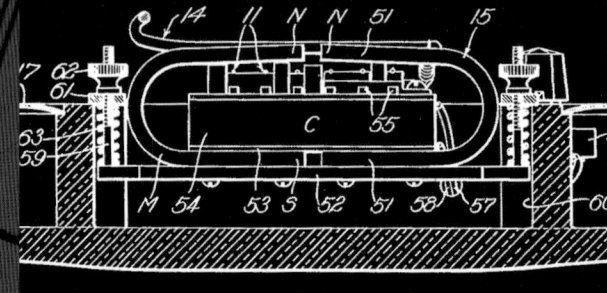

"The way that they wound them back then was definitely different, using smaller sewing-machine motors and hand-held wire, and more erratic winding techniques, so that maybe you'll have more windings at the bottom of the pickup and less windings at the top of the pickup. That influences the tone of the pickup. How tightly you hold that wire influences it, too."
MIKE ELDRED, CORONA, CA, APRIL 2008

the development of the pickup

As with the development of the solid-body electric guitar in the middle part of the last century – a story with which players today are generally more familiar – the development of the electromagnetic guitar pickup was driven largely by the shifting styles of and performance outlets for the music that benefited from it.

Look back to 1920 and the guitar really was a minority instrument on the performance bandstand, even within the realm of stringed instruments. There were plenty of skilled players around, certainly, and plenty of elegant, highly refined designs, from Gibson's Lloyd Loar models to a myriad Martin offerings, but once you got a piano, percussion, a string section, and half a dozen horns up onstage alongside it, the poor guitar struggled badly to be heard. The banjo was considerably more piercing, and even the mandolin cut through better when chorded vigorously or tremolo-picked for single-note lines; the guitar, however, in the band context at least, really was functional only as a rhythm instrument, and even then probably wasn't heard much past the front edge of the dance floor when the rest of the orchestra was really pumping. If you wanted to give a gifted guitarist a solo, you had to drop out most of the rest of the orchestra to accomplish it. But great guitarists were out there, and they wanted to play. In order to be heard, too, they needed a way to make their six-strings louder.

The early solution came in an acoustical form, namely, the thin, spun aluminum cones that gave the first resonator guitars of the 1920s their unprecedented volume-producing capabilities. The first National 'tri-cone' guitars of 1927 were produced in Los Angeles, CA, as a result of the collaboration between the vaudeville guitarist and self-styled inventor George Beauchamp, instrument manufacturer John Dopyera, and tool-and-die plant proprietor Adolph Rickenbacker. Beauchamp brought his ideas for an amplifying horn to make the guitar louder (originally conceived as something akin to the horn used to amplify early gramophones); Dopyera refined it into the more compact, more effective system of three cones mounted within the body of a hollow steel guitar; and Rickenbacker manufactured these bodies and cones. Their combined efforts did increase the volume of the guitar beyond anything the acoustic instrument was previously capable of producing, and briefly embodied a revolution that was welcomed by Hawaiian and blues players in particular. And although the instrument could be considered redundant – in volume-production terms, at least – just nine years later when Gibson launched the ES-150, our wayside sojourn with Beauchamp and Rickenbacker in particular

the development of the pickup

remains directly relevant to the development of the pickup itself. Before following the thread of their catalytic impact on the birth of the guitar pickup, however, let's take a brief detour to explore the further dabblings of another formidable name in instrument design that has likewise already been dropped into our narrative.

In 1924 the guitar designer Lloyd Loar left Gibson, the company for which he had introduced some of the most revered archtop guitar and mandolin designs of all time, and by the early 1930s had launched the ViViTone company with fellow ex-Gibson employee Lewis Williams right there in Kalamazoo, MI, where he primarily explored efforts to amplify stringed instruments (his company and its instruments were also referred to, appropriately enough, as Acousti-Lectric). Loar developed a pickup that appears crude by today's standards, but which was nevertheless well ahead of its time, and fitted it to numerous instruments in the ViViTone line, which included a guitar, mandolin, viola, mandola and mandocello (as well as a clavier, a keyboard instrument with its tone produced by hammers hitting tuned steel bars instead of strings).

As seen on one surviving example of a ViViTone mandolin, the pickup's workings are contained in a sliding drawer that can be removed from the upper side of the instrument, and it functions by transmitting the vibrational energy of the strings through the wooden bridge to two long screws beneath it that extend to the pickup coil mounted in the bottom of the 'drawer'. As such, Loar's pickup would appear to perform in a manner akin to the piezo-electric pickups often used to amplify acoustic guitars today, although it does take the form of the electromagnetic (aka magnetic) pickups which would become standard for electric guitars proper. Being both ahead of the curve trend-wise and, history-wise, rooted in the years just prior to and the early years of the Great Depression, ViViTone was doomed to failure, but Loar's efforts with the company show how one preeminent instrument designer of the time was pegging the future of the instrument to the development of reliable amplification.

Another early name in the history of the electric guitar, Stromberg-Voisinet, introduced another and somewhat differently conceived instrument in 1928. Sold in a set with an accompanying amplifier, the Stromberg Electro was a flat-top acoustic guitar equipped with a transducer to pick up the vibrations of the soundboard, rather than those of the bridge – as in Loar's ViViTone instruments – or the strings themselves, as with guitars of the near future equipped with electromagnetic pickups. These instruments were short-lived, sales hit hard no

FACING PAGE **One of George Beauchamp's early Spanish electric guitar concepts.**

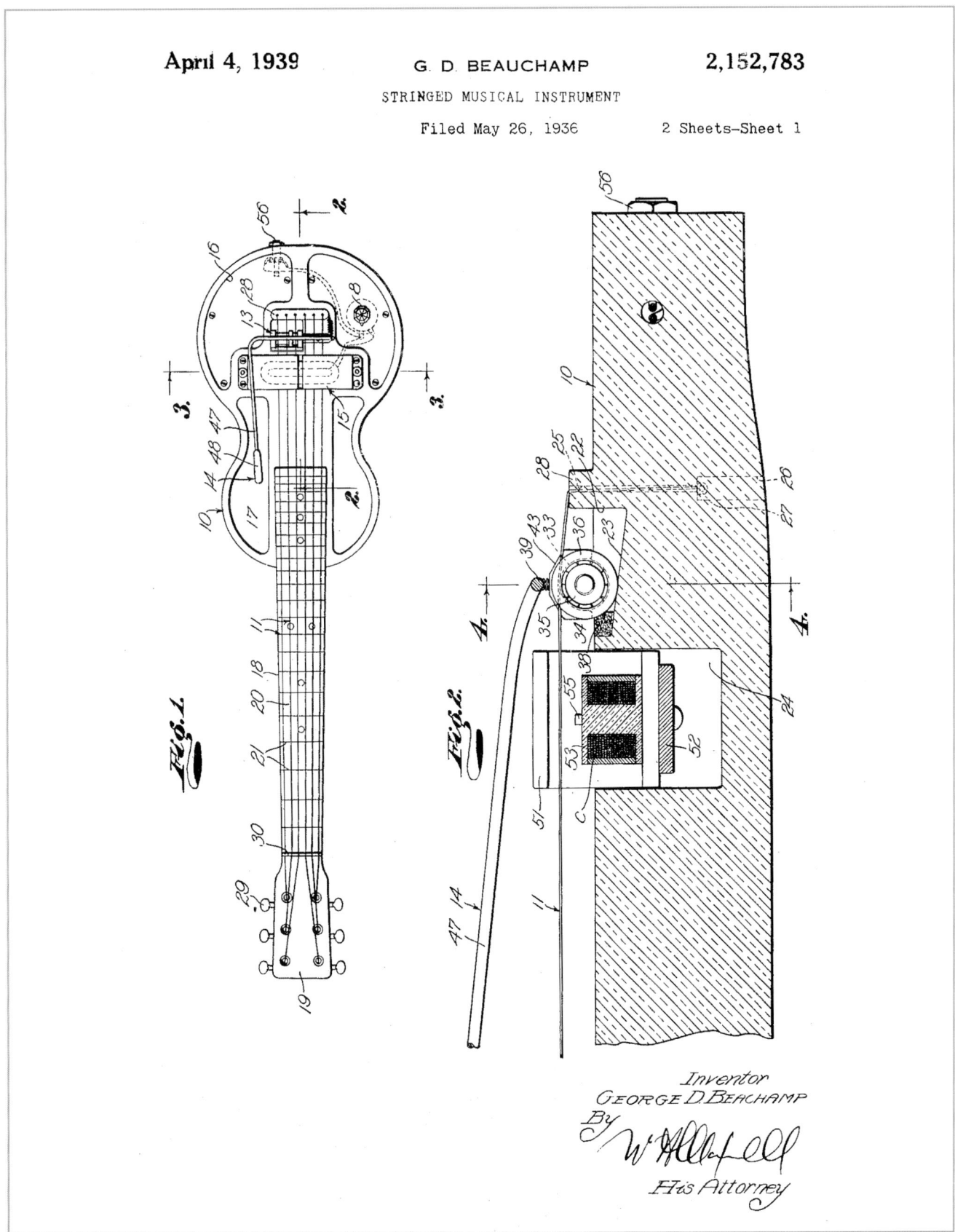

the development of the pickup

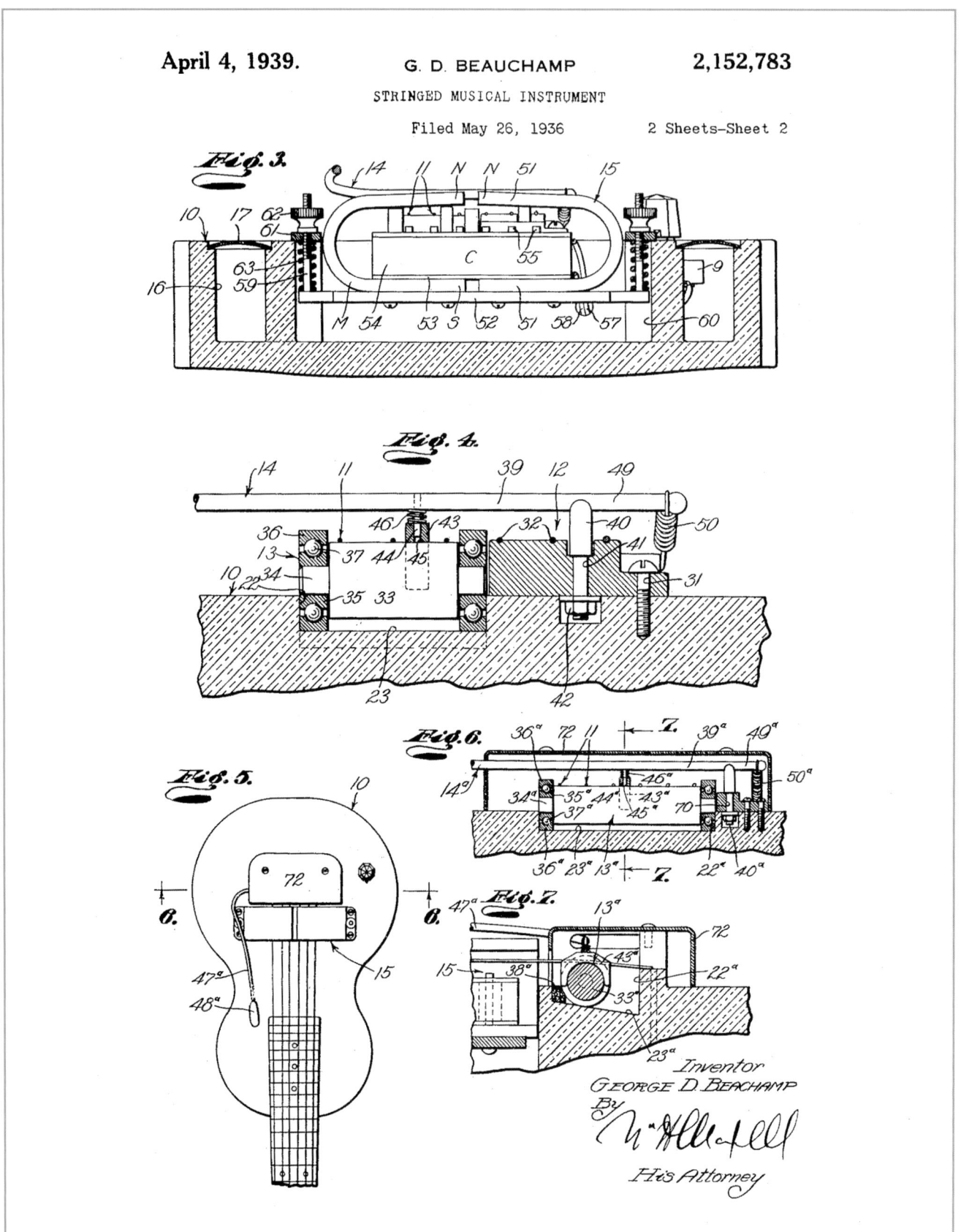

14 the guitar pickup handbook

the development of the pickup

doubt by the onset of the Depression, although the Stromberg-Voisinet company lived on as Kay, which became one of the world's largest manufacturers of both electric and acoustic guitars.

Meanwhile, back in California, Beauchamp and Rickenbacker were paving a smoother road toward the magnetic electric guitar pickup. Almost simultaneously with his brainstorm about making a guitar louder with the use of a horn device, which was refined into the resonator cone, Beauchamp had been considering the notion of an amplified guitar. He was experimenting with microphones and amplified public address (PA) systems as early as the mid 1920s, and adapted an electric phonograph pickup (the needle and cartridge assembly) to be used on a test unit, a one-string guitar crudely made from a 2x4-inch board. The unit was a far cry from revolutionary, but it worked, it was a first step down that long road.

During his diversions as general manager of National String Instrument Corporation, Beauchamp got to know a nephew of owners John and Louis Dopyera's by the name of Paul Barth, who was also working at National, but shared an interest in the grander notion of the amplified guitar. Around 1930 the pair began pursuing their goal of developing an electromagnetic pickup that would be functional with a guitar. They constructed their own coil-winding machines, first out of a washing machine motor, then a sewing machine motor, and completed their pickups with a pair of horseshoe magnets mounted side-on in mirror image, to form a 'tunnel' of sorts through which the strings passed. The coil itself was affixed at the bottom of these double arches, and contained six steel pole pieces to further focus the magnetic field beneath the individual strings.

The eponymous 'horseshoe pickup', in use by Rickenbacker into the mid 1950s, was ready to go by 1931, when Beauchamp and Barth roped in Harry Watson from National to construct a basic test-bed guitar for the unit. The crude wooden instrument, a Hawaiian-style six-string with a small, round body and unusually long neck, has become known as the 'Frying Pan', and ungainly or not, was the first guitar to carry an electromagnetic pickup. Beauchamp and Barth turned to Adolph Rickenbacker to help them produce a sturdier cast-aluminum version of the instrument, and later that same year the trio formed the Ro-Pat-In company, which was later renamed Electro String. Lap-style aluminum Frying Pans hit the market in 1932 (Beauchamp and Barth had lost their jobs at National in a shake-up of the company the previous year), and initially carried the Electro name on the headstock. Later that same year, the company also released some

FACING PAGE **A detailed cross section of the "horseshoe pickup" George Beauchamp developed for Rickenbacker, as mounted on a solidbody Spanish electric gutiar.**

the development of the pickup

Spanish-style Electro guitars (that is, guitars played in the traditional, upright manner) using traditional wooden archtop guitars bought in from other manufacturers, usually Harmony or Kay, and mounted with horseshoe pickups.

Early efforts sold poorly, but Electro String persisted. In 1934 the partners decided to change the brand on the headstock to Rickenbacher, the original Germanic form of the Anglicized Rickenbacker, perhaps because they thought the association with Adolph's cousin, the famous World War I flying ace Eddie Rickenbacker, would help boost sales. Soon after, they further utilized Adolph Rickenbacker's tool-and-die plant to manufacture both Hawaiian and Spanish-style semi-solid electric guitars out of molded Bakelite, in slightly more conventional guitar shapes. Slowly, the electric guitar – and therefore, the magnetic pickup – began to catch on. Sales increased gradually as musicians developed more faith in the radical new format, and the Bakelite Rickenbacher Model B Hawaiian in particular is regarded as a seminal lap-steel. Around this time, some other manufacturers dared to dip a toe in the waters of what was looking more and more like a promising market.

Beauchamp was awarded a patent for the horseshoe pickup in 1937, and shortly afterward Barth was likewise granted a patent for a similar add-on version that could be retrofit to most any archtop acoustic guitar. Having become disenchanted with the electric guitar business, however – which was clearly a hard row to hoe throughout the 1930s when the Great Depression left musicians with little spare cash to spend on expensive and unproven new instruments – Beauchamp sold up his interest in the company and departed Electro String in 1940. A life-long lover of fishing and the gear that went with it, he had applied for and was awarded a patent for a new type of fishing lure, and began making plans to manufacture the design. But not long after parting ways with Barth and Rickenbacker, Beauchamp suffered a heart attack while out at sea on a fishing trip and died.

Like most American instrument manufacturers of the time, Electro String ceased its production of guitars from 1942 to 1946 to concentrate on the necessities of the war effort. In the late 1940s the company returned with a range of Spanish and Hawaiian models, but Adolph Rickenbacker was likewise growing disenchanted with the guitar industry. In 1953, he and his remaining partners sold the Electro String Music Corporation, complete with its horseshoe pickup design and the rights to the Rickenbacker brand name (now with the Anglicized second 'k'), to FC Hall, the proprietor of a radio and television service and supply company most commonly known as Radio-Tel. Radio-Tel had been an

FACING PAGE **Armand Knoblaugh's 1935 design for an early humbucking pickup for the Baldwin company.**

the development of the pickup

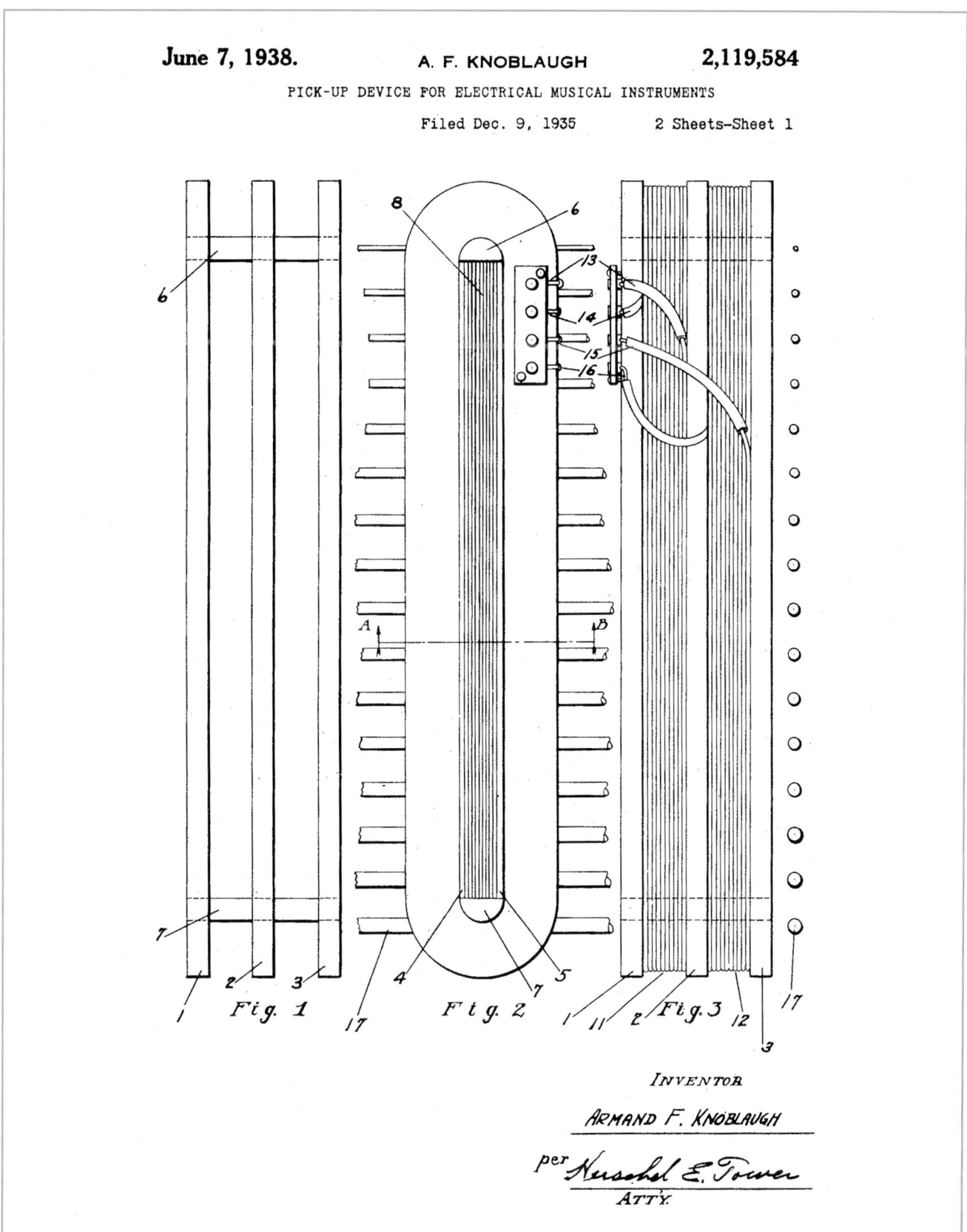

early distributor of Fender guitars and amplifiers, and Hall saw the potential in the electric guitar business. Under his guidance, Rickenbacker as we know it today would flourish. Soon after the takeover, solid-bodied wooden Spanish electric guitars arrived in shapes that clearly presage the Rickenbacker solids of later years, and today. Early on, these still carried Beauchamp and Barth's seminal horseshoe pickup, and although Rickenbacker pickups would soon evolve to the 'toaster top' and 'button top' variants that the brand is more famous for, the ungainly horseshoe unit remains a tonal icon with many players today, lap-steelers in particular.

The Ro-Pat-In/Electro String/Rickenbacher efforts are particularly interesting to us in the context of this book, and that of the electric guitar in particular, because Beauchamp and company approached the task from the pickup-end first. Their efforts focused on the electric instrument first and foremost, and they constructed the guitar to suit the pickup design they had settled on, which also, arguably, led them to release what can reasonably be considered the first 'solid' electric guitar (their aluminum, pressed steel, and Bakelite instruments had hollow chambers within them for weight-reduction purposes, but were not 'acoustic' in terms of a hollow-bodied instrument intended to resonate with acoustic energy).

As the electric movement began to show some legs, established guitar manufacturers – those who naturally approached the challenge from the perspective of the traditional, wood-bodied, acoustic instrument – pursued their own means of entering the race. The most prominent of these is Gibson, which released a cast-aluminum Electric Hawaiian lap-steel guitar in 1935, the E-150 (later EH-150, a model number it shared with its accompanying amplifier). The following year, the company debuted its Electric Spanish ES-150, which is widely acknowledged as the first production electric from a major guitar manufacturer.

Around the same time, however, the lesser-known Epiphone company introduced its own Electraphone (later Electar) range of non-cutaway archtop Spanish and lap-style Hawaiian electric guitars, which were fitted with horseshoe pickups acquired from Electro String. By 1939, both Gretsch and Epiphone were marketing electric guitars with their own pickups, although the former's Electromatic Spanish model was actually manufactured by Kay (formerly Stromberg-Voisinet) in Chicago. The pickups on Zephyr, Coronet and Century models from Epiphone were large, oval-shaped units, which later in the year were adapted to take adjustable pole pieces, making them the first such

the development of the pickup

pickups available. Despite the innovation, Gibson was by this time clearly pulling ahead in the game; already recognized as the pre-eminent manufacturer of archtop guitars, its electrics were fast becoming the professional's choice for amped-up requirements, too.

Although our journey here involves an exploration of electromagnetic pickups used on electric guitars, it's worth visiting a few other significant designs along the way, even those that are all but forgotten, and perhaps even went tragically unsung in their day. One such detour should pay brief homage to the father of the humbucking pickup … and right here where you're anticipating the name Seth Lover, I'm going to delight in throwing out instead the unfamiliar moniker Armand F. Knoblaugh, a designer working for the Baldwin Company of Cincinnati, Ohio. A good 21 years before Gibson was awarded a patent for Seth Lover's humbucking pickup, Baldwin was awarded a patent for a humbucking pickup design filed on the company's behalf by Knoblaugh in 1935. Sure, the unit was intended primarily to amplify the electric piano, but Knoblaugh's application also states that it can be used on other instruments that employ vibrating steel strings, so it wouldn't be much of a stretch to adapt it to the guitar. Here's the kicker though – the application states:

The principal object of my invention is the elimination of effects caused by stray magnetic fields and such elimination of the device of my invention, without affecting its sensitivity to the motion of the adjacent magnetized strings. For example, let the coils [figs 11 and 12] be identically constructed and be connected in series in an opposite sense … The induction of electromotive forces by stray magnetic fields into coil 12 is then counterbalanced, part by part, by the induction of equal and opposite electromotive forces into coil 11, with the result that any reproduced extraneous noises, such as hum, are essentially eliminated. (A.F. Knoblaugh, Patent Number 2,119,584)

Knoblaugh's design used two stacked coils rather than two placed side by side, and the concept of a 'hum-bucking' choke transformer was already commonplace in radio and amplification technology – as both Seth Lover and Ray Butts would site in regard to the inspiration for their own humbucking pickups two decades later – but it's an impressively advanced piece of design, nevertheless. And, having been awarded a patent in 1938, it was there on file for any future pickup inventors to discover.

While the horseshoe pickup was already proving successful in its own way by the mid 1930s, its utility was limited by the cumbersome arrangement presented by the two large magnets that gave it its name. It's impossible to pick

the development of the pickup

the strings right above this pickup, and very difficult to do so near its front or back edge, and the traditional palm-muting technique for dampening strings also has to be adapted considerably on any instrument carrying one of these. Gibson's first pickup had a magnet structure that's almost as ungainly as that of the horseshoe pickup that beat it to the market by a good four years, but the boys from Kalamazoo tucked their elongated magnets out of the way by mounting them within the body of the ES-150, with only the coil and blade-style pole piece protruding through a mounting hole cut in the guitar's top. As such, the 'Charlie Christian' pickup, so-called for its use by the pioneering electric-jazz guitarist who took up these Gibson guitars soon after their introduction, looks much like a slightly archaic version of our contemporary magnetic pickups. But don't let this tip-of-the-iceberg coil assembly fool you; there's one honking big magnet assembly hovering under the center of the guitar's arched top.

Designed by Walter Fuller, the Christian pickup is held in place by three adjustable screws that can be used to raise or lower the entire assembly, the heads of which are visible in the top of any old ES-150. The unit changed slightly during the years of its existence, from 1936 to 1940; it was born with a single one-piece blade pole piece, then had a single blade but with a notch under the B string, then three separate pole pieces under the treble strings, and finally six notches. In 1940 Gibson introduced a more compact magnetic pickup to replace the Christian, with six fixed individual pole pieces in a coil with a soapbar shaped cover. Used only until the war-time production hiatus in 1942, this looks a little like Gibson's most famous single-coil pickup, the P-90, but has a few crucial differences. Introduced in 1946, the P-90 is sometimes given the distinction of being the first pickup with adjustable pole pieces, although the Epiphone pickup available before it actually claims that prize. Even so, the P-90 was a far more widely available adjustable-pole pickup, and although it seems a minor point today, it was a major feature for its time. After World War II, Gibson ramped up production and was eventually blitzing the market in a big way, and for a while the P-90 appeared on everything. For Gibson, this was the sound of jazz, dance band, country, and the newfangled rock'n'roll – all of it.

The P-90 was – and remains – a fat, round, warm-sounding pickup for a single-coil unit, although it also possesses a flattering, slightly gritty treble response and more aggressive mids than what we usually think of when 'single coil' is mentioned. They aren't over-blessed with clarity, but when used judiciously can nevertheless present a snappy, musical performance with good definition. Put a slightly over-wound P-90 in the neck position, however, in a big

the development of the pickup

jazzbox in particular, and you risk inducing a tonal bud bath (which, hey, in some circumstances can be just what you're looking for). Midway through the 1950s, Gibson started seeking a cure for this, although it soon turned its attention to bigger fish. In 1950, one upstart in the electric guitar business introduced a whole new world of bright to the fledgling sound of amplified music. Just a few years later, longstanding Gibson competitor Gretsch was making major inroads into the rock'n'roll and country markets in particular, with new guitars equipped with the twangy, clear-sounding DeArmond 200 pickup, known as the DynaSonic in Gretsch literature (DeArmond is another big player in the pickup world, responsible for everything from basic pickups on beginners' guitars to some of the most revered add-on jazzbox pickups of all time, as we shall see later in the book). Gibson president Ted McCarty set engineer Seth Lover the task of producing a pickup with the clarity and treble response of a DeArmond 200 or a Fender Telecaster bridge pickup, and in 1954 the results of this venture appeared in the neck position of the new Les Paul Custom as the Alnico V pickup (or 'Staple' pickup). These units, which also feature on some archtop models of the mid 1950s, look much like P-90s from a distance, and even use the same plastic 'soapbar' covers, but instead of the threaded steel pole pieces, Alnico Vs use six individual rectangular alnico magnets as pole pieces (hence their name), which are adjustable via six individual screws that run alongside them, much as are the Gretsch's DeArmond/Dynasonic pickups. Putting the magnets within the coil as pole pieces themselves changes the magnetic field of the pickup and elicits a brighter response, as we shall explore in further chapters, and as such Lover succeeded at his task. In another year, however, McCarty would set his sights on another Gibson first – the humbucker – the arrival of which would overshadow the Alnico V.

Meanwhile, as mentioned, Leo Fender introduced his Esquire (later Broadcaster, later Telecaster) in 1950, with a pickup that would arguably set the benchmark for single-coil tone. This pickup, developed from Fender's earlier work with solid-bodied lap-steel guitars, lacked adjustable pole pieces, although the entire unit was more easily height-adjusted than many other pickup of the day. And leaving out any height-adjustment facilities for the individual alnico rod pole pieces (as included on the DeArmond 200, and later the Gibson Alnico) enabled Fender to produce a sturdy, compact unit with a narrow coil and magnetic field that further enhanced its treble response, and to do so more affordably than the competition. Other factors revolving around the Tele bridge pickup's mounting structure further enhanced its twang factor, as we shall see later in the book, but suffice to say for now that – successful rock'n'roll tone being something of a brightness war in the realms of guitar and amp design – the Fender pickup quickly became the one to beat, however scoffed at the arrival of the guitar that housed it might have been.

With a range of pickups on the scene, including the Gibson P-90, the DeArmond 200 (aka Gretsch DynaSonic), Fender's Telecaster pickups and, by 1954, Stratocaster pickups, and the Rickenbacker 'toaster top' pickup that replaced the horseshoe pickup in the mid 1950s, by 1956 we really did have on hand all the major designs that have remained the pre-eminent tonal benchmarks of the past 50-plus years. Aside from, of course, a pair of hallowed pickups that were hailed as major advances in their day, two units that are outwardly similar, yet quite different tonally. In 1957 Gibson introduced the production version of its 'Patent Applied For' humbucking pickup, while Gretsch unveiled its new Filter'Tron, and both were displayed for the first time at the NAMM Show in Chicago that same year. With the arrival of these dual-coil units, and the concept of hum-canceling finally established, all of the major formats in pickup design were finally on the scene. Which is not to say that great strides wouldn't yet be made – or, indeed, that breathtaking new developments aren't ahead of us still – but it's astounding to think that the golden age that brought us not only rock'n'roll but so much seminal jazz, blues, and country music also ushered in the milestones of pickup design that, in many players' estimations, still offer the majority of the most desired pickups on the planet.

Sure, there's life beyond the sting of a vintage Strat pickup, the rich purr of a PAF, or the biting twang of a Tele bridge pickup, and we'll explore all that 'spice of life' stuff here, too. Without a doubt, there's plenty of validity in the world of ceramics, for one thing. Most players are at least somewhat aware of the high-gain ceramic pickups that became popular in the 1970s and which retain a place in the world of rock, metal and thrash guitar today. Perhaps further from the front of guitarists' collective consciousness are other avenues for ceramics, such as Leo Fender's own work at G&L (which remains available today in that company's current models); or the new, rather refined approach easing musical tones from this 'modern magnet' that has been taken by winders such as Bill Lawrence or Joe Barden. Undeniably, there are a lot of preconceptions to dispel in this arena.

The 1990s and 2000s have also seen enormous advances in noise-free (which is to say, less noisy) pickups in single-coil-sized casings. The dual-coil humbucker in sheep's clothing (that is, beneath a Strat pickup cover) has been with us for some time, but in the past decade-and-a-half many creative

the development of the pickup

manufacturers have worked to attain a more genuine vintage single-coil tone from these formats – chasing it in some creative new ways – and have largely achieved the goal. Active and low-impedance pickups have also played their part. While they have never achieved the widespread popularity that Les Paul no doubt envisioned when he convinced Gibson to put them on the Les Paul Personal and Professional models way back in 1969, they have won the hearts and ears of more than a few players, and have been the stock in trade of the successful EMG pickup line, for one.

So, while the principles and the approximate format were all in order by the mid 1940s, and the majority of the most significant designs were with us by the late 1950s, the electromagnetic pickup has continued its evolution in the 50-plus years since. Certainly the majority of smaller manufacturers today seem to be concentrating their efforts on out-Fendering Fender, or out-Gibsoning Gibson, by way of creating the 'ultimate vintage pickup', but plenty of creative winders are also seeking new avenues to tonal versatility and purity, regardless of what has gone before. Now let's plunge into the wires and magnets, and try to discover something about what makes this very real, yet invisible, force do its thing.

THE ANATOMY OF THE PICKUP

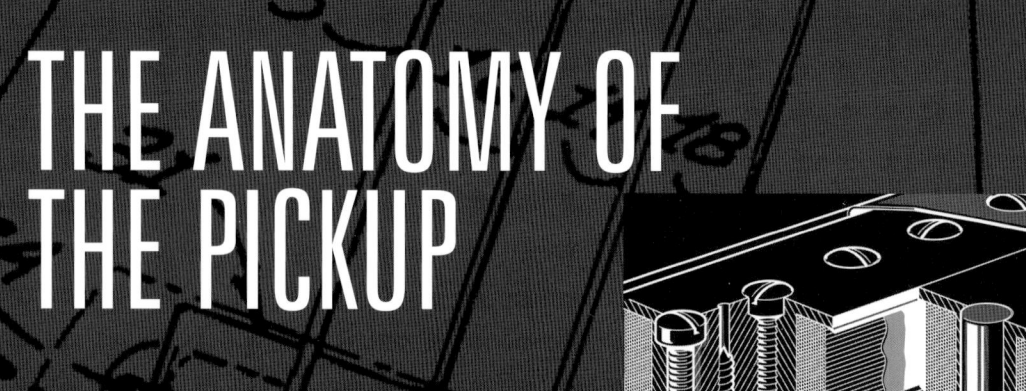

"Any metal object breaking a magnetic field will induce a current in the coil. It's just that iron happens to be the best. You can use aluminum strings and it will still generate some signal, it just wouldn't be as powerful as ferrous."
KENT ARMSTRONG, GRAFTON, VT, MAY 2008

the anatomy of the pickup

Guitar pickups function according to quite simple, although really rather amazing, electromagnetic principles. And while the vast majority of the pickups that concern us work in exactly the same way – in scientific terms, that is – a myriad little variations in their design and construction will lead them to sound very different from each other once mounted into your guitar. As ever in the realm of guitar tone (and all things guitar-tone related, such as amps, speakers, effects, and all the individual components of the guitars themselves), the nuances, the minutiae, work together to determine the voice of each type of pickup, even if the electromagnetic devices are themselves all functioning in 'the same' way. Tweak an ingredient or two and you trigger a chaos-theory style fluttering of the butterfly wings that results in an entirely different sounding pickup and, therefore, guitar. Let's begin as if they all do work the same, however, and examine the electrical principles behind their function, then we'll move on to dissect the variables in some detail.

Be aware as you read this book – and this chapter in particular – that I am not an electrical engineer, nor am I a guitar tech by trade, nor a pickup designer. I'm a guitarist and a writer, so I'm approaching this subject out of the personal fascination of a fellow musician, rather than as a craftsman who labors at the design, manufacture, or repair of these components. Toward the end of *Guitar Pickups*, however, we'll talk to some of the top practitioners in the trade to get their points of view on a wide range of pertinent pickup-related subjects.

As electromagnetic devices go, guitar pickups are down there at the end of the scale marked 'basic'. They are far simpler than another electromagnetic musical device that's familiar to most people, the speaker (also loudspeaker, or driver), and also slightly simpler than a passive dynamic microphone such as a Shure SM57. A speaker employs an electromagnetic coil within a fixed magnet to create a push-me/pull-you relationship between the two that pumps a paper cone in a flexible suspension and puts sound waves into the air. A guitar pickup works somewhat the reverse of this, but only requires about half the parts, and certainly no moving parts. Also, as a passive device, it requires no power source in the actual sense, although the low-voltage signal that it creates must be amplified by an active, powered device in order to be heard. Which, at the end of the chain, involves being pumped back through a speaker. Ah, the circle of life … or, of feedback, if you're a guitarist (and it's so easy to see where feedback comes from, when you look at it like this).

A pickup does the reverse of many electromagnetic devices that we might be more familiar with in everyday life, such as speakers, small electrical motors, microphones, and so forth. Instead of receiving an electrical signal and translating it into motion by manipulating magnetic forces, a pickup senses motion (string vibration) and, through this motion's disruption of its magnetic field, translates that motion into an electrical signal. In short, electromagnets can translate an electrical signal into motion by exerting magnetic force, or translate motion into an electrical signal; pickups do the latter.

A guitar pickup consists of just two main 'active ingredients', if you will, alongside a collection of other inactive ingredients that mostly help to hold it together (although sometimes these supposedly inactive ingredients do interact with the pickup's magnetic behavior and, therefore, affect the way it sounds, as we shall see later in this chapter). The actives are the magnet(s) and the wire coil. The inactives are the coil former, or 'bobbin', and a number of other parts that are used in some designs but not in others, including a base plate, cover, pole-adjustment screws, wooden (or other) spacers used to keep certain parts from contacting each other, and wax or paraffin used to seal the coil to keep out moisture and dampen vibrations. All pickups use solder to connect the coil wire to the wire leads that extend toward the guitar's controls. Also, as we shall see, the magnet can take a lot of different forms, many of which include multiple parts, and even multiple parts of different types of materials, with magnet(s) and steel working together to configure the pickup's magnetic field.

The Invisible Power

The next time an acquaintance tells you they don't believe in anything they can't see, sit them down with a couple of magnets attached to some children's toys. As a structure housing a magnet, sometimes many magnets, any pickup mounted in a guitar will exert a magnetic force – an unseen, but very real, force that radiates from the pickup itself in patterns determined by the shape and structure of that particular pickup. We're all so familiar with magnets that it seems like no big deal: opposite magnetic poles will attract and 'stick' to each other; like poles will repel each other. But stop taking it for granted for a minute, and it's an incredible thing. It occurred to me perhaps most profoundly a few years ago while helping my infant son, Freddie, line up his Thomas the Tank Engine train cars on their slotted wooden track. All at once, the simple fact that attempting to hitch one car to another the wrong way around would repel the other car, rather than give the expected 'click' of the magnetic connection, seemed a major revelation. It was a principle that I was well familiar with, but it suddenly hit me: there's a force there, just as real as it is invisible.

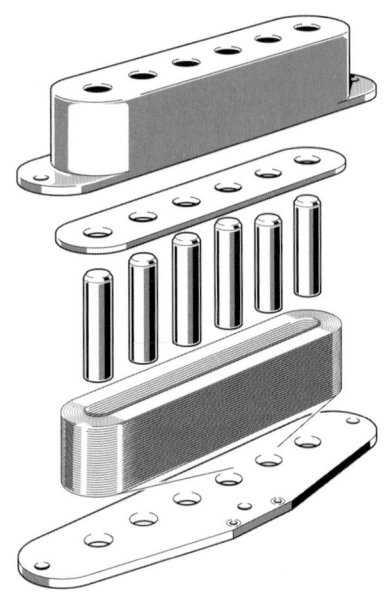

Whatever their design, most pickups contain certain basic elements essential to their function. This single-coil pickup comprises, from top to bottom, a cover, top plate, magnetic pole pieces, coil, and bottom plate. Variations to this might include a "bobbin" in place of top and bottom plates, and a bar magnet mounted beneath a set of steel pole pieces.

the anatomy of the pickup

Dad: *"Look, Fred, look! Isn't that amazing! If you try to connect them the wrong way this car will push the engine all the way around the track without touching it!"*
Fred: *"Yeah, dad, I know. They're called magnets."*

Maybe I just have a brain that's more easily amused than that of a two-year-old, but I still find magnetism an amazing thing. I mean, man, you'd think you could *do something* with that invisible power. Well, it turns out you sure as hell can.

Given the pickup(s) mounted in our guitars, and the magnetic fields they exert, it makes sense that any reactive metal that moves within that field is going to cause a reaction from the magnet. Hit your steel strings, they vibrate and therefore 'push' against the magnet's force, and the coil converts the magnets' sensing of that disturbance into the electrical signal that carries the sound of the guitar to the amplifier. Yeah, it's still totally amazing that that electrical signal transfers precise musical notes and not just some blur of white noise or static. Not to sound like some navel-gazing stoner here, but *c'mon*... this is just breathtaking, wonderful, elemental stuff. Celebrate its glorious mystery with me here. And that's really it: vibration within magnetic field, magnet is acted upon by vibration, and therefore reacts; coil of wire placed correctly within/around that magnetic field senses that reaction; guitar signal. Tone, baby.

As you can imagine, a whole heck of a lot depends on the way in which that magnetic field is disrupted, and this accounts for a big portion of the variables in the entire equation of the guitar pickup. Another heck of a lot depends on, well, every little factor regarding how the pickup was made. Let's lay out a few of the major variables so we've got them all in view, then we'll dive into each in some detail.

Different string types will affect the magnetic field differently, according to the type of steel they are made from, their condition, their gauge, and other factors.

Different magnet structures (or magnet-and-pole piece structures in many designs) will respond differently, because they are creating different types and shapes of magnetic fields in the first place.

Different sized or differently structured pickups will present different magnetic fields and, therefore, will present different readings of the strings' vibrations to the coil.

Different types of coils will translate the disrupted magnetic field differently, and therefore send a differently-shaped signal down the wire to the amp (and of course differing numbers of turns of wire in an otherwise similar coil will also lead two of the 'same' pickups to produce different signals).

How many of each type of the above variable have we got? Well, several, at least. Say we can think of, conservatively, five quite different types of steel strings (not even considering gauge), five magnet/pole piece structures, five different shapes of pickups, and five different styles and shapes of coils (not even accounting for greatly differing numbers of turns, and wire gauges). Multiply these – that's five cubed (five to the power of four, or 5^4) – and we've already got 625 possible pickup types, given the potential combinations of these variables. Given the many sub-variables I have hinted at already, there are bound to be a lot more than that (by which I mean, in many cases, two or more pickups of the same make and model, but which – being imperfect devices, made by humans – are built slightly differently). Got one Stratocaster with a little air bubble between a layer of windings in a particular place in the coil? That's going to sound a little different than the one next to it without the bubble, or with a larger gap in a different place, or with 500 fewer or 500 more turns of wire. I'm talking tonal minutiae here, sure, but that's why we convened this meeting in the first place, and it all adds up.

Of course the guitar itself – that is, everything about the guitar minus the pickups an the strings, which we have already accounted for above – collectively contributes the largest variable of all, which is why you can't just bolt a good Stratocaster pickup or Gibson PAF to a plank of wood and sound like a '57 Strat or a '59 Les Paul. The instrument's general design, the wood it's made from, whether it's a 25½-inch or 24¾-inch or 22½-inch scale length, bolt neck, glued in or 'through' neck, its weight, its density, its resonant characteristics, the hardware used on it – especially the string anchors – the bridge and the nut – all play an enormous part in how it sounds, the way those strings vibrate and, therefore, the frequency content of that electrical signal that our simple little electromagnetic coil sends down the pipeline to the amp. But we know that, right? We're not of the 'the pickups are the only components that matters' school of thought; we know better than that. Yet we are here to talk about pickups, so let's take the enormous (and I mean gargantuan) influence of the whole damn guitar for granted, and move on to the variables that directly affect the pickups themselves.

Strings

Having just sidestepped the mammoth variable of the guitar itself, I'm going to start off with a look at a set of components that, being a 'consumable', are not actually constituent parts of the pickup, and are not even a 'fixed' component of the guitar. Throughout this chapter, however, we are discussing the pickup with regard to its ability to produce a signal that carries our guitar sound, and the strings' vibrations are where that all starts. Even though the strings don't contact the pickup, they interact with it in a very real, very tangible way. In fact … let's backtrack a moment to say that, looked at with the blinders off, the strings do contact the pickup: they push against the invisible, yet very real, magnetic force that the unit exerts – that unseen yet magnificent power that is the real courier between plucked note and electromagnetic component. The string is the interloper into that magical, magnetic zone, bless its heart, and as such is the trigger for all the action. The strings' type, gauge, make-up and condition, therefore, play critical parts in the way our electromagnetic device perceives our tone.

Gauge is far and away the most pertinent factor in string selection for the vast majority of players, and most at least put in a little thought in this department with regard to how the thickness or thinness of their strings feels against their fingertips. Beyond that, other than maintaining the awareness that new strings sound bright and old strings sound dull, many guitarists don't give much thought to their strings with regard to composition and the ways in which different metals used in their manufacturing can elicit different sounds. Prior to 1970, when the cost of nickel went through the roof, the majority of strings were wound with pure nickel wire wrapped around a plain steel core. Although nickel is magnetic, it reacts less with a pickup's magnetic field than the metals in many other types of steel strings. As a result, pure nickel-wrapped strings produce a warmer, mellower tone than some other modern types of strings, a sound that is beloved of many players seeking 'vintage' rock, blues and jazz tones.

Post-1970, strings wrapped with nickel-plated plain steel wire have been the norm, and pure nickel-wrapped strings virtually died out for a time. The higher plain-steel content in these gives them a little more volume and a brighter voice (while they also display more bright-to-dull polarity between their fresh and old states, and therefore appear to 'dull out' quicker and to have less longevity than pure nickel strings). Other modern types such as chrome and stainless-steel-wound strings are brighter and more powerful still.

Armed with this understanding, many guitarists aim quite sensibly to craft their tone right from the strings upward. A guitar that is potentially harsh, with treble spikes and a brittle edge to the upper mids might be tamed with pure nickel-wrapped strings. A guitar that's too mellow and restrained might be perked up with chrome or stainless steel strings of the type that are sold as 'power brights'. Get that vibrating steel interacting with your pickups in a tonally favorable manner in the first place, and it's a lot easier to fine-tune your sound all the way down the line, sweetening it in an additive fashion as desired, rather than having to apply reductive corrective measures.

On top of this, be aware that different shapes of wraps will interact differently, too. Round wounds, the most common strings in use, resonate most fluidly thanks to their pliant, round structure, and therefore reside at the top of the brightness scale. Flatwounds, made with 'ribbon' shaped wraps (that is, wire with a rectangular cross section), occupy the other end of the scale and exude warmth and a distinct roundness in the lower register. Somewhere in between, half-round or 'ground round' strings use round wraps that have been flattened on one side. As expected, they are a little mellower than full rounds, a little brighter than flatwounds.

Magnet Type and Structure

Many, many different types of magnets are used in pickup manufacture, and the same types are very often used in differently constructed pickups, too, and every turn of the design wheel results in a different sound. Makers most commonly use alnico and ceramic magnets, but some other types of 'rare earth' magnets such as neodymium and samarium cobalt are also used in some newer designs.

Even if we examine a dozen different makes of pickups that are all made with Alnico II magnets, for example, we will often find that the actual magnets themselves are different shapes, lengths, weights, densities, and strengths. Any difference in the type of magnetic material will alter the 'gauss' of the magnet, that is, the extent to which the magnetic field reaches out beyond the pickup itself. The size of magnet used, however, and the way in which this magnet is built into the pickup as a whole and its position in or below the coil will also affect the reach of the magnetic field, so even the exact same magnet material will result in two different magnetic fields in differently structured pickups.

First off, as most players know, there are two main categories of magnets

the anatomy of the pickup

used in pickup manufacturing: alnico and ceramic. For now, think of alnico as the 'vintage voiced' magnet and ceramic as the 'modern voiced' magnet, but there are exceptions to the rules in both camps. With that in mind, it's important to be aware that similar magnets of each type are used in very different ways in different pickup designs, so we don't want to make any assumptions that 'alnico pickups all sound like …' and so forth.

Alnico magnets used in pickup manufacturing come in four different flavors, labeled with roman numerals II through V. As it happens, II and V are the more common of the quartet, with III and IV occasionally used by some makers, specialist and 'boutique' shops in particular, where designers are seeking to really dial in a sound according to magnet characteristics. Each type of alnico is differentiated according the composition of the alloy, and the numbers ascend according to the strength of the magnet. The short definition of alnico usually tells you it is made up of aluminum (around 10 percent), nickel (around 18 percent), and cobalt (around 12 percent), but those approximate percentages also tell you there's something missing. Often ignored are the less romantic ingredients: copper (around 6 percent) and iron (54 percent). Some alnico also contains a small quantity of titanium and traces of niobium.

Whatever the exact ingredients – and even, for example, two different batches of 'Alnico II' will arrive with slightly different proportions of these – Alnico II, III, IV and V do tend to exhibit slightly different magnetic characteristics and, therefore, sounds. The weakest of them, Alnico II is a little softer and sweeter than the others. Alnico III is still rather soft but perhaps a little richer and slightly bolder. Alnico IV tends to be noticeably punchier than II and III, with more definition in the highs, while Alnico V is bolder, clearer, and more aggressive still. Keep in mind this is a little like trying to compare lobster stew from two excellent but different restaurants: "Mmm, Chez Bertrand's lobster stew is rich and silky, with a gently peppery finish." "Oh yeah? Well, Petit Pierre's lobster stew is richer still, with lemon-butter notes and an enticing marjoram nose." You could probably plug in a guitar loaded with pickups made with Alnico II, III, IV or V magnets and describe all of them as any of the above. And, *gasp*, you might even elicit similar flavors from yet another pickup made with ceramic magnets. But in close comparison, all else being equal, yes, these characteristics tend to play through enough for them to be accepted in the tone industry.

As mentioned at the top of this section, any of these types of alnico can be procured in a range of sizes and shapes, according to what a pickup manufacturer seeks to do with them. Different shapes and sizes will lead to

the anatomy of the pickup

Fender Telecaster

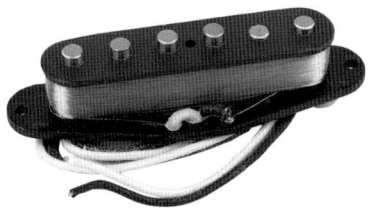
Fender Stratocaster

Gibson P-90 "soapbar

differing magnetic strengths and, therefore, slightly different tonal responses. Alnico magnets are most visible as the pole pieces of Fender single-coil pickups, where six are used in each of the traditional Stratocaster and Telecaster units, one visible under each string. As used in these great designs from the golden age of pickups, the magnets are inserted right into the bobbins (or more accurately, the 'flatware', the flat fiber top and bottom of the pickup), and therefore contained right within the coil itself. The other most popular pickup types, the Gibson PAF-styled humbucker and Gibson P-90, also use alnico magnets, but they are hidden beneath the pickup, or rather, between the bottom of the bobbin and a base plate that holds the entire structure together. These pickups use alnico bar magnets – one magnet in the case of the PAF, two in the P-90 – which transfer their magnetic properties to steel pole pieces that run through the coil(s), so the poles you see on these pickups are not the magnets themselves, although they do react with the magnetic field.

Pickups manufactured with pole pieces that are made from actual magnets sound different from pickups made with magnets mounted below them, transferring their magnetism to steel pole pieces placed within the coil. The sounds of the different major makes and models of pickups that employ these basic design differences will be examined in detail as we encounter each of them in the *Manufacturers' Profiles* chapters that follow, but I can provide some broad guidelines here to help us formulate some sonic images.

This magnet in the coil vs. magnet beneath (outside of) the coil dichotomy really is one of the baseline variables in pickup design, and plays a big part in determining the tonal character of any pickup. In short, using pole pieces that are made from actual magnets and placing these within the coil tends to add to the clarity, definition and overall brightness of the pickup. This rule applies whether you are using six (or 12) individual alnico or ceramic magnet pole pieces, or a single bar magnet as a blade-style pole piece (or a pair of them in the case of a humbucker). On the other hand, using steel pole pieces connected (in the electromagnetic sense, at least) to a magnet placed beneath the coil makes for a fatter, grittier and somewhat more 'raw' tonality. Again, these are broad guidelines, but they tend to hold true across a wide cross-section of both types of pickups. For a head-to-head comparison of these differences, we can look to a Gibson P-90 and a Fender Jazzmaster pickup. Both are approximately the same shape and nominally use the same numbers of turns of wire, but the P-90 has threaded steel pole pieces and a pair of alnico bar magnets mounted beneath the coil, while the Jazzmaster pickup has six fixed, individual pole

the anatomy of the pickup

pieces made from alnico rod magnets. The former sounds a little more furry and raw – although often very sweetly so – while the latter sounds bright, clear and twangy. We will keep this design variable in mind when analyzing almost all of the pickups to follow in this book.

While the magnet beneath/magnet within dichotomy accounts for two major breeds of pole piece, those made from steel and from the magnet material itself, there are other variations besides. The most obvious is the blade pole piece, which – as per its description – employs a single fillet of steel rather than six individual pieces for each coil. Such blades are only of steel, not magnet material, and run through the coil to contact a magnet beneath, as most familiarly seen in pickups by Joe Barden, Bill Lawrence, and some designs from Seymour Duncan. Even Gibson's early Charlie Christian pickup is a single-blade unit.

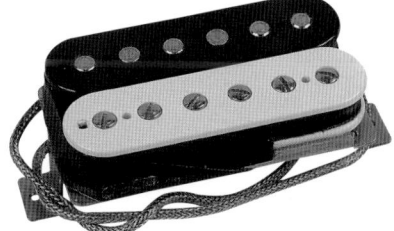

Gibson PAF-style

An unseen magnet 'blade' of sorts is also used in some designs, however, such as the Gibson Firebird pickup, a mini humbucker that uses an alnico bar magnet within each coil of dual-coil structure, or the Danelectro 'Lipstick Tube' pickup, a single-coil pickup with its coil wound around a bar of alnico. Given their 'magnet within' construction, both of these pickups, although very different from each other, offer a bright, well-defined presentation. As they employ the full bar magnet as a hidden 'blade' pole piece of sorts, they are also quite different from Fender's classic version of the magnet-within-coil design.

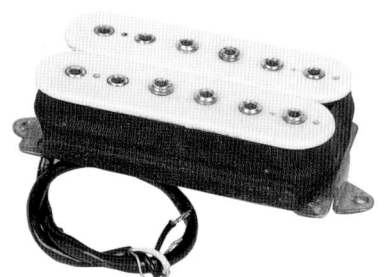

DiMarzio Super Distortion

Other makers have used more unusual pole piece structures. The California equipment manufacturer, Carvin, has made many humbuckers with two rows of tightly packed hex-screw poles, which essentially form an adjustable "blade" of sorts. Another unusual pole piece arrangement is found on G&L's Magnetic Field Design (MFD) and Z-Coil pickups, which have adjustable threaded center poles within sheathed outer poles. Each of these, and others, are the efforts of creative designers to tweak the magnetic fields of their pickups and, therefore, the way they respond to string vibration.

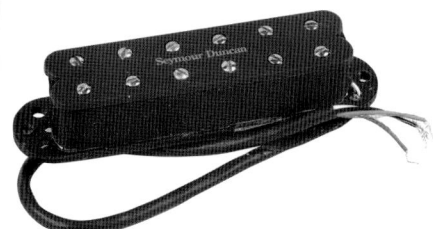

Seymour Duncan Lil'59

All of the above design variables apply likewise to pickups that are made with ceramic magnets, although ceramic pickups do tend to be magnet-plus-steel-pole constructions more often than magnet-pole-piece constructions. Ceramic magnets have developed an unfavorable reputation in some circles, probably duo to the over-wound, high-gain 'distortion' type pickups that populated the replacement pickup market in the late 1970s and '80s. Sticking a ceramic magnet in an already over-wound Strat or PAF style pickup designed with alnico magnets instantly cranks up the heat for monstrous rock drive, but making the change without due consideration to the other variables that will

the anatomy of the pickup

Joe Barden Danny Gatton T-Style neck & bridge

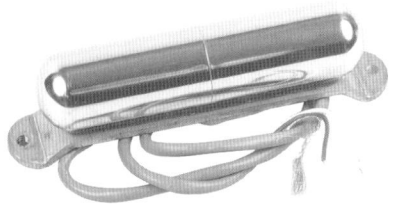

Kent Armstrong "Split Tube" replacement

simultaneously shift in the result can often yield a thick, muddy sounding pickup with shabby lows and clipped highs – which is exactly how too many of these replacement pickups sounded.

Hot, over-wound ceramic pickups have their place, certainly, but using one to define 'the ceramic pickup' does a disservice to dozens of other excellent designs that employ ceramic magnets. A number of excellent sounding G&L pickups, for example, including many designed by Leo Fender himself, use ceramic magnets, as do highly respected 'boutique' pickups from both Joe Barden and Bill Lawrence, and plenty of excellent designs from DiMarzio and Seymour Duncan. While the latter two makers do tend more often to use ceramic magnets in pickups intended for heavy rock and metal players – although they do so today with due consideration of the full range of factors associated with ceramic magnets – many pickups from G&L, Barden and Lawrence aim to attain vintage-voiced sweetness and unprecedented clarity in pickups that appeal to jazz, blues and country players as much as to rockers.

The designers of more nuanced ceramic pickups achieve their success by redrawing the blueprint, to some extent at least, and conceiving their pickups from the ground up with the properties of ceramic magnets in mind. This means, among other things, adjusting the number of wire turns considerably downward, in most cases, to maintain a broad frequency response and achieve a clean, dynamic performance. Simply substituting ceramic for alnico as a 'hotrodding' effort, as was often done in the early days, usually results in a slamming but flat voice, and works for little else than super-high-gain rocking. Redrawing all the parameters accordingly and working with ceramic's strengths, these makers produce pickups that are nuanced, musical, and extremely well defined. Depending upon what you do with them, you can convince your ears that they are 'vintage' sounding, or entirely 'modern'. They are, simply, something different. New designs using rare earth magnets have also appeared in recent years. Tom Anderson uses neodymium in some of his more contemporary styled pickups, and Bill Lawrence has employed samarium cobalt in a range of pickups designed for Fender. Magnets made from these rare materials are very expensive, but also extremely powerful – as much as seven times as powerful as ceramic magnets of a comparable size – so much less magnetic material is required in the construction. By and large, such magnets contribute to pickups that exhibit high fidelity and a broad frequency response, which is generally achieved in designs in which the magnetic field presents a minimum of interference with string vibration.

the anatomy of the pickup

Ultimately, what the detractors of these high-end ceramic or rare earth pickups might hold against them most is their unfamiliarity. A player's first experience with something like a set of Joe Barden S Deluxe pickups can be daunting. Guitar and amp settings and playing style all need to be adjusted, to some extent, to account for the clarity and resolution that high-fidelity ceramic pickups such as these will confront you with, and sometimes the experience is just too revealing for some players to enjoy. Which is not to say that the relative softness, roundness and compression of a 'vintage-style' pickup is either superior or inferior; as with everything gear-related, they are all questions of taste and perception. The issues that matter most are what you do with it, and what the results sound like to you.

Differently Sized and Structured Pickups

This far into the game you're already getting the idea that every little change in the template triggers a change in the way a pickup will sound. The overall structure and size of the unit are biggies in the equation, and even with all else being equal, just molding that clay into different shapes will give you a different tonal performance.

DiMarzio Virtual Vintage

Some pickups use 'bobbins' as coil formers, which are pre-molded formers with channels down the center that provide space to insert the pole pieces and an insulating wall around which the wire will be wound, along with a flat top and bottom section that will provide protection for the coil. The dual bobbins of a Gibson humbucker or the single wide bobbin of a P-90 fit this description. Others, such as Fender single-coil pickups, don't have a bobbin as such (although the term is still sometimes used), but use flatware – the familiar top and bottom fiber plate – to hold the alnico magnet pole pieces in place, while the coil wire is wound directly around these magnets. Not only will the type of former used to shape the coil affect the pickup's tone, but so will the shape of either configuration.

DiMarzio Fast Track

Take one coil former for a Fender Jazzmaster pickup and one for a Stratocaster pickup, load them with six alnico pole pieces cut from the exact same rod, and wind them back-to-back with the exact same number of turns of wire from the same spool. Now load them in turn onto the same test-bed guitar, and play. They will sound different. They will have sonic elements in common, of course, but there should also be enough noticeable differences to make you think of them as two different types of pickups ... which they are.

Just winding that wire around a differently shaped bobbin changes the way

the anatomy of the pickup

the coil performs. We'll look at that from a few other angles below, but as far as the shape/performance ratio is concerned, a big part of it goes back to the basics of the electromagnetic device. Compiling this structure around a different framework, and thereby rendering the ultimate shape of the device differently, also changes the structure of the magnetic field – invisible though it might be – and leads to pickups that read string vibration slightly differently. The wider pickup shape contributes to a wider 'magnetic window', if you will, which samples vibrations from a wider region along the length of the strings. A longer sample of the vibrating strings means more competing frequencies which, when blended, lead to a little phase cancellation and, therefore, a slightly warmer, less defined, less brightly focused sound. I'm talking extremes here, and of course a single coil vintage Jazzmaster pickup is still a pretty bright and focused-sounding pickup. But it does sound different from a narrower pickup made with exactly the same ingredients.

Let's sidetrack a minute to consider how this sampling of a longer section of the strings' vibration leads to a different sound coursing through your pickup. You already know how your guitar's strings sound different at different locations along their length; this is why we have pickups in different positions and select them with a switch to achieve different sounds. But even with just one pickup selected you can pick your strings at different locations along their length between bridge and neck and hear how the tone changes in each place. Start at the back and pick steadily, moving just a few millimeters at a time, and you will notice that the change is constant and steady.

Blend the sound from a range of those positions and you've got a sound that's different than that perceived from a narrower, more tightly focused portion of the strings. Of course, the most obvious example of this is the humbucking pickup. Consider the classic example, Gibson's PAF humbucker. Its two narrow, side-by-side coils react with string vibration most intensely from two narrow regions just a little over ¾-inch apart, while also picking up a little of the vibration between these two regions and a little beyond either side of them. A vintage PAF and a vintage P-90 both use alnico bar magnets, and have about the same total number of turns of wire, give or take a few hundred, and will give you about the same DC resistance reading (within a fairly broad range that encompasses both types of these inconsistent early pickups). They sure do sound different, though, and the differences in their shape and construction partly account for this. Sure, they are also different in many other ways, and we're not even addressing the noise issues at the heart of the whole humbucking *raison d'etre*,

the anatomy of the pickup

but this is an easy case in point regarding pickup shape and response. The P-90, like the Jazzmaster pickup, also uses a wide coil and therefore reacts with a magnetic field that is again different from that of a Strat or Tele pickup. Again, of course, they are different in many other ways besides, but it all comes together to determine what they are, and how they sound.

The position of the coil and the magnet structure in relation to the strings also contributes to sonic changes. For example, consider two P-90 pickups with the tops of their pole pieces exactly the same distance from the underside of the strings, but one pickup is mounted low into the body of the guitar with the threaded pole pieces extended toward the strings, while the other is raised up to lift the entire pickup closer to the strings. The two will sound slightly different. The same applies to two identical Gretsch Dynasonic pickups, one with its adjustable alnico pole pieces raised toward the strings, the other with the entire pickup boosted up toward the strings, with an extra mounting ring used as a shim, for example. The ways in which they sound different are largely down to the ears of the player, but the low pickup/extended pole pieces scenario is often described as 'twangier', while the raised pickup scenario is 'fuller', to put it simply.

To a great extent these three variables – (1) Magnet Type and Structure and (2) Differently Sized and Structured Pickups (as just discussed), and (3) Different Types of Coils, to follow – all work hand in hand, and in some ways the lines between their functions are blurred. What I'm really trying to do is build up the big picture of these variables, while keeping in mind their constant interaction. And it's that interaction that leads to the geometric progression of tonal variations when you start twisting the tweak wheel a few notches on one variable after another. It really is like chaos theory in so many ways: the beating butterfly wings of a simple change of alnico type at one end echoes forward to a tonal hurricane at the other end.

Different Types of Coils

We approach this one knowing that we've already discussed coils in a range of contexts, but there's plenty more to say. The most obvious factor here is the number of times the wire is wrapped around the coil former, or bobbin, to make the complete coil. Most guitarists are at least a little aware of this factor, and many will know that increasing the turns of wire means a higher DC resistance reading, which in turn increases the output of the pickup (more about DC resistance readings later).

Note, however, that in addition to increasing the power of any given pickup, wrapping more wire in the coil also changes its voice. After a point, as you add turns, you increase midrange response but attenuate treble and bass; the reverse applies for removing turns of wire from a nominal, tonally acceptable 'standard' number of turns. Up to a point, increasing a pickup's midrange aggression by adding more wire can work to the advantage of a weak pickup with a harsh, brittle treble response, as the high strings will sound smoother and fuller with an increase in output coupled to a decrease in pure highs. Along the way, though, the lower wound strings – which perhaps sounded just right as they were, treble-balance wise – will round out too, and grow toward sounding muddy and indistinct if the increase in winds is taken to extremes.

Given the dimensions of many traditional bobbins, there's a limit to how much wire you can load into many coils anyway. Stack enough turns of 42-gauge wire tightly onto a standard Stratocaster pickup, for example, to get it up to around 7.5k to 8k ohms and you have pretty much filled the thing up. The next step is to change up to a thinner wire and wind a coil with 43-gauge wire. This solution fits not only the needs of pickup hotrodders, but also of manufacturers who are dealing with smaller bobbins and need to load in enough wire for merely adequate output levels. Changing wire gauge changes your pickup's tone, too, and while using a thinner wire might let you really pack the coil, it will also result in a pickup that sounds different even from one with either the same number of turns of thicker wire, or wound to the same DC readings but with thicker wire.

Once again, what works for each player is a matter of taste. Take as a case in point, though, a standard Fender Telecaster pickup set. The pickup set on this guitar is unusual – in fact, totally unique among the field of classic electric guitars – in that its bridge and neck pickup are of very different designs. Look at the average pair from the mid 1960s, at the very start of the CBS era, by which time Fender's pickup-winder counter readings had become standardized: bridge pickups averaged 7,500 turns of 42-gauge wire for an average DC resistance reading of around 6.4k; neck pickups were wound with an average 7,500 turns of 43-gauge wire for a reading of around 7k. This would imply a hotter neck pickup, which on most guitars would lead to a major imbalance between pickup outputs since the neck position is a 'louder' position acoustically in the first place. But any Tele player will tell you that, if anything, those neck pickups tend to be a little dull and weak sounding when compared to the twang-o-matic bridge pickup in a good Telecaster. W'happen? Well, they are differently constructed pickups, part of which is their use of different wire gauges, and they just sound different.

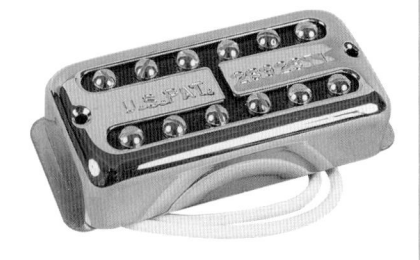

Gretsch Filter'Tron

the anatomy of the pickup

For another exception that proves the rule, take the Gretsch Dynasonic pickup of the mid 1950s (manufactured by Rowe as the DeArmond 200 model). These single-coil pickups were wound with very fine 44-gauge wire, and I have measured original examples with DC readings from anywhere in the upper 8k range to beyond 13k ohms. High-output pickups? Not by the contemporary meaning of the term, no. They certainly can have a kick to them, but great examples are characterized more as bright, jangly, clear, and fat. Even though at the hotter end of the range they give you specs that read like those of hotrod style 'distortion' pickups, they are a classic clean pickup, with a broad frequency response and excellent note definition throughout the range.

The variables of coil construction, however, include many, many factors beyond mere wire gauge and number of turns, although those are biggies within any given design. The precision with which any given wire was wound onto the coil former will also affect the way the coil performs. This accounts for a whole bundle of variables in and of itself:

The tightness or looseness of the coil will affect its sound. Some players and manufacturers attribute some of the 'magic' of good vintage-style reproduction pickups to a degree of looseness in the wind, which translates to a slightly microphonic pickup. Not a coil so loose that wire is flopping around and the coil is changing shape, nor one that exhibits so much microphony that you're getting excessive feedback howl even at moderate volumes. But a touch of microphony can contribute to a 'lively' sounding pickup, and when a coil is acting both as a microphone that pickups up direct guitar-body resonance in addition to its electromagnetic sensing of string vibration, it's conceivable that it is producing a richer, more complex signal.

The neatness and consistency with which the turns of wire are laid into the coil, or layered, is also attributed with certain sonic properties. More precisely, the reverse is generally credited with producing a certain magic. The term 'scatter wound' describes a coil that has been wound with a degree of 'calculated randomness', if you will. Manufacturers that employ this technique site the arguably 'sloppy' winding of some vintage Fender pickups, where wire was not layered up wrap upon wrap, precisely, as it formed around the bobbin, but occasionally made skips and jumps up and down the horizontal plane. Sloppy or not, this scatter winding is also accredited with a liveliness of tone, and many modern manufacturers seek to reproduce it. Others, of course, will boast of the superior precision and regularity of their turns, and credit this with superior sounding pickups.

In another way, the care with which wire is wound onto the bobbin can greatly affect the final result. Very fine wire will stretch slightly if pulled too tightly around the ends of the bobbin, which are narrower than the sides. If you stretch 42-gauge wire, it becomes something like 43- or 44-gauge wire, and even if this happens only for brief passes at the ends of the bobbin the change will affect the DC resistance and the performance of the pickup.

Variables within variables, my friends. You're getting used to it by now, but it does make your head spin after a time.

We have discussed the fact that different gauges of coil wire will result in coils that perform differently. Along with the wire itself, even the coating used to insulate it plays a part in determining how the pickup performs. While the very fine wire wrapped around the bobbin of any pickup might look like bare wire, it actually has an insulating coating, and would short out otherwise. The wire within the insulation does the muscle work, of course, but the type and degree of insulation acts as a variable in the coil's performance by affecting how tightly and thickly/thinly the wire can be wound as well as determining the overall outer diameter of the wire, insulation included. The overall thickness of the wire and its contribution to the way the coil builds up will affect the inductance and capacitance of the coil. Arguably, the insulating material also affects mechanical vibration, and therefore resonance, within the pickup, according to how hard/brittle or absorbent it is.

Since the wire used to wind pickup coils is so fine, its insulation must be baked on, rather than applied as a sheath as is the more familiar plastic or PVC insulation which most of us are familiar with from larger-gauge wire. The most commonly used coatings are Formvar, plain enamel, and polyurethane, and each results in a slightly different thickness of insulation. Formvar-coated wire was used in Fender Stratocaster pickups until about 1964, when the company changed to plain enamel, and this slightly thicker, heavier Formvar therefore is the coating material you will hear bragged about most in the literature of contemporary winders keen to point out how rigidly they adhere to vintage Fender Strat specs. Gibson, on the other hand, used plain enamel-coated wire for both its P-90 single coils and PAF humbucking pickups, as did Fender for its Telecaster pickups, so this type of wire has come to be and essential ingredient of any repro PAF or vintage-style Tele pickup. On one hand, many great pickup-makers will tell you that 'wire is wire. On the other, many others will expound at length on the fact that, while wire may be wire, the coating it carries will both vary in thickness according to the material it is made from, and affect the

the anatomy of the pickup

inductance and capacitance of the coil according to that thickness, so in these ways a change in insulation coating material can indeed change the sound of the pickup in a very real way.

In an effort to dampen unwanted vibration and microphony within the coil and between constituent parts of the pickup, and to keep out unwanted moisture, many manufacturers dip their pickups in hot wax or paraffin – a process called 'wax potting'. The wax settles in between and around the windings, as well as the formers and spacers and any hardware used to assemble the pickup, and forms a cohesive sheath that is also resistant to mechanical vibration. Whether a pickup is potted or not, or how thoroughly it is potted, can also affect its sound and performance. Players are more aware of the performance aspect of this procedure, or, more precisely, the resultant feedback howl that an absence of wax potting can sometimes lead to.

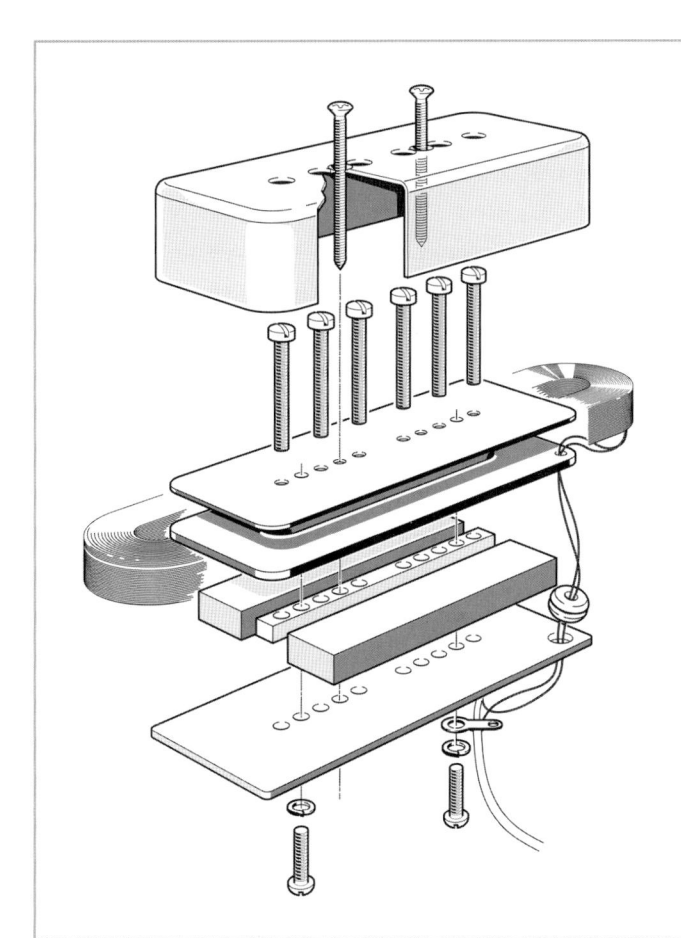

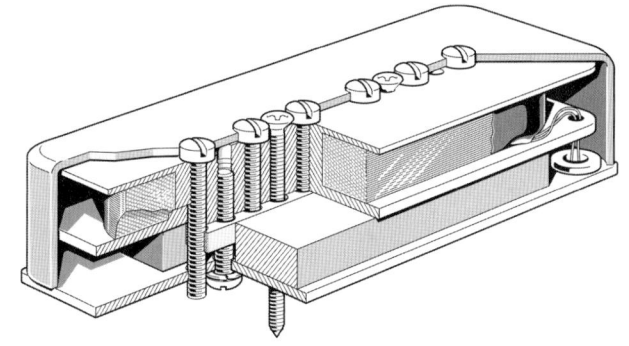

P-90 Soapbar

The original Gibson 'soapbar-style' P-90, and the many contemporary replacement models for this pickup manufactured by other makers, uses a coil wound around a wide, shallow plastic (or butyrate) bobbin, through which six adjustable threaded steel pole pieces pass. Beneath the bobbin, they also thread through a steel bar that provides contact with the two bar magnets mounted either side of it. Coil and magnets are held in place by a steel bottom plate with two mounting bolts. The plastic cover is held in place by two long screws that pass through the entire assembly and into the body of the guitar, providing the adjustable mounting for the pickup. (Note that the 'dog-ear' P-90 pickup is made the same way, but its base plate has two mounting tabs, one at either end, through which screws pass to mount the pickup to the body, while also holding the cover on the pickup itself.)

Take two identical pickups, pot one and leave the other unpotted, mount both in similar guitars and play them in front of a loud amplifier, and very often the unpotted pickup will squeal if you get too close. This isn't the harmonic feedback that can be used to creative effect, but the squealing howl-round of a feedback loop that is a pure nuisance. Many unpotted pickups can sound great, and many vintage pickups – notably Gibson PAF humbuckers and P-90s – were not originally potted, so this hot-wax bath hasn't always been considered an absolute necessity. Sometimes you even encounter a non-potted pickup that was wound tightly and well, and has remained so, and will stand up to high-volume playing with minimum squeal. More often than not, however, potting is a necessary procedure for pickups that are going to be used in high-gain, contemporary rock situations.

Beyond the performance and potential squeal nuisance aspects of potting, however, the procedure can also have a slight affect on the overall tone of any pickup. Since many vintage pickups were not potted, some modern manufacturers avoid potting certain repro-style pickups to help retain a lively, active feel in their newly made units. Others accept that a potted pickup really is required in many playing situations, but pot them minimally so as to avoid over-dampening the coil. What you can get away with in an un-potted pickup really does seem to be a matter of luck, to some extent. I once owned a late '60s Gibson SG Special that had P-90s that were so microphonic you could sing into them and be heard loud and clear through your amp, but the guitar could wield gorgeous harmonic feedback when coaxed toward the amp, and was remarkably resistant to howl. Come to think of it, that was one of the best sounding P-90 equipped guitars I've ever had, too. On the other side of the coin, I also once owned a beautiful '63 Telecaster that had a gorgeous, fat yet twangy sounding bridge pickup, but it would squeal horribly anywhere within about ten feet of an amp at gig volumes. There was nothing for it but to get that pickup potted, and it still sounded great afterward – but without the squeal.

Potting, therefore, is another nuance of the pickup-maker's art, and while necessary at times, is more than just a yes/no decision, with a lot of finesse involved, and some gray area too.

Measurements and Common Specifications

Having built up our ghost of a pickup to a specific size, shape, and design, we inevitably will want to measure it. We guitarists are funny that way. If we can't affix a specification or a readout to any given piece of equipment, we're often

the anatomy of the pickup

just not happy with the simple realization that "it sounds good" so we should just get on with playing and stop worrying about it. Some of us, anyway. Talk to any considerate pickup manufacturer and they'll tell you that DC resistance readings – the most common spec associated with pickups – tell you little or nothing about how a pickup will actually sound. That said, we often don't have much else to go on, other than wiring pickup after pickup into a test-bed guitar and playing them to find out. And many manufacturers don't give us much other than DC resistance to go on, other than their own floral promotional descriptions of the components.

While this spec doesn't, indeed, tell you everything about how any given pickup will sound, it does perhaps give you some clues about, for example, six similarly designed Stratocaster pickups, made with the same materials. Attach six different DC resistance readings to these, and you can guess that the 4.85k ohm pickup might sound a little thin, bright and under-gunned in the bridge, but

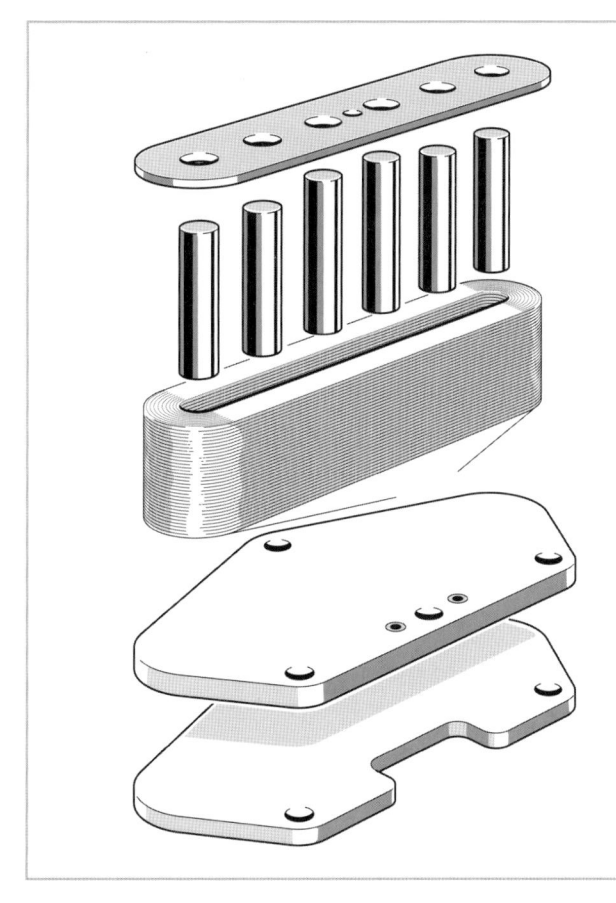

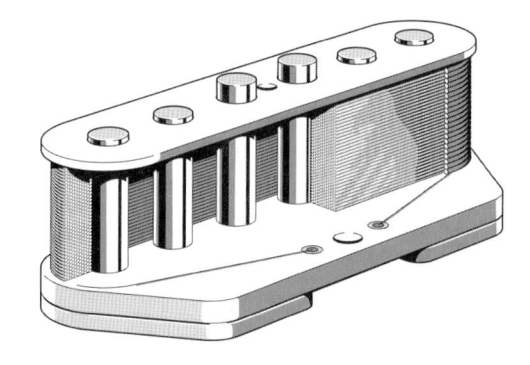

T-Style Single Coil

The original Fender Telecaster single-coil pickup (and similar replacements made by a range of manufacturers today) is a more complex design than it might at first appear, and traditionally it works in conjunction with the steel bridge plate to which it is mounted. A 'bobbinless' coil is wound directly around six fixed pole pieces made from alnico rod magnets, which are held in place by top and bottom plates cut from a semi-rigid fiber material (sometimes plastic or other synthetic material in later examples). A further thin steel base plate is held to the bottom fiber plate by the magnetism of the pole pieces and the tackiness of the wax with which the pickup is potted. This base plate is tapped with three holes, into which mounting bolts passed through the bridge plate are threaded. These pickups carry no cover, so the coil is traditionally wrapped with black or white string for protection (sometimes modern examples use tape).

snappy and round in the neck; the 7.2k ohm pickup is likely to sound a little too fat in the neck, but will be twangy and thick in the bridge, or gutsy and aggressive in the middle position, and so on.

Generalizing more broadly, however, about a wide range of pickups' power, or so-called 'output', by using DC resistance as a yardstick can be misleading. A pickup's resistance doesn't measure anything being 'put out' at all, but is a static measure of its coil at rest, taken with a specially designed meter, and simply reads the number of turns of X gauge of wire that have been wrapped around the coil. More or less turns of wire in a coil of a specific design will yield a more or less powerful result, respectively, but comparing the resistance readings of a Strat pickup, a Tele pickup, a Gibson P-90, and a Gretsch Filter'Tron will get you nowhere. Even if all read exactly 6.5k ohms they would sound very different, and even exhibit distinctly different output levels. Also, since DC resistance readings

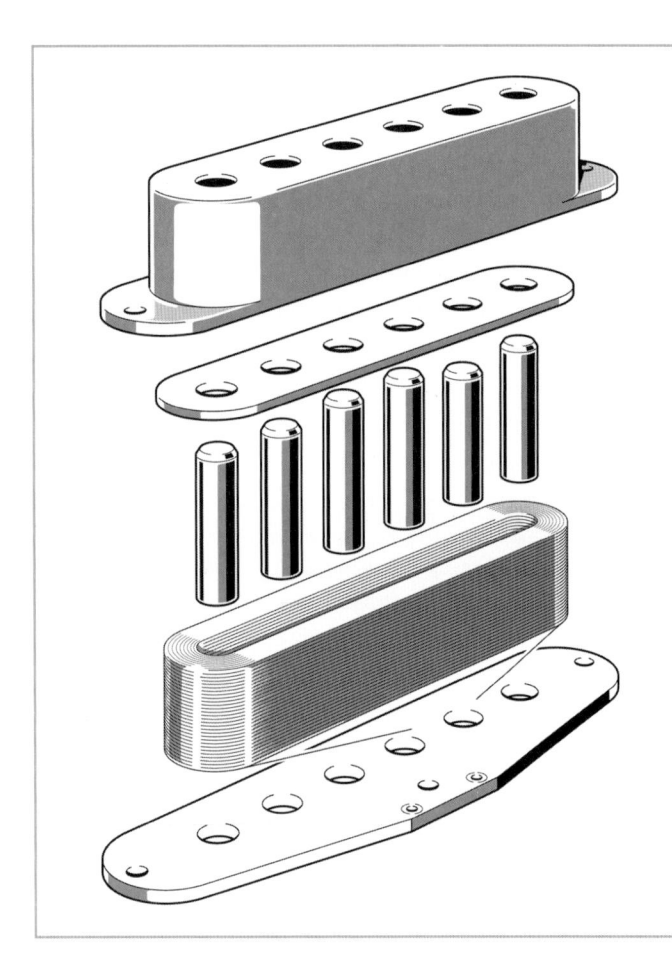

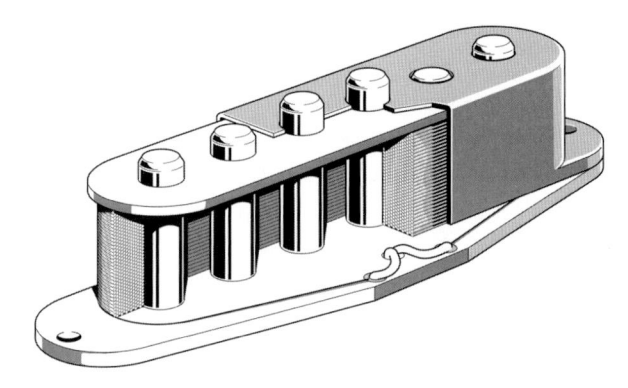

S-Style Single Coil
The original Fender Stratocaster single-coil pickup, versions of which are now used on a wide range of electric guitars, is essentially a 'bobbinless' design. A top and bottom plate (made from semi-rigid fiber in original examples, and from plastic or other synthetic material in some later designs) hold alnico rod magnet pole pieces in place, and the coil wire is wound directly around these magnets. A plastic cover protects the coil from grime, sweat, and general wear and tear.

the anatomy of the pickup

are taken with the pickup 'at rest', all bets are off once you strum those strings and set things in motion. When the coil reacts to the strings' vibration in the pickup's magnetic field it generates an AC signal, and its DC resistance changes as a result. Different pickups with approximately the same DC resistance react differently in use, so this measurement is of limited use in comparing X to Y to Z. (If you've got a digital multi-meter handy, try this: set it to the 20k position in the OHMs field, plug in a short jumper cord, connect the meter's positive probe to the hot tip of the cord's dangling plug and the negative to the shaft of the plug, switch to either bridge or neck pickup alone with volume and tone up full, and take your reading. Now strum. See how it fluctuates? Now change the meter to a setting for AC 200V or even DC 200m. With the strings still your reading should be '000', but when you strum the numbers should roll up a little. That's your pickup's coil generating its low-voltage signal. It's no use, by the

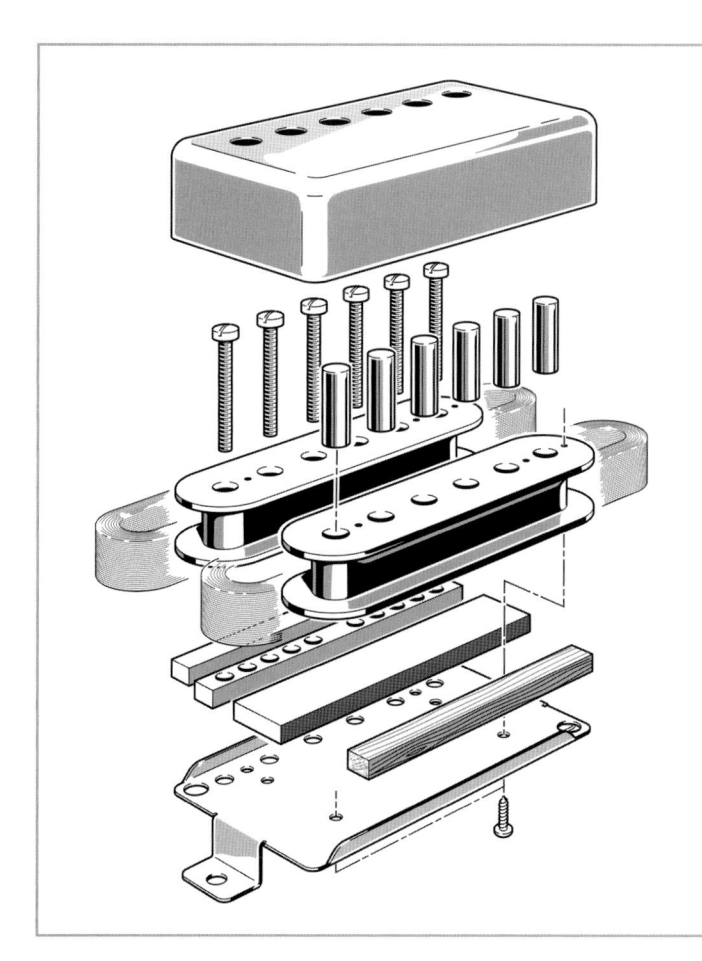

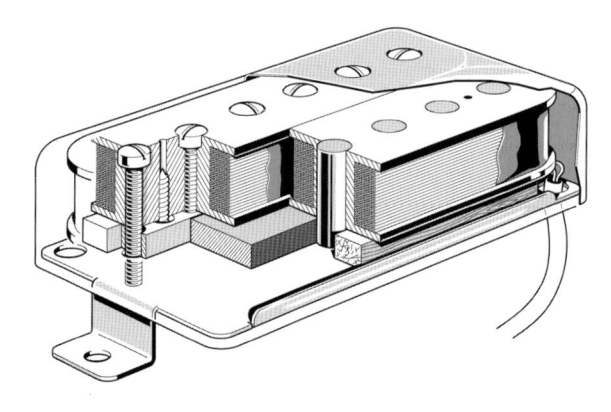

Humbucker
The majority of traditional, full-sized humbuckers are made in the approximate image of the Gibson PAF humbucker. The notable elements of these are the two side-by-side coils wound around plastic (or butyrate) bobbins, fixed steel slug poles in one coil and threaded adjustable steel poles in the other, a steel bottom plate that holds the works together, and often a cover, traditionally made of thin nickel silver. The threaded poles pass through a threaded steel bar that provides their contact with the single bar magnet mounted between them (beneath the coils), while the slug poles contact the magnet directly. A spacer, traditionally made of maple, takes up the extra space on the far side of the slug poles and provides another surface for that coil to rest upon.

the guitar pickup handbook

way, trying to make anything of this 'output' read out, and this isn't any accurate way to measure output in any case, it's just an interesting exercise – and rather fascinating to see a visual example of a coil at work.)

The factors that tell us more about how a pickup is likely to sound are all those we have discussed above. In short, the numbers will only take you so far, but a description of how the pickup was made, and with what materials, will get you into the ballpark at least. To paint an even more detailed picture, you need to bring other numbers into play, ones that aren't so easily read by the conventional $20 multi-meter from Radio Shack. A pickup's AC impedance and its resultant inductance, which is measured in Henries, say a bit more about how it might sound than its raw DC resistance does, and give us some clues about the 'meat' and 'body' of its tone. The relationship between inductance and magnetic strength are also important factors. Beyond these, a pickup's resonant frequency can also be a clue to its basic voice. When plugged into a standard guitar cord, most pickups have a resonant frequency in the 2,000 Hz to 5,000 Hz

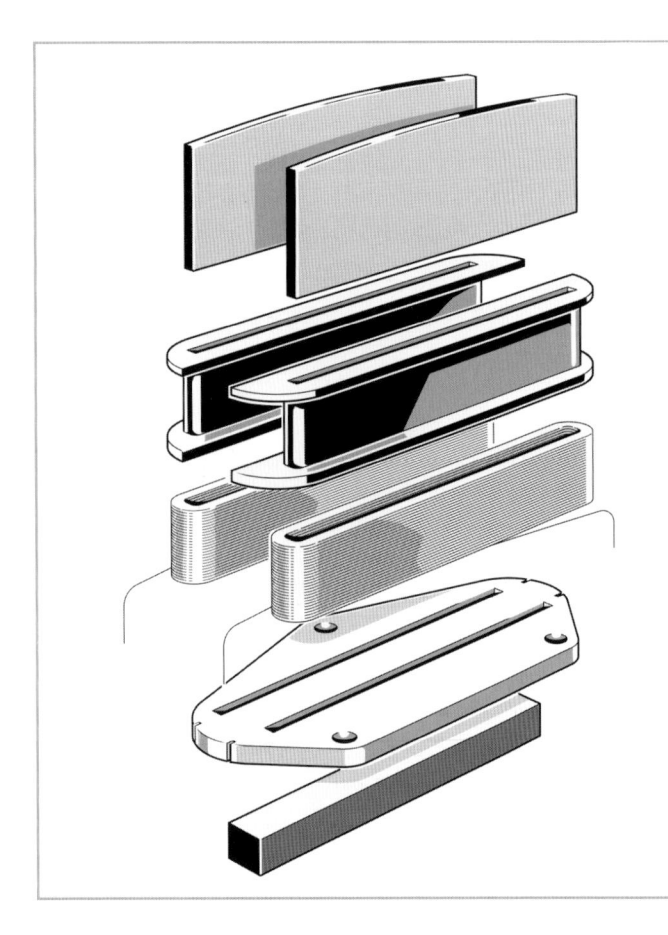

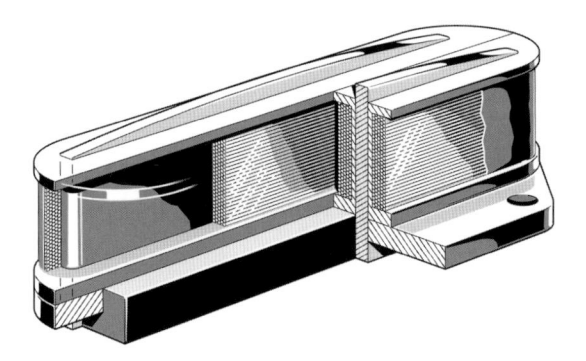

Dual Rail
Dual rail-style humbucking pickups made to fit into a single-coil-sized mounting employ two narrow, side-by-side bobbins with channels slotted through the center, through which steel 'blade' pole pieces pass to contact a separate magnet mounted below. In most designs, a separate bottom plate holds the coils, magnet and poles together. Note that different manufactures make this type of pickup somewhat differently, with the magnet inserted into a slot in the bottom plate in some designs, and simply mounted to the underside of the plate in others. To illustrate this, our exploded view shows the latter, while the cross-section view shows the former.

the anatomy of the pickup

range. At extreme lows in this range pickups are likely to be overly dark and dull sounding; at extreme highs, they will tend to be brittle and harsh.

So, knowing the specs might get you somewhere: scrutinizing the DC resistance, inductance, and resonant frequency, and contemplating them in combination with the magnet type and structure, coil configuration, pole piece design and configuration, and the basic structure of the pickup will almost always give you a rough idea of how the thing is going to sound and perform. But you're not looking for 'a rough idea', are you? No, you want to *pin down* your tone. In the end, all you can really do is wire up the thing and play it, and of course you need to do so in the guitar in which you intend to use it in order for the assessment to be of any value for you. That said, the more you know about how pickups are put together, what goes into them, and what kinds of statistical read outs they are likely to give you, the better you can narrow down your search for that next critical component from thousands of possibilities to just a few dozen. You're getting there already, so hang on tight and keep driving.

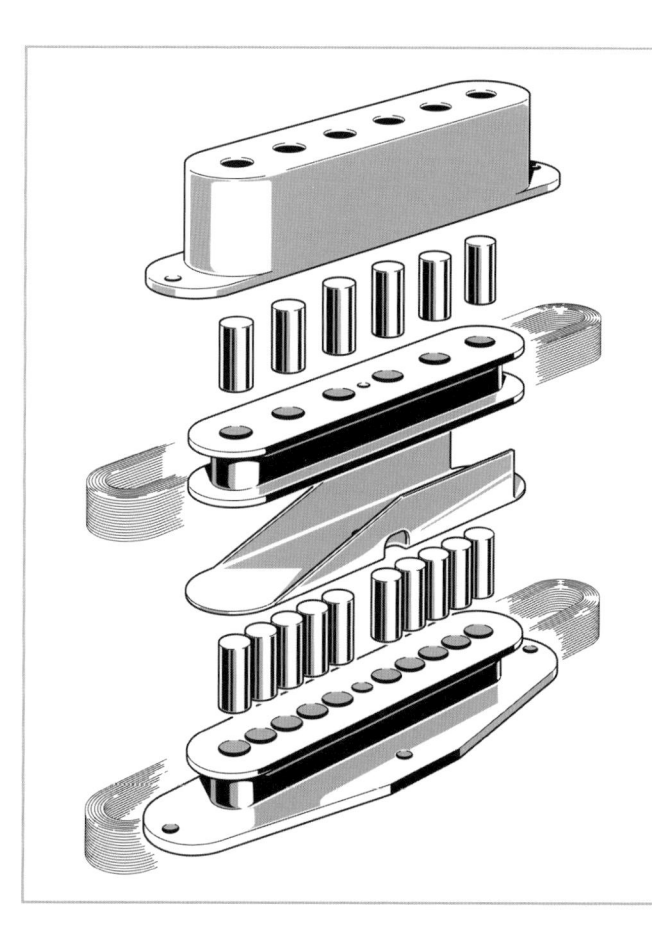

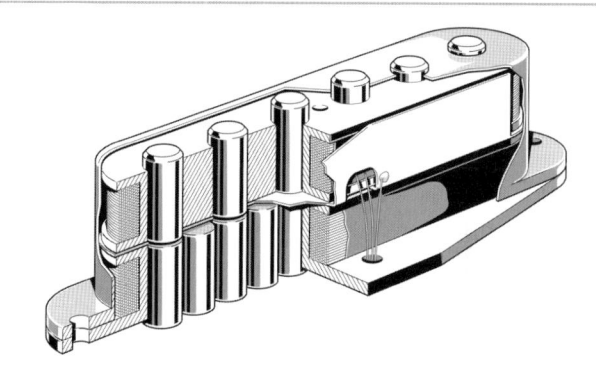

Stacked Humbucker
One of the early solutions to the puzzle of achieving single-coil tone in a noise-canceling design, stacked humbuckers have been made in a number of different ways. Some – early examples of the breed in particular – use a pair of 'piggybacked' coils through which long alnico rod magnets pass, and which are wound reverse phase/reverse polarity to negate the 60 cycle hum from each, while passing on the summed signal from both. Some newer designs, of which our illustration is one, use a shallower noise-reducing coil with 'dummy poles' on the bottom that serves to eliminate hum, without contributing anything to the tonal output of the pickup. A larger coil on top, loaded with alnico magnet poles, to generate the guitar signal. There is usually some form of steel shielding between the two coils to further reduce unwanted noise.

MANUFACTURERS' PROFILES — THE 'BIG FOUR'

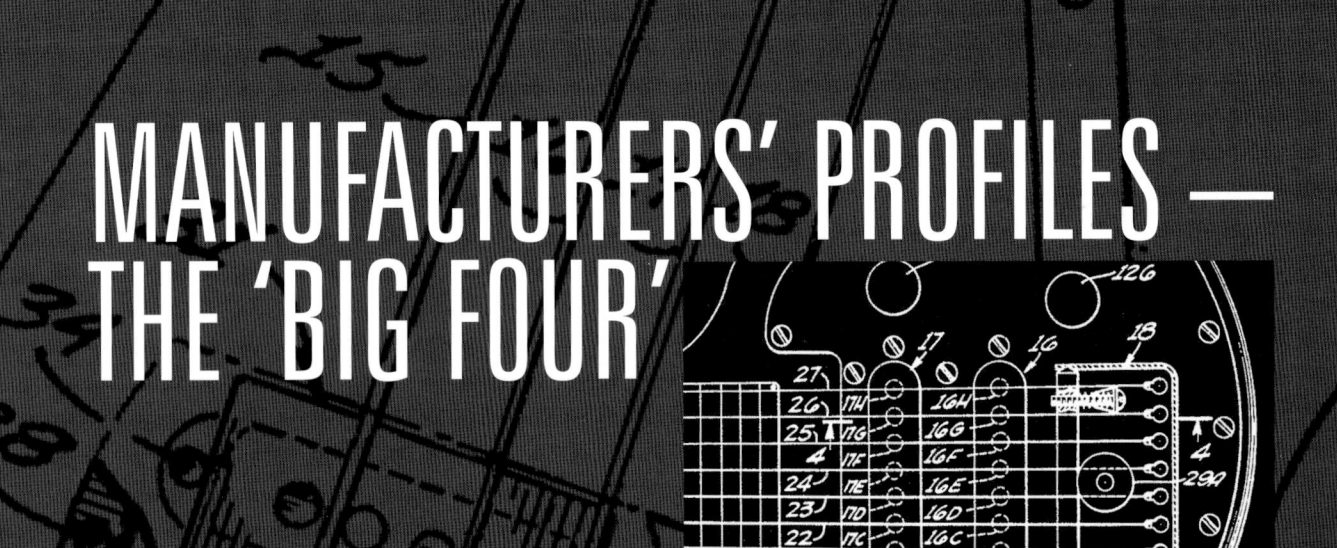

"Essentially what it boils down to is, magnetism is magnetism. It doesn't matter where you get it, it's how you apply it."
JOE BARDEN, MANASSAS, VA, MARCH 2008

manufacturers' profiles – the 'big four'

It's time to dig into the histories and specific creations of the manufacturers that have brought so many great tonal icons to the guitar world, right alongside a few clunkers and oddballs that are often no less interesting. In this chapter, we'll look at what I call the 'Big Four' of American pickup development for the 20th century: Rickenbacker, Gibson, Fender, and Gretsch. These guitar-makers really laid the foundations for electromagnetic tone, and I'd guess that some 90 percent or more of pickups in use today can trace their roots to designs that originated in their workshops. In the next chapter, we'll look at other guitar-makers who have contributed to the art, as well as manufacturers that specialize in after-market replacement pickups. The spec boxes included here are intended to detail what information is available on these pickups, although the inconsistencies in many early examples means there's often quite a wide range of readings applicable in certain categories. Approximate dates of the designs' origination are given, where useful for reference, and current-manufacture pickups are also indicated. In cases where reissued examples of an original, vintage design are not specified themselves, it can be assumed that the reissue is a fairly close replica of the original.

Rickenbacker

The Introduction to this book already covered a lot of the early history of Rickenbacker, which was really the first viable manufacturer of guitars equipped from the factory with electromagnetic pickups, and the only surviving company to have begun even before Gibson's entry into the electric guitar market. Although Rickenbacker has its roots in George Beauchamp and Paul Barth's efforts with electromagnetic pickups of as early as 1930, and its first products hit the market in the form of the Electro brand Model 22 'Frying Pan' lap-steel and Spanish-style guitars, the name as we know it today didn't land on a headstock until around 1949, although the company switched from Electro to the Germanic 'Rickenbacher' spelling in 1934. Nevertheless, Rickenbacker's ascension by fits and starts into the mainstream of the electric musical instrument market, and the simple fact of its longevity, make it the longest surviving manufacturer of electric guitars, and more to the point here, of electromagnetic pickups, beating Gibson by a healthy four years, or two if you discount the Electro years.

Unsurprisingly, early Rickenbacker pickups are archaic looking beasts, too, but they sure pack a punch. Many a tone-minded player still swears by the sonic

manufacturers' profiles – the 'big four'

girth and depth produced by a Rickenbacker 'horseshoe pickup', the name given to the final result of Beauchamp and Barth's undertakings, which remained the company's cornerstone pickup for a surprisingly long stretch of time, from the early 1930s until the mid 1950s. These pickups retain their legendary status in steel-guitar circles in particular, where lap-steel players continue to discuss their unique and stellar tonal properties to this day. But Rickenbacker even used the pickups on a number of Spanish-style guitars (ie upright guitars, played traditionally) while they were still being manufactured, including some of the first of the new era of solid-body models of the 1950s. Issued by the new owner of Rickenbacker, Francis Hall, who had bought the parent company Electro String Music Corporation from Adolph Rickenbacker in 1953, guitars in the Combo series display many of the trademarks of the later, more famous Rickenbackers of The Beatles and The Byrds, but carry these ungainly horseshoe pickups rather than the more compact units that would follow them. The up-market Combo 800 model of 1955 even carried a dual-coil horseshoe pickup, a sort of basic humbucker, the individual coils of which were designed to enhance bass and treble response respectively.

For pure tonal prowess these horseshoe units might have survived until today, but for their awkwardness in playing. It is impossible to pick right over the pickup itself, and palm muting of the strings is made extremely difficult (similarly awkward to playing an early Les Paul with 'wrapunder' trapeze tailpiece, for example). For this reason, although this is a book about electric guitar pickups and not lap-steel pickups as such, early Rickenbacker lap-steel usually make easier – and more common – proposition for sampling the horseshoe sound. If you do come across one of the rare Ricky guitars with horseshoe pickup, though, it's worth plugging it in if you get the opportunity. For recorded examples of horseshoe tone, check out David Lindley's work with Jackson Browne, or much of his live and studio recording with El Rayo-Ex.

Horseshoe pickups were constructed from two U-shaped hardened cobalt steel magnets, an alloy that differs somewhat from alnico. These so-called horseshoes were positioned with their open ends nearly touching, with a coil mounted within the 'tunnel', so that the guitar strings passed over the coil but under the topmost sides of the two U channels. The coils were wound with very fine 44-gauge wire, and steel pole pieces passed through the coil to contact the lower arms of each U magnet. These are hot sounding pickups with a lot of bite and definition, but also plenty of warmth ... a sound unto themselves.

Rickenbacker really seems to be 'the company with the nicknamed pickups'.

FACING PAGE **Rickenbacker's groundbreaking "Frying Pan" electric guitar, with horseshoe magnetic pickup, patent filed 1934, granted 1937.**

manufacturers' profiles – the 'big four'

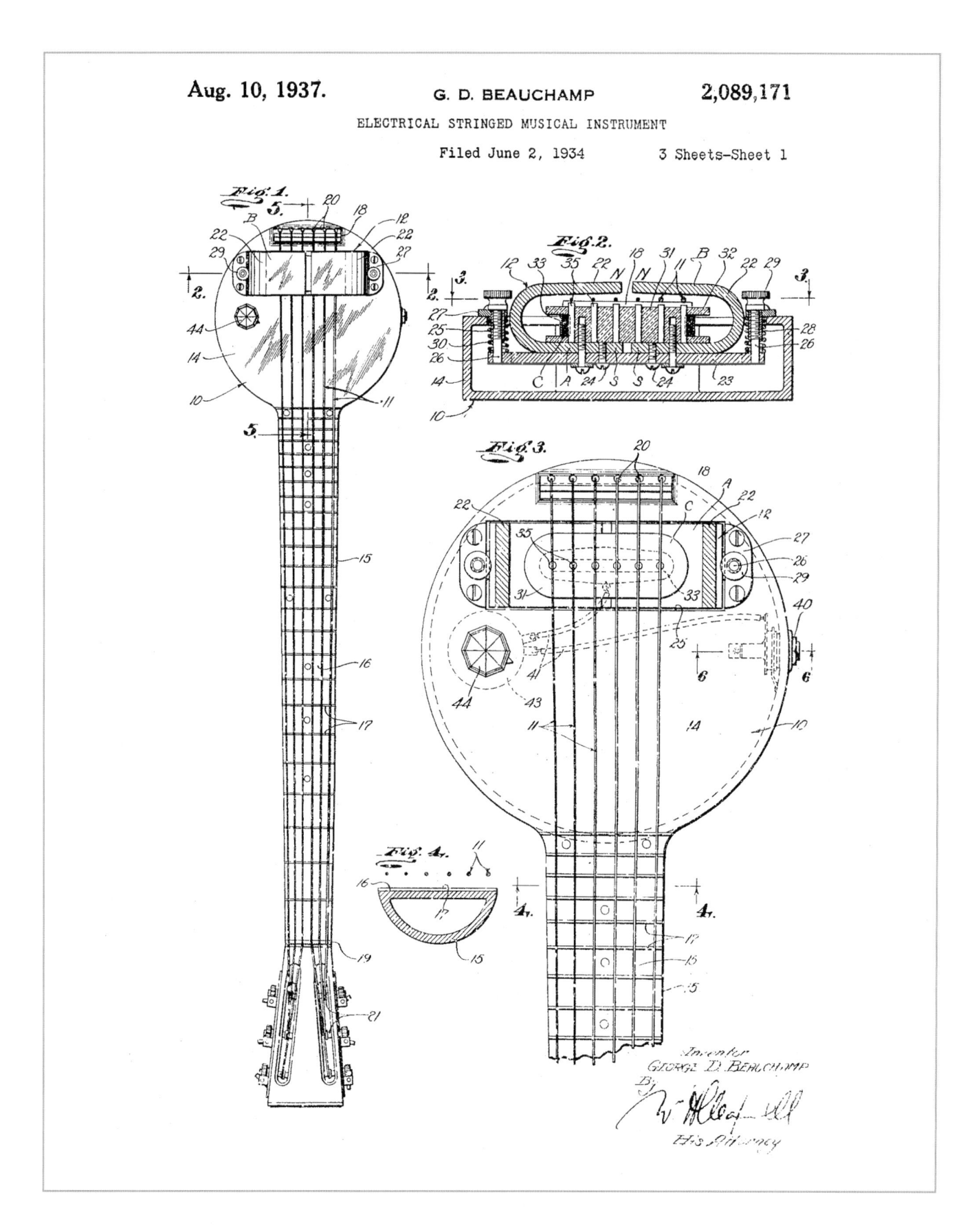

Aug. 10, 1937.　　　　G. D. BEAUCHAMP　　　　2,089,171
ELECTRICAL STRINGED MUSICAL INSTRUMENT
Filed June 2, 1934　　　3 Sheets-Sheet 1

Inventor
GEORGE D. BEAUCHAMP
By
His Attorney

manufacturers' profiles – the 'big four'

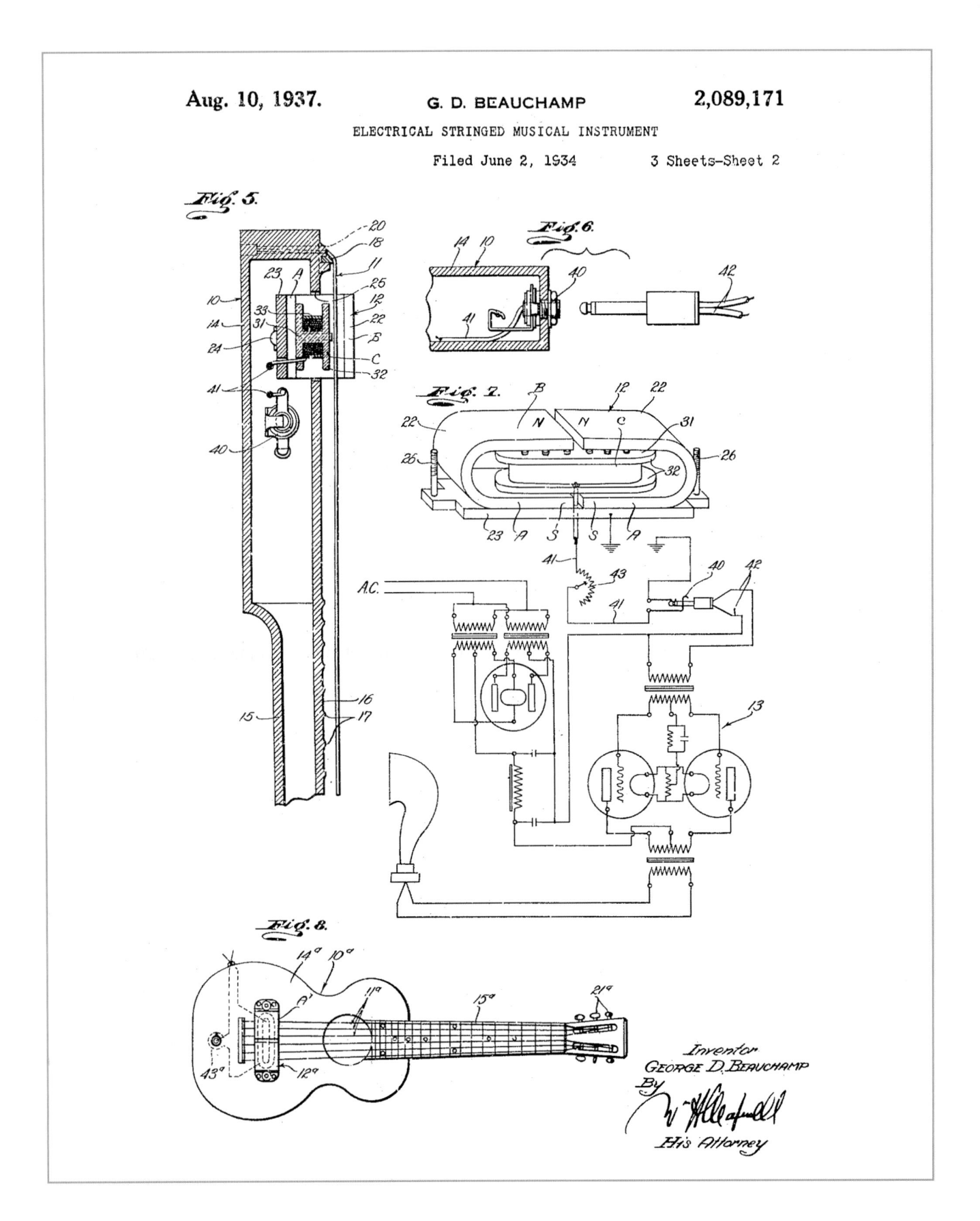

Aug. 10, 1937.   G. D. BEAUCHAMP   2,089,171
ELECTRICAL STRINGED MUSICAL INSTRUMENT
Filed June 2, 1934   3 Sheets-Sheet 2

Fig. 5.
Fig. 6.
Fig. 7.
Fig. 8.

Inventor
GEORGE D. BEAUCHAMP
By
His Attorney

manufacturers' profiles – the 'big four'

Although the horseshoe pickup is legendary for being the first widely-used magnetic pickup on a production-model electric guitar, the company's most famous pickup of all time is undoubtedly the 'toaster top' model introduced in late 1957 or early '58, which Rickenbacker was evolving toward with a number of short-lived designs for more compact pickups in the middle of the decade. The toaster top is the units you see on the 325 played by John Lennon in the early 1960s, the 360/12 played by George Harrison and Roger McGuinn, or the 1997 and 1998 models (the export versions of the 335 and 345) played by Pete Townshend in the early and mid '60s. Outwardly, these pickups are easily mistaken for a mini-humbucker type, but the 'slots' that given them the 'toaster top' nickname, really just black inlays recessed into the covers, fall either side of a single row of six individual alnico magnet pole pieces which run under the chrome center bar of the cover. These otherwise fairly traditional single-coil pickups are wound with very fine 44-gauge, Formvar-coated wire, to a DC resistance that measures anywhere between around 7k and 8.5k ohms in a range of vintage samples, but upwards of 10k ohms and beyond in some cases (the occasional use of 42- and 43-gauge wire has also been reported; note that very early examples from the 1950s were often as low as 5k ohms). The housings of these pickups are shock-mounted to the top of the guitar with a small rubber grommet at each corner to reduce microphony that might be induced by direct vibrations from the body of the guitar.

Toaster tops are bright, twangy, archetypically jangly pickups, but vintage examples aren't without a little poke and bluster when you wind them up high. Listen to the gritty *krang* that Pete Townshend gets from the toaster tops in many early Who recordings and you'll hear that these aren't necessarily tame, polite pickups. Clean up the amp and lighten up on the attack, however, and they will also deliver sweet, crystalline jangle as heard in much of Roger McGuinn's best playing. Latter-day Rickenbacker has manufactured some fairly accurate toaster top reproductions for its reissue models over the years, although the most common complaint about these is that, if anything, they have been a little *too* hot, when compared to vintage examples. The simple mod of partially unwinding these units to bring them back down into the 7k–8k range is popular in some purist circles.

In any case, Rickenbacker's next significant pickup design was intended to cater specifically for hotter rock sounds. The 'High-Gain' pickup, introduced in 1969, inevitably acquired the nickname 'button top' for its row of six, button-shaped pole pieces. These steel poles ran through a traditional single coil to

FACING PAGE **Beauchamp's design for a version of the horseshoe pickup mounted to a more conventional hollowbody Spanish guitar, patent filed 1934, granted 1937.**

contact a pair of ceramic magnets mounted beneath. Retaining the high turns ratio of 44-gauge wire while using ceramic magnets and steel polls increased the output of these new pickups significantly, but while their hot performance was deemed suitable to emerging rock styles of the day, they don't tend to be favored by fans of classic vintage Rickenbacker tones. That said, they made plenty of significant music at the hands of the Rickies played by Paul Weller in The Jam, or Peter Buck with REM, in the band's early period in particular, and they do still capture a degree of 'the Rickenbacker sound', if one that's hotter and grittier. Rickenbacker as also used other in-house pickup designs over the years, including a humbucker styled much like a dual-coil button-top unit, but fans of the classic guitar models from this maker tend to dwell most on the tonal splendor of the toaster top, or the button top for more aggressive sounds, while steel players continue to wax lyrical about the tone of the horseshoe pickup. Rickenbacker also currently offers a narrow dual-coil humbucker housed in the same size cover as the toaster and button top, and which fits the same footprint.

● Rickenbacker 'Horseshoe' (c.1931)
Type: single coil
Magnet: two hardened cobalt steel U-shaped magnets (1½-inch wide pre-war, 1¼-inch wide after World War II)
Wire: 44 gauge, Formvar coated
Resistance: 10k ohms
Pole pieces: steel within coil
Sound: bright yet fat, lots of drive and sustain with good definition

● Rickenbacker 'Toaster Top' (1957, specs circa early 1960s)
Type: single coil
Magnet: six individual alnico rod magnets
Wire: 44 gauge, Formvar coated (42- and 43-gauge occasionally reported)
Resistance: 7k–10k ohms (reissues tending toward the higher readings)
Pole pieces: alnico rods
Sound: bright, clear, crisp, yet without unpleasant harshness

● Rickenbacker High-Gain ('Button Top')
Type: single coil
Magnet: ceramic
Wire: 44 gauge, Formvar coated
Resistance: 7k–10k ohms
Pole pieces: individual steel poles
Sound: hot, punchy, slightly gritty, midrange-forward

manufacturers' profiles – the 'big four'

Gibson

The biggest name in guitars to have remained continually in operation from the late 19th century until now, Gibson was also one of the most significant players in the early days of the electrification of the instrument. In the mid 1930s Gibson offered an add-on pickup that could be mounted to its archtop guitars, but these are extremely rare units. Guy Hart originally developed Gibson's first built-in pickup for use on lap-steel guitars, namely the aluminum-bodied E-150 (later EH-150) of 1935. Known, in this form, simply as the 'bar pickup', it would be far better known as adapted for use on the ES-150 in 1936. The first mass-produced electric guitar from an established manufacturer, the ES-150 was taken up a year later by early jazz great Charlie Christian, an association that would give this pickup its name.

Gibson's so-called Charlie Christian pickup is almost as cumbersome of design and construction as the Rickenbacker horseshoe pickup that preceded it, although the majority of the Christian's bulk is hidden beneath the top of the hollow-body archtop guitar that carried it. In place of the Ricky pickup's two U-shaped cobalt steel magnets the Gibson unit used a pair of four-inch- to five-inch-long cobalt steel bar magnets, which were positioned out of site, mounted by three bolts to the underside of the guitar's top. The magnets contacted a thin, copper and nickel-plated and chromed mild-steel blade pole (or poles, in later examples) that extended through the central core of a wide bobbin. Around this was wound a coil made from anything from 38- to 41-gauge plain enamel coated wire – thick stuff compared to the magnet wire in use today – with enough turns to produce a fairly low resistance reading of around 2.5k to 4k ohms. The low gauss of the cobalt steel magnets of the day necessitate the seemingly excessive size of the two bars used, in a structure that all together weighed around 2lbs. While the whole construction combined to produce adequate output levels, these pickups often sound brighter, clearer, and more well-defined than you might expect.

The pickups on the first ES-150s used a consistent, straight blade pole piece, but in 1938 the blade was notched below the B string to compensate for its increased output relative to the other strings (remember, guitarists were still using a wound G string in those days). In 1939 the ES-250 was released with a version of the pickup that had five notches in the blade. The magnet structures varied over the years, too, with shorter magnets coming into use after 1936. Also, Gibson generally used a different magnet structure entirely in its EH (Electric Hawaiian) lap-steel guitars, employing a single large magnet attached

manufacturers' profiles – the 'big four'

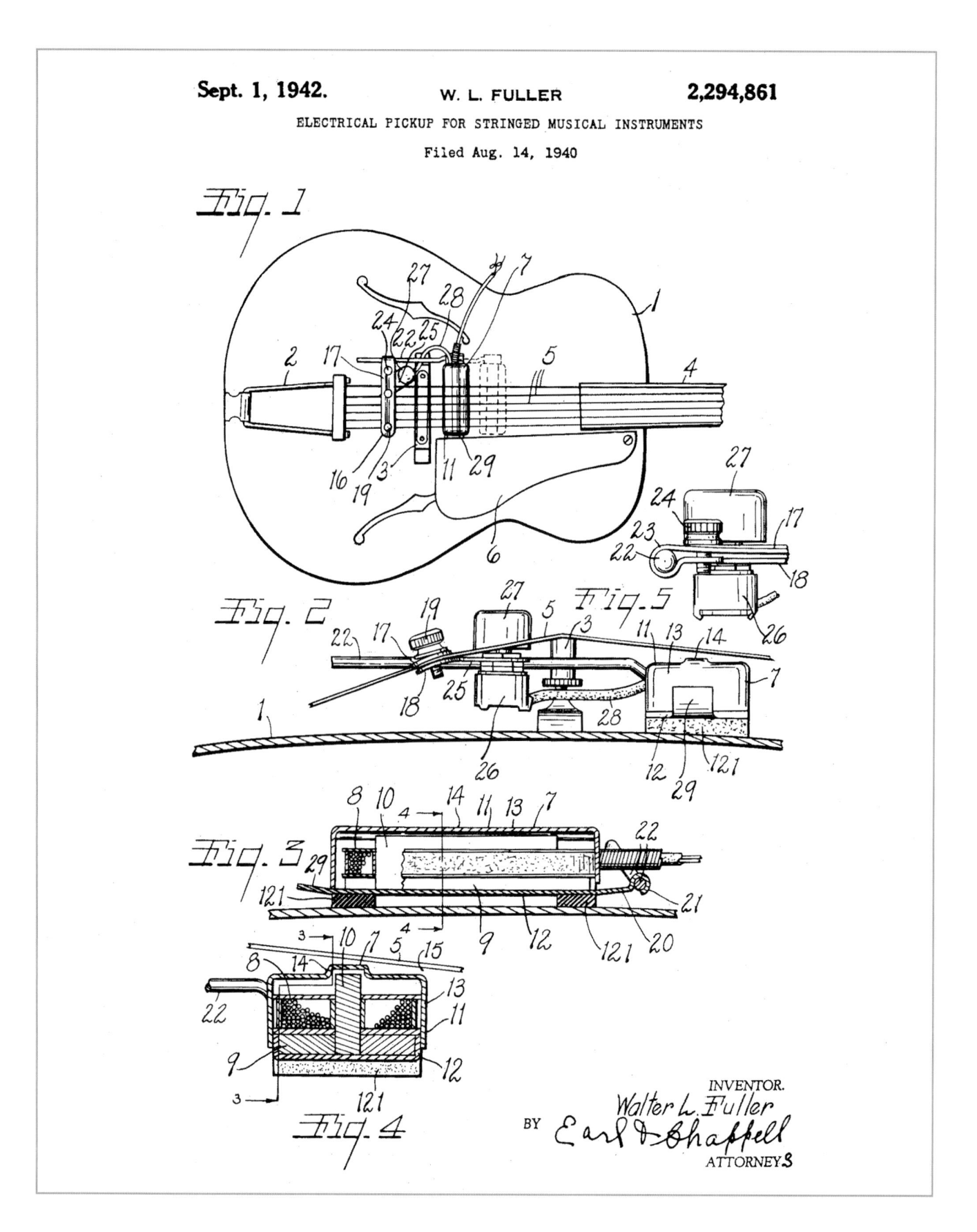

Sept. 1, 1942. W. L. FULLER **2,294,861**
ELECTRICAL PICKUP FOR STRINGED MUSICAL INSTRUMENTS
Filed Aug. 14, 1940

Fig. 1
Fig. 2
Fig. 3
Fig. 4
Fig. 5

INVENTOR.
Walter L. Fuller
BY Earl D. Chappell
ATTORNEYS

manufacturers' profiles – the 'big four'

directly under the coil. Variances in the design of these pickups create differences in their tonal character, naturally, but they do tend to have a signature sound in common, which is generally described as a rich tone with plenty of girth, haloed in surprising high-end clarity.

The Charlie Christian pickup was available from Gibson by custom order from the mid 1950s to the mid 1960s, and also showed up on the ES-175DCC (for Charlie Christian, of course) of the late 1970s. Oddly enough, the pickup has also been extremely popular for use in the (highly modified) neck position of the Fender Telecaster with some jazz and country-jazz players, a craze that was started when the late, great picker Danny Gatton used just such a configuration in the late 1970s and early '80s.

The P-90, Gibson's most beloved single coil, arrived in 1946 after guitar production ramped up again in Kalamazoo after the end of the war. It is often described as being the first production pickup with adjustable pole pieces, although early examples had fixed pole pieces. In another condemning 'although', Gibson itself had introduced an earlier unit with six individual, adjustable threaded steel poles on the 1940 ES-300, and Epiphone had a pickup with adjustable poles as early as 1937. The odd, 7-inch-long pickup was mounted on a slant and ran from about one-inch shy of the bridge under the high E string, to around a quarter-inch short of the neck under the low E string, and encased a mammoth coil under which was mounted a mammoth bar magnet. These were extremely short-lived, though, as guitar production ceased after 1941 for the war effort.

Oddities and exceptions aside, the P-90 is an undeniable and enduring classic. From the pre-Les Paul days we know it as mounted in the 'dog-ear cover', a plastic cover named for the triangular extensions at either end by which it was screw-mounted to the top of archtop guitars (and, later, budget models like the Les Paul Junior). In this configuration pickup height is not adjustable, although added shim-rings – or taller or shorter covers – were used to lift the entire pickup closer to, or drop it further from, the strings as required. The adjustable pole pieces were intended mainly to enable fine balancing of string-to-string output levels, although many players use them to increase overall output, rather than raising the pickup itself. (This works, to an extent, but many knowledgeable techs will tell you that a P-90 sounds better when the entire unit is raised toward the strings as required, rather than when the pole pieces alone are raised.) The 'soapbar' covers that arrived with the solid-body Les Paul in 1952, on the other hand, afforded an easy means of raising and lowering the

FACING PAGE **Slightly later version of an add-on pickup for archtop guitar by Gibson, patent filed 1940, granted 1942.**

manufacturers' profiles – the 'big four'

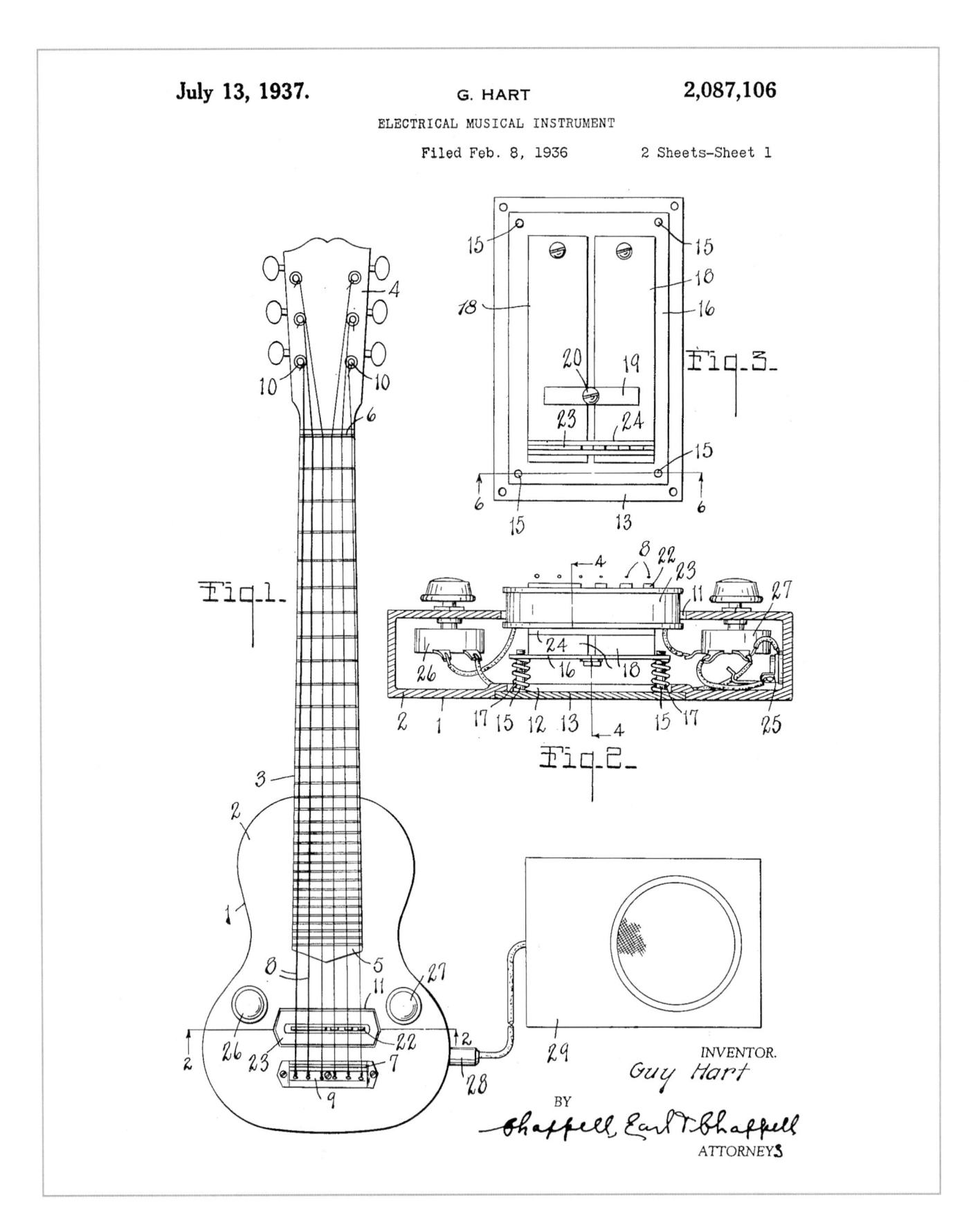

July 13, 1937. G. HART 2,087,106
ELECTRICAL MUSICAL INSTRUMENT
Filed Feb. 8, 1936 2 Sheets-Sheet 1

INVENTOR.
Guy Hart
BY
Chappell Earl T. Chappell
ATTORNEYS

manufacturers' profiles – the 'big four'

entire pickup, with the adjustment of two mounting screws that ran between the A and D and the G and B poles and into the body.

Either cover hides the same basic pickup, made from a wide bobbin wrapped with approximately 10,000 turns of 42-gauge plain enamel coated wire. Six threaded steel pole pieces run through the bobbin's central channel, and contact a pair of Alnico III or IV (and later Alnico V) bar magnets mounted beneath, all of which is held in place by steel base plate. Given the guitars it has appeared on, and the music is has made, the P-90 has proved itself something of a do-it-all pickup in the 60-plus years of its existence. Classic country, jazz, blues, rock'n'roll, and heavy rock tracks have all been cut on guitars carrying P-90 pickups, but its core tone is probably predisposed toward rugged, grungy rock more than anything else. While the P-90 can have a certain sweetness, it is most known for its gutsy, somewhat aggressive, mid-forward performance, and few would argue that it has a particularly refined sound, although good examples are not without some clarity and definition. Prior to the electric guitar boom of the early 1950s though, this was one of the only games in town, and players embraced the P-90 – and the great Gibson guitars it came on – with a tight, sweaty grip.

Despite the P-90's success, Gibson president Ted McCarty, for one, must have noticed that the sound was perhaps a little raw for some tastes. Either that, or a purely market-driven need to compete with upstart Gretsch's new electrics, which carried bright, twangy DeArmond 200 pickups, led him to task engineers Seth Lover and Walter Fuller in the early 1950s with developing a new unit with better definition and enhanced treble response. To achieve this, Lover – an electronics expert and former military radio technician – employed a principle that we explored in the previous chapter. He put pole pieces cut from alnico bar magnets right into the central channel of the coil of a pickup that was otherwise fairly similar to a P-90, and gave them individual adjustment screws alongside each chunk of alnico to enable height adjustment. In this, they were extremely like the DeArmond (Gretsch Dynasonic) pickups with which Gibson intended to compete, right down to the complex 'monkey on a stick' adjustment mechanisms, although the beveled rectangular pole-piece tops gave them a slightly different look to the DeArmonds, which had rod-shaped alnico pole pieces.

The alnico poles provided the desired increase in twang and high-end definition, and the resultant 'Alnico V' pickup, as they have become known, (also sometimes called the 'staple' pickup, for the appearances of its rectangular pole pieces) appeared most famously in the neck position of the elegant new Les

FACING PAGE **Gibson's Charlie Christian pickup, designed by Guy Hart.**

manufacturers' profiles – the 'big four'

Paul Custom in 1954, but was also used in all positions on a number of high-end Gibson archtop electrics of the mid 1950s such as the Super 400CES, L-5CES, and Byrdland. The Les Paul Custom retained a P-90 in the bridge position, where a little more grit and grind could arguably be an asset, but gained some clarity focus from the Alnico in the neck selection, a position that can naturally be prone to woolly or boomy tones with a poor pickup match. It's often said that these were intended to be more powerful pickups, too, although that doesn't entirely follow through in side-to-side comparisons with standard P-90s, and vintage examples of both types vary widely in any case. Both the Alnico V and the P-90 were wound to the same specs, and give an average DC resistance reading of around 8k ohms. As such, the two make an excellent case study for the differences that having the magnet *in* the coil and *below* the coil can make.

An interesting and effective design, the Alnico V probably deserved to be a longer-lived alternative to the P-90, but many players encountered problems with it thanks to the built-in adjustment facility that was originally intended to aid them in getting the most out of the unit. Give a guitarist the means of making their guitar a little hotter, and they'll usually jump on it. Rather than using the adjustable pole pieces to balance string-to-string output levels as intended, many players just cranked the poles up as close to the strings as they could get them, to the point where individual magnets exerted a pull on the steel strings and inhibited their vibration, causing wolf tones and a duller sound overall. Herein lies another difference between the P-90 (steel poles, magnets below) and the Alnico V (magnets for poles): you can adjust the threaded steel poles of the former up pretty high toward the strings, within reason, or even lift the entire pickup, without interfering unduly with string vibration; get an actual magnet close to the string, though, and it will literally start to pull on it, and choke your tone. This is a factor that in-the-know Stratocaster players are particularly aware of, and most are careful of their neck pickup height adjustments as a result.

In any case, the Alnico V pickup was soon overshadowed by the biggest thing to hit the scene since the advent of the electromagnetic pickup. Around 1955, at the urging, once again, of Gibson president Ted McCarty, Seth Lover and Walt Fuller began working on the idea of a hum-rejecting guitar pickup. Both Gibson's main pickup of the day, the P-90, and the Alnico V that Lover and Fuller had developed a few years before, were great, full, distinctive sounding pickups, but like all single-coil designs were prone to picking up unwanted hum and noise from external electrical sources. Being familiar with tube amplifiers, Lover was well aware of how a choke (a coil in the form of a small transformer) could help

FACING PAGE **P-90 pickup. Gibson was late applying for a patent for this pickup.**

manufacturers' profiles – the 'big four'

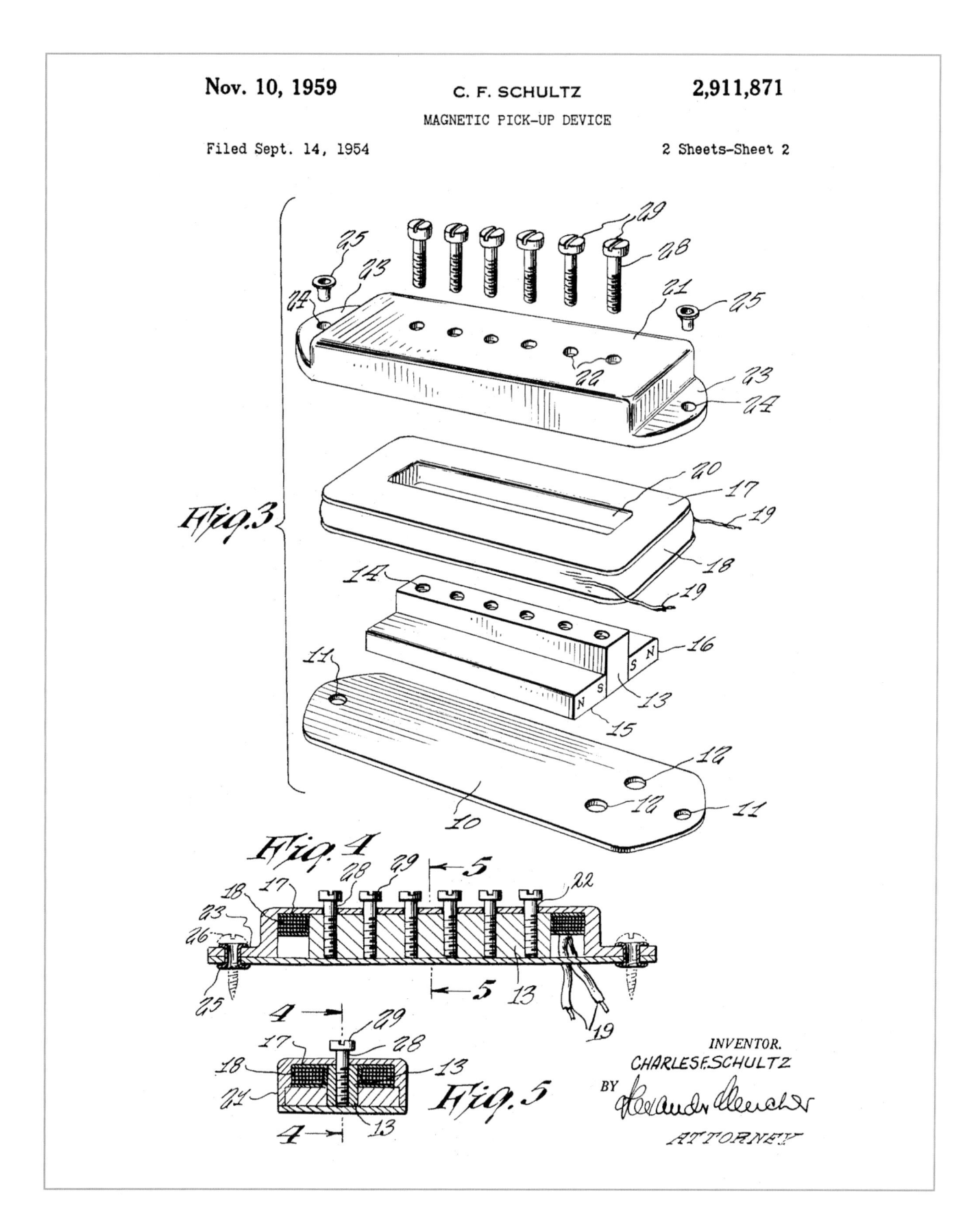

Nov. 10, 1959 C. F. SCHULTZ 2,911,871
MAGNETIC PICK-UP DEVICE
Filed Sept. 14, 1954 2 Sheets-Sheet 2

Fig. 3

Fig. 4

Fig. 5

INVENTOR.
CHARLES F. SCHULTZ
BY
ATTORNEY

manufacturers' profiles – the 'big four'

filter out hum induced by an amp's power supply, and began working toward applying the same logic to guitar pickups. The concept wasn't entirely new, and other innovative designers had applied similar thinking to pickups for electric instruments, but none had yet achieved the simple elegance – and tonal success – that would follow Lover's device.

His solution took the form of a double-coil pickup, in which two similar but reverse-wound coils with opposite magnetic polarities were placed side-by-side and wired together in series. As a result, this configuration rejected much of the hum that single-coil pickups reproduce – which is eliminated when the signals from two 'mirror image' coils are summed together – but passed along all of the guitar tone. In addition to the benefits regarding noise rejection, the double-coil pickup's side-by-side coil alignment produced a warm, rich sound that came across as bigger and rounder than that of the average single-coil pickup. Lover also added a cover made of thin metal to the pickups, to further reject electrostatic interference. Often referred to as nickel, these covers were actually made from German silver, also sometimes called 'nickel silver', which is an allow of copper, zinc and nickel.

Gibson dubbed Lover's new creation the 'humbucker' for its ability to 'buck' electrical hum and, aware that it was a unique device in the fledgling industry, applied for a US patent to protect the design. The first variations of the unit appeared in the form of a triple-coil humbucker, used on Gibson lap-steel guitars in 1956. When double-coil humbuckers first appeared on the Les Paul Goldtop and Les Paul Custom in 1957, they carried stickers that read "Patent Applied For", to warn off would-be copyists while the company awaited the patent. Pickups of the era, therefore, are given the nickname 'PAF', which applies to any pickup carrying the "Patent Applied For" sticker that all Gibson humbuckers wore between late 1956 or early '57 and late 1962. In fact a US patent was granted in July 1959, but Gibson continued to apply these stickers for another two years. One theory is that the company still didn't want potential copyists to have access to the design, as they could easily have done by searching for the patent number at the US Patent Office (when the patent number stickers finally appeared on humbuckers late in 1962, the number was in fact for a bridge patent – a simple mistake, or a further deterrent to the competition?). The second theory is that Gibson was just using up the many "Patent Applied For" stickers it had already printed up, and perhaps had already applied to a stock of pickups.

Gibson's PAF humbucker turned the industry's thinking on its ear, and offered players unparalleled levels of sound and performance that set the

FACING PAGE **The early form of Gibson's humbucking pickup.**

manufacturers' profiles – the 'big four'

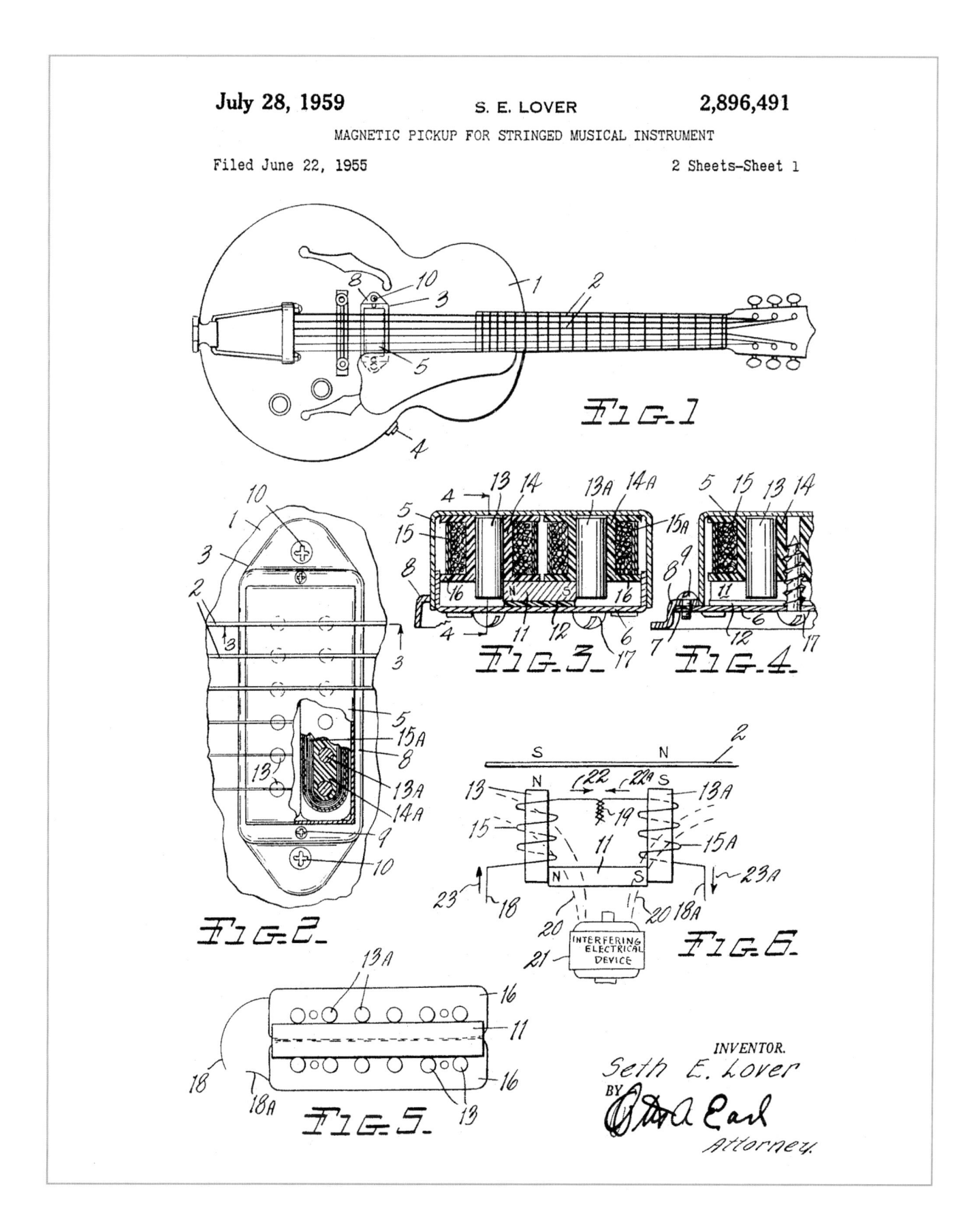

July 28, 1959   S. E. LOVER   2,896,491
MAGNETIC PICKUP FOR STRINGED MUSICAL INSTRUMENT
Filed June 22, 1955   2 Sheets—Sheet 1

INVENTOR.
Seth E. Lover
BY
Attorney.

manufacturers' profiles – the 'big four'

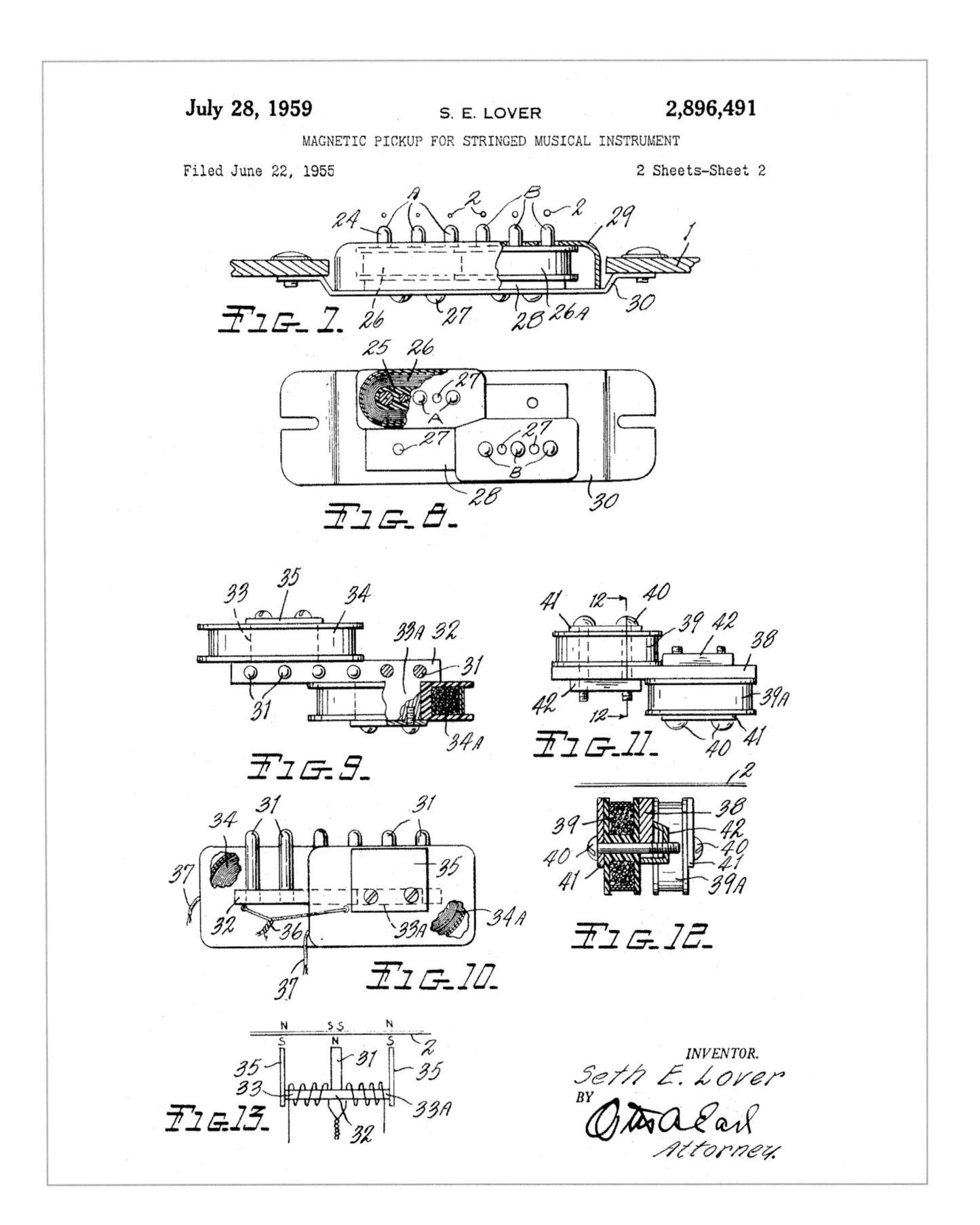

July 28, 1959 — S. E. LOVER — 2,896,491
MAGNETIC PICKUP FOR STRINGED MUSICAL INSTRUMENT
Filed June 22, 1955 — 2 Sheets-Sheet 2

Fig. 7.
Fig. 8.
Fig. 9.
Fig. 10.
Fig. 11.
Fig. 12.
Fig. 13.

INVENTOR.
Seth E. Lover
BY
Otto A. Earl
Attorney.

manufacturers' profiles – the 'big four'

standards for pickup design forever after. Check out the five-figure sums that players and collectors are willing to pay for an original pair of PAFs on the vintage market, or the way players flock in droves to accurate reproductions of these hallowed humbuckers, and you get an inkling of the impact they have had on the guitar world. Imagine how they must have appeared back in the mid 1950s when they appeared on their first Gibson guitars, in an era when your choice in pickups was single coil or … another single coil. Vintage enthusiasts are prone to waxing lyrical about virtually any guitar or component from the 1950s or early '60s, but the PAF has attained a status elevated above any classic piece of gear, other than, perhaps, the hallowed 1958–60 Les Paul 'Bursts' on which they most famously appeared. And while a great proportion of vintage gear worship might rightly be attributed to myth and bluster and the sheer scarcity of the piece being idolized, most players' experiences with authentic Gibson PAFs show us there is definitely something in the water.

A friend of mine, freelance writer and guitarist Nathaniel Riverhorse Nakadate, who pens articles regularly for *The ToneQuest Report*, *Vintage Guitar Magazine*, *The Fretboard Journal*, and a multitude of mainstream surfing magazines, recently had the opportunity to play a hand-picked and mint selection of original late 1950's Les Pauls from an esteemed collection. He also taste tested numerous vintage PAFs with David Wilson of *The ToneQuest Report*, in search of a pair to slip into his own '59 historic burst reissue. As always, the Riverhorse was game for sharing his findings, so allow me to sidetrack you through one player's recent first-hand experiences with a boatload of glorious, original Gibson PAF pickups:

FACING PAGE **Variations on the design for Gibson's humbucking pickup, as filed with the original patent application in 1955.**

"As with any tone-chasing endeavor, I went into this with an open mind, yet admittedly with a few general expectations of what most likely would occur based on 26 years of firing up guitars. That said, I sure as hell wasn't prepared for what I discovered and heard in those true vintage PAFs, not even remotely.

"Perhaps what caught me the most off guard was the astounding clarity of the vintage PAFs. The low E string held firm and clear, beyond resonant when hit hard, and chords were more so a joint chorus heading toward a common goal, with each note ringing clear, so damn clear. The best ones measured in the 7.0 to 7.5 range for the necks, and obviously the bridge position allowed pickups which were stouter to shine.

"They do not push the front end of the amps around like modern

production pickups, the new efforts have gotten this all wrong. To be fair, though, some players may prefer pickups that have more apparent signal level, but my take is that you lose a lot of the perceived magic, and limit the capacities of the amp for warm cleans, garner too much midrange in lieu of full bass to treble spectrums. Speaking of treble, the treble on these is round and sweet as can be, not a hint of the obliterating harsh spike we often have to suffer through with the modern offerings. Amazing, inspiring.

"They are also extremely height sensitive, and actually prefer sitting down deep into the body, where they deliver a much woodier tone. There is an enormous readjustment of you ears when you have a pair of these at your disposal. They demand players to pay attention to the details of how they approach and attack the notes. Once you know what these are capable of, and feel what they do in your hands, it is difficult to play new production pickups any more.

"These are simply tools, no doubt, a means to an end where the most important goal should be expression of emotion and creating music, not gear snobbery, but I have found when operating on a world-class level of tone such as this, they allow you to reach back deep into the recesses of your mind and heart, and actually connect those thoughts, translate them into music utilizing your fingers as conduits, and fire away like no tomorrow. A single good PAF can cause a lot of dreams to come true."

Heady stuff, and you can tell the man has been stung, and stung bad. As with a handful of other 'Holy Grail' grade pieces of guitar gear out there, some time spent with a pair of good PAFs in the right guitar will just about spoil you for anything else.

Just as the myriad variables applied to the wide world of pickup-making create enormous differences in sound and performance between different types of pickups, each of these variables seems to have hit right on the mark to produce a little form of magic in original Gibson PAF humbuckers. That said, not all PAFs were created equally, although players who know them well will tell you that examples of each type are capable of sounding just about as glorious. Seth Lover specified Alnico V for use in his new humbuckers, but for the first five years of these pickups' existence Gibson variably used Alnico II, III, and V with a fervent disregard for any pretense of consistency. After 1961, the pickup department went with the plan and stuck with Alnico V. At around the same time, Gibson also changed to shorter bar magnets, using magnets of 2⅜-inch

manufacturers' profiles – the 'big four'

rather than the 2½-inch magnets used from 1956 to early '61. Some say the reduction in magnet size was to compensate for the consistent use of a slightly stronger magnet, Alnico V. Most authorities on pickups would likely confirm, however, that other variables would still have post-1961 PAFs coming off the line with greatly varying output levels, and a range of factors would make any efforts to tweak power levels by shortening magnets by ⅛-inch a rather futile exercise. Also, rather than just using shorter versions of the same bar magnets, the post-1961 'short magnets' are also just a bit narrower and thinner than the longer magnets used before.

In theory, Gibson standardized its humbucker's resistance at 7.5k ohms around 1961, but post-1961 PAFs – just like those made from 1956 to 1961 – will still give you a wide range of readings. Like most vintage pickups, the number of winds given the coils in original PAFs made from 1956–62 varied greatly and, as a result, so did their sound. Coil-winding counts supposedly got more accurate toward the end of the PAF's existence, with the goal being 5,000 turns per coil of 42-gauge plain enamel wire, but like most pickup-makers of the day, reports from employees at the Gibson plant back in the day indicate that the two coils were still generally wound 'until they were full'. I recently had the opportunity to play half a dozen vintage Gibson guitars with PAF pickups myself, all dating between 1958 and 1961, and to take resistance readings from some of them. Some examples from that selection include:

Guitar	Neck	Bridge	(Middle)
1958 Flying V	7.51k	7.5k	
1959 ES-335	8.52k	8.4k	
1959 Les Paul	8.2k	8.8k	
1961 SG/Les Paul	7.6k	8.15k	
1962 SG/LP Custom	8.2k	7.86k	7.47k

They all sounded glorious, if different (of course the very different guitar designs, woods, and hardware complements contributed to this too). To put it crudely, the main impression is perhaps that, if you have only ever played modern and relatively high-output humbuckers, a good original PAF *doesn't sound like a humbucker at all*. It will sound clear, bright, even slightly jangly, and with a tantalizing metallic edge to the notes, but also rich, vocal, and multi-textured. If anything – if, for example you're a single-coil player and have never experience a real PAF – it sounds more like the mental image in guitarists' collective

manufacturers' profiles – the 'big four'

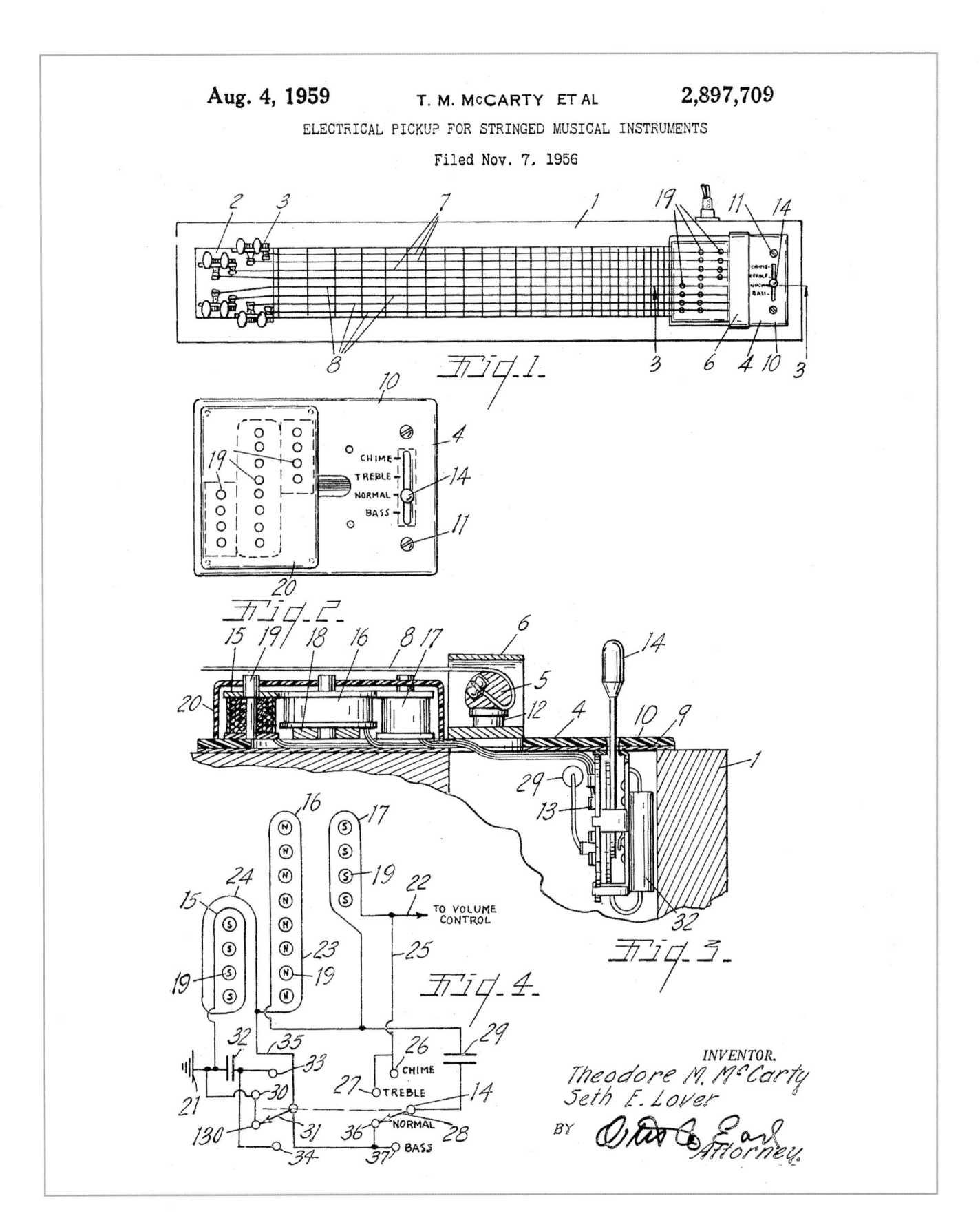

manufacturers' profiles – the 'big four'

consciousness of the sweetest, richest Stratocaster neck pickup tone, another of the most beloved tones on the planet for pure juicy goodness. In short, they aren't 'hot' pickups, although they'll get behind your hot playing right quick, rammed through a tweed Twin or a cranked Marshall JMP50. And that's because, well, they're *not* hot. As evidenced by Gibson's guide specs for original PAFs, and by my own readings above, they fall very much in the same range as the average P-90 from the same era, and very often below the P-90's nominal 8k mark, too. They are different pickups, sure, very different, so just comparing DC resistance only gets us so far, but any player who has had his hands around guitars carrying pickups of each type knows an original P-90 will hit your amp as hard as an original PAF any day, and will in some cases sound muddier and 'fatter' because of it's increased grit factor, although the humbucker's wider magnetic window will often have a PAF sounding a little warmer, too, which sometimes fools the ear into thinking it's hearing heat, gain.

One of the predominant determining variables in the manufacture of vintage pickups, the inconsistency of the number of turns of wire given each coil, affects PAFs from two perspectives: as already mentioned, it makes each pickup a little different from the next one on the line, but also makes each coil a little different from the one lying next to it in the very same pickup. The use of slightly unbalanced coils, compounded by the fact that one coil used adjustable steel pole pieces while the other carried fixed steel slugs, meant that these could never achieve perfection in their hum-canceling duties – since the very definition of the true humbucker requires two *equal but opposite* coils to get the job done. On the plus side, however, this imbalance is also attributed with some of the PAF magic, and helps a good PAF sound a little richer and more intricately textured than does a similarly constructed pickup with perfectly balanced coils. Better balanced coils will contribute to what a lot of players describe as 'smoothness' in a humbucker, but a good PAF is pretty smooth already; what the imbalance helps to achieve, on the other hand, is a little more bite and edge, and therefore clarity, something a lot of players value in a pickup like this. Also, note that the coils were *not* wax potted in original PAFs, and the slight microphony that this sometimes imparts to their performance is often credited with contributing to their noted 'liveliness'.

The PAF's mild steel base plate also plays a part in its sound, although a greater role, a factor that players soon discovered they could tweak to their own tastes, is played by the German silver covers. These metal covers raise the capacitance of the pickup and darken the tone slightly. Lover has stated that he

FACING PAGE **Three-coil humbucker for lap-steel.**

designed the pickup with this factor very much in mind, but players soon discovered that they would eek out a little more high-end response by loosening the two solder connections between the cover and the base, and removing the covers entirely. Gold-plated covers, it's worth noting, raise the capacitance further still, so removing these will have an even greater impact on the sound of a PAF-style humbucker.

A purely cosmetic variable is found in the color of the bobbins used, made from a form of plastic called butyrate (sometimes buterate). Black bobbins were the norm from the beginning, but in early 1959 the suppliers of these occasionally ran out of the dying agent used to make the black butyrate, and supplied them in cream instead. Lifting the covers on PAFs from this period occasionally reveals one cream and one black bobbin, a configuration known as 'zebra coils', or – the most prized of all – double cream bobbins. The color has no affect on the sound of the pickups, although there's some indication, as reported by David Wilson in his intensive study of the Gibson PAF in the *ToneQuest Report* of April 2008, that Gibson was also supplied with some off-spec coil wire at around the same time, and many white bobbins were consequently wound with plain enamel wire that was actually a little finer than the specified 42 gauge. As we have already learned, finer wire allows you to fit more windings around the bobbin; the theory seems to hold water, since many zebra and double-cream PAFs do measure on the high side, in the upper 8k and even the lower 9k range.

A good two years after receiving its patent for the new humbucking pickup, Gibson started replacing the "Patent Applied For" stickers on the bottoms of its pickups with stickers that read "Patent No 2,737,842", which was actually the patent awarded in 1956 for the combined trapeze tailpiece and bridge used on the original version of the Les Paul in 1952 and early '53 (the patent for the pickup, awarded in July 1959, is number 2,896,491). There's a considerable crossover period between the PAF pickups and the 'Patent Number' pickups, as they have come to be known, and I have seen examples of the latter sited from late 1961, with examples of the former from late 1962. Regardless of the sticker, for the first year or so of what we consider to be the era of the Patent Number humbuckers, from around mid 1962 to mid '63, the pickups were all still made the same, regardless of the sticker. Some time after 1962, however, a number of changes were gradually made to these units. The wires between coils, visible between the bobbins from the end where the black paper tape covers each individual bobbin rather than both bobbins together, were now one black and

manufacturers' profiles – the 'big four'

one white wire, rather than the two black wires used up until this point. Another alteration occurred during the course of 1963 when Gibson started using polyurethane-coated coil wire in place of the plain enamel-coated wire. Although the wire within the coating was, in theory, the same stuff, many toneheads will claim that a change in the insulating coating in and of itself can affect the sound of a coil; more practically speaking, a change in coating also means a minute change in the thickness of the wire, and this in itself will affect the way the wraps fall in to place as the coil is wound.

Many of these contributing factors to the tonal palette of the PAF are in the realm of minutiae, certainly, but when you're discussing a component as revered and rarified as Gibson's humbucker from 1956 to 1962, every little piece of the puzzle has significance. The saying 'the whole is greater than the sum of its parts' applies here in spades; with a pickup so special that no one has quite achieved an entirely accurate and sonically satisfactory recreation of the original, you've got to consider the importance of every little factor, however microscopic.

Early Patent Number pickups are still very highly regarded, and players in the know are fully aware that the only thing standing between these units and a late PAF pickup is the sticker… and an extra $1,000–1,500 a pair. Later Patent Number pickups are still highly regarded, too, although toward the mid 1960s these humbuckers had evolved far enough from the original PAF formula to no longer benefit from the beatifying glow reflected off the originals. Patent Number pickups were made into 1965, during the course of which Gibson changed the pickups again, and used a different style of black plastic bobbin notable for the distinct "T" impressed into the top. Known as 'T-top' pickups, these carried the same decal reading "Patent No 2,737,842", but had white wires between the coils, rather than the white and black of the later Patent Number pickups. Gibson humbuckers were also now being wound to a more consistent 7.5k ohms, thanks to a new fully automated coil-winding system that was introduced some time after 1965. T-tops of this configuration were made until 1975, when Gibson started stamping the pickups' steel base plates themselves with the *real* patent number for their humbucking pickup, rather than sticking on the decal with the misleading tailpiece patent. As with just about everything related to vintage guitar gear, it seems, Gibson humbuckers follow a chronological curve that represents the depletion of desirability of these parts. From PAF, to early Patent Number, to later Patent Number, to first-generation T-top, to second generation T-top, the lust factor traces a significant decline from version one to version two, then a sharp and sharper fall-off after that. Come the arrival of the 1970s, with the era of the T-tops well entrenched and Gibson, under Norlin, producing guitars to put them in that are among the least well-regarded of the company's history, pickups that still follow the basic form and dimensions of the PAF have been reduced to 'just an ordinary humbucker' status.

The other significant pickup of Gibson's vintage years is the Mini-Humbucker… more accurately described as Mini-Humbuckers. Although from the outside these all have about the same dimensions, the compact humbucking pickups used in Gibson-made Epiphone guitars between 1960 and 1962, in Gibson Firebirds from 1963, and Gibson Les Paul Deluxes from 1969 are all quite different pickups.

The first of these has become known as the PAF Mini-Humbucker in some circles, as it carries the same "Patent Applied For" sticker as Gibson's full-sized PAF. Gibson acquired these Mini-Humbuckers from Epiphone, and they appeared on models such as the Sheraton and Sorrento. While these pickups are constructed similarly to a shrunken-down PAF, they are also different in many ways other than size. They do, however, mount similarly to a full-sized humbucker, rather than being rather awkwardly suspended in a cut out P-90 cover as were later Mini-Humbuckers of the type used in the Les Paul Deluxe of 1969 and after. Sonically, the Epiphone Mini PAFs (and LP Deluxe Minis, for that matter) are noted for their lower output and brighter response – the latter a factor of their narrower magnetic window and, well, their lower output. While they can't be said to capture the full-sized PAF tone in a more diminutive package (as, no doubt, some owners would hope), they are nevertheless considered to be fine sounding pickups in their own right.

The Firebird Mini-Humbuckers that arrived on Gibson's radical new reverse-bodied electric in 1963 appear outwardly to be Epiphone-style Mini-Humbuckers with sold covers to hide the adjustable pole pieces, but in fact they are completely different pickups. These pickups were designed with two similar coils, each of which was wound around an Alnico II bar magnet. As with the Alnico V of the 1950s – or indeed Fender's Telecaster, Stratocaster, and Jazzmaster pickups, or Gretsch's DeArmond-made Dynasonic – placing the magnet right within the coil sharpened the treble response of these pickups, and increased their overall twang factor considerably. It seems Gibson was gunning for Fender's hip'n'groovy early 1960s designs in every way with the Firebird – the reverse-body styling aped a flipped-over Jazzmaster body, while the custom color offerings likewise attacked a Fender stronghold in the market

manufacturers' profiles – the 'big four'

– and the pickups themselves served to come closer to the bright, twangy, cutting tonality of many Fenders than any Gibson before it, while maintaining the advantage of hum-canceling performance, something Fender hadn't yet achieved in a guitar pickup. For some, the sound of these Firebird pickups was just too cutting and shrill, and they can definitely have some spike to them, but they achieve the goal of brightness and definition, and certainly help you slice through the mix.

The Mini-Humbuckers that appeared on the Les Paul Deluxe of 1969 are perhaps more infamous than famous, being the pickup that kept an oddly belligerent-seeming Gibson from bringing back the Les Paul that players were *really* clamoring for, namely the Les Paul Standard with full-sized humbuckers. But again, they are decent sounding pickups in their own way. Like the Epiphone variation before them, they achieved the end of producing a brighter, cleaner performance – something perhaps lacking in some of the indistinct sounding T-top humbuckers of the era – while still being capable of rocking when pushed. These Mini-Humbuckers carried an Alnico V bar magnet beneath two coils wound with polyurethane-coated 42-gauge wire, one with fixed slug pole pieces, the other with threaded adjustable slot-head pole pieces. Both the Epiphone and LP Deluxe Mini-Humbuckers, and the Firebird Mini-Humbucker, were given an average of about 4,250 turns of wire per coil, and yield readings of between 6k and 7k.

In the late 1960s Gibson, at the urging of Les Paul himself, newly back in the fold, dabbled in low-impedance pickups, which were coming into their brief heyday around that time. Paul argued, quite rightly, that low-impedance pickups had a much broader frequency response, partnered with a lower noise floor, than standard pickups, and insisted – quite wrongly – that they would be a revolution in the guitar world. These units can be plugged straight into the low-impedance inputs of recording desks or live sound mixers, but require some form of preamp to boost them to levels required for input into guitar amplifiers, as well as a small transformer for conversion from low to high impedance. Gibson's low-impedance pickups appeared on the short-lived Les Paul Personal and Professional models in 1969 (alongside the Les Paul Bass), the Les Paul Recording of 1971, and the thinline Les Paul Signature of 1974. The first wave of these required a special cord with built-in transformer for connection to a guitar amp, while the second wave had the low-to-high-Z transformers built into the guitar. All failed spectacularly to set the guitar world alight, although a few guitarists here and there have found them useful (names escape me at the moment). None of them were helped, I'm sure, by the staid, brown mahogany finishes applied to the models, nor by the confusing array of controls and switches that some included, mounted on (arguably ugly) plastic control plates.

We have crossed the threshold from vintage to post-vintage Gibson pickups, but to get here I skirted around one other creation of the late 1950s, the Melody Maker pickup. These are too often described as being 'like a Fender pickup', although in truth they are really quite different. They do share their narrow-single-coil dimensions with Fender's outwardly similar Stratocaster and Mustang pickups, and have another commonality in their magnet-in-the-coil tone, but the Melody Maker pickups were made with a single Alnico V bar magnet with a coil of 42-gauge plain enamel wire wrapped around it, rather than with the six individual alnico pole pieces that Fender used. The first versions, introduced in 1959, were ⅞-inch wide, although in 1960 they were reduced to ⅝-inch wide. As you can guess from the specs so far, these are bright, cutting, twangy pickups, and actually pretty hot too, for narrow single coils, with an average DC resistance reading of around 7.25k ohms. They never achieved the classic status of the P-90, or certainly the PAF or early Patent Number pickups, but are beloved of plenty of players.

As something of a sideline to Gibson pickup history, it's worth noting one valiant early effort at reproducing a more accurate PAF humbucker, within the constraints of Norlin-owned Gibson's new Nashville plant. The popularity of original 1958–60 Les Paul Standards had sunken in with the corporate decision-makers, slowly as ever, it seems, and in 1980 Gibson decided to produce a reissue of sorts, although the result was far short of the accuracy achieved by recent Les Paul reissues from the Gibson Custom Shop. Along with reproducing the guitar, Gibson also decided to reproduce the pickup, and assigned an engineer in the Nashville plant by the name of Tim Shaw with the task of doing so. This being the darkest era of the Norlin reign, Shaw wasn't given the budget for a full-on reproduction, but using some revamped bobbins, Gibson's current 42-gauge polyurethane-coated coil wire (rather than more accurate, and more expensive, plain enamel-coated wire), and Alnico V magnets, he created what is generally regarded as a pretty darn good sounding humbucking pickup, compared to whatever else was available at the time, at least. Having studied the number of turns on original PAFs, largely from existing documents, Shaw kept the resistance of these pickups down to around 7.5k, which is a little lower than many other humbuckers of the late 1970s and early 1980s. The 'Shaw humbucker' appeared first on the Les Paul Heritage 80, Heritage 80 Elite, and

manufacturers' profiles – the 'big four'

Heritage 80 Award, and a few other reissues after, apparently including the ES-335 Dot Reissue of the following year.

The whole Les Paul-amp stack-stadium rock equation of the early 1970s led a lot of people toward a 'hotter is better' mentality, which is in part what gave birth to the thriving after-market pickup business (that and, it's fair to say, the mediocrity of many guitar manufacturers' in-house pickups in the 1970s). With players yanking out stock pickups and wiring in third-party options that promised more sustain and thicker overdrive (and, sadly, very often delivered … be careful what you wish for), Gibson saw an opportunity to get in on the act themselves, and jumped in head first in the early 1980s with the Dirty Fingers humbucker. Wound to within an inch of its life with around 8,000 turns per coil of super-fine 44-gauge plain enamel coated wire for a resultant resistance reading of around 16k ohms, and hiding three – yes three – hefty ceramic bar magnets between bobbins and base plate, this was one filthy, hot, raunchy hard-rock pickup, and no mistakin'. Dirty Fingers pickups gave select Gibsons such as the Flying V, Explorer, ES-347 and 335-S of the era a thundering, mid-soaked attack and the ability to drive high-gain amps of the era close to meltdown. For sweet cleans, ethereal jangle, or rich, vintage blues tones, look elsewhere.

Gibson segued from vintage to contemporary via a broad range of flavors. Currently the company makes a little of something for just about every taste, including some of the best PAF reproductions it has yet produced, and some very respectable vintage-style P-90s too.

Between its three lines of vintage-style reproduction humbuckers – '57 Classics, BurstBuckers, and BurstBucker Pros – Gibson today seeks to account for all tastes in PAFs. The '57 Classic and '57 Classic Plus are calibrated to yield a PAF-like tone in the neck and bridge positions respectively. Each design features Alnico II magnets, vintage plain enamel-coated wire, nickel-plated pole pieces, nickel slugs, maple spacers and vintage-style, two-conductor, braided wiring. Unlike original PAFs, however, the '57 Classics' coils are wax potted to combat microphony and feedback squeal at high volumes so, while vintage voiced, they are arguably more suited to high-gain playing, too. The number of windings in the two coils are also equally matched, an enhancement that provides a creamy, balanced performance that many players enjoy, but which does stray from the haphazard nature of the mismatched coils of the originals.

The '57 Classic is wound to a DC resistance toward the lower range of the scale for original PAF pickups, for a warm, round, rich tone from the neck position with plenty of definition and clarity, and an open, clear, textured vintage voice from the bridge position (the pair in a Gibson Memphis ES-335 Dot that I have on hand hear read 8.04k bridge, 7.94k neck, meaning they're not calibrated to the extent that many modern neck/bridge sets are, but readings will of course vary). The '57 Classic Plus is wound toward the hotter end of the PAF scale in homage to the originals that received extra windings to fill up the bobbins, and it provides an excellent volume balance with the neck unit, and a little extra bite and sizzle from the bridge position, without sacrificing definition and the legendary smooth PAF treble response. Both models carry "Patent Applied For" stickers on the bottom plate just like the originals.

If we say the '57 Classics provide 'modified vintage' performance, Gibson's BurstBucker aims to take matters one step further by reproducing some of the inconsistencies that are credited with contributing a certain magic to original Gibson humbuckers from 1957–62. Available in three output strengths, BurstBuckers are made with unpolished Alnico II magnets and unpotted coils that are wound to slightly different numbers of turns, like the originals. While using two slightly mismatched coils depletes a humbucking pickup's noise-canceling abilities slightly, it also gives the pickup a little more edge than can be achieved with perfectly balanced coils, as described above regarding original PAFs – a sound you could even say comes a little closer to achieving the bite of a good single-coil pickup. The BurstBucker 1 is slightly underwound to achieve an output toward the lower-medium end of the PAF range, an output that brings it in just slightly below the '57 Classic. It is intended for either position, but is particularly considered to improve clarity in the neck position, with the added bonus of good volume balance when paired with a BurstBucker 2 in the bridge. The '2' has a slightly hotter output in the range of the '57 Classic, for more grind and sustain from the bridge position. Or, pair a BurstBucker 2 in the neck with a BurstBucker 3 in the bridge – the hottest of the trio – for a guitar that offers good balance and a vintage voice that is still accurate, but biased toward the hotter end of the PAF scale.

Finally, BurstBucker Pros are based on the original BurstBuckers and available in two output strengths, calibrated to match neck and bridge positions (with outputs akin to those of the BurstBucker 1 and 2). They employ Alnico V magnets for a little extra sting and punch, and feature wax-potted coils to combat potential squeal and microphony. Like the BurstBuckers they use two coils with unmatched windings to retain a little extra sonic edge in their 'enhanced vintage' performance. In addition to a pretty accurate sounding P-90 reproduction, Gibson also offers the P-94, a P-90 design in a standard

manufacturers' profiles — the 'big four'

humbucker mounting, a pickup that has become popular with many players wanting to achieve fat-single-coil sounds from guitars that shipped with full-sized humbuckers. Both use Alnico V magnets and enamel-coated wire, and are sold individually or in sets calibrated for neck and bridge.

Gibson's Modern Classics range of humbuckers comprises the company's longstanding line of 'workingman's humbuckers', as used on the majority of Gibson USA guitars (whereas the Gibson Custom and upscale Gibson USA guitars carry the BurstBuckers and '57 Classics). Comprising the 490R, 490T, and 498T 'Hot Alnico', this set takes its cue from the '57 Classic, but rolls the output and midrange grind upward a few notches to create a pickup more suited to modern music styles. The 490R uses Alnico II magnets and features pole-piece spacing suitable to the string spread at the neck position, while also being calibrated for balanced volume when matched with a slightly hotter 490T in the bridge position (a pickup also made with Alnico II magnets). Hotter still, the 498T 'Hot Alnico' uses a punchier Alnico V magnet and modified coil windings to provide even more oomph in the bridge position, and is considered ideal for rock lead work. Another step up the scale, Gibson has also recently introduced the Angus Young Signature humbucker. Calibrated to the bridge position in particular, it aims to achieve a 'hot PAF' tone, and employs an Alnico V magnet and slightly over-wound, double-wax-potted coils to get there.

Gibson's first ever signature pickup, the Tony Iommi humbucker, takes us right into the heavy metal territory you might expect from a component developed for Black Sabbath's lead guitarist. The third hottest pickup in Gibson's lineup, it uses over-wound coils that are double potted with wax and epoxy resin to eliminate microphony, and a patented custom magnet configuration. Next up the scale are the 'Hot Ceramics' offerings, the neck-intended 496R, and the 500T for the bridge position. As the name implies, both use ceramic magnets, along with extra windings to push the crunch and wail toward the extreme … if not quite there. That place is reserved for our old friend the Dirty Fingers, back with a vengeance at the request of Blink-182 guitarist Tom DeLonge, who selected it out of a cast of thousands for use in his Signature model guitar. As it was in the beginning – or, the beginning of high-output ceramic pickups at Gibson, anyway – the Dirty Fingers is yet again the most powerful pickup made by the big boys in Nashville, and a long way down that road from Kalamazoo and the original PAF humbucker.

manufacturers' profiles – the 'big four'

● Gibson 'Bar' (Charlie Christian Pickup)
Type: single coil
Magnets: two cobalt steel bar magnets, mounted beneath the guitar's top
Wire: 38 to 41 gauge, plain enamel coated
Resistance: 2.5k to 5k ohms
Pole pieces: steel within coil
Sound: bright, fat, rich, surprisingly well defined

● Gibson P-90
Type: single coil
Magnet: Alnico III (early on, in particular) or Alnico V
Wire: 42 gauge, plain enamel coated
Resistance: 7.5k to 8.5k ohms
Pole pieces: individual threaded adjustable steel pole pieces
Sound: thick, slightly gritty, with serious midrange presence, reasonable high-end response

● Gibson Alnico V (or 'Staple')
Type: single coil
Magnet: six individual Alnico V bar magnets (occasionally Alnico III?)
Wire: 42 gauge, plain enamel coated
Resistance: 7.5k to 8.5k ohms
Pole pieces: individual alnico magnets, adjustable via adjacent screws
Sound: thick and powerful like the P-90, but with a little more 'twang' and clarity

● Gibson 'PAF' Humbucker
Type: double coil
Magnet: Alnico II, III or V (V more consistently post-1961)
Wire: 42 gauge, plain enamel coated
Resistance: 7.25k to 9k ohms
Pole pieces: six adjustable threaded steel poles in one coil, six fixed steel slugs in the other coil
Sound: deep, clear, multidimensional – the 'tone of tones'. Warm and rich in the neck, biting and aggressive in the bridge

● Gibson Melody Maker
Type: single coil
Magnet: Alnico V bar magnets
Wire: 42 gauge, plain enamel coated
Resistance: 7k to 7.5k ohms
Pole pieces: alnico bar magnet serves as 'blade' pole
Sound: bright and punchy, with a little grit but good definition

● Gibson 'Patent Number' Humbucker
Type: double coil
Magnet: Alnico V
Wire: 42 gauge, plain enamel coated 1962 to early '63, polyurethane coated after mid '63
Resistance: 7.25k to 9k ohms
Pole pieces: six adjustable threaded steel poles in one coil, six fixed steel slugs in the other coil
Sound: much like PAF above until mid '63; still similar afterward, if 'slightly less so'

● Gibson Firebird
Type: double coil
Magnet: two Alnico II bar magnets
Wire: 42 gauge, plain enamel coated
Resistance: 7k ohms
Pole pieces: alnico bar magnet in each coil serves as 'blade' pole
Sound: edgy, bright and percussive

● Gibson 'Patent Number T-top'
Type: double coil
Magnet: Alnico V
Wire: 42 gauge, polyurethane coated
Resistance: 7.5k to 8.5k ohms
Pole pieces: six adjustable threaded steel poles in one coil, six fixed steel slugs in the other coil
Sound: thick, fairly aggressive, honking midrange presence

● Gibson Mini-Humbucker ('Les Paul Deluxe')
Type: double coil
Magnet: Alnico V
Wire: 42 gauge, polyurethane coated
Resistance: 6.5k to 7.5k ohms
Pole pieces: six individually adjustable steel poles in one coil, six fixed steel slugs in the other
Sound: bright, cutting and percussive, but not without a little smoothness

manufacturers' profiles – the 'big four'

● Gibson 'T-top'
Type: double coil
Magnet: Alnico V
Wire: 42 gauge, polyurethane coated
Resistance: 7.5k to 8.5k ohms
Pole pieces: six adjustable threaded steel poles in one coil, six fixed steel slugs in the other coil
Sound: thick, fairly aggressive, honking midrange presence

● Gibson Dirty Fingers
Type: double coil
Magnet: three ceramic bar magnets
Wire: 44 gauge, plain enamel coated
Resistance: approximately 16k ohms
Pole pieces: six adjustable threaded steel poles in each coil
Sound: super-heavy, thick, aggressive and compressed when hit hard

● Gibson '57 Classics
Type: double coil
Magnet: Alnico II
Wire: 42 gauge, plain enamel coated
Resistance: 7.8k to 8.1k ohms
Pole pieces: six adjustable threaded steel poles in one coil, six fixed steel slugs in the other coil
Sound: clear, creamy, smooth, well balanced

● Gibson BurstBucker
Type: double coil
Magnet: Alnico II
Wire: 42 gauge, plain enamel coated
Resistance: 7.5k to 8.2k ohms
Pole pieces: six adjustable threaded steel poles in one coil, six fixed steel slugs in the other coil
Sound: rich, well textured, slightly 'edgier' than 57 Classics

● Gibson BurstBucker Pro
Type: double coil
Magnet: Alnico V
Wire: 42 gauge, plain enamel coated
Resistance: 7.5k to 7.8k ohms
Pole pieces: six adjustable threaded steel poles in one coil, six fixed steel slugs in the other coil
Sound: similar to standard BurstBucker, but smoother and better balanced

● Gibson P-94
Type: single coil (mounted in humbucker-sized housing)
Magnet: Alnico V
Wire: 42 gauge, plain enamel coated
Resistance: 7.5k to 8.5k ohms
Pole pieces: individual threaded adjustable steel pole pieces
Sound: thick, slightly gritty, with serious midrange presence, reasonable high-end response

● Gibson 490R & 490T
Type: double coil
Magnet: Alnico II
Wire: 42 gauge, plain enamel coated
Resistance: 7.5k to 9k ohms (+/-)
Pole pieces: six adjustable threaded steel poles in one coil, six fixed steel slugs in the other coil
Sound: thick, creamy, fairly hot; 'T' offers more midrange aggression

● Gibson 498T Hot Alnico
Type: double coil
Magnet: Alnico V
Wire: 43 gauge, plain enamel coated
Resistance: 13k to 14k ohms (+/-)
Pole pieces: six adjustable threaded steel poles in one coil, six fixed-steel slugs in the other coil
Sound: thick, hot, sizzling highs and aggressive midrange

● Gibson 496R & 500T Ceramics
Type: double coil
Magnets: ceramic (three in the 500T)
Wire: 42 and 43 gauge respectively
Resistance: N/A
Pole pieces: six adjustable threaded steel poles in one coil, six fixed-steel slugs in the other coil
Sound: hot and hotter, ceramic crunch and grind for contemporary rock

manufacturers' profiles – the 'big four'

- **Gibson P-94 (P-90 specs in humbucker-sized housing)**
Type: single coil
Magnets: Alnico V
Wire: 42 gauge, plain enamel coated
Resistance: 8k ohms (+/-)
Pole pieces: individual threaded adjustable steel pole pieces
Sound: thick, slightly gritty, with serious midrange presence, reasonable high-end response

- **Gibson Tony Iommi Signature**
Type: double coil
Magnets: three ceramic bar magnets
Wire: N/A
Resistance: N/A (+/-)
Pole pieces: fixed steel slug poles in both coils
Sound: aggressive hot ceramic humbucker tone

- **Gibson Angus Young Signature**
Type: double coil
Magnet: Alnico V
Wire: N/A
Resistance: N/A
Pole pieces: six adjustable threaded steel poles in one coil, six fixed steel slugs in the other coil
Sound: in the ballpark of the 498T, with perhaps more nuance

Fender

A young upstart radio repairman from the Fullerton district of Los Angeles, CA, by the name of Leo Fender began manufacturing pickups for lap-steel guitars in 1945 in partnership with local musician and former Rickenbacker employee Doc Kauffman, under the short-lived K&F brand. Fender had opened a record store and radio repair shop in Fullerton six years earlier, and his business had swiftly segued into repairing instruments and PAs for, and soon renting them to, the many musicians who were flocking to the boomtown for work. It was no great stretch for Fender to begin manufacturing equipment himself, and – with the entertainment industry ramping back up after the war effort – there was certainly a demand for his services. Fender and Kauffman had gotten to know each other during the war years through just such a confluence of circumstances, and had filed a patent for an early pickup and solid-bodied steel guitar (which also, in fact, could be played as a Spanish-style guitar) in 1944. The early design featured a coil that the instrument's strings would pass right through (somewhat, but not entirely, like Rickenbacker's horseshoe pickup), but Fender soon refined the design to something that would look far more like the narrow single-coil pickups familiar to us from most of his electric guitars of the following decade.

After Kauffman departed in 1946, Fender established Fender Manufacturing, which he renamed Fender Electric Instrument Company the following year, by which time he was already making surprisingly advanced guitar amplifiers, the

manufacturers' profiles – the 'big four'

descendents of which would set the standards for generations of tube amps to come. We're more familiar with the models today as applied to the early amps – Champ, Deluxe, Princeton, Champion – but these were sold in sets with lap-steels that carried the same names. Check out any of those early steels, and you'll see pickups that are easily recognized as Fender designs: tidy and slim of build, bright and cutting of tone, this is where the Fender sound really started. Well before Leo's first production solid-body Spanish guitar hit the scene in 1950, his Champion carried a pickup that was very much like the one we would come to know as the Broadcaster (or Esquire, and later Telecaster) bridge pickup, while the Champ carried something not dissimilar to the Broad/Telecaster neck pickup.

Even though Fender really started to coin it for real in the early 1950s with his Spanish guitars, he learned his tricks from the Hawaiian lap-steel crowd, and decided early on that this was the sound that would propel the Spanish electric to acceptance, and genuine success. Very insightful of Mr. Fender. For while Gibson had its sound, and was certainly a big player in the market, the three most desirable factors in an electric guitar sound at the time were treble, treble, and treble, and Fender's new creations were *bright*. Their impressive clarity and definition went a long way toward cutting through the predominantly warm, rounded amps and lo-fi mixes of the day, and took the guitarist another step closer to center stage, letting him cut it with the horn players – which was, to a great extent, the impetus for the development of the electric guitar in the first place.

The first Fender pickup of great interest to us six-stringers, the Broadcaster bridge pickup, was wound with as many as 10,000 turns of 43-gauge plain enamel-coated wire. Very early in production, however, Fender changed to 42-gauge plain enamel-coated wire for these pickups, and this is the coil wire generally referred to when vintage Telecaster or Esquire bridge pickup specs are discussed. Approximately 9,200 turns of wire on a hand-guided winder gave these pickups a DC resistance reading in the 6.8k to 7.8k ballpark. Although it might appear otherwise from a quick glance at these pickups, Fender didn't use 'bobbins' as such, but a pair of fiber plates, top and bottom, made from a similar material to that the company was using for its amps' circuit boards, and for the early black pickguards on the guitars themselves. These were held in place by the six non-adjustable Alnico V rod magnets used as pole pieces, and the coil was wound right around this construction (with a thin insulating barrier of tape used to keep the fine coil wire from catching or shorting out on any rough imperfections on the magnets' surfaces). Add to this uncomplicated

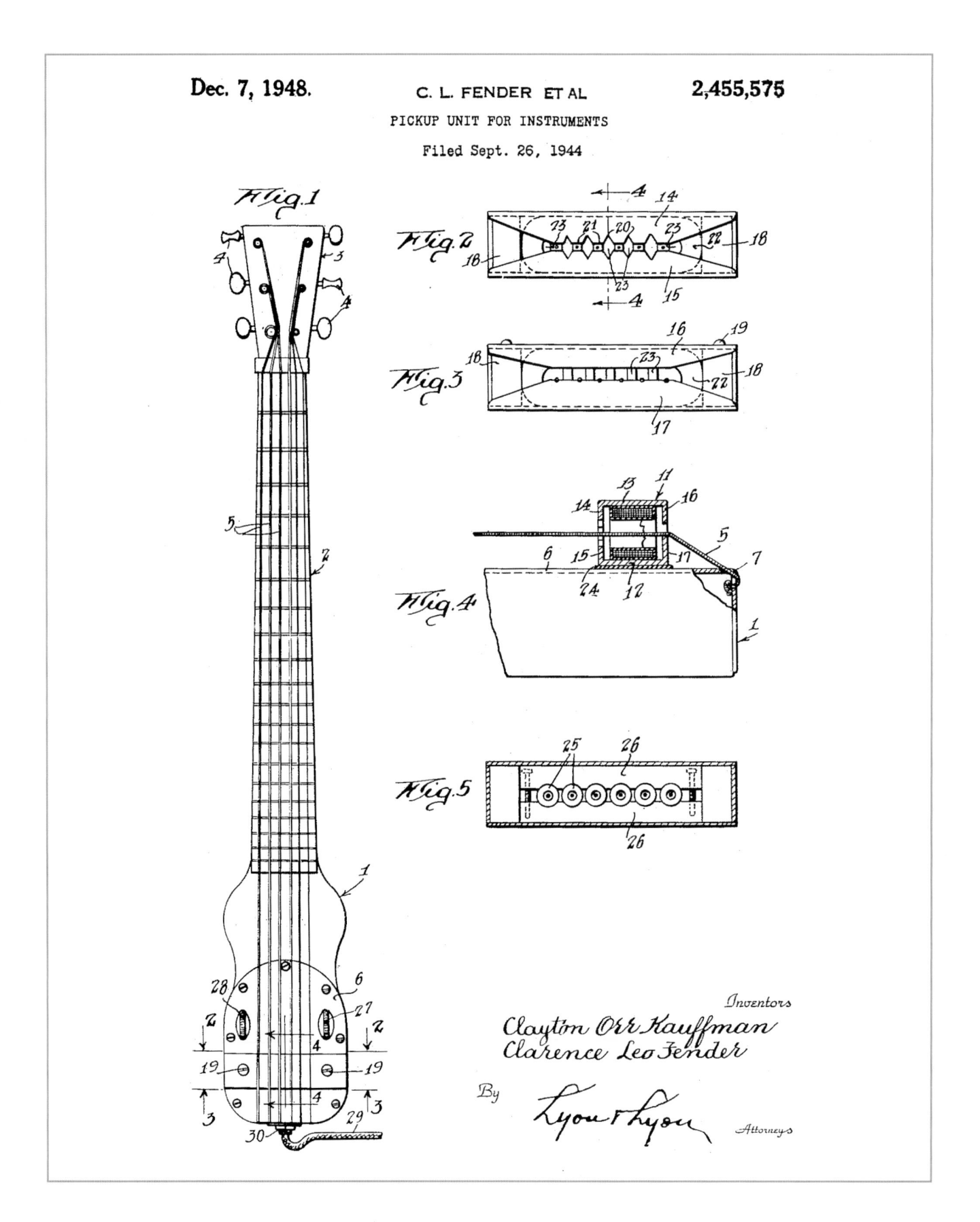

Dec. 7, 1948. C. L. FENDER ET AL 2,455,575
PICKUP UNIT FOR INSTRUMENTS
Filed Sept. 26, 1944

Inventors
Clayton Orr Kauffman
Clarence Leo Fender
By Lyon & Lyon
Attorneys

manufacturers' profiles — the 'big four'

construction the legendary copper-plated, tin base plate (originally zinc), and twang history is made.

As basic as these pickups are, nothing else sounds quite like them, and original examples from 1950 to the mid '60s have become highly prized as a result. But the unique Telecaster bridge pickup tone makes a great lesson in the 'everything contributes' nature of guitar tone in general. More than just the result of the pickup design itself, the Tele twang is a factor of the way the unit is mounted, and of course of the design of the guitar itself. The pickup hangs in a 'semi-floating' steel bridge base, which is screwed to the body at its back edge only. On top of this (literally) the three basic saddles transmit string vibration into the bridge plate, which transmits it – via pickup-mounting screws that are threaded right into the base plate – which is in contact with the bottoms of the pole pieces, while also just a thin fiber base plate away from the coil itself – into all of the critical electro-magnetic workings of the pickup. Talk about resonance and vibration characteristics – the Tele bridge pickup is getting it from all angles. The Tele's through-body stringing enhances the sustain element of this tone, as well as its overall body and presence, while the guitar's light swamp ash body and maple neck go a long way toward maximizing its snap and jangle. Spanky, bright, cutting … just call it 'twangy', and everybody knows what you're talking about.

As the mid 1960s rolled along Fender got closer to standardizing its pickup specs, which mainly meant restricting turns of wire down to around 7,500 to 8,000 turns, and as a result the Telecaster got a little weaker, although they remained rich and full-throated performers. Resistance readings in the 6.25k to 7k range are more common for 1960s examples. In 1965, Fender also changed the bottom base plate to light gray fiber, which conveniently helps to delineate post-CBS pickups. Light gray base plates changed to dark gray in 1968. In 1983, Fender dropped the base plate from bridge pickups used on its Standard Telecaster, finally taking the unit a major step away from its vintage design. As is so often the case with original components verses contemporary renditions that have evolved from them, however, most Telecaster fans will agree that modern pickups don't capture quite the same magic of vintage examples from the 1950s and '60s.

Once again, we can contribute this to a number of factors, which include the materials used and the way in which the pickups were constructed. A certain 'happy accident' factor in the way the wire was hand-guided onto the coils is credited with some of the liveliness and general sonic mojo of all early Fender pickups, and sure, there's probably a little of this holding sway. I guess such

FACING PAGE **Leo Fender – lap-steel pickup, c'44.**

thinking is proved out in the very best of the originals that you occasionally hear, where some magic ratio of coil-wire length, coil construction (its relative looseness or tightness, and general shape), and magnet strength all coalesce to produce splendiferous tone. By the same logic, though, there are plenty of vintage examples that fail to hit that magic ratio, and which therefore sound less than spectacular. This does follow through, to some extent, so perhaps the 'happy accident' theory holds some water. This brings in the great task of the reproduction pickup manufacturers, which is to achieve a consistent production of pickups that sound like the best of various types of vintage units, but more of this a little later in the book. I will say that the best of the vintage 1950s and early-60s Esquires and Telecasters with original pickups that I have played have walked all over even good reissues and/or contemporary guitars with the best reproduction vintage-style pickups installed, but … the best of these reproductions sound damn good indeed, and come closer to the Tele thang than, for example, many (or any?) of the best reproduction PAF-style humbuckers do to the real thing. Again, there are a lot of factors at play here – the guitars themselves, for one – so this is a very rough judgment, and one that I wouldn't want you to stake the farm on.

Broadcaster neck pickups were wound with 43-gauge plain enamel-coated wire from the start, just like the earliest bridge pickups, but the neck units stayed that way, right through the Telecaster years and beyond. There's an obvious and practical reason for this: these are tiny little pickups, and you can't get a lot of 42-gauge wire around them, or not enough to produce an adequate output, anyway. Fender could fit more turns of 43-gauge wire onto this pickup, 8,000 turns of which, more or less (as ever), resulted in a resistance of around 7.25k to 8.25k in most examples. Now, the two very different pickups in the Telecaster make a great case study in the fact that DC resistance alone will not tell you how a pickup will sound, or even provide an accurate indication – absent of other factors – of how powerful a pickup will be. Traditional Tele neck pickups average 7.5k to 8k, while their counterparts in the bridge average 7k to 7.8k, but any twangmaster worth their salt will tell you which is louder and more powerful. They'll also tell you that any guitar with two very similar pickups in the neck and bridge positions will give you a lot more guts from the neck position, where the strings vibrate in a wider arc and produce more energy themselves. This is another case in point regarding trying to compare apples to oranges where pickups are concerned: the 43-gauge wire in the Telecaster neck pickup's coil means that its resistance reading cannot be taken on the same scale as the

manufacturers' profiles – the 'big four'

bridge pickup, wound with 42-gauge wire, nor do similar readings indicate similar tones.

Many fans of the twang rave in particular about Esquire pickups, and you occasionally see claims (usually from guitar dealers with Esquires to sell) about 'the hotter pickups Fender used in vintage Esquires', but these are essentially the same units that were put into the Telecasters being made right alongside them. There are a few factors in the construction and wiring of the single-pickup model, however, that give some Esquires more tonal girth. One is a purely physical characteristic: the lack of a pickup in the neck position means there is no magnetic force there to pull against the strings' aforementioned wide vibrational arc at that point, and to thereby dampen the tone, however slightly (or considerably, if that pickup is adjusted too close to the strings). The other is the Esquire wiring, which is designed to provide three different sounds from one pickup at the flick of a switch. Switch selections on the Esquire give you: forward – preset 'bassy sound' (aka 'jazz sound') created by a simple two-capacitor network; middle – normal bridge pickup through volume and tone controls; back – pickup with tone control bypassed. That third selection, which bypasses the tone control, adds a little extra gusto to the pickup's sound, since routing through a tone control always adds a little capacitance, even when the pot is rolled fully 'on', and creates the perception that Esquire pickups are 'hotter'.

The pickup that arrived on the revolutionary Fender Stratocaster of 1954 was not wildly unlike the Telecaster bridge pickup, without the base plate. Most notably, however, these were given fewer windings than Tele bridge pickups, and wound with 42-gauge Formvar-coated magnet wire which, despite being the same gauge, came out thicker than the wire wound on Tele bridge pickups thanks to its heavier coating (plain enamel-coated wire was used in the mid 1960s, and polysol-coated wire later in the '70s). Fender, like many manufacturers of the day, was going for the bright, sparkling, well-defined performance that would help a guitarist stand out amid a large ensemble, and this was another pickup aimed at achieving it. Original Stratocaster pickups of the 1950s and '60s were given from around 7,500 to 8,000 turns of wire, and display a DC resistance reading from the mid 5k ohms to the lower 6k ohms, descending, in general, from readings toward the higher end of the range in the '50s to the lower end of the range by the mid '60s. These are not powerful pickups, and the bridge units are notoriously under-gunned against those fitted in the neck position, but they can still sound glorious in all positions. The Strat neck pickup is one of the all-time tonal icons, particularly as wielded by a number of blues masters, from Eric Clapton to Buddy Guy to Stevie Ray Vaughan. This is a sound that shows us how a bright, clear, low-output single-coil pickup, when placed in a position that provides warmth, depth, and beefy volume levels from the guitar itself, can result in a surprisingly rich, throaty tone. In other words, the neck position, where those strings are shimmying with *mucho gusto* and interacting with the magnetic field in a mighty way, makes up for what the weak-looking Stratocaster single-coil pickup design might seem to lack on paper, and guitar and pickup work together here to give us lots of juice, no mistake.

Contemporary makers of this type of pickup usually offer them, wisely, in calibrated sets, which means the middle is a little stronger than the neck, and the bridge is a little stronger than the middle. This results in more balanced output levels between the positions, with a little extra gusto from the bridge, the position rock'n'rollers are likely to flip to for cutting lead breaks. Stratocaster players have always sought to balance neck/middle/bridge output levels in their own way, of course, by staggering the pickup heights, with the bridge set highest, middle down a little, and neck down further still. Setting the neck pickup down into the pickguard more than the others also helps to minimize its pole pieces' pull on the strings, which can seriously impede your tone when you get this pickup up close to those vibrating wires. Imperfect beast though it might be, the Stratocaster pickup has nevertheless established a legendary sound, one so beloved that players have found ways to work within its limitations. As much as reproduction-style units have sought to improve on some of the Stratocaster pickup's acknowledged flaws, and Fender itself has introduced many modifications to the form, original examples from Stratocasters made between 1954 and the mid '60s are still extremely desirable, and very expensive, when you can find them.

There's a lot of talk about the 'beveled magnets' used in vintage Strat pickups, meaning that the edges of the top ends of the Alnico V pole pieces, when viewed closely, can be seen to have been ground away at an angle. Some players consider this another factor of the vintage-Strat tone, although removing such a slight amount of material from the magnet would have a minimal affect on the pickup's performance, and would certainly play less of a part in a vintage Strat's overall tone than would many, many other variables. Primarily, this beveling was done to make it easier to push the magnets into the fiber top and base plates. Until 1974 the pole pieces in Strat pickups were also staggered in an attempt to balance their outputs, with the D tallest of all, the G following it, then the A and D on a par, and the B and E shortest (lowest) of all. In 1956 the

manufacturers' profiles – the 'big four'

pattern changed so that the G was tallest and the D fell just beneath it, and in 1974 Fender switches to flush pole pieces. As with Telecaster pickups, Fender also changed to dark gray, then light gray fiber base plates during the course of the 1960s, and dropped cloth-covered black and white (later yellow) wire in mid 1968 for PVC-covered wire.

The Jazzmaster pickup was Fender's next significant development after the Strat pickup. The new unit, introduced in 1958, chased the core Fender goals of clarity and brightness by again using individual Alnico V pole pieces set within the coil, but uses a wider and shallower coil with slightly more turns (around 8,500) of 42-gauge Formvar-coated wire to attain a slightly thicker, warmer sound. The variation of form works to some extent, and Jazzmaster pickups do sound a little fatter and more mid-rangey than Strat or Tele pickups, but they don't entirely achieve the classic jazz tone that Leo was after with the design. In fact, the size and shape of the Jazzmaster coil, and the number of turns of wire its coil was given, is not far from the standard for Gibson's P-90 single coil, but the differences between them account for the Jazzmaster's twang and definition verses the P-90s grit and thump.

A more unusual proposition arrived on the Jaguar of 1962. The Jaguar was aimed squarely at the surf crowd that had flocked around the thicker-sounding Jazzmaster and, to some extent (surf master Dick Dale being a case in point) the Stratocaster, and its unusual pickups were designed to capture the bright, percussive tone that defined this instrumental music genre. Jaguar pickups look something like Stratocaster pickups framed in steel 'claws', but they are different in other ways besides. They were given a few more turns of wire than Strat pickups in many cases, upwards of around 8,500 turns of 42-gauge Formvar-coated wire, and have a different cover that displays the mounting 'ears' above the pickguard. The visible steel claws are actual 'U' channels that the pickups sit within, and which were intended to help focus the magnetic field. In fact, the added steel, which is in contact with the Jaguar pickup's Alnico V pole pieces at the bottom of the unit, do increase these pickups' inductance somewhat, much as does the Telecaster bridge pickup's base plate. The other notable vintage Fender single coil, the Mustang Pickup, was made much like the Stratocaster pickup, although with flush Alnico V pole pieces and slightly fewer turns of 42-gauge wire, which was originally Formvar-coated, and later plain enamel-coated. These bright, cutting pickups tend to read around 5.5k ohms on average, and a pair of them can be surprisingly versatile in a little Mustang, especially given the model's on/off/reverse-phase switching options. Of course

manufacturers' profiles – the 'big four'

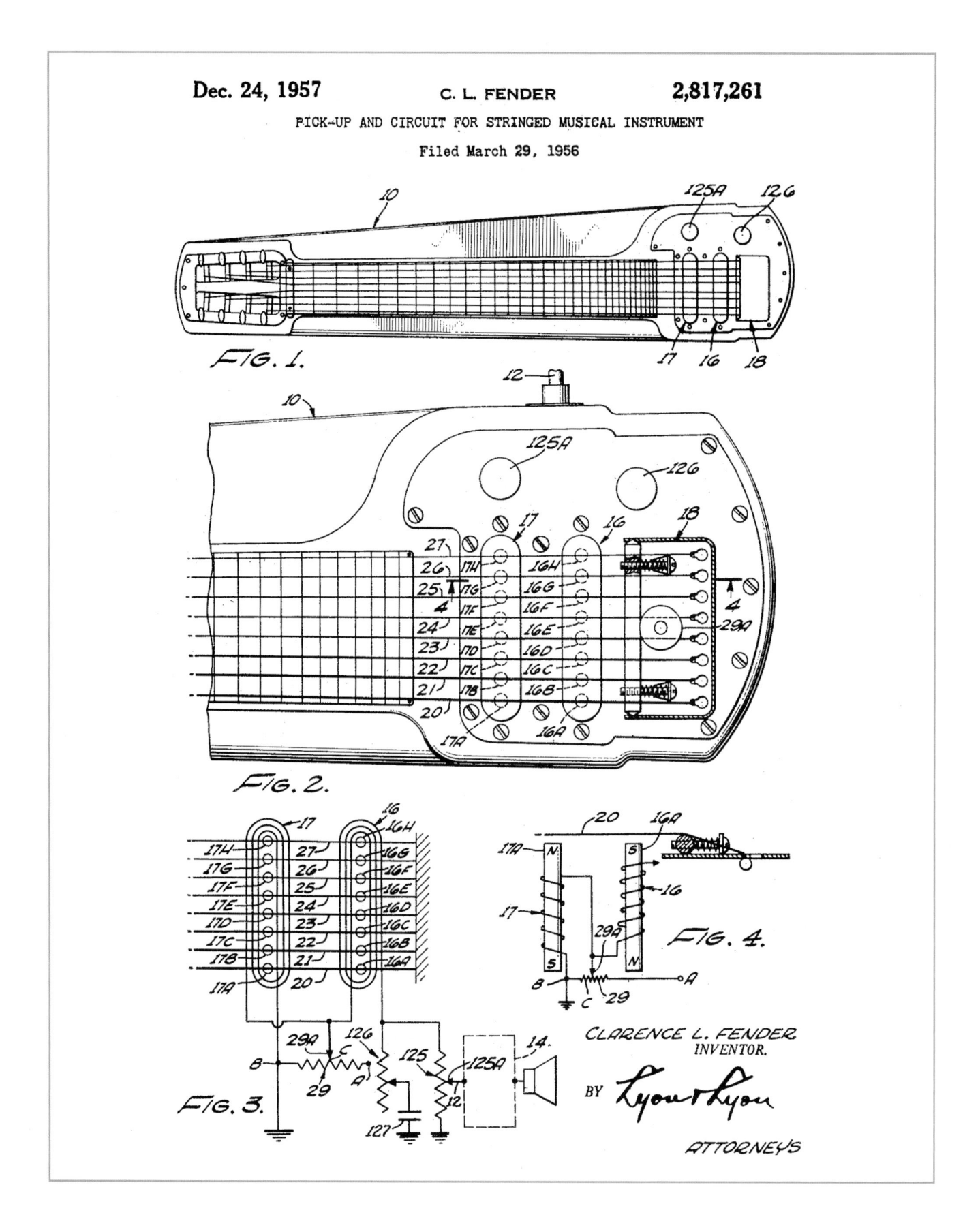

Dec. 24, 1957 C. L. FENDER 2,817,261
PICK-UP AND CIRCUIT FOR STRINGED MUSICAL INSTRUMENT
Filed March 29, 1956

CLARENCE L. FENDER
INVENTOR.
BY Lyon & Lyon
ATTORNEYS

manufacturers' profiles – the 'big four'

that guitar's shorter 24-inch scale length also furs up the sound somewhat, which means these low-powered pickups can sometimes give the impression of having a little more warmth than Strat pickups. This is a good case in point regarding 'the Fender pickup sound' when considered against 'the Gibson pickup sound': along with the pickups' predisposition toward an enhanced treble response, the Stratocaster and Telecasters' 25½-inch scale length also accentuates sparkle, clarity and high harmonics. Putting a Telecaster pickups on a Les Paul won't get you exactly the same breed of twang as a Tele, just as putting a PAF on a Stratocaster won't give you the same kind of juicy rock lead tones you get from a Les Paul.

A look at some of the unrealized inventions of guitar-makers from the golden years, and of Fender in particular, can make a fascinating study in the directions in which some of these visionaries thought the electric guitar, and the pickup in particular, might be headed. Leo Fender, for one, seemed to have been obsessed in the late 1950s and early 1960s with developing a smoother-sounding pickup. In the claims listed for a patent filed August 13 1957 but not granted until January 17 1961, Fender cites the need to eliminate from current pickup designs "a number of effects ... which are undesirable in certain situations." Among these, he lists, "firstly, a strong, and relatively harsh, twang or percussive sound followed by a very rapid decay or attenuation to a much lower sound level." (In other words, the classic 'Fender sound', many would say!) "Such effects also include, secondly, a slow beating or tremolo effect, caused by rotation of the plane of vibration of the string." His cure – described in words and pictures in the application for patent number 2,968,204 – involved a pickup with seven pole pieces to capture the vibrations of the six strings, each of which would therefore run between two pole pieces.

We never saw this unit on a production guitar, but portions of the thinking might sound and look familiar. The 'strings between poles' design was applied to the Precision Bass pickup, a patent application for which was filed in 1959, and granted shortly after that for the above pickup, in March 1959.

While most Fender fans mark the company's sale to CBS, concluded in early 1965 after negotiations begun the year before, to mark the start of a period when the company would start seeking to do things cheaper, and in greater numbers, Leo Fender himself seems never to have been willing to rest upon his laurels. Leo Fender's contract with CBS as an R&D consultant was up in 1970, and following the expiration of a non-compete clause in the Fender sale, he first did some design work for the new Music Man company, then eventually

FACING PAGE **Fender – lap-steel humbucker, '56. Not all of Leo Fender's pickup design work was applied to 'Spanish' electric guitars, and many innovations continued to be directed toward steel guitars. This patent, for a dual-coil pickup with humbucking capabilities and various switching options, shows Fender was thinking of hum rejection in the mid 1950s, even though the company wouldn't produce a humbucker for traditional Spanish electric guitar until well into the post-CBS years.**

manufacturers' profiles – the 'big four'

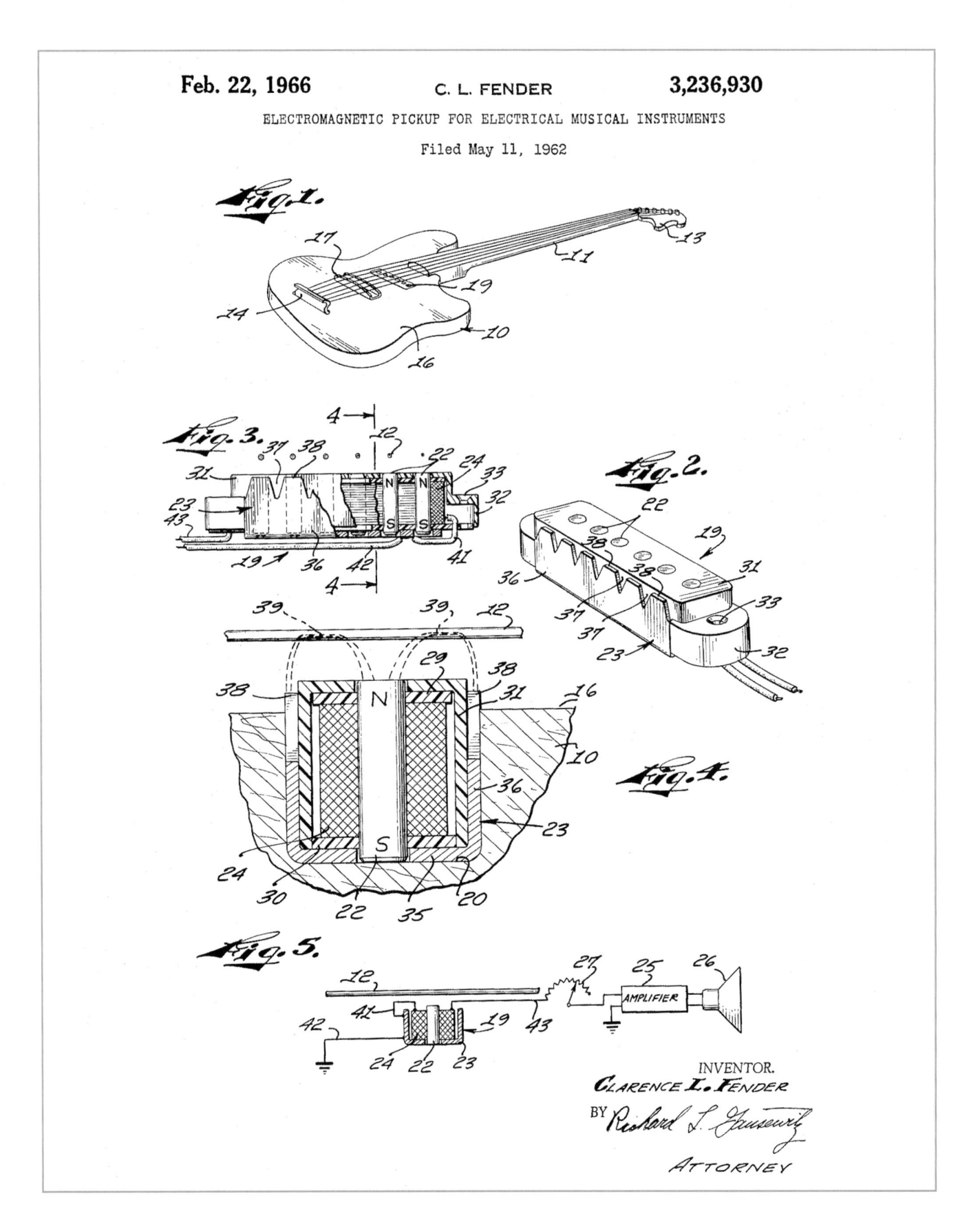

Feb. 22, 1966   C. L. FENDER   3,236,930
ELECTROMAGNETIC PICKUP FOR ELECTRICAL MUSICAL INSTRUMENTS
Filed May 11, 1962

INVENTOR.
CLARENCE L. FENDER
BY Richard S. Gausewitz
ATTORNEY

manufacturers' profiles – the 'big four'

established the G&L guitar company in 1980 along with George Fullerton (G&L = George and Leo), where he revived a lot of his forward-looking designs, both in pickups and other aspects of guitar construction. In the next chapter, Fender's pickup work with G&L shows just how intent the founder of one of the seminal sounds in rock, blues, and country guitar was on moving the technology forward. He also seemed to enjoy filing patent applications for just about anything under the sun, which included some procedures long in use by other pickup-makers, but apparently not patented previously. Among these, was a patent Fender filed – and was granted – for the wax-potting process used to seal pickups from unwanted moisture and microphonic vibration (patent number 4,885,970). Despite his declining health, Fender continued his intensive R&D work with G&L right up until his death on March 21 1991.

Fender, the company, finally got into the humbucker game in an effort to produce its own breed of juicy rock lead tone in 1970, and did so with the help of a major name from the annals of Gibson history. Appearing first in the neck position on the Custom Telecaster, then as a pair on the revamped Thinline Telecaster model of 1972, Fender's 'Wide Range Humbucking Pickup', as it was officially known, was designed by Seth Lover, father of the Gibson PAF humbucker. Although it looks outwardly like another PAF-inspired design, but with the adjustable pole pieces offset three-each in the side-by-side coils, it is in fact a considerably different design. Not wanting to merely copy his work for Gibson (which, it has been said, is pretty much what CBS-owned Fender wanted from him), Lover concocted a design that used pole pieces made from cunife magnets, an alloy of copper, nickel, and iron that is soft enough to be threaded. Six more threaded cunife magnets, again staggered three and three, are hidden beneath the chromed cover, but these are installed in the coils with their slotted ends down, since they are not adjustable with the cover in place. These pickups were wound with some 5,000 turns of 42-gauge polysol-coated wire per coil, resulting in a fairly hot DC resistance reading of around 10.5k ohms. Despite these specs, the cunife magnets help to keep them brighter than a similarly hot PAF-style humbucker with an alnico magnet mounted beneath steel pole pieces, and these pickups retain a degree of characteristically Fenderish brightness as a result, which was one of Lover's main goals in the first place.

Like so many other big-name guitar-makers, Fender realized in the early 1980s – dark days for the company under CBS, as they were for Gibson under Norlin – that the surest road to renewed success was the one that headed back over the ground the company covered so thoroughly in the 1950s and early '60s.

FACING PAGE **Leo Fender's design for the Jaguar pickup, patent filed 1962, granted 1966.**

manufacturers' profiles – the 'big four'

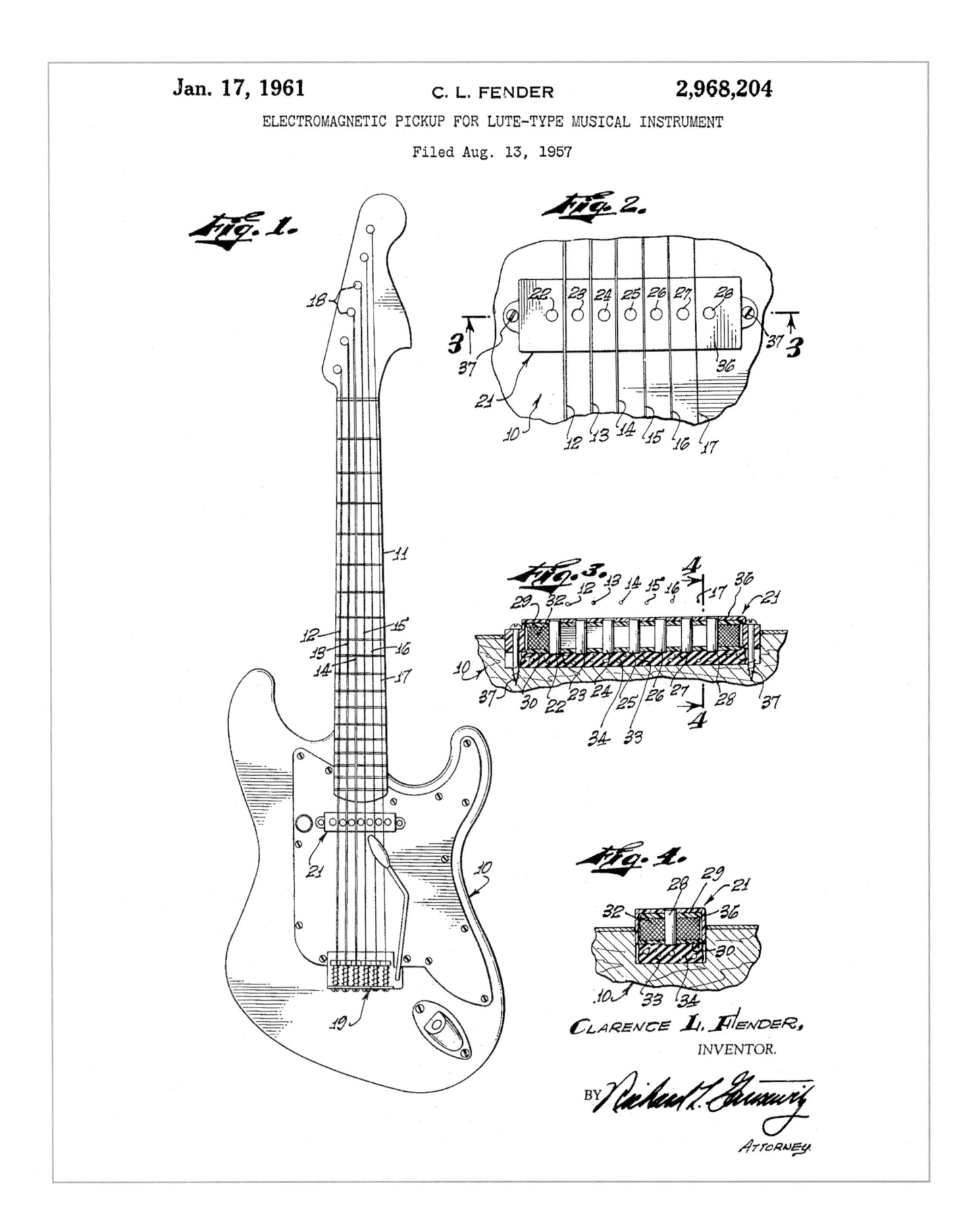

Jan. 17, 1961 C. L. FENDER **2,968,204**
ELECTROMAGNETIC PICKUP FOR LUTE-TYPE MUSICAL INSTRUMENT
Filed Aug. 13, 1957

CLARENCE L. FENDER,
INVENTOR.

BY *Richard [signature]*
ATTORNEY.

manufacturers' profiles – the 'big four'

In 1985 CBS sold Fender to a group of the company's managers and other investors, one of whom was Dan Smith, who had already been a prime mover in getting Fender onto the reissue track in the early 1980s. Of course any good reissue program required a close look at vintage pickups in order to accurately reproduce these crucial components, and slowly but surely Fender worked its way back to creating the best possible reproductions of its original Telecaster and Stratocaster pickups. Come the 21st century, and this effort has culminated in a wide range of vintage-styled pickups – some as accurate as possible, some modified to suit different players' desires – that together represent the great diversity among even untouched original examples. For as we know, there's no such thing as *the* great 1957 Stratocaster pickup', just *a* great 1957 Stratocaster pickup', given that they all varied so much in the first place.

Many current-production pickups used on Fender USA guitars fall under the Custom Shop banner, although some of the special concoctions used on the higher-end Custom Shop guitars themselves are not available as after-market replacement pickups. Among these, and one of the most popular series of Fender pickups of the modern era, is the Texas Special, which aims to give you hot blues and gnarly twang respectively in its Strat and Tele guises. Both varieties use Alnico V magnets and are over-wound into 6.5k to 7k territory for the Strat bridge pickup (calibrated sets with middle and neck at 6.5k and 6.2k), and 10.5k for the Tele bridge pickup. Fat '50s Strat pickups are also popular, and offer staggered, hand-beveled Alnico V magnets within coils wound with traditional 42-gauge Formvar-coated wire to land just on the hot side of the range of readings found from vintage pickups, at around 6.2k ohms for the bridge unit. These aim to capture a traditional vintage-Strat tone, while getting you past any chance of the thin or spiky treble response that even some great original Stratocasters will exhibit in certain situations. The Custom '54 Strat set uses a similar magnet and wire formula, but offers a little more disparity between bridge and neck/middle, topping out at around 6.4k on the bridge pickup and 5.9k on the other two. Finally, the Custom '69 Strat offers the weaker Stratocaster pickups that were more common in the Hendrix era. These are wound by noted Fender pickup-maker Abigail Ybarra, who has worked for Fender since the late 1950s, and they use the staggered Alnico V magnets and enamel-coated wire of the period, partnered with the light gray base plates and lower 'standardized' coil turns of the late 1960s to produce pickups that read around 5.8k in all positions.

Telecaster players seeking a more traditional breed of twang than that

FACING PAGE **Leo Fender's design for a pickup with reduced string pull, to produce a smoother tone.**

manufacturers' profiles – the 'big four'

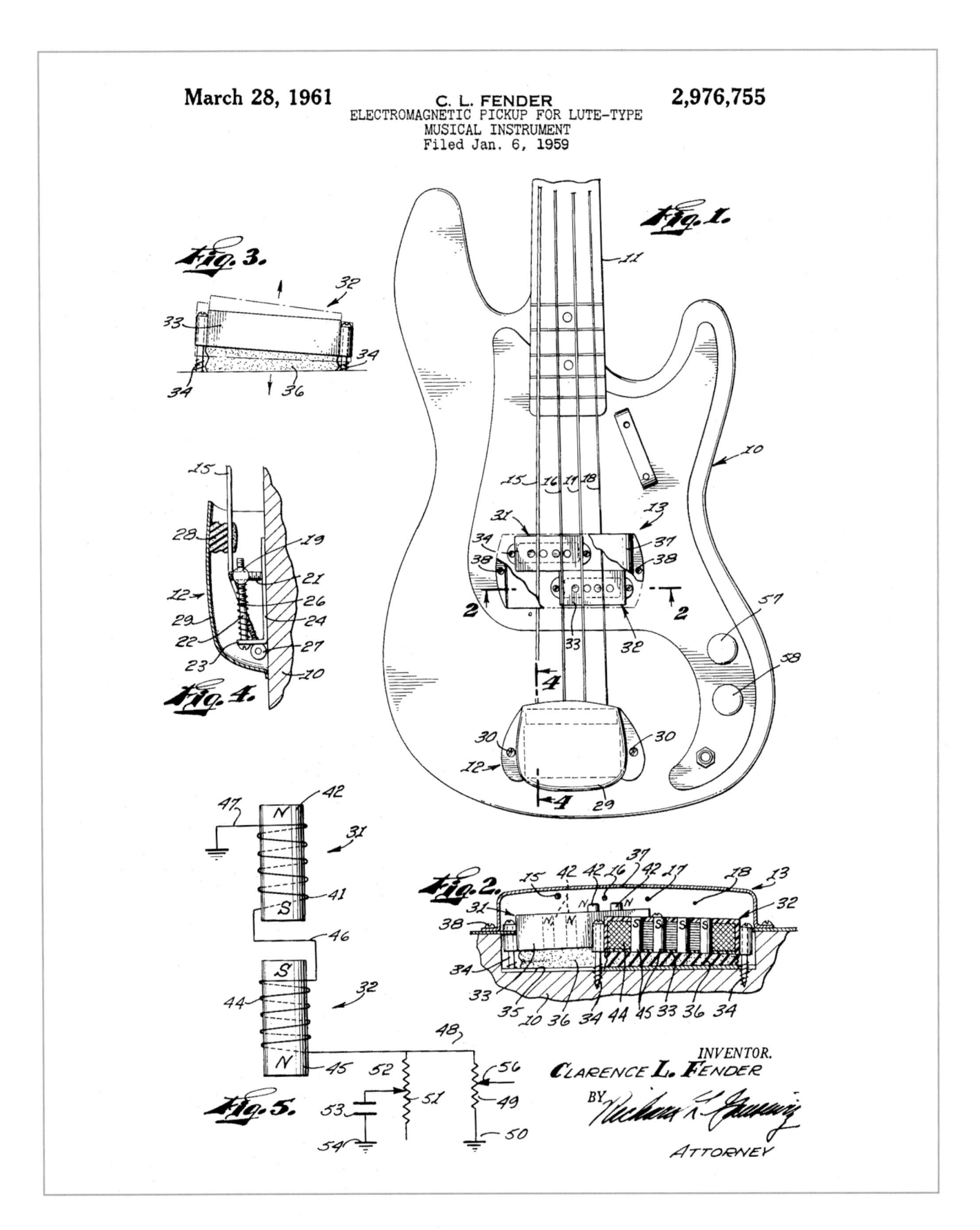

March 28, 1961   C. L. FENDER   2,976,755
ELECTROMAGNETIC PICKUP FOR LUTE-TYPE
MUSICAL INSTRUMENT
Filed Jan. 6, 1959

INVENTOR.
CLARENCE L. FENDER
BY
ATTORNEY

manufacturers' profiles – the 'big four'

delivered by the beefy Texas Specials can find it in the Custom Shop Nocaster set. The bridge unit is wound with 42-gauge enamel-coated wire to a DC resistance of around 7.75k, while the neck pickup reads 7.9k from a coil wound with 43-gauge wire. Both use Alnico III magnets. As discussed above regarding Telecaster pickups, not that these resistance readings can be deceiving: inductance readings of 3.7 Henries for the bridge pickup and 2.35 Henries for the neck pickup help to tell more of the story, the moral of which is that the former still has a lot more punch than the latter, despite its 0.15k higher resistance. Also worth noting is that the Nocaster bridge pickup comes with a zinc base plate, as did the original Broadcaster and early Telecaster pickups, rather than the copper-plated steel base plate of units made after the very early 1950s (and many modern types, such as the Texas Special above).

A few other Custom Shop Telecaster pickups of interest are not offered for sale as replacement parts. One of these is the Broadcaster pickup, which has flush magnets and is wound with 43-gauge wire like the originals to a resistance of around 9k ohms, a level that still retains more sharp twang than a 9k bridge pickup wound with 42-gauge wire would offer. Another is a pickup that aims specifically to combat 'dull Tele neck tone syndrome', a unit called the Twisted Tele neck pickup. Designed by former Custom Shop employee Alan Hamel, the Twisted Tele uses extra long Alnico V magnets (magnets taken from stocks used for the Jazz Bass pickups, in fact), and is wound with 42-gauge Formvar-coated wire – rather than the 43-gauge traditionally used for these pickups – to achieve a DC resistance reading in the 5.8k to 6.1k range. Given the long magnets and heavy wire, the Twisted Tele achieves a bright, full tone in the neck position, despite its seemingly low resistance, that many players equate with a great Stratocaster neck-pickup sound. Which, as it happens, was exactly Fender's goal with the unit. Although it can't be bought separately, look for it in plenty of Fender's higher-end Telecasters.

A wide range of other current-manufacture pickups from Fender USA caters for a broad range of tastes. Original '59/'62 Strat pickups couple a fairly low resistance of around 5.6k with a pretty beefy inductance for a Strat pickup (3 Henries) for a classic bright, cutting sound with good body, while the Tex-Mex Stratocaster pickup – originally designed for the Jimmy Vaughan Tex-Mex Stratocaster – beefs up the classic formula a little more. The SCN Strat and Tele pickups – for Samarium Cobalt Noiseless – designed in 1995 by noted pickup guru Bill Lawrence, use a rare and unusual magnet material, Samarium cobalt, for their pole pieces, in combination with traditional bar magnetic material

FACING PAGE **A continuation of Fender's patent application for a pickup with reduced string pull, as applied to the Precision Bass.**

beneath. The magnet structures are designed to produce a wider, softer magnetic field which doesn't impede string vibration, and contributes to a full-sounding yet characteristically 'Fenderish' pickup. They are fairly 'hot' pickups that nevertheless retain good clarity and high-end detail, along with a hum-canceling performance. Hotter still, the Hot Noiseless Strat set, designed for Jeff Beck and now available as after-market pickups, go the stacked-humbucker route and employ ceramic magnets for some serious oomph. Their cousins, the Vintage Noiseless Strat pickups, use Alnico V magnets for a more vintage-voice performance. A Vintage Noiseless Telecaster set does the same for plank spankers, while the recently redesigned Original Vintage Telecaster pickups aim for authenticity in a '50s-style Tele pickup, using Alnico III magnets, enamel-coated 42-gauge and 43-gauge wire in bridge and neck respectively, and enough coil turns to bring them up to 7.2k and 7.7k.

Another notable new-generation 'Fender' pickup is not a Fender design at all, really, and not even a pickup in the traditional sense of the electromagnetic units discussed in this book, come to think of it. Fender-Lace Sensors, which were designed by Don Lace and are manufactured by Actodyne General, Inc (assignees of the patent for them), appear outwardly to be traditional Stratocaster single coils with no visible pole pieces, but under the hood lurks an entirely different form of pickup. Rather than using electromagnetic coils to sense the vibration of steel strings, they sense the emission of acoustic energy from the strings' vibration and translate that into an electrical signal. Their structure is very different from that of any traditional pickup; Lace Sensors use 36 tiny, low-energy particle magnets and 36 'comb teeth' in place of pole pieces, all of which are shielded by what Lace calls its 'radiant Field Barrier system', which helps to eliminate electrical interference and 60-cycle hum, and also focuses the magnetic field. Unlike many other alternative pickups designs, however, they are still passive devices, although they offer an impressive signal-to-noise ratio and a very broad frequency response, yet, when desired, can still produce fairly traditional single-coil Strat pickup tones. They are available in a range of outputs, indicated by color, from an emulation of an authentic 1950s Stratocaster sound to a hot contemporary sound, via a little of anything in between. While vintage-minded tone freaks tend to turn their noses up at any design that departs radically from foundations laid in the 1950s and '60s, it's worth keeping in mind that Lace Sensor Golds ('Classic '50s') have been the favorite of Eric Clapton for many years, and have also been used by Buddy Guy and Jeff Beck. Lace Sensors were available exclusively on Fender guitars from

FACING PAGE **Donald Lace's 1987 design for the pickup that would originally be known as the Fender-Lace Sensor.**

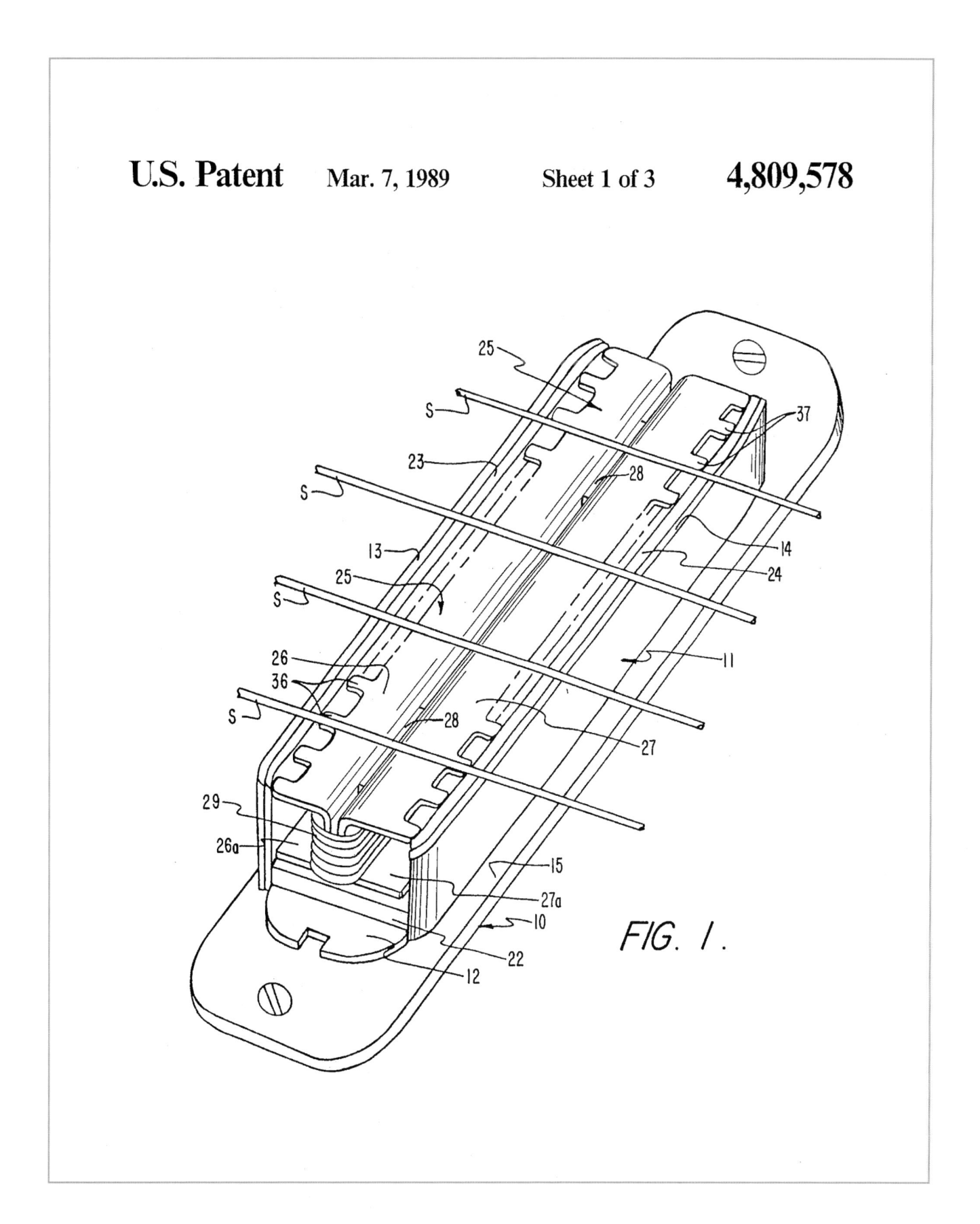

manufacturers' profiles – the 'big four'

U.S. Patent   Mar. 7, 1989   Sheet 1 of 3   **4,809,578**

FIG. 1.

FIG. 2.

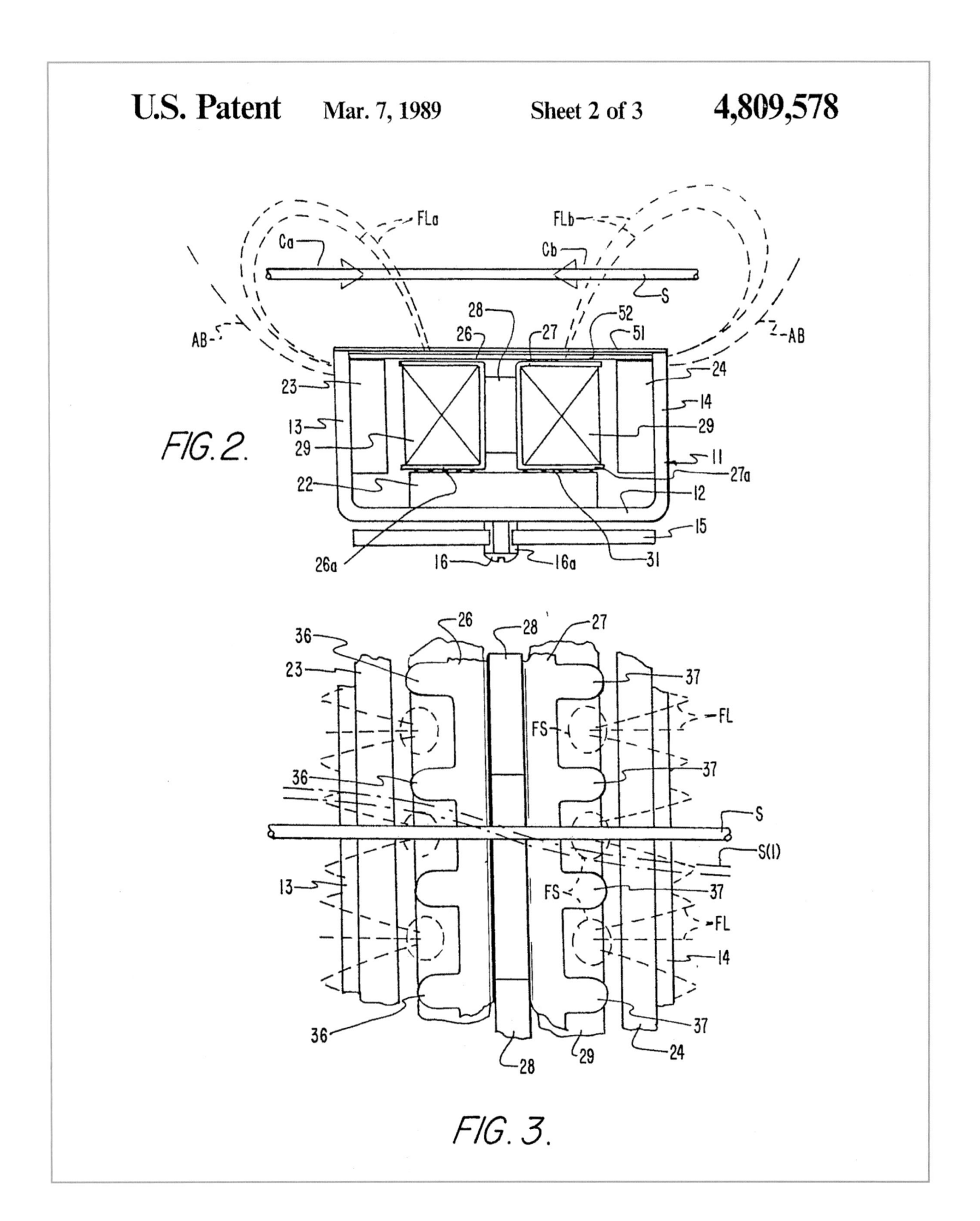

FIG. 3.

manufacturers' profiles – the 'big four'

1985 to 1996, but can now be used by other manufacturers, and are also available to be purchased separately.

In addition to the reproductions of Fender's 'Wide Range Humbucking Pickup' that come in some period-appropriate Telecaster reissues, Fender also offers the Atomic Humbucker, a more traditional, PAF-inspired design aimed at the classic rocker that uses Alnico II magnets and 42-gauge enamel-coated wire to achieve a resistance of around 7.8k neck and 9.2k bridge.

Of course, in addition to being available from Fender, traditional Fender Telecaster and Stratocaster pickups have provided an enormous inspiration to 'boutique' pickup winders, who seem to be finding Tonesville something of a boomtown these days, and they are therefore available in every nuanced shade under the sun, thanks to the efforts of some major producers and backyard-shed winders alike.

FACING PAGE **The continuation of Lace's patent application, with illustrations to display the magnetic field created by the Lace Sensor pickup.**

● Fender Broadcaster Bridge
Type: single coil
Magnet: Alnico V
Wire: 43 gauge, plain enamel coated
Resistance: 8k to 9k ohms
Pole pieces: individual alnico rod magnets, flush tops
Sound: bright, clear, percussive and well defined

● Fender Broadcaster/Telecaster Neck
Type: single coil
Magnet: Alnico V
Wire: 43 gauge, plain enamel coated
Resistance: 7k to 8k ohms
Pole pieces: individual alnico rod magnets, flush tops, covered
Sound: clean, round, good definition

● Fender Telecaster Bridge
Type: single coil
Magnet: Alnico V (very occasionally Alnico III in 1954)
Wire: 42 gauge, plain enamel coated
Resistance: 6.8k to 7.8k ohms
Pole pieces: individual alnico rod magnets, staggered tops
Sound: bright, well defined, with firm lows and smooth highs, and a little sizzle and good midrange punch, esp. at upper readings. Archetypal 'twang' (can vary widely)

● Fender Stratocaster
Type: single coil
Magnet: Alnico V
Wire: 42 gauge, Formvar coated
Resistance: 5.6k to 6.4k ohms
Pole pieces: individual alnico rod magnets, staggered/beveled tops
Sound: bright, clear, cutting; glassy and bell-like in the bridge, throaty and round in the neck (can vary widely)

● Fender MusicMaster/DuoSonic
Type: single coil
Magnet: Alnico V
Wire: 42 gauge, Formvar coated
Resistance: 6k ohms +/–
Pole pieces: individual alnico rod magnets, flush tops (unseen under plastic cover)
Sound: bright, clear, glassy and bell-like, while fairly rich too

● Fender Jazzmaster
Type: single coil
Magnet: Alnico V
Wire: 42 gauge, Formvar coated
Resistance: 6.5k ohms +/–
Pole pieces: individual alnico rod magnets, flush tops
Sound: cutting and well defined, but fairly thick and rich sounding, with some high-end sizzle

the guitar pickup handbook

manufacturers' profiles – the 'big four'

● Fender Jaguar
Type: single coil
Magnet: Alnico V
Wire: 42 gauge, Formvar coated
Resistance: 6.5k ohms +/−
Pole pieces: individual alnico rod magnets, flush tops, pickup sits in U-channel steel 'claw'
Sound: clear, full, bright, and decently 'round'

● Fender Wide Range Humbucker
Type: double coil
Magnet: cunife
Wire: 42 gauge, polysol coated
Resistance: 10k ohms
Pole pieces: six individual threaded cunife magnets per coil (three adjustable in each coil, the other three installed slot-down)
Sound: thick, rich, powerful, yet with appealing high end

● Fender Custom '54 Strat
Type: single coil
Magnet: Alnico V
Wire: 42 gauge, Formvar coated
Resistance: 5.9k to 6.5k ohms (neck to bridge)
Pole pieces: individual alnico rod magnets, beveled and staggered tops
Sound: classic clear, bell-like Strat tones, with extra kick in the bridge

● Fender Custom '69 Strat
Type: single coil
Magnet: Alnico V
Wire: 42 gauge, polysol coated
Resistance: 5.8k ohms (all positions)
Pole pieces: individual alnico rod magnets, beveled and staggered tops
Sound: transparent highs, recessed midrange, thumping lows

● Fender Custom Shop Fat '50s
Type: single coil
Magnet: Alnico V
Wire: 42 gauge, Formvar coated
Resistance: 6k to 6.3k ohms (neck to bridge)
Pole pieces: individual alnico rod magnets, beveled and staggered tops
Sound: clear, ringing highs, slightly scooped mids, enhanced bass

● Fender Texas Special Strat
Type: single coil
Magnet: Alnico V
Wire: 42 gauge, plain enamel coated
Resistance: 6.2k to 6.5k-7.1k ohms (neck to bridge)
Pole pieces: individual alnico rod magnets, beveled and staggered tops
Sound: bright and well defined, but with extra midrange punch and sizzle compared with classic Strat pickup (ie 'Texas blues' tone)

● Fender Custom Shop Texas Tele
Type: single coil
Magnet: Alnico V
Wire: neck 43 gauge, 42 gauge, plain enamel coated
Resistance: 9.5k ohms neck, 10.5k ohms
Pole pieces: individual alnico rod magnets, staggered tops in bridge unit, flush in neck unit
Sound: thick, fat and aggressive, but with a degree of Fender single-coil character (i.e. 'Texas blues' tone)

● Fender Custom Shop Nocaster
Type: single coil
Magnet: Alnico III
Wire: neck, 43 gauge; bridge, 42 gauge, plain enamel coated
Resistance: neck, 7.9k ohms; bridge, 7.72k ohms
Pole pieces: individual alnico rod magnets, flush tops on both pickups (zinc base plate on bridge pickup)
Sound: bright, clear, slightly sizzly twang tones with smooth midrange

● Fender Original '57/'62 Stratocaster
Type: single coil
Magnet: Alnico V
Wire: 42 gauge, Formvar coated
Resistance: 5.6k ohms
Pole pieces: individual alnico rod magnets, beveled and staggered tops
Sound: classic clear, bell-like Strat tones

manufacturers' profiles – the 'big four'

● Fender Vintage Noiseless Strat
Type: stacked single coil-sized humbucker
Magnet: Alnico V
Wire: plain enamel coated, gauge N/A
Resistance: 9.8k ohms
Pole pieces: individual alnico rod magnets
Sound: bright, well-defined Strat tones with a little added thickness, with hum-canceling benefits

● Fender Hot Noiseless Strat
Type: stacked single coil-sized humbucker
Magnet: ceramic
Wire: plain enamel coated, gauge N/A
Resistance: 10.4k ohms
Pole pieces: individual steel slugs
Sound: hot, thick, high-gain, improved sustain and midrange aggression

● Fender Vintage Noiseless Telecaster
Type: stacked single coil-sized humbucker
Magnet: Alnico V
Wire: neck, 43 gauge; bridge, 42 gauge, plain enamel coated
Resistance: neck, 12.2k ohms; bridge, 8.6k ohms
Pole pieces: individual alnico rod magnets
Sound: hum-canceling performance with typical Telecaster tones, thickness and frequency range slightly expanded

● Fender SCN Strat
Type: single coil-sized humbucker
Magnets: combination of Samarium Cobalt and traditional moderator bar
Wire: N/A
Resistance: bridge, 11.6k ohms; neck and middle, 6.5k ohms
Pole pieces: individual Samarium Cobalt magnets
Sound: hum-canceling performance with extended frequency range, good clarity and definition

● Fender SCN Tele
Type: single coil-sized humbucker
Magnets: combination of Samarium Cobalt and traditional moderator bar
Wire: N/A
Resistance: bridge, 13.8k ohms; neck, 12k ohms
Pole pieces: individual Samarium Cobalt magnets
Sound: hum-canceling performance with extended frequency range, good clarity and definition

● Fender Tex-Mex Stratocaster (current)
Type: single coil
Magnet: Alnico V
Wire: 42 gauge, polysol coated
Resistance: bridge, 7.4k ohms; neck and middle, 6.4k ohms
Pole pieces: individual alnico rod magnets, staggered tops
Sound: classic sparkling highs, good warmth, extended output for more midrange aggression

● Fender Vintage Telecaster Bridge
Type: single coil
Magnet: Alnico III
Wire: neck, 43 gauge; bridge, 42 gauge, plain enamel coated
Resistance: neck, 7.7k ohms; bridge, 7.2k ohms
Pole pieces: individual alnico rod magnets; staggered tops bridge (with copper-plated steel base plate); flush tops neck
Sound: classic blend of warmth and edge, commonly defined as 'twang'

● Fender-Lace Sensor Stratocaster
Type: low-noise unconventional single coil
Magnet: ceramic
Wire: N/A
Resistance: Gold, 5.8k ohms; Silver, 7.1k ohms; Blue, 12.8k ohms; Red, 14.5k ohms
Pole pieces: 36 individual steel teeth in a 'comb' configuration
Sound: from bright, percussive 'vintage Strat' tones (Gold), to singing high-output tones (Red), all with extended frequency range and low-noise operation

● Fender Atomic Humbucker
Type: double-coil humbucker
Magnet: Alnico II
Wire: 42 gauge, plain enamel coated
Resistance: neck, 7.9k ohms; bridge, 9.2k ohms
Pole pieces: six threaded steel poles in one coil, six fixed steel slugs in the other
Sound: broad, warm, smooth in the neck position; more biting and aggressive in the bridge, with increased midrange honk

manufacturers' profiles – the 'big four'

Gretsch

This guitar manufacturer nearly rivaled even Gibson in the jazz guitar market at one time, but because it bought in its pickups from another manufacturer until the late 1950s, the company comes into play quite late in our consideration of the electromagnetic pickup. German immigrant Friedrich Gretsch established the Fred Gretsch Manufacturing Company in New York City in 1883 to make drums and banjos. His son Fred – who headed the company after his father's death in 1895 – added guitars to the line in 1933, when it became clear the instrument was surpassing the banjo in popularity, and his son, Fred Gretsch Jr., would eventually pilot the company through its golden era, supported not by the endorsement of the jazz players that first elevated Gibson's profile, but by country and rock'n'roll players who would become the pop-music stars of the 1950s.

Gretsch electrics, from the first Gretsch-made electric guitar, the Electromatic Spanish model of 1949 (pre-war Gretsch electrics were manufactured by Kay) to the Duo Jets and 6120s that Cliff Gallup, Chet Atkins and Eddie Cochran took to stardom in the 1950s, all carried out-of-house pickups, however, until the arrival of the Filter'Tron humbucker in 1957 and '58. Prior to that, Gretsch pickups were supplied by Rowe Industries of Toledo, Ohio, a company that manufactured a number of pickups designed by Harry DeArmond, including the DeArmond 200 (see the relevant section in the following chapter for other DeArmond designs). Known in the guitar-maker's literature as the DynaSonic (you'll notice I use the names interchangeably), this is the archetypal Gretsch pickup of the early rock'n'roll years. Bright and clear, yet also quite sweet and fairly powerful, the DynaSonic is the 'other breed of twang'; it sports plenty of cut and definition, along with big, firm lows, decent muscle too, and a round, musical fatness that often surprises players unfamiliar with the pickup.

It's a fairly complicated design, but extremely effective at doing what it does. The pickup uses individual pole pieces made from fairly wide-diameter Alnico V rod magnets, but enables them to be adjustable by attaching separate brackets to the bottoms of each, through which passes a threaded, spring-tensioned adjustment screw. The result looks a little like the piston and valve arrangement on a straight-six hotrod engine, and has been dubbed the 'monkey on a stick' design for its high contraption factor. The adjustment screws, seen offset alongside the pole pieces through the top cover of the pickup, also fool some players into thinking they are looking at a humbucking pickup. It works, though, and since you can't thread alnico rod magnets (not practically speaking,

manufacturers' profiles – the 'big four'

anyway) this is one way of making the DeArmond 200's pole pieces adjustable, rather than keeping them fixed and static as in Fender pickups. This was clearly the inspiration for the adjustable pole pieces in Gibson's Alnico V pickup of 1954, too, although designer Seth Lover used rectangular bar magnets for pole pieces to avoid resembling the DeArmond too closely.

The coils in these DeArmonds – the bobbins of which had to fit a lot of gadgetry into their center channels – were wound with 44-gauge wire to a DC resistance of around 10k ohms, and sometimes more (I have seen original examples that measured anywhere from 8k to 12k). While this would imply a supercharged output, however, remember that the super-fine magnet wire moves the goalposts, and, with the help of the fat alnico poles, these pickups retain plenty of brightness and clarity, along with firm lows and a smooth midrange, as any Gretsch player will tell you. Their beefy inductance readings of around 3.35 Henries hold with this assessment, too. As used on Gretsch guitars, these DeArmonds always wore black tops, although the same pickups with white tops were used in many Guilds, Levins, Martins, and some others.

For many Gretsch fans, the DynaSonic epitomizes 'that great Gretsch sound', beloved of vintage rock'n'roll and rockabilly players in particular. Others look to the pickup that followed for the epitome of tonedom *a la* Gretsch, a unit regarded by many as the only humbucker with twang: the Gretsch Filter'Tron.

In so many ways, Chet Atkins was for Gretsch what Les Paul was for Gibson. Atkins not only provided the company with its first really major endorsement from a popular recording artist, but made considerable input regarding guitar and pickup design during his years as a Gretsch artist (paralleled, too, are the wrong turns both artists took model-wise in later years: consider the Gretsch Super Chet vs. the Gibson Les Paul Signature/Artist/Recording models). As the mid 1950s rolled on by, Atkins wanted a smoother sounding pickup for his signature models, the 6120 Chet Atkins Hollowbody and 6121 Chet Atkins Solidbody, and he started urging his recent acquaintance, amp-maker Ray Butts, to work on something for him. Not really a 'twanger' as such anyway, Atkins is said to have found the DynaSonic too harsh and bright sounding, and wanted something rounder, richer, and fuller. While he was at it, Butts decided that hum-canceling capabilities wouldn't be a bad thing either, and Chet's dissatisfaction with the way the strong magnetic pole pieces in the DynaSonic could impede string vibration when set high indicated that a design with the magnet below, charging adjustable steel pole pieces, would be the way to go.

Butts is reported to have begun development on the pickup that would

manufacturers' profiles – the 'big four'

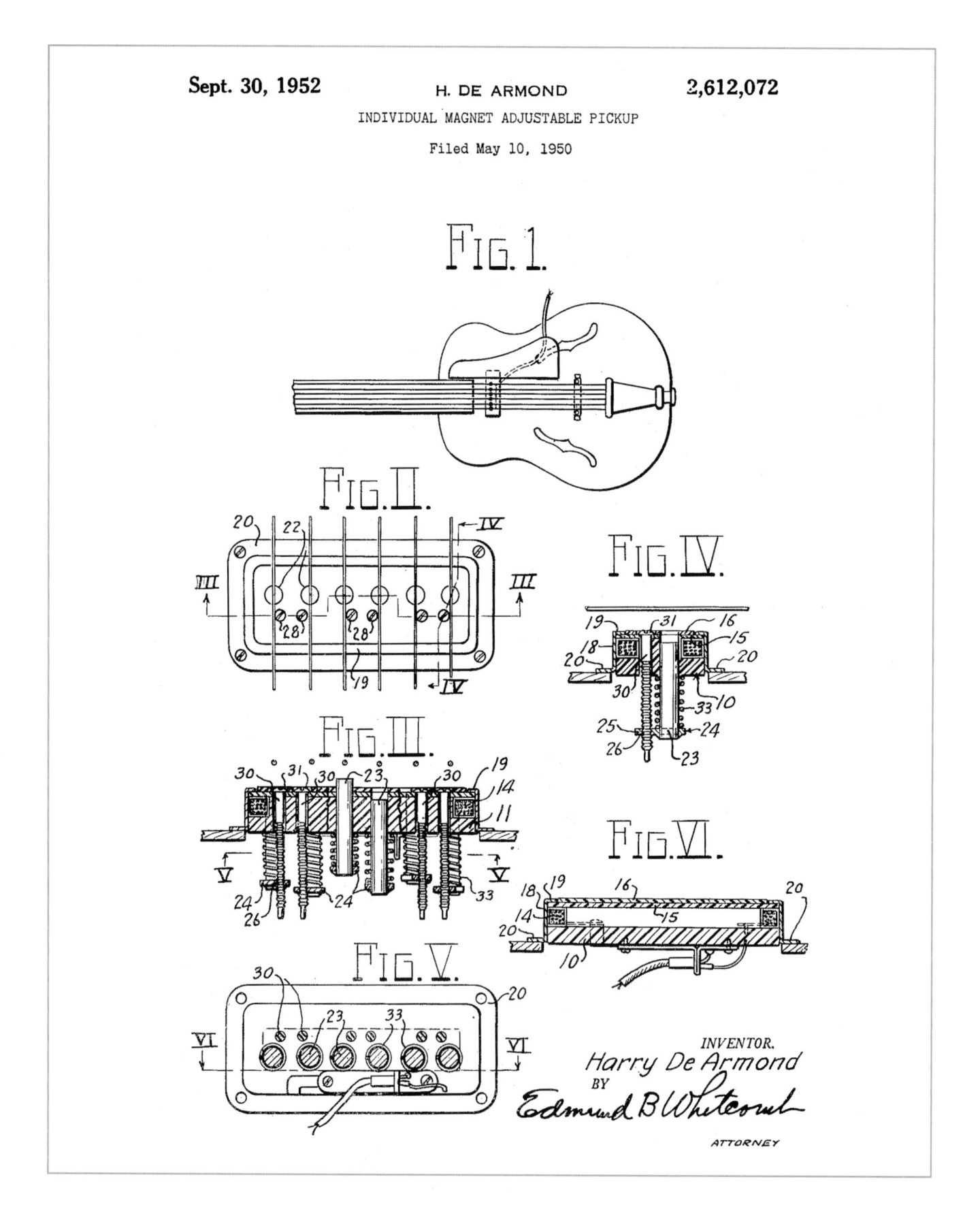

Sept. 30, 1952   H. DE ARMOND   2,612,072
INDIVIDUAL MAGNET ADJUSTABLE PICKUP
Filed May 10, 1950

INVENTOR.
Harry De Armond
BY
Edmund B Whitcomb
ATTORNEY

manufacturers' profiles — the 'big four'

become the Filter'Tron ('FILTERs out elecTRONic hum') as early as 1954 or '55, but Gretsch was slower getting the humbucker into a production model than Gibson was. The new Gretsch pickup carried a pair of side-by-side coils that were, in theory at least, more identical than the pair in the Gibson PAF, given that they both used a row of six adjustable threaded steel pole pieces – although as ever back in the day, coil winding specs were somewhat inconsistent. The pickup carried an Alnico V bar magnet between the bottoms of the two coils, each of which was wound with only about 3,000 turns of polyurethane-coated 43-gauge copper wire for a combined DC resistance of only around 4k to 5k for both coils together. Each of these two coils is narrower than those in Gibson's classic humbucker, and so is the pickup's magnetic window. As a result, in addition to being less powerful than a PAF the Filter'Tron also has sweeter, clearer highs. So, despite the move from DeArmond 200/DynaSonic pickups to the new Filter'Tron humbuckers, Gretsch guitars maintained a high twang factor, with a little growl in there when played through a pushed tube amp. While DynaSonics are the sound of Cliff Gallup, Eddie Cochran (although he had a P-90 in the neck position), Duane Eddy, vintage Bo Diddley, and early-era George Harrison with The Beatles, Filter'Trons are the sound of Chet Atkins at his peak, Brian Setzer, Stephen Stills, and George Harrison on many of mid-period Beatles tracks. Although noted for their trebly bite, both pickups can rock plenty well, too: witness the use of Filter'Trons by AC/DC's Malcolm Young and The Cult's Billy Duffy, and – it goes without saying – Mike Nesmith of The Monkees; or of DynaSonics by X's Billy Zoom and … well, he's the only one I can think of, but he kicks out enough furry for a room full of Filter'Tron players.

Despite apparently having arrived at his humbucking pickup design along parallel but separate lines at around the same time that Seth Lover had for Gibson, if not earlier, Ray Butts applied for his patent a little later, and was later in receiving it. Gretsch introduced the Filter'Tron at the summer NAMM show of 1957 – by which time Gibson's humbucker was already on the market – and it was standard equipment in everything except the Clipper by 1958. Gretsch and Gibson disputed the 'first humbucker' claim for a time, and Butts pointed out that he had photographs of Atkins using the pickup as early as 1954, but ultimately each company decided to drop any challenge of the other's design.

Instead, Gretsch hit the marketing angles with its typically grandiose verbiage; the new pickup, dubbed the Filter'Tron Electric Guitar Head (Gretsch typically related its pickups to the 'heads' of tape recorders), and claimed in company catalogs that, "The finest engineers in the country were engaged in

FACING PAGE **DeArmond – '50 "indiv. Adj. Magnet poles pickup" aka DeArmond 200/Gretsch DynaSonic.**

manufacturers' profiles – the 'big four'

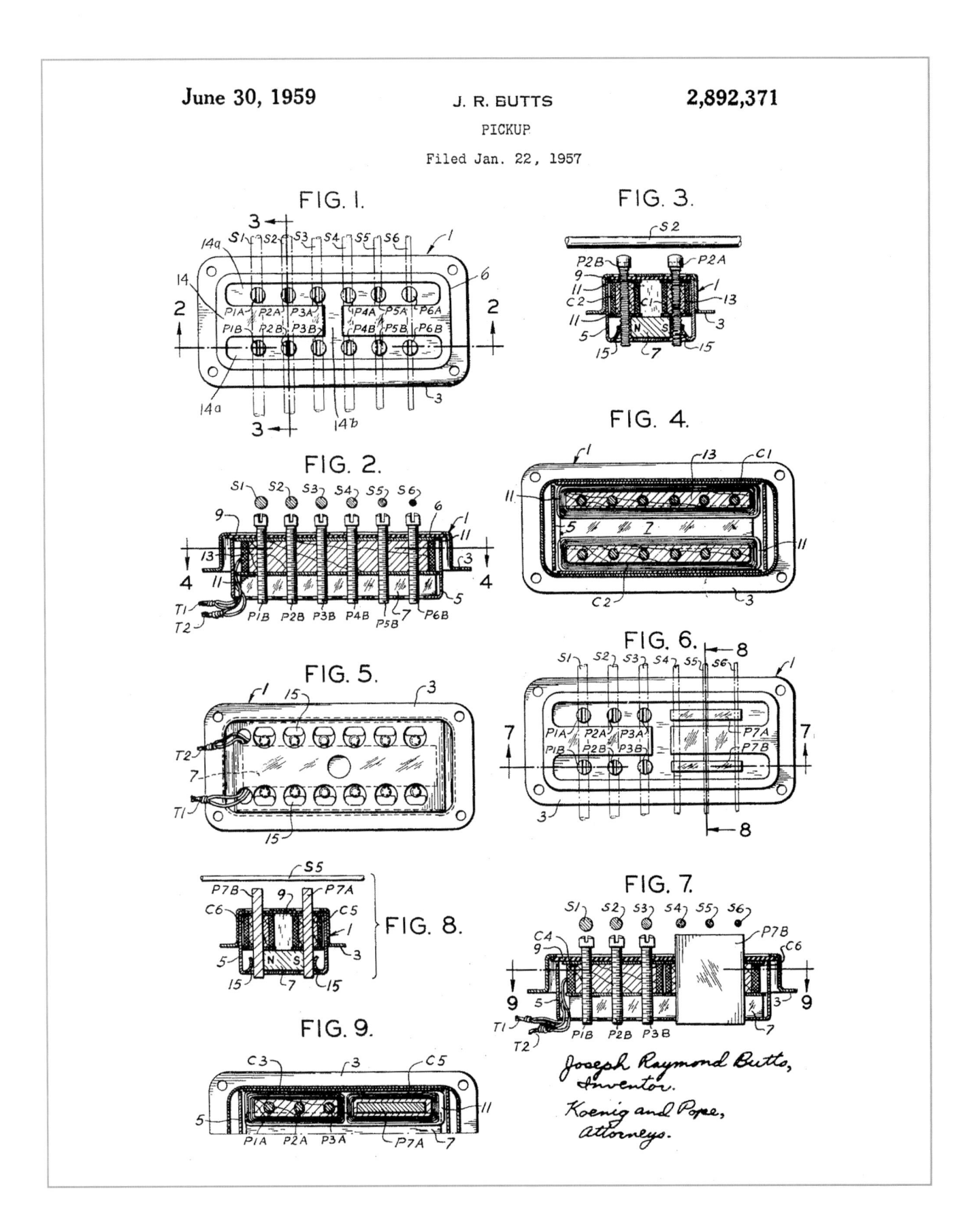

June 30, 1959   J. R. BUTTS   2,892,371
PICKUP
Filed Jan. 22, 1957

manufacturers' profiles – the 'big four'

the development of the Filter'Tron and their main object was to produce the greatest sound with as many color combinations as possible." In fact, Ray Butts alone had developed the pickup at the urging of Chet Atkins, and had brought it to Gretsch after its completion ... but maybe that just didn't sound as good in the marketing literature. Filter'Tron pickups carried no cover inscriptions in their first year, then bore the legend "Pat. Applied For" for the following two years, and the actual patent number itself after 1960. Later in the 1970s and into the early '90s, Filter'Tron pickups were made with ceramic magnets, and while they were more powerful as a result, many Gretsch fans consider that this introduced a major departure from the classic sound of the component (a change that paved the way for the great reproductions of TV Jones that have set the standard for that tone today).

Rather than returning to Rowe/DeArmond for the single-coil pickups used on lesser models, and having established a pickup-winding works with the Filter'Tron, Gretsch introduced its own standard in-house single-coil unit in 1960 with the HiLo'Tron (earlier versions of the down-market Clipper used a transitional single-coil pickup with a solid plastic cover and no visible pole pieces). Also soon available on guitars such as the Single and Double Anniversary, the Corvette, and others, the HiLo'Tron is a low-output single-coil constructed with six adjustable steel pole pieces, an Alnico V bar magnet beneath, and a coil wound with 43-gauge wire to a resistance of around 3.5k ohms, give or take a few hundred. The single-coil HiLo'Tron was housed in a humbucker-sized cover that looked a lot like a Filter'Tron cover without the central bars between the coils. From underneath, it's just a narrow single-coil bobbin, with bar and rigging to hold the magnet in place. For a long time – or, I should say, in the early years of the rediscovery of the glories of vintage Gretsch guitars, before the nuances of genuine vintage tone really became appreciated – HiLo'Trons had a rotten reputation as being thin, underpowered pickups. Then some players discovered that driving a cranked tube amp with an otherwise thin, underpowered pickup can often yield a fat, rich tone. Go figure.

In 1964, Gretsch also introduced the Super'Tron humbucker, a modified version of the Filter'Tron. It was housed in the same cover, but used a parallel pair of 'blades' instead of individual pole pieces (later layers of thinner laminated blades, in two pairs); otherwise, it was essentially identical. Super'Trons have their fans too, but they never knocked the Filter'Tron off its throne as king of the Gretsch humbuckers. The blade-style poles 'hold onto' string vibration more than narrow individual threaded steel poles when the player executes extreme

FACING PAGE **Ray Butts (ie Gretsch) – Filter'Tron humbucker.**

manufacturers' profiles – the 'big four'

bends, and also influences the frequency response of the pickups somewhat, making Super'Trons more aggressive in the midrange.

The 1970s were a dark period for many major guitar manufacturers, and their pickups, but while Fender and Gibson produced single coils and humbuckers that were less stellar than their seminal models of two decades before, if still on the same road at least, Gretsch efforts slid right off tone highway into a far deeper ditch. To avoid slogging down a blind alley, let's agree to ignore the Gretsch humbuckers of the 1970s, as appeared on limp beasts like the TK 300, Committee, Super Chet, and, well, the Beast BST-1000. Bought in either from DiMarzio or forgotten Japanese suppliers, these Gibson-style humbuckers were entirely un-Gretschy, and of little interest in a discussion of the company's other significant pickup designs.

As with any other guitar manufacturer with a past worth recalling, however, Gretsch guitars have surged forward in recent years primarily by looking backward. And with the resurgence of the reissue line years, largely driven by very well-regarded reproductions manufactured in Japan, has come the renewed availability of somewhat more accurate vintage-style Gretsch pickups. In 2002, Fender Musical Instruments Corp. acquired all manufacturing and distribution of Gretsch products, and has therefore also handled pickup manufacturing since that time too, whether offshore or in-house. Currently available are new versions of the DynaSonic, High Sensitive Filter'Tron, Hot Rod Filter'Tron, and HiLo'Tron, all of which are regarded as fairly accurate reproductions, if not necessarily dead-on with all specs when compared to vintage originals (a degree of inaccuracy that guitar players have come to accept, given how difficult it frequently is to obtain stocks of parts – alnico magnets, wire, fabricated metal components – that are identical to those originally used in many pickup designs). Gretsch enthusiasts today are also well aware, and generally in very high regard, of the pickups designed and manufactured by TV Jones (detailed separately in the following chapter). Jones's reproductions are widely considered to be the best course to authentic vintage Gretsch tone in many cases, so much so that Gretsch itself, under Fender, has bought in many TV Jones pickups for upscale new and reissue models.

Another 'Gretsch' pickup of recent years, the DeArmond 2k that appeared on many DeArmond by Guild guitars, is really not a Gretsch unit at all. See the DeArmond section in the following chapter for more details. Current-manufacture Gretsch DynaSonic pickups are made for Fender in Japan, while a popular substitute is also manufactured by Seymour Duncan in the form of the Dyno-Sonic.

manufacturers' profiles – the 'big four'

● Gretsch DynaSonic
(original c.1950: see DeArmond 200, following chapter)

● Gretsch Filter'Tron
Type: double coil humbucker
Magnet: Alnico V
Wire: 43 gauge, polyurethane coated
Resistance: 3.5k to 4.5k ohms
Pole pieces: six threaded steel pole pieces in each coil, all individually adjustable
Sound: bright, rich, well defined, but with good balance and sizzle; 'twang' for the humbucker crowd

● Gresch HiLo'Tron
Type: single coil
Magnet: Alnico V
Wire: 43 gauge, polyurethane coated
Resistance: 3.5k ohms +/–
Pole pieces: six threaded steel 'grub screw' pole pieces, all individually adjustable
Sound: bright, rather thin but well balanced, recessed mids, firm lows

● Gretsch Super'Tron
Type: double-coil humbucker
Magnet: Alnico V
Wire: 43 gauge, polyurethane coated
Resistance: 3.5k to 4.5k ohms
Pole pieces: steel blade poles (non-adjustable), made from laminated sheets in later units
Sound: bright, rich, slightly more mid-forward than its predecessor the Filter'Tron

● Gretsch High Sensitive Filter'Tron
Type: double-coil humbucker
Magnet: Alnico V
Wire: 43 gauge, polyurethane coated
Resistance: 4k to 4.8k ohms
Pole pieces: threaded steel pole pieces, all individually adjustable
Sound: trebly without undue harshness, good balance and depth

● Gretsch Hot Rod Filter'Tron
Type: double-coil humbucker
Magnet: Alnico V
Wire: 43 gauge, polyurethane coated
Resistance: 5k to 6k ohms
Pole pieces: threaded steel pole pieces, all individually adjustable
Sound: enhanced midrange and output compared to High Sensitive Filter'Tron

● Gretsch DynaSonic
Type: single coil
Magnet: Alnico V
Wire: 44 gauge, polyurethane coated
Resistance: 7k to 8k ohms
Pole pieces: alnico rod pole pieces with 'monkey on a stick' adjustment screws
Sound: bold, bright, percussive – a thick yet twangy single-coil sound

OTHER GUITAR AND PICKUP MAKERS

"Sometimes a pickup that doesn't have as much output as another will actually sound louder than a higher-wind pickup. The higher-wind pickup will be distorting the amp, but the one that is clearer has more treble, so it just rides right over the top of that and you hear everything you're doing."

JASON LOLLAR, VASHON, WA, APRIL 2008

other guitar and pickup makers

The groundwork for the vast majority of pickup designs still in use today was laid in the middle part of the 20th century by just a handful of guitar-makers, namely Gibson, Rickenbacker, Gretsch, and Fender. Other manufacturers have brought significant designs to the table, however, or have come forward in recent years as respected makers of after-market replacement pickups. While the formulae that many of them follow do owe a lot to the original work of the 'Big Four', they pursue their work in reproduction-style pickups with a fervor and an attention to detail that has earned them respect among players. Others have continued to push the envelope, and declare passionately that the state-of-the-art in pickup development was not behind us by 1960, but is still ahead of us in the 21st century, and these pioneers also deserve their entry into the annals of tone. This chapter discusses other guitar and pickup manufacturers worthy of consideration, and details some of their more original or outstanding developments. Rather than taking them chronologically as in the previous chapter, an alphabetical listing seems more appropriate here (by last name, where a maker's own name is applicable).

Please note that the vast majority of after-market pickups intended to replace specific original models look very much the same from the outside, however well they might attain their goal, so I won't lists specs for all such units. Detailed specs and descriptions will be available from the individual makers. I will, however, list the unique or more original creations from these manufacturers, along with a few more unusual twists on the vintage template.

Alembic

One of the first manufacturers to heavily push the notion that the electric guitar – and the pickup – could still be vastly improved upon was Alembic. This California company heralded a brave new world of active electronics, low-impedance pickups, and high-fidelity instruments from the time of its inception in 1969, and for a while even had a major impact on the designs and directions of many major manufacturers around the world. From the perspective of the early 1970s you'd be forgiven for thinking that the passive guitar with high-impedance pickups would have gone the way of the dodo by the 21st century, if not long before. But of course the Alembic way of doing things didn't tickle every player's fancy, and plenty of major artists continue to make great music on archaic-styled creations that have their blueprints lodged firmly in the 1950s.

Founded by Ron and Susan Wickersham, who were soon joined by early

other guitar and pickup makers

partner Rick Turner, Alembic began as a pro audio consultancy that serviced many of the big name artists in the San Francisco Bay area, including Jefferson Airplane, The Grateful Dead, Crosby, Stills, Nash & Young, and others. Turner and the Wickershams' work segued into modifying guitars with active electronics and, eventually, building such instruments themselves. Their guitars are noted for their highly polished, multi-wood, through-neck construction; their pickups – which Alembic calls 'Activators' – are noted for not looking like a whole lot of anything from the outside, but hiding a few good tricks inside. Alembic pickups appear to follow 'single coil' and 'humbucker' shapes, but are really a thing unto themselves. An excellent signal-to-noise ratio is achieved by making them low impedance and running them through an efficient onboard preamp; early guitars often included an active 'dummy coil' between pickups to rejected hum without contributing anything to the brew tonally. The arrangement presents a clear, clean signal and broad frequency range to the amp, all of which was manipulated by onboard tone-shaping and switching circuitry of unprecedented complexity. Alembic coils come in two flavors, 'standard' or 'narrow', which describes the distance between each of the two 'sensing coils' for each string, this pair taking the place of the conventional pole piece in a standard pickup. Standard-spaced coils are about an inch apart, and narrow a little under half-an-inch, and the size of this magnetic window, or 'aperture', helps determine the voice of the pickup. Rather than using traditional wax dipping, Wickersham and Turner sealed the coils of their pickups with cyanoacrylate to dampen vibrations, and shielded them against electrostatic interference with copper laminate on the tops and bottoms, along with copper sheeting on the sides (a construction referred to as a 'Faraday cage').

As a result of all this, Alembic guitars are known for capturing every nuance of a player's technique, with little or none of the furring and forgiveness offered by vintage-styled, high-impedance alnico pickups, and minimal hum or noise. While, as so described, the low-impedance thing might sound like a universal good in the realm of pickup design, it just ain't rock'n'roll to some players. Alembic guitars (and low-impedance pickups coupled with active electronics) tended to catch on with many artists who used a lot of complicated processing and played through enormous sound systems – or who DI'd right into the board while recording and relied on a lot of studio effects for their sound shaping – but were condemned as cold, harsh, and brittle by some of the types of players who enjoyed the sweet, juicy blur of an old Strat and a tweed Bassman (or, insert your vintage rig of choice here).

other guitar and pickup makers

It's worth noting that there's a distinct divide between guitarists and bassists in the high-fidelity stakes. Even rock bassists often want both their pickups and amps to produce a full, firm, undistorted frequency range from their instruments, while guitarists of most genres want a little grit and gristle introduced all along the way. This book doesn't have the scope to deal with bass pickups, but I mention this as some partial explanation as to why Alembic basses seem to have reached a much wider acceptance in the guitar community than their six-string electric guitars. They are superlative instruments – and pickups – without a doubt, but they just don't fit (or perhaps, go too far beyond) many players' basic idea of 'the electric guitar'. Specs for Alembic pickups won't be published here, since they are not like any 'standard' passive, high-impedance pickups in any sense that would provide useful for comparison. Suffice to say that a range of models are available to cater to different sonic needs, all of which offer a wide range of tonal variables given the EQ filters and preamps they are coupled with.

Tom Anderson Guitarworks

After working as a custom builder for Schecter, Tom Anderson started up his Guitarworks in 1984, and quickly developed a reputation for turning out high-quality instruments. Unlike many low-production makers, however (or, lower-than-the-majors at least), Anderson's quest to create "the world's finest feeling, sounding and playing electric guitars" – as the company's early ads stated – includes winding their own pickups, rather than buying them. All are available to purchase separately for installation in other makes of guitars.

Anderson pickups are traditional passive, high-impedance units in a range of familiar shapes. They are not intended as accurate clones of any particular vintage pickups, although some types do aim to capture vintage-style tones, usually with a little twist. Other than the pickups used on the Classic T and The Classic models, which are Tele- and Strat-style guitars respectively, Anderson pickups are characterized more by their over-wound coils and large-diameter pole pieces, and are largely designed for high-output performance for contemporary rock styles. By enlarging the poles and recalculating the string spacing between them, Anderson has sought to create a balanced magnetic field that isn't prone to end-string drop out like some traditional units (which results in softer reproduction of the low and high E strings), coupled with a low magnetic pull on the strings. Other than the Classics used on Anderson's the Strat-styled model, these pickups are supplied without covers. Note, too, that

Tom Anderson's TM bridge pickup

other guitar and pickup makers

the bridge pickup in the Classic T model is *not* mounted in a semi-floating bridge plate as on the original Fender Telecaster, but is mounted directly into the body with three adjustable screws, without use of a base plate.

The Anderson pickup roster is extensive, and caters to just about every requirement in gain and tone. Furthermore, each series within the humbucker and single-coil lines carries a number of variations in strength to balance between neck, bridge, and middle positions, or the simple desire for a little more or less output within a particular sonic range. The HO, HF, and HC series use Alnico II magnets and aim at anything from vintage to hotrodded-vintage PAF-style performance. The high-output, ceramic-magnet H is fuller and fatter, and the HN is the super-high-output series of the line, and uses powerful, high-clarity neodymium magnets to get the job done. Within each group, blue, yellow, and red versions account for different output strengths. Anderson humbuckers are also supplied with four-conductor wiring, and designed to provide convincing single-coil sounds when split.

These brief details already hint at a pickup-maker that is willing to stray from the classic template, and a few words from Tom Anderson himself further bear out this conclusion. Regarding the H series humbucker, he points out that the ceramic magnet "is oriented 90 degrees different than all other humbuckers I know of. The magnet is vertical in between the coils and polarized through the thin side. It makes for a very strong field in the coil, but one that's very weak at the strings." Anderson adds, "the DC reading on those models will be very deceiving. They will be much lower than you would expect to see for the output and tone they produce. For example, the H1- (the lowest-output humbucker in the range) at about 3.5k ohms is as hot or hotter than a 7k ohm vintage humbucker." Although wire gauge specs are not published on a per-model basis, Anderson confirms that all coils are wound with wire that's between 41 and 44 gauge.

Anderson's single coils follow a similarly innovative line. The VA vintage Strat-style and TV vintage Tele-style pickups, for example, are both made with Alnico V magnets and wound with formvar and polysol-coated wire respectively. The SD, SA, SF, TD, and TF series, on the other hand, are all made with neodymium magnets. Other than the clearly declared aims of the vintage-voiced models, the majority of Anderson single-coil pickups aim toward versatile, contemporary sounds. The SD (Tele-style equivalent TD) and SA are hum-canceling units, the latter with a slightly bigger midrange presentation that's recommended for semi-hollow (chambered) guitars. The SN series has a big,

Tom Anderson's VA pickups on an Anderson Classic

other guitar and pickup makers

contemporary scooped-mid sound, while the ST series offers similar voicings in a tapped pickup that gives a brighter, thinner single-coil tone at the flip of a switch (the TT is the tapped Tele version). Finally, Anderson also offers the M series of mini-humbucking pickups, which employ neodymium magnets and polysol coil wire, and the P series of soapbar-style single-coil pickups, made with Alnico II and polysol wire.

● Tom Anderson H Series
Type: double-coil humbucker
Magnet: ceramic
Wire: gauge N/A, polysol coated
Resistance: a range of outputs calibrated to pickup position
Pole pieces: individual, fixed
Sound: contemporary humbucker tone, from clear and open, to hot and punchy.

● Tom Anderson H0 Series
Type: double-coil humbucker
Magnet: alnico II
Wire: gauge N/A, polysol coated
Resistance: a range of outputs calibrated to pickup position
Pole pieces: individual, fixed
Sound: vintage humbucker tone, calibrated for neck and bridge positions.

● Tom Anderson HF & HC Series
Type: double-coil humbucker
Magnet: alnico II
Wire: gauge N/A, Formvar coated
Resistance: a range of outputs calibrated to pickup position
Pole pieces: individual, fixed
Sound: modified-vintage-voiced contemporary humbuckers, calibrated to a range of output requirements.

● Tom Anderson HN Series
Type: double-coil humbucker
Magnet: neodymium
Wire: gauge N/A, polysol coated
Resistance: N/A
Pole pieces: individual, fixed
Sound: high-gain rock pickup with increased midrange punch and thick, thumping lows; available in two outputs, HN3 and HN3+, as 'hot and hotter' for bridge position.

● Tom Anderson M Series
Type: double-coil mini humbucker
Magnet: neodymium
Wire: gauge N/A, polysol coated
Resistance: a range of outputs calibrated to pickup position
Pole pieces: individual, fixed
Sound: full and punchy, with a little extra high-end zest; M1, M2 and M3 for low-med, medium, and med-high outputs.

● Tom Anderson P Series
Type: soapbar-sized single coil
Magnet: alnico II
Wire: gauge N/A, polysol coated
Resistance: a range of outputs calibrated to pickup position
Pole pieces: adjustable steel
Sound: from open, clear, crisp and mid-forward, to barking and aggressive ('hotrodded soapbar tone').

● Tom Anderson SA Series
Type: noise-free single coil (Strat-sized pickup)
Magnet: neodymium
Wire: gauge N/A, polysol coated
Resistance: ranging from the medium-output SA1 to the high-output SA2+
Pole pieces: N/A
Sound: similar to the SD series, with added midrange (intended for semi-hollow or chambered electric guitars.

● Tom Anderson SD Series
Type: noise-free single coil (Strat-sized pickup)
Magnet: neodymium
Wire: gauge N/A, polysol coated
Resistance: ranging from the low-output SD1- to the high-output SD2+
Pole pieces: N/A
Sound: open, round, soft and clean with SD1-; thick, broad and punchy with SD2+ at the top of the range.

other guitar and pickup makers

● Tom Anderson SN Series
Type: standard single coil (Strat-sized pickup)
Magnet: neodymium
Wire: gauge N/A, Formvar coated
Resistance: a range of outputs calibrated to pickup position
Pole pieces: N/A
Sound: wide, round single-coil tone with scooped mids and firm lows. (NB: ST is the tapped version of this series).

● Tom Anderson TD Series
Type: noise-free single coil (Tele-sized pickup)
Magnet: neodymium
Wire: gauge N/A, polysol coated
Resistance: ranging from the low-output TD1- to the high-output TD3+
Pole pieces: N/A
Sound: the neck-intended TD1- is full, warm and well defined (lower-output TD0 is even cleaner in the neck); bridge position TD2 is clear and twangy; TD3 or TD3+ are fat and gnarly in the bridge.

● Tom Anderson TN Series
Type: standard single coil (Tele-sized pickup)
Magnet: neodymium
Wire: gauge N/A, Formvar coated
Resistance: a range of outputs calibrated to pickup position
Pole pieces: N/A
Sound: big, open tone with scooped mids and firm lows, bell-like highs. (NB: TT is the tapped version of this series).

● Tom Anderson TV Series
Type: single coil Tele-type pickup
Magnet: Alnico V
Wire: gauge N/A, polysol coated
Resistance: ranging from vintage clean to vintage hot
Pole pieces: individual alnico rod magnet pole pieces
Sound: TV1 neck pickup is round, clear and balanced; TV3R is a hot-vintage, reverse-wound bridge pickup.

● Tom Anderson VA Series
Type: single coil Strat-type pickup
Magnet: Alnico V
Wire: gauge N/A, Formvar coated
Resistance: ranging from vintage clean to vintage hot
Pole pieces: individual alnico rod magnet pole pieces
Sound: from the clean, clear, bell-like Strat tones of the VA1, to the thicker Tele-like midrange grind of the VA3.

other guitar and pickup makers

Kent Armstrong

With son Kent having carried on the tradition of innovative component design and manufacture that was begun by his father, Dan, in the late 1960s, the Armstrong name is going strong well into two generations. Kent Armstrong moved to New York City as a teenager in 1967, where he attended high school by day and worked in Dan's repair shop on 48th Street in the guitar district by night. When other work called his dad to California in 1970, Kent stayed on to run the shop. Slowly but surely, Armstrong focused his interest on pickups in particular, a specialization that was extremely well timed, given that one Bill Lawrence was also working in the shop at that time, and was happy to teach the young repairman what he could about the art of magnets and wire. Just a year later, however, Dan decided to close the New York business and head off for London – and he took Kent and his brother along with him. From 1971 until 2001, when he moved to Vermont, Armstrong lived and worked mainly in the UK.

Although Armstrong's early work naturally involved a lot of rewinds of standard pickups (a service he occasionally still performs), and he has designed and manufactured many replacements for the classic single-coil and humbucker types, he has developed a reputation for invention and originality and has designed and built a great many bold new types of pickups in his nearly 40 years in the business (read the full interview with Kent Armstrong in the *Meet the Makers* chapter for more details in his own words). From pioneering ultra-thin floating jazz pickups, such as the 11/32-inch-deep Kent Armstrong Hand Made '2-D' Pickup – made with his own unique 'bobbin-less' coils that are sealed in epoxy resin – to the hundreds of OEM pickups he has designed for major guitar manufacturers around the world, Armstrong is one of the industry's most prolific creators of pickups.

Kent Armstrong continues to hand-build many pickups in his own workshop to custom order, although in 1995 he signed a deal with the Korean manufacturer Dong Ho Electronics to design a comprehensive line of original and replacement pickups, which are sold as OEM to guitar manufacturers, as well as being distributed exclusively by WD Music Products, Inc. Of these, many are affordable good-quality replacement and upgrade pickups that fall in to the popular categories: vintage or hotrodded Strat and Tele pickups, humbuckers and P-90s, and dual-rail 'hot' and 'cool' single-coil-sized humbuckers for Fender-type guitars. I won't detail those here, but will look at a few of the other more original Kent Armstrong models available through WD. Armstrong is also the designer and manufacturer of the reproduction pickup used on Burns guitars,

other guitar and pickup makers

● **Kent Armstrong Jazz Humbucker**
Type: thin double-coil humbucker
Magnet: alnico
Wire: gauge N/A, polysol coated
Resistance: 8k ohms
Pole pieces: rail, covered and non adjustable
Sound: add-on floating pickup; round, sweet, mellow jazz tones with ample cut and string definition; available for neck mount or pickguard mount

● **Kent Armstrong Jazz Slimbucker**
Type: ultra-thin double-coil humbucker
Magnet: alnico
Wire: gauge N/A, polysol coated
Resistance: 8k ohms +/−
Pole pieces: rail, covered and non adjustable
Sound: more affordable mass-production version of the Handmade '2-D' Pickup and similar to standard Kent Armstrong Jazz Humbucker, above, but only ⅜-inch thick to fit archtop guitars with low string clearance at the neck

● **Kent Armstrong Split Tube**
Type: single coil
Magnet: alnico bar
Wire: N/A
Resistance: 4.9k ohms
Pole pieces: bar magnet within coil (enclosed)
Sound: Kent Armstrong's replacement for the Danelectro/Silvertone 'Lipstick tube' pickup; bright, lively and clear

● **Kent Armstrong Split Tube Hot**
Type: single coil
Magnet: ceramic bar
Wire: N/A
Resistance: 7.9k ohms
Pole pieces: bar magnet within coil (enclosed)
Sound: hot replacement for Danelectro/Silvertone 'Lipstick Tube' pickup; bigger, fatter sound with more midrange aggression

● **Kent Armstrong Mini Split Tube**
Type: single coil
Magnet: alnico bar
Wire: N/A
Resistance: 4.9k ohms
Pole pieces: bar magnet within coil (enclosed)
Sound: Kent Armstrong's version of the Danelectro/Silvertone 'Lipstick Tube' pickup designed to fit Stratocaster-sized pickup route and mounting; bright, lively and clear

● **Kent Armstrong Burns Tri-Sonic V**
Type: single coil (bobbin-less tapewound coil)
Magnet: two isotropic ferrite bars (an alternative ceramic)
Wire: N/A
Resistance: 6.4k ohms
Pole pieces: fixed individual steel
Sound: a thick yet bright and cutting single coil tone, with good body and some growl when pushed

● **Kent Armstrong High Output Humbucker**
Type: double-coil humbucker
Magnet: ceramic
Wire: N/A
Resistance: 15k ohms
Pole pieces: individual, fixed
Sound: hot humbucking tones aimed at contemporary rockers; thick mids, stinging highs, aggressive attack

● **Kent Armstrong Kentron N**
Type: double-coil humbucker
Magnet: alnico
Wire: N/A
Resistance: 5k ohms +/−
Pole pieces: steel, individually adjustable
Sound: Kent Armstrong's rendition of the Gretsch Filter'Tron; a bright, low-output humbucker with good string definition and a lively, focused character

other guitar and pickup makers

the Tri-Sonic V, which is also extremely popular with any guitarist seeking to nail the sound of Brian May's famous DIY guitar 'Red Special', which carried a set of original Burns single coils from the good old days. Otherwise, regarding handmade pickups, Armstrong is willing to tackle just about anything a customer wants to request.

Joe Barden

Visionary pickup designer and manufacturer Joe Barden's name is inextricably linked with that of an equally visionary guitarist, Tele virtuoso Danny Gatton. It's an association that has no doubt brought Barden some business over the years (as he explains in his own words in the full interview in the *Meet the Makers* chapter that follows), but along with that has also arguably narrowed the workaday player's perception of what Barden pickups seek to achieve.

Barden originated the dual-rails design to fit a narrow-aperture humbucking pickup in a single-coil-sized mounting, but because some makers who followed him have been more prolific in the market, his own creations are often mistaken for the high-output types of twin-blade pickups that commonly adopt this look, such as Seymour Duncan's very popular Hot Rails units for Stratocaster and Telecaster. In fact, Joe Barden pickups are more high-fidelity than high-output, and don't aim to slam the front end of the amp the way other overwound twin-blade ceramic 'buckers do. Instead, they are optimized to present a high-definition, full-frequency tone with as low a noise floor as possible. In use, they offer extreme sensitivity to the nuance and dynamics of a player's style, and therefore can take some getting used to, but many major artists who are fans of Barden's pickups declare that they couldn't go back to anything else after becoming accustomed to the definition and sensitivity that these pickups provide. "Like taking the blanket off the amp," is the description I have encountered again and again, and having spent some time with this in my test Stratocaster to record a few tracks for the accompanying CD I know exactly what these players are talking about. These pickups might not be for everyone, and certainly some players might miss the appealing softness and squash of a vintage low-output alnico single coil, for example. But if you think a traditional electromagnetic pickup with a robust, hi-fi response and low noisefloor might be interesting, it could be worth giving these a try.

Barden met Danny Gatton in 1975, became the guitarist's self-appointed roadie/assistant for a time, and rewound his first pickup in April 1980. By the end of that year he had manufactured, from scratch, pickups that would be used by

Joe Barden Danny Gatton T-Style Set

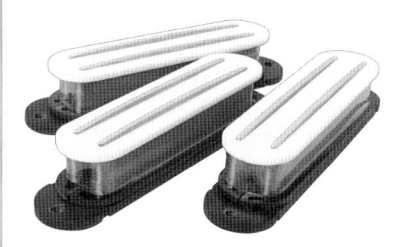

Joe Barden S-Deluxe Set in white.

other guitar and pickup makers

Gatton, Thumbs Carllile, Bonnie Raitt, and others, although these were still of a single-coil style with a split-blade pole piece, and prone to picking up major hum by Barden's own admission. Around 1982 Barden developed his groundbreaking single-coil-sized, twin-blade humbucking design in a Stratocaster-style pickups, soon adapted to Telecaster, and eventually to full-sized humbucker. This is the line, with a few refinements, that he continues to offer today.

By using the ceramic magnets' power with due consideration for all aspects of his pickups' design, coupling them with low-wind coils, and compensating with inductance levels adequate to voice the pickups as desired, Barden has created a super-low-noise unit that is bright and dynamic, and offers an extremely wide frequency response. These are not 'hot' or 'distortion' humbuckers, although they do offer a very high output (despite DC resistance readings that are only in the 4k ohms range) without sacrificing clarity and definition. Joe Barden pickups could be described as producing a 'contemporary' sound, certainly, but it's one that has won over many players known for fat, 'vintage-styled' tone – and major chops.

Through the late 1990s and early 2000s, Barden also worked as a road tech with a number of major touring bands, notably Aerosmith and Bruce

Joe Barden HB humbucker

● Joe Barden Danny Gatton T-Style
Type: Tele-sized slim double-coil humbucker
Magnet: ceramic bar
Wire: 42 gauge
Resistance: bridge, 4.42k ohms; neck, 4.10k ohms
Pole pieces: two fixed steel blades
Sound: from bright, gutsy, twangy and well defined in the bridge to round, rich and clear in the neck, all with a distinctly 'vintage' foundation, but coupled with a broad, linear frequency response.

● Joe Barden S-Deluxe
Type: Strat-sized slim double-coil humbucker
Magnet: ceramic bar
Wire: 42 gauge
Resistance: bridge, 4.21k ohms; middle and neck, 4.11k ohms
Pole pieces: two fixed steel blades
Sound: from bright, gutsy and well defined in the bridge to round, rich and clear in the neck and middle, yet all with a distinctly 'vintage' foundation, but coupled with a broad, linear frequency response.

● Joe Barden HB (and HB Two Tone)
Type: humbucker
Magnet: ceramic bar
Wire: 42 gauge
Resistance: bridge, 4.5k ohms; neck, 4.2k ohms
Pole pieces: two fixed steel blades
Sound: thick, rich, creamy and more 'humbuckerish' than Barden's T-Style or S-Deluxe models, but with good clarity and definition; the Two Tone model is tapped to yield and authentic single-coil tone as its alternative selection.

other guitar and pickup makers

Springsteen & The E-Street Band. His pickup-making venture was recently restructured, with MI executive Frank Troccoli taking the position of CEO, and is currently going strong in Manassas, VA, where Joe Barden Engineering offers the full range of Barden handmade pickups, and a small selection of other related products such as Telecaster bridge plates and saddles.

Bare Knuckle

This British pickup-maker is a recent addition to the scene, but has developed a good reputation in a relatively short period of time. Founded by Tim Mills in 2003, and based in Falmouth in the Southwest of England, Bare Knuckle is a small operation run entirely by guitar players, with about half a dozen employees (at the time of writing) laboring at the craft of hand-building mainly vintage-reproduction style pickups. Instead of slotting their pickup models into the more generic types of categories that many manufacturers use – 'vintage' or 'hot blues', for example – Bare Knuckle names them according to seminal tones that players might be trying to capture. Thus their Apache Stratocaster replacement pickup offers '50s-era twang in the vein of Hank Marvin (guitarist with The Shadows, who logged a major instrumental hit with the single 'Apache'), their The Boss Telecaster set implies Springsteenesque bite and grind thanks to a 8.2k ohm bridge pickup, their Abraxas Humbucker aims at vintage-era Santana lead tones, and so forth.

"I started the business out of frustration-having been a pro player for many years," says Tim Mills. "I'd had enough of trying various pickups that never seemed to do what they claimed and felt the market was right for a well-thought-out range of hand-wound pickups that went from original spec through to contemporary models, all built with an attention to detail and consistency that I felt was lacking in what was available up to that point."

Bare Knuckle also makes a number of more original contemporary-styled pickups, and currently manufactures two Signature Series pickups, the Steve Stevens 'Rebel Yell' Humbucker and the Geoff Whitehorn 'Crawler' Humbucker, plus a P-90 designed to fit a standard humbucker route, the Mississippi Queen HBP90.

other guitar and pickup makers

● Bare Knuckle Steve Stevens 'Rebel Yell'
Type: humbucker
Magnet: Alnico V
Wire: 42 gauge plain enamel
Resistance: neck, 8.3k ohms; bridge, 14.4k ohms
Pole pieces: six adjustable threaded steel screws in one coil, six fixed individual steel slugs in the other
Sound: increased midrange power and punch over standard PAF-style designs, with added growl and a balanced harmonic richness.

● Bare Knuckle Geoff Whitehorn 'Crawler'
Type: humbucker
Magnet: Alnico V
Wire: 43 gauge plain enamel
Resistance: bridge, 15k ohms (or as set with calibrated neck pickup)
Pole pieces: six adjustable threaded steel screws in one coil, six fixed individual steel slugs in the other
Sound: vintage-toned high-power humbucker intended to clean up well with guitar volume rolled down, or push the amp with volume up full.

● Bare Knuckle Holydiver
Type: humbucker
Magnet: Alnico V
Wire: N/A
Resistance: 16k ohms
Pole pieces: six adjustable threaded steel screws in one coil, six fixed individual steel slugs in the other
Sound: '80s style 'hotrodded humbucker' with driving midrange for rock lead tones.

● Bare Knuckle Cold Sweat
Type: humbucker
Magnet: ceramic
Wire: 42 gauge
Resistance: 14k ohms
Pole pieces: six adjustable threaded steel screws in one coil, six fixed individual steel slugs in the other
Sound: firm bass, added definition and extended high-end cut in a contemporary humbucker.

● Bare Knuckle Miracle Man
Type: humbucker
Magnet: ceramic
Wire: N/A
Resistance: 17.5k ohms
Pole pieces: six adjustable threaded steel screws in one coil, six fixed individual steel slugs in the other
Sound: high-powered ceramic humbucker designed for maximum drive for contemporary rock playing.

● Bare Knuckle Nailbomb
Type: humbucker
Magnet: Alnico V
Wire: 43 gauge plain enamel
Resistance: 16k ohms
Pole pieces: six adjustable threaded steel screws in one coil, six fixed individual steel slugs in the other
Sound: harmonically saturated 'blizzard of nails' rock humbucker tone.

● Bare Knuckle Warpig
Type: humbucker
Magnet: Alnico V
Wire: N/A
Resistance: 22k ohms
Pole pieces: twelve adjustable threaded steel Allen-key poles (six in each coil)
Sound: super-hot'n'heavy humbucker sounds for nu-metal guitar styles.

● Bare Painkiller
Type: humbucker
Magnet: ceramic
Wire: N/A
Resistance: 15.6k ohms
Pole pieces: six adjustable threaded steel screws in one coil, six fixed individual steel slugs in the other
Sound: powerful ceramic humbucker voiced for classic British metal.

other guitar and pickup makers

● Bare Knuckle Trilogy Suite
Type: single coil
Magnet: Alnico V
Wire: "special gauge" enamel coated
Resistance: bridge, 15.5k ohms; middle and neck, 11.2k ohms
Pole pieces: six fixed, flat-top alnico bar magnets
Sound: Strat replacement with big lows and balanced highs, slightly recessed mids.

● Bare Knuckle The Sinner
Type: single coil
Magnet: Alnico V
Wire: "special gauge" enamel coated
Resistance: 21k ohms (or as a calibrated set)
Pole pieces: six fixed, flat-top alnico bar magnets
Sound: super high-powered Strat replacement for high-gain metal guitar styles.

● Bare Knuckle Mississippi Queen HBP90
Type: single coil
Magnet: bridge, Alnico V; neck, Alnico IV
Wire: 42 gauge plain enamel
Resistance: bridge, 7.9k ohms; neck, 7k ohms
Pole pieces: six fixed adjustable threaded steel bolts
Sound: vintage-voiced P-90 tones in a humbucker-sized housing.

Burns

Founder James Burns made guitars for other companies in the late 1950s, and founded Burns London Ltd in 1960, although the company would change hands frequently over the course of the next couple of decades. The best-loved and most sought-after of British made pickups, the original Burns Tri-Sonic pickup, is not a copy of any standard American design – as are so many others – but a thing unto itself. These single-coil pickups were made with a pair of isotropic ferrite magnets beneath a bobbinless tapewound coil with steel pole pieces, all encased in a thin metal cover. The result was a thick, ballsy sounding pickup that nevertheless had good definition and a sweet high-end response, a sound often described as being a cross between a P-90 and a more traditional Strat-style single-coil pickup, with noticeably more output than the latter. Their metal covers could sometimes become loose and vibrate microphonically, but also seemed to boost the magnetic field and fatten up the tone somewhat.

The Tri-Sonic is partly responsible for the surprisingly gnarly yet twangy tone of vintage Burns models such as the Marvin, Vista Sonic, and Bison, and was the pickup that Queen guitarist Brian May settled on for the 'Red Special' that he and his dad built from a mahogany mantle-piece, after the pickups that May had wound himself proved insufficient for his rock antics. The present-day Burns London Ltd is once again offering a wide range of guitars, including many reproductions of models of the early 1960s, although the pickups – re-engineered by Kent Armstrong (see above) – are now manufactured in Korea by Dong Ho Electronics.

> ● **Burns Tri-Sonic (c.1960s)**
> **Type:** single coil (bobbinless tapewound coil)
> **Magnet:** two isotropic ferrite magnets
> **Wire:** N/A
> **Resistance:** 6k ohms +/–
> **Pole pieces:** fixed individual steel
> **Sound:** a thick yet bright and cutting single coil tone, with good body and some growl when pushed

Carvin

Known to many as 'that mail-order guitar company', Carvin has a long history of pickup manufacture that dates back to the company's origins as a lap-steel and amp-maker of the 1940s. Lowell C. Kiesel founded the company in Los Angeles in 1947 and originally sold instruments under his own name, but two years later made three major changes in his operation when he changed to mail-order only, changed the company name to Carvin (for his sons CARson and GaVIN), and moved to nearby Covina, California. In the early 1950s guitars were supplied by Kay and Harmony, and by the late '60s bodies were coming from companies in Japan and then Germany, but all of these were outfitted with Carvin's own pickups, most notably a type called the AP6 that looked much like a squared-off Gibson P-90 soapbar-style unit with fixed pole pieces first, and adjustable poles a few years later. These Carvin-made 'soapbar' single coils were the pickups that Semi Mosley used on pre-Mosrite guitars such as those he build for Joe Maphis and Larry Collins, and also appeared on early versions of his Ventures-model Mosrite guitars.

In 1976 Carvin began making its most recognizable pickup of the modern era (well, early modern), the M22 Hex-Pole humbucker, by which time it was also making its own guitars (including set-neck models in 1978). These were a generally PAF-like dual-coil humbucker, but one that had a row of 11 small threaded hex-screw pole pieces in each coil, which could be adjusted for super-fine tweakage of string output balance. In the late 1970s Carvin boasted that its high-output version of the M22 was the hottest humbucker available on the

Carvin Twinblade humbuckers in black and zebra

other guitar and pickup makers

● Carvin AP11
Type: single coil
Magnet: ceramic
Wire: N/A
Resistance: 4.3k ohms +/–
Pole pieces: 11 adjustable Philips-head steel poles
Sound: bright and clear single-coil tone

● Carvin S60T/N
Type: single coil
Magnet: Alnico V
Wire: N/A
Resistance: 7.6k ohms +/–
Pole pieces: single fixed blade
Sound: aggressive single coil with more midrange than AP11

● Carvin TBH60
Type: single-coil sized dual-coil humbucker
Magnet: ceramic
Wire: N/A
Resistance: 7.8k ohms
Pole pieces: two fixed blades
Sound: punchy and hot, with muscular midrange

● Carvin AP13 Series
Type: single coil (for 7-string guitar)
Magnet: ceramic
Wire: N/A
Resistance: 4.3k ohms +/–
Pole pieces: 13 adjustable hex-screw steel poles
Sound: bright and clear single-coil tone

● Carvin C22 Series
Type: dual-coil humbucker
Magnet: Alnico V
Wire: N/A
Resistance: four ascending models from 7.2k ohm C22N to 13.6k ohm C22B
Pole pieces: 11 adjustable Philips-head steel poles in one coil, 11 fixed poles in the other
Sound: contemporary take on PAF humbucker with novel coil adjustment; C22N is the super-hot lead pickup, heavy on the midrange

● Carvin H22 Series
Type: dual-coil humbucker
Magnet: Alnico V
Wire: N/A
Resistance: neck, 7.3k ohms; bridge, 8.4k ohms
Pole pieces: 11 adjustable Philips-head steel poles in each coil
Sound: low to middle-output contemporary humbuckers with full, rich tone (Alan Holdsworth signature pickup)

● Carvin M22 Series
Type: dual-coil humbucker
Magnet: Alnico V
Wire: N/A
Resistance: four ascending models from 7.2k ohm M22V to 13.9k ohm M22SD
Pole pieces: 11 adjustable hex-screw steel poles in each coil
Sound: from sweet and clean to hot and aggressive

---

market. This formula has been retained into the 21st century, although Carvin also carries a full range of low- and high- output humbuckers and single coils, among them the M22 and H22, the Alan Holdsworth signature pickup. In 2008 the company introduced its first humbuckers with chrome covers (also in black and gold), the S22 series. These retain the 22-pole structure of the others, and are similar internally to the C22 and H22 range. All models available to purchase separately as replacement pickups to fit guitars other than Carvin's own. Ever since the late 1970s or early 1980s Carvin has forged a market with rock and fusion players in particular, and has numbered Frank Zappa, Jefferson Starship's Craig Chaquico, Rush's Alex Lifeson, and British virtuoso Alan Holdsworth

other guitar and pickup makers

among its endorsees. The company now has outlet stores in Hollywood, Santa Ana, Sacramento, and Covina, while the main factory is located in San Diego.

Danelectro/Silvertone

Guitars carrying the Danelectro and Silvertone brands have employed a wide range of pickups over the years, but the company is far and away most famous for one single design: the 'Lipstick Tube' pickup. This was the only pickup of note on Danelectros from their arrival in the mid 1950s right up until the company's demise in 1969. It appeared on the majority of Danelectro-made Silvertones sold by Sears during this era too, although Silvertone guitars made by other companies did carry other pickups.

Danelectro was founded in the late 1940s by Nathan I. 'Nat' Daniel, who by then already had been in the industry for ten years, as a manufacturer of guitar amplifiers that supplied a number of retail companies, including major catalog companies such as Sears and Montgomery Ward. He began manufacturing solidbody electric guitars for Sears under the Silvertone name in 1954, and introduced the first of his classic Danelectro guitars, the U-1 and U-2, two years later. To make the pickups for these basic, affordable guitars, Daniel wound a coil of wire around an alnico bar magnet, and enclosed the arrangement within two actual chromed metal lipstick-tube tops that were placed end to end. A relatively low turn count of 42 gauge wire resulted in DC resitance readings in the 3.75k to 4.75k ballpark, and that combined with the alnico bar magnet within the coil and the narrow magnetic window yielded a bright, snappy, percussive pickup, but one with smooth highs rather than any prominent harshness, and an appealingly scooped midrange, with firm if not over-present lows.

Add these to the fine poplar-and-Masonite tonewoods of the Danelectro guitars and you'd expect a thoroughly underwhelming soundstage... but the

● **Danelectro Lipstick Tube**
Type: single coil
Magnet: Alnico V
Wire: N/A
Resistance: from around 3.75k to 4.75k ohms
Pole pieces: enclosed alnico bar
Sound: bright, clear and percussive; definitely a low-output single coil tone, but with an appealing frequency range overall

other guitar and pickup makers

combination actually sounded pretty good. Jimi Hendrix, Jimmy Page, Eric Clapton and Stevie Ray Vaughan have all wrangled a Danelectro or Silvertone with Lipstick Tube pickups to good effect, and reproductions of the pickups themselves became popular with guitar-makers such as Charvel, Jackson and Chandler in the 1990s, not to mention Jerry Jones, a company that made Danelectro-styled models.

Shortly after Nat Daniel's death in 1994 the Evets Corporation bought the rights to use the Danelectro name, and after testing the waters with a line of pedals, reintroduced reproductions of many of the original guitar models in 1998, complete with Lipstick Tube pickups. As we have seen time and time again in this 'every variable matters' field of electronics, few reproductions are quite like the originals of some 40 years or more before, but the new Lipstick Tubes do come pretty close, although they tend to be wound toward the weaker side of the spectrum when compared to original examples, ohming out at around 3.75k. As such, however, they do work well to offer a more powerful tonal option in the series-wired 'blow' mode that many Danelectro reissues offer in the middle position of the pickup selector switch, or paired closely together in a reverse wound/reverse polarity set to make a switchable humbucker, like that on the discontinued Hodad model.

DeArmond

The name didn't appear on the headstock of a guitar until the late 1990s, and even then it arrived on a Korean-made import, but DeArmond pickups were among the most highly respected units available from the 1930s to the '70s, and during that time Row Industries, their manufacturer, was among the industry's most prolific makers. Harry DeArmond, born January 29 1906, was a self-proclaimed inventor who applied his skills early in the field of electromagnetic pickups. His FH and FHC add-on pickups for archtop guitars (and their siblings the RH and RHC for flat-tops) – all advertised as "microphones for stringed instruments" – were manufactured by Rowe in Toledo, Ohio, in the mid 1930s, and became among the most popular attachable pickups for players venturing into the brave new world of electric guitar. The RH and RHC models, and similar DeArmonds that followed, came to be known as the 'monkey on a stick' pickups because they were either mounted to a rod that clamped to the strings behind the bridge and extended toward the fingerboard, or to a rod that attached with screws to the edge of the fingerboard itself. Either could be adjustable for ideal position – and therefore tone – by sliding back and forth between neck and

other guitar and pickup makers

bridge, and carried Volume and sometimes a Tone control mounted in a separate housing (the flat-top versions were clamped into the guitar's soundhole, and had a small built-in 'trim pot' style Volume control). Each employed individual pole pieces made from Alnico II rod magnets within a shallow coil of wire, all contained within a chrome-plated brass cover. DeArmond also put a lot of thinking into the problem of balancing the varying output levels of different strings, and fell upon the idea of producing pickups with less magnetic energy under the B string, which was usually the loudest in the day, when low E, A, D, and G were all wound strings.

In the 1950s DeArmond introduced one of the most revered pickups of all time among archtop jazz guitarists, the Model 1000 Rhythm Chief and Model 1100 Adjustable Rhythm Chief, the former identified by its red inlay and enclosed pole pieces, the latter by its six visible adjustable slot-head pole pieces. Both were still adjustable in the positioning sense, in that they retained the 'monkey on a stick' mounting arrangements. These units represented a marked improvement in tone and fidelity and, given the added bonus that they could be mounted on a valuable instrument without major modification, they became perhaps the most popular add-on pickup for players who wanted to electrify high-end acoustic archtop guitars such as those by D'Angelico, Stromberg, Gibson, and Epiphone.

Although it gives little away from the outside, the Rhythm Chief is quite a complex pickup on the inside. The alnico pole pieces of the non-adjustable version differ in size and diameter to balance string outputs, and to the same end the 44-gauge wire is wound first around the E, A, D, and G poles for a number of turns, before being further wrapped around the full six poles. I don't have one to hand and haven't been able to track down reliable resistance readings, but all indications are they ohm out somewhere in the 5k range. Given the very fine wire in the coil, they aren't very powerful pickups by any means, but they translate a clear, clean, flattering tonality for jazz guitar, and have earned their reputation as a classic in this genre. And while these are seminal jazz pickups, they have also served many blues artists well: Elmore James used a Model 1000, and Muddy Waters used an FHC (or was it FH?) on his archtop acoustics before moving to solidbody electric guitars.

Shortly before the Rhythm Chief's arrival, however, DeArmond introduced its most notable built-in pickup for electric guitar, the Model 200, also known as the Gretsch DynaSonic when used on that maker's guitars (see the Gretsch entry in the previous chapter for further details). With its pole pieces made from

FACING PAGE **DeArmond** – add-on pickup, pickguard mounted. Similar thinking in the B model pickups, for 'Balanced B string'.

other guitar and pickup makers

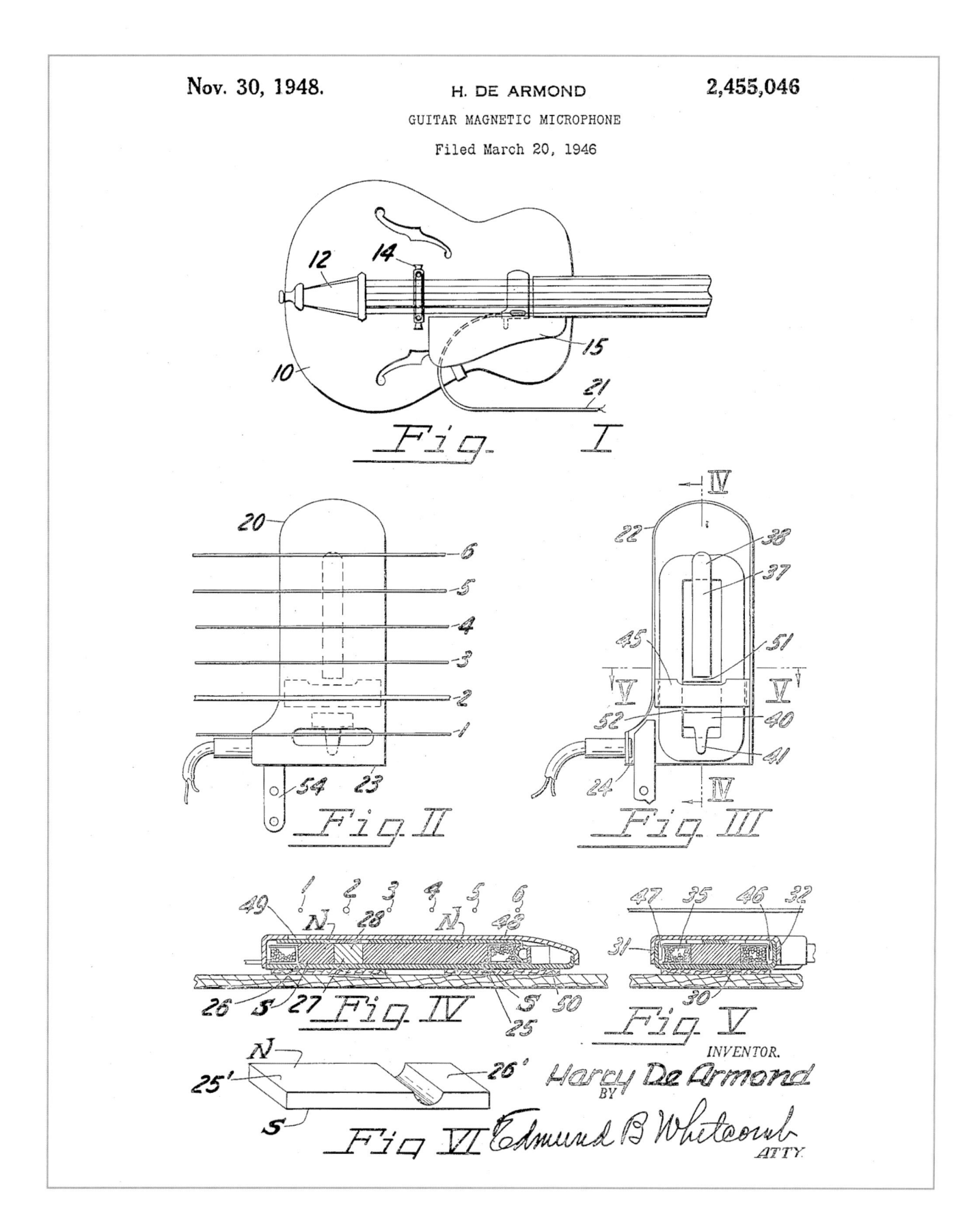

Nov. 30, 1948. H. DE ARMOND 2,455,046
GUITAR MAGNETIC MICROPHONE
Filed March 20, 1946

Fig. I

Fig. II

Fig. III

Fig. IV

Fig. V

Fig. VI

INVENTOR.
Harry De Armond
BY Edmund B Whitcomb
ATTY.

other guitar and pickup makers

individual Alnico V rod magnets (adjustable via a different form of 'monkey on a stick' arrangement … clearly a trait of old Harry) the Model 200 went a long way toward achieving DeArmond's goal of balancing string-to-string output levels, while also achieving the bright, cutting, high-definition sound that most guitar-makers were looking for in the day. Partnered with a wide coil wound with 44-gauge wire to a DC resistance reading that averaged in the 10k+ ballpark it was also a pretty fat, rich sounding pickup, with a silky, smooth high-end response and firm lows, rather than the treble spike associated with some twangy single coils. This pickup, as much as any factor in the guitars themselves, deserves a lot of credit for establishing what became known as 'the Gretsch sound', and it did similar tricks for guitars by Guild, Levin, Martin, and Kustom that it appeared on in the 1950s and '60s.

Two other vintage DeArmond pickups that have become prized in recent years are units that you could have laid your hands on for peanuts in the past. The 'gold foil' and 'silver foil' pickups used on many guitars from Harmony, Silvertone, Airline and others in the late 1950s and '60s have developed a real following, and have come to be worth almost as much as the guitars they're attached to, in many cases. Named for the foil inserts in their tops (and referred to in some Harmony literature as Golden-Tone pickups) these are fat, clanky, percussive, and generally 'lo-fi' sounding pickups … and surprisingly groovy tone machines as a result. They aren't refined, but really pack some mojo, and are real favorites in the vintage-blues community in particular. They use wide, flat coils, wound with either 43- or 44-gauge wire, and can read anywhere from 8k to 11k+ ohms. Specs vary widely, as do the appearances of the many variations of these pickups themselves. Magnets in many of these pickups were – *gasp!* – rubber bars impregnated with ferrite magnetic material, a distant cousin of the flexible magnetic material that holds your dentist's business card to your fridge. These aren't especially powerful, so these gold foil and silver foil DeArmonds' high resistance readings belie their relatively low outputs. Again, mucho mojo in any case, and they have become much loved oddities of the electromagnetic sphere.

Before his death in 1999 Harry DeArmond logged some 100 or more pickup designs, and was a true maverick and pioneer of his field. In addition, he also invented many other devices for use with the guitar, including what is widely acknowledged as the first external effects pedal, the Model 800 Trem Trol tremolo unit of the late 1940s. One other pickup worth mentioning here is a DeArmond in name only, and wasn't a Harry DeArmond design. The DeArmond

FACING PAGE **DeArmond – '50 "indiv. Adj. Magnet poles pickup" aka DeArmond 200/Gretsch DynaSonic**

other guitar and pickup makers

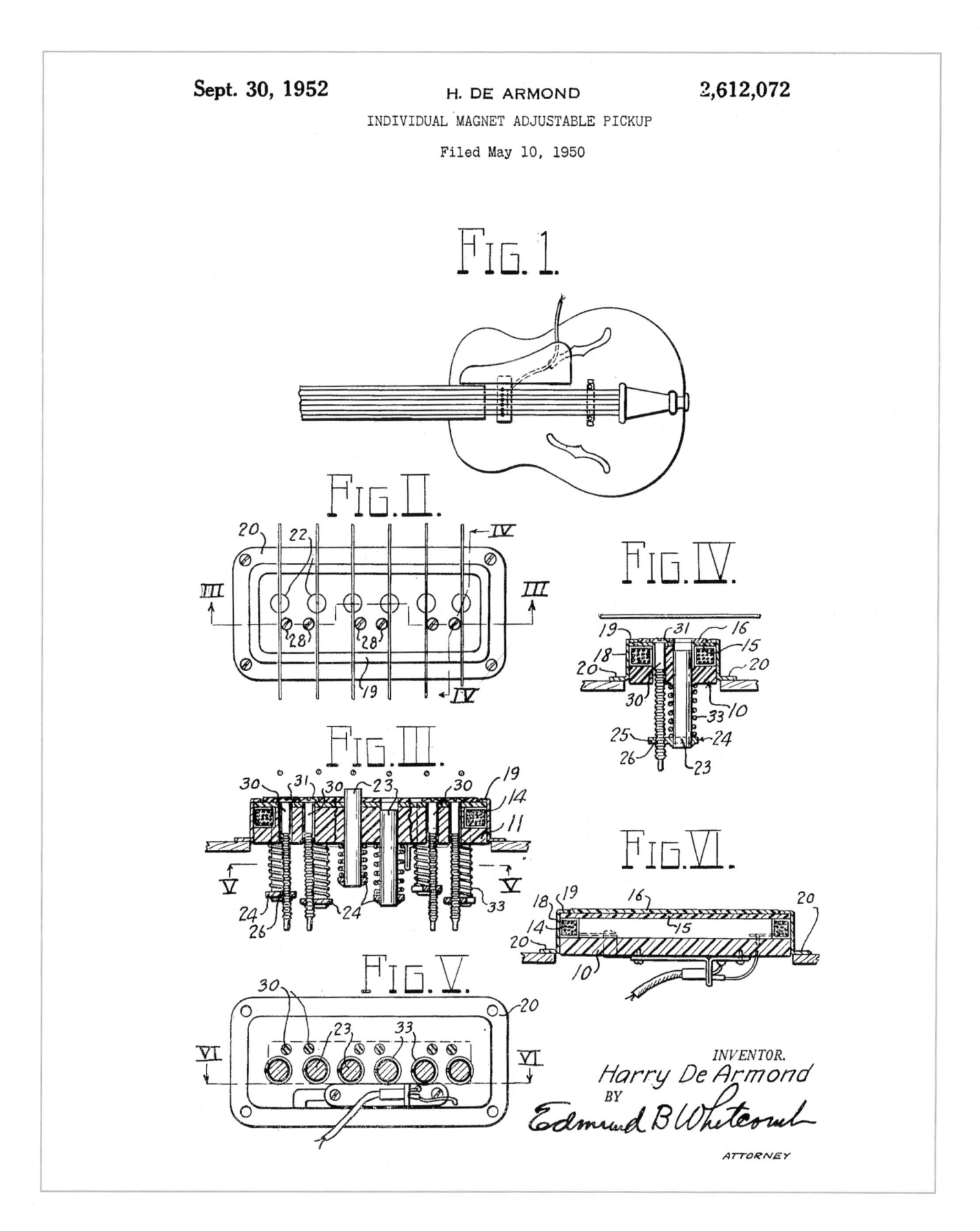

Sept. 30, 1952   H. DE ARMOND   2,612,072
INDIVIDUAL MAGNET ADJUSTABLE PICKUP
Filed May 10, 1950

INVENTOR.
Harry De Armond
BY
Edmund B. Whitcomb
ATTORNEY

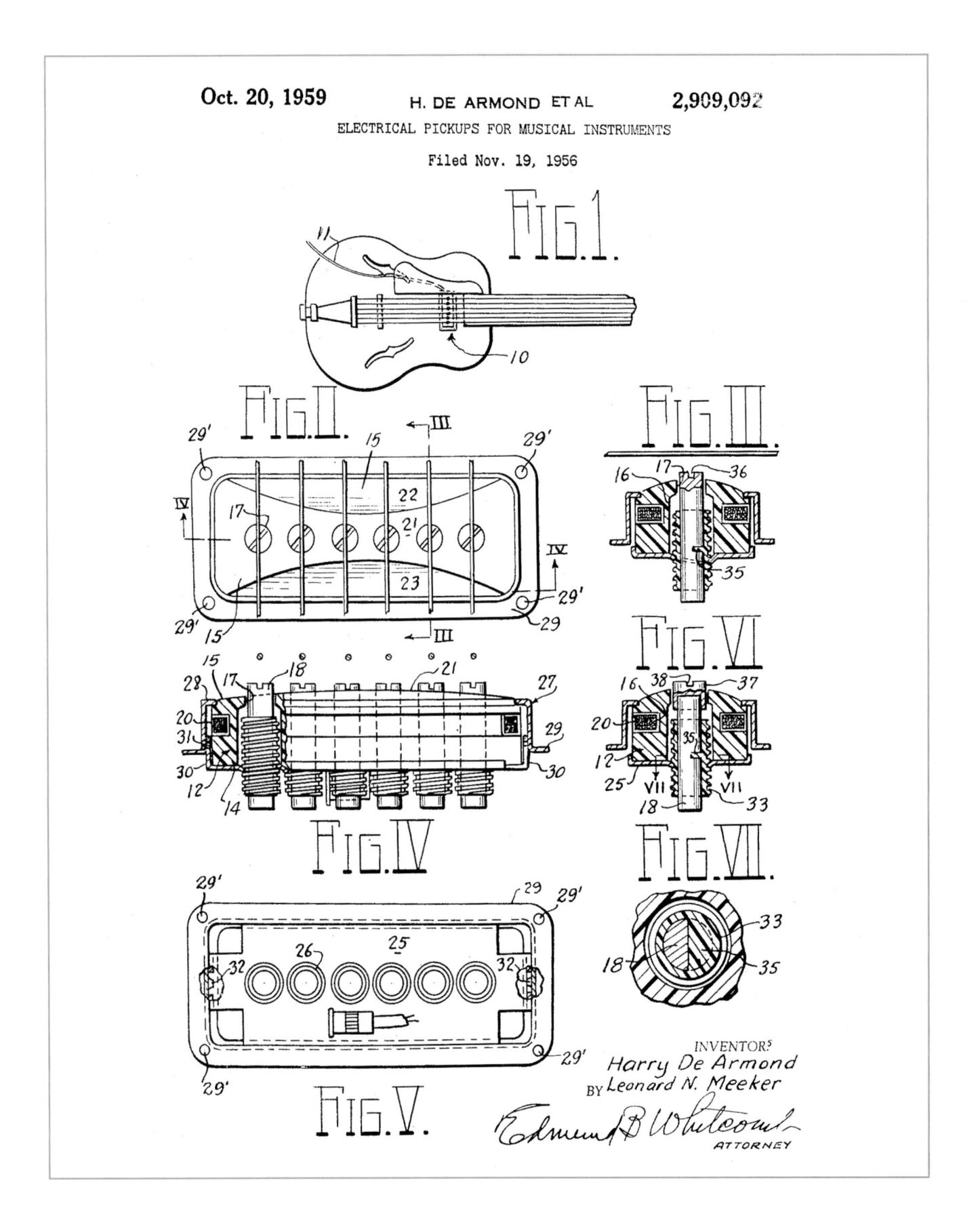

Oct. 20, 1959   H. DE ARMOND ET AL   2,909,092
ELECTRICAL PICKUPS FOR MUSICAL INSTRUMENTS
Filed Nov. 19, 1956

INVENTORS
Harry De Armond
BY Leonard N. Meeker
Edmund B Whitcomb
ATTORNEY

other guitar and pickup makers

2K pickup that appeared on DeAremond-brand pickups retailed by Fender in the late 1990s and early 2000s was made to look like the DeArmond Model 200 (aka Gretsch DynaSonic) originally used on Gretsch and Guild guitars, but is in fact an entirely different structure under the cover. Its adjustable pole pieces are steel slugs rather than alnico magnets, and they contact an alnico bar magnet mounted beneath the coil. As such, they follow the Gibson P-90 formula more than the Model 200 formula, but they aren't bad sounding pickups in their own way … just don't expect them to emulate a DynaSonic.

FACING PAGE **DeArmond** – compact pickup with "thread sheaths" for individually adjustable magnet poles.

● DeArmond Model 1000 Rhythm Chief
Type: single coil
Magnet: Alnico II
Wire: 44 gauge
Resistance: from around 4.5k to 5.5k ohms +/−
Pole pieces: unlike-sized alnico poles
Sound: clear and well defined; low-output, but rich and round.

● DeArmond Model 1100 Adjustable Rhythm Chief
Type: single coil
Magnet: Alnico II
Wire: 44 gauge
Resistance: from around 4.5k to 5.5k ohms +/−
Pole pieces: individual threaded steel poles
Sound: clear and well defined; low-output, but rich and round.

● DeArmond Model 200 (aka Gretsch DynaSonic)
Type: single coil
Magnet: Alnico V
Wire: 44 gauge
Resistance: from around 8.5k to 12k ohms
Pole pieces: individual alnico pole pieces mounted to adjustment screws
Sound: round, rich, and muscular – predominantly a 'twang' pickup, but on the fat and beefy side of that genre.

● DeArmond RH and RHC
Type: single coil
Magnet: Alnico II
Wire: 44 gauge
Resistance: from around 4k to 5k ohms
Pole pieces: individual alnico poles
Sound: clean and clear, with a low output but a flattering frequency response.

● DeArmond by Guild (Fender) Model 2K
Type: single coil
Magnet: alnico
Wire: N/A
Resistance: 8k ohms +/−
Pole pieces: individual steel poles mounted to adjustment screws
Sound: thick and punchy, with a muscular midrange and appealing highs.

other guitar and pickup makers

DiMarzio

Founder Larry DiMarzio repaired his first pickup in 1970 (or attempted to, a failed effort you can read about in the full interview with Larry DiMarzio and Steve Blucher in the *Meet the Makers* chapter), designed his Super Distortion humbucker in 1972, and officially established DiMarzio Pickups in 1975 as the first company dedicated solely to manufacturing after-market replacement pickups. Like other makers that would follow in that decade, DiMarzio's early efforts – notably the Super Distortion humbucker and FS-1 single coil – sought to achieve the high-gain rock sounds that many players were seeking from replacement pickups. The line has expanded, however, into a full range of vintage, modified-vintage, and hotrod-contemporary models to suit the vast needs of a pickup-hungry playing public.

DiMarzio's original impetus was to overcome the weak pickup/low-gain amp equation to give rock guitarists a means of achieving natural overdrive without the aid of a distortion pedal. Of course, in the mid 1970s players still had pretty easy access to plenty of original vintage pickups (and the guitars they came on) for clean playing, so the high-gain market was where it was happening, and this premise gave the New York-based company a major head start in the field. The Super Distortion humbucker and single-coil models used ceramic magnets and threaded steel Allen-key poles, along with overwound coils, to achieve the drive required to push the front end of a tube amp into distortion. Its single-coil sibling the SDS-1, introduced in 1978, followed a similar format to provide one of the only means of getting an anemic CBS-era Stratocaster to really rock out alongside contemporary humbucker-loaded guitars of the hair-band era. That same year, the seminal Pre B-1 did the same for the Telecaster, although in an alnico-magnet package this time, with a whopping 14.2k DC resistance. The X2N, the company's highest-output humbucker with distinctive wide-bar pole pieces and a resistance reading of a generous 16k ohms or so, hit the scene in 1979, when it set forth to slamming the inputs of unsuspecting tube amps on hard-rock stages across the globe.

The PAF Pro of 1986 embodied the 'modified vintage' thinking behind many DiMarzio products by achieving a PAF-style alnico vibe with added definition and cut for rock playing. An offshoot of the design arrived in 1989 in the guise of FRED, another humbucker using an Alnico V magnet, with a little more output (and a DC resistance of around 10k ohms compared to the PAF Pro's c.8.9k resistance) plus a voice that offers more harmonic sparkle and saturation. This model became the main bridge pickup of shred virtuoso Joe Satriani for many

DiMarzio Chopper T humbucker for Telecaster

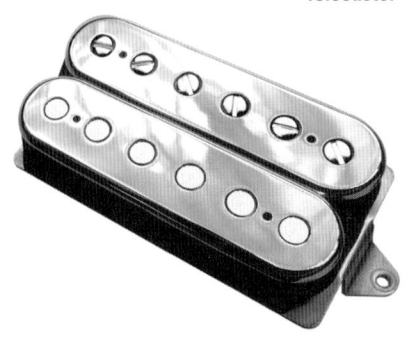

DiMarzio Air Classic with camouflage top plate

FACING PAGE **Larry DiMarzio – stacked single-coil-sized humbucker.**

U.S. Patent   Apr. 17, 1984   Sheet 1 of 3   4,442,749

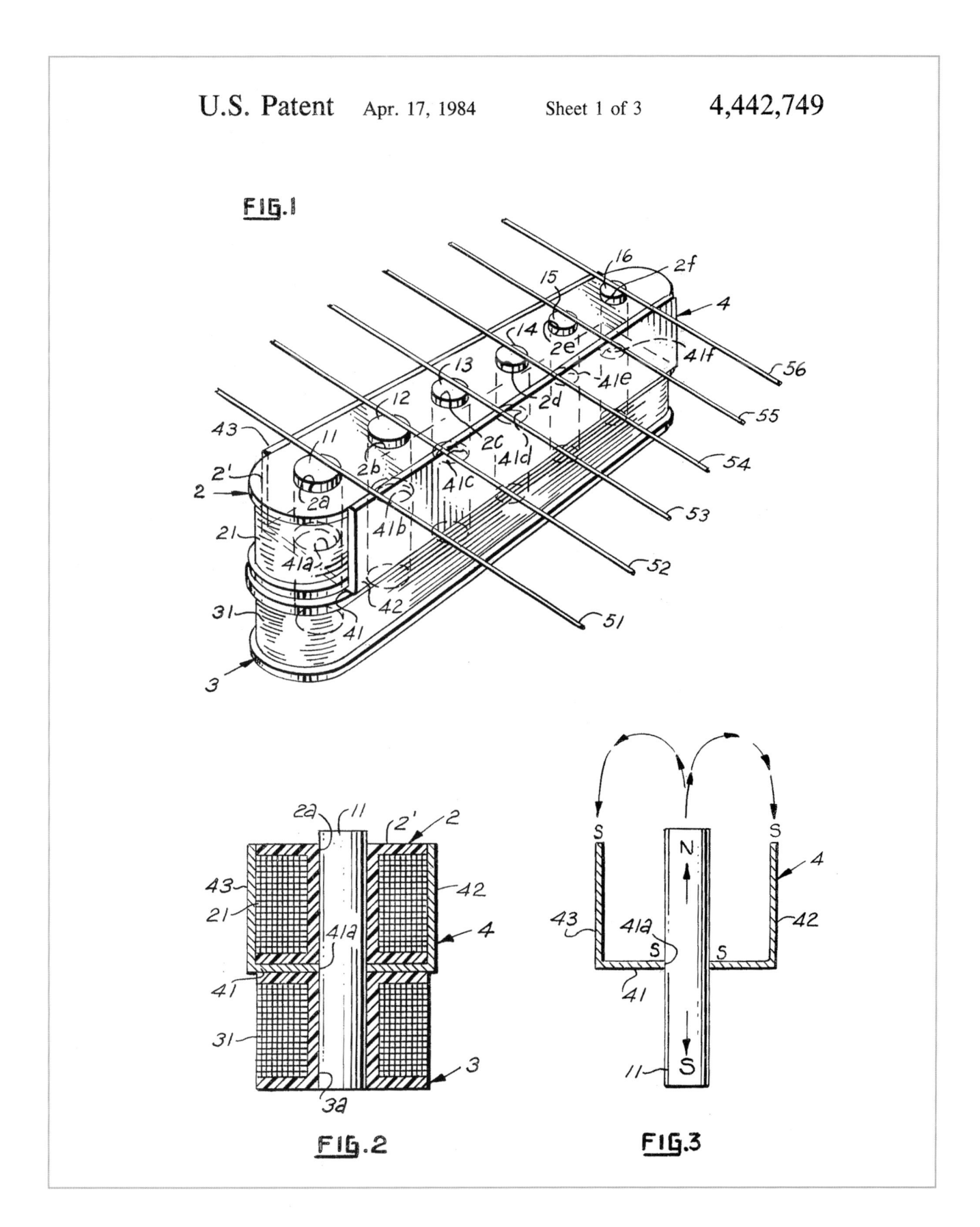

FIG.1

FIG.2

FIG.3

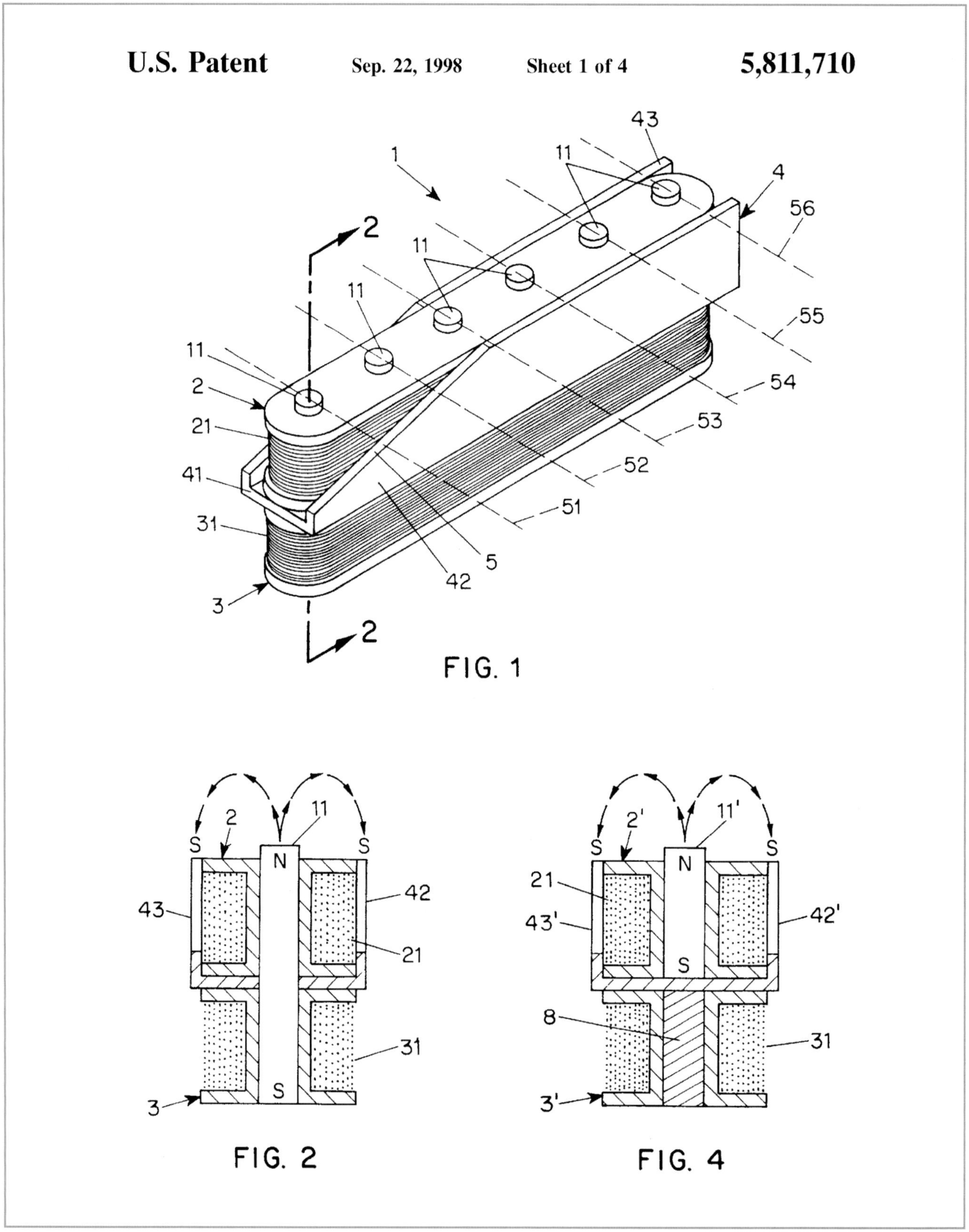

FIG. 1
FIG. 2
FIG. 4

other guitar and pickup makers

improved, so there is far less sonic interaction between the two. The weaker lower coil, still an effective noise inductor (and therefore eliminator) thanks to its steel 'dummy' poles, interferes less with the tone-bearing signal produced by the top coil, and with a little tweaking of the formula DiMarzio has managed to create a hum-cancelling pickup that sounds far more like a conventional single-coil pickup. Also, rather than having the high resistance of the two summed coils of the HS-2, at around 14k ohms, the Virtual Vintage '54 Pro, for example, clocks in at around 7.5k once the top coil is wired to the shallower bottom coil, which has a resistance reading of only around 20 percent that of its mate.

DiMarzio, and his associate Steve Blucher, have also experimented extensively with ways of enhancing the tone and noise-rejection capabilities of conventionally shaped humbucking pickups, the results of which are seen in a number of inventions whose rather traditional looks belie what's really going on inside the bobbins. Humbuckers such as the Air and D-Activator ranges, for example, make use of the practice of winding two side-by-side coils in a traditional looking 'bucker with different gauges of wire, and thereby tuning them to different resonances, to produce a more detailed harmonic response and a clear, full-frequencied voice. To detail one, the Air Norton introduced in 1995 benefits from two different patents awarded to DiMarzio – one for coils wound with dissimilar gauges of wire, one for a magnet and pole-piece structure with reduced string pole – to perform its distinctive sonic tricks.

Today DiMarzio makes more than 70 pickup models for guitar, not even counting calibrated variations for neck and bridge positions or pickups for bass and acoustic guitar. The company does offer many vintage-voiced pickups to suit a booming market in that direction, but its main impetus is still toward contemporary and high-gain pickups for the rock market, many made with ceramic magnets. In addition to tapping the vast replacement pickup market, DiMarzio pickups are also original equipment on guitars by a number of major manufactures, Ibanez and Ernie Ball/Music Man among them.

FACING PAGE **Drawing of DiMarzio's Virtual Vintage design in a patent filed March 1997, granted 1998.**

DiMarzio Fast Track

other guitar and pickup makers

● DiMarzio Breed
Type: humbucker
Magnet: Alnico V
Wire: N/A
Resistance: 17.5k ohms (neck version, 10k ohms)
Pole pieces: six individually adjustable threaded Allen-head steel poles in each coil
Sound: fat, warm rock humbucker with a punchy midrange.

● DiMarzio D Activator
Type: humbucker
Magnet: ceramic
Wire: N/A
Resistance: bridge, 11.41k ohms; neck, 8.9k ohms
Pole pieces: six individually adjustable threaded Allen-head steel poles in each (dissimilarly wound) coil
Sound: a medium-output ceramic humbucker with a rich harmonic content; designed as a passive alternative to other active humbucking pickups on the rock market (most likely intended to rival EMG pickups, popular with many metal players).

● DiMarzio D Activator-X
Type: humbucker
Magnet: ceramic
Wire: N/A
Resistance: bridge, 14.5k ohms; neck, 11.3k ohms
Pole pieces: single steel bar pole in each (dissimilarly wound) coil
Sound: a high-output ceramic humbucker for sizzling lead sounds full up, but decent clarity wound rolled off on the guitar volume; designed as a passive alternative to other active humbucking pickups on the rock market (most likely intended to rival EMG pickups, popular with many metal players).

● DiMarzio D Sonic
Type: humbucker
Magnet: ceramic
Wire: N/A
Resistance: 12k ohms
Pole pieces: fixed, single-steel bar pole in one coil, six individually adjustable threaded Allen-head steel poles in the other
Sound: a high-output humbucker with two dissimilar coils for enhanced brightness and definition in down-tuned guitars when mounted bar-toward-bridge, or enhanced warmth and presence when mounted with poles toward bridge.

● DiMarzio Dual Sound
Type: humbucker
Magnet: ceramic
Wire: N/A
Resistance: 13.5k ohms
Pole pieces: six individually adjustable threaded steel Allen-head poles in each coil
Sound: hard-hitting, high-output ceramic humbucker for thick, compressed lead tones (four-conductor version of original Super Distortion, for series/parallel switching options).

● DiMarzio Evolution
Type: humbucker
Magnet: ceramic
Wire: N/A
Resistance: 13.84k ohms (neck available, c.13k ohms)
Pole pieces: six individually adjustable threaded steel Allen-head poles in each coil
Sound: fat, aggressive, and loud ceramic humbucker for high-gain shred.

● DiMarzio Evo 2
Type: humbucker
Magnet: ceramic
Wire: N/A
Resistance: 12.81k ohms
Pole pieces: six individually adjustable threaded steel Allen-head poles in each coil
Sound: as Evolution (above) with increased headroom and dynamics, designed to clean up well with volume rolled down.

other guitar and pickup makers

● **DiMarzio Steve's Special**
Type: humbucker
Magnet: ceramic
Wire: N/A
Resistance: 17k ohms
Pole pieces: six individually-adjustable threaded steel Allen-head poles in each coil
Sound: high-gain ceramic humbucker with a broad frequency spectrum rather than the usual aggressive mids and thumping compression; enhanced lows and highs married to recessed mids.

● **DiMarzio Super Distortion**
Type: humbucker
Magnet: ceramic
Wire: N/A
Resistance: 13.68k ohms (Super 2 for neck, 8.7k ohms; Super 3 hotrod for bridge, 25k ohms)
Pole pieces: six individually adjustable threaded steel Allen-head poles in each coil
Sound: crunchy, gutsy midrange with major aggression (see Steve's Sepcial, above, and reverse it). DiMarzio's original high-output humbucker from the early 1970s. Super 2 is for neck position, Super 3 is super-super-high output.

● **DiMarzio Tone Zone**
Type: humbucker
Magnet: Alnico V
Wire: N/A
Resistance: 17.3k ohms
Pole pieces: six individually adjustable threaded slot-head steel poles in one coil, six fixed steel slugs in the other
Sound: high-output alnico humbucker that seeks to offer a broader, more PAF-voiced tonality.

● **DiMarzio X2N**
Type: humbucker
Magnet: ceramic
Wire: N/A
Resistance: 16k ohms
Pole pieces: fixed steel bar blade pole in each coil
Sound: 1970s era high-output ceramic humbucker, for smashing mids and scorching hard-rock lead tones.

● **DiMarzio Air Norton**
Type: humbucker
Magnet: Alnico V
Wire: N/A
Resistance: 12.5k ohms
Pole pieces: six individually adjustable threaded slot-head steel poles in one coil, six fixed steel slugs in the other
Sound: medium-output alnico humbucker with a smoother, rounder rock voice than the Tone Zone; employs patented magnet structure designed to reduce string pull.

● **DiMarzio Air Zone**
Type: humbucker
Magnet: Alnico V
Wire: N/A
Resistance: 16.5k ohms
Pole pieces: six individually adjustable threaded slot-head steel poles in one coil, six fixed steel slugs in the other
Sound: medium-output alnico humbucker designed as a more vintage-voiced version of the Tone Zone (not a high-output humbucker, despite resistance reading); employs patented magnet structure designed to reduce string pull.

● **DiMarzio FRED**
Type: humbucker
Magnet: Alnico V
Wire: N/A
Resistance: 10k ohms
Pole pieces: six individually adjustable threaded steel Allen-head poles in each coil
Sound: medium-output humbucker with extended sparkle and harmonic range.

● **DiMarzio Mo'Joe**
Type: humbucker
Magnet: Alnico V
Wire: N/A
Resistance: 9.8k ohms
Pole pieces: six individually adjustable threaded steel Allen-head poles in each coil
Sound: medium-output humbucker designed to be a little hotter and fatter than FRED (see above; remember, resistance readings can be misleading).

other guitar and pickup makers

● DiMarzio Norton
Type: humbucker
Magnet: Alnico V
Wire: N/A
Resistance: 12.5k ohms
Pole pieces: six individually-adjustable threaded slot-head steel poles in one coil, six fixed steel slugs in the other
Sound: enhanced midrange punch and extended high-end harmonics in a medium-output humbucker.

● DiMarzio PAF Joe
Type: humbucker
Magnet: Alnico V
Wire: N/A
Resistance: 8.5k ohms
Pole pieces: six individually-adjustable threaded steel Allen-head poles in each coil
Sound: a clear, warm, focused medium-output humbucker, originally designed for Joe Satriani's neck position requirements.

● DiMarzio PAF Pro
Type: humbucker
Magnet: Alnico V
Wire: N/A
Resistance: 8.5k ohms
Pole pieces: six individually-adjustable threaded steel Allen-head poles in each coil
Sound: enhanced presence, cut and definition in a medium-output humbucker.

● DiMarzio Air Classic
Type: humbucker
Magnet: Alnico V
Wire: N/A
Resistance: 8.6k ohms bridge, 8.3k neck
Pole pieces: six individually-adjustable threaded slot-head steel poles in one coil, six fixed steel slugs in the other
Sound: round, full-frequencied low-output humbucker set, with magnet structure designed to reduce string pull.

● DiMarzio Bluesbucker
Type: humbucker
Magnet: Alnico V
Wire: N/A
Resistance: 9.8k ohms
Pole pieces: six individually-adjustable threaded slot-head steel poles in one coil, six fixed steel slugs in the other
Sound: hum-cancelling pickup employing Virtual Vintage technology and voiced like a P-90, designed to fit conventional humbucker route.

● DiMarzio EJ Custom
Type: humbucker
Magnet: Alnico V
Wire: N/A
Resistance: bridge, 7.8k ohms; neck, 7k ohms
Pole pieces: six individually-adjustable threaded slot-head steel poles in one coil, six fixed steel slugs in the other
Sound: clear, bright, well-defined sounding low-output humbuckers, originally designed to Eric Johnson's request to make them sound like Gretch Filter'Trons.

● DiMarzio Humbucker From Hell
Type: humbucker
Magnet: Alnico V
Wire: N/A
Resistance: 5.8k ohms
Pole pieces: six individually-adjustable threaded steel Allen-head poles in each coil
Sound: low-output humbucker designed to cancel fewer frequencies with coils summed than traditional humbucker; bright, open and clean.

● DiMarzio PAF 36th Anniversary
Type: humbucker
Magnet: Alnico V
Wire: N/A
Resistance: bridge, 8.6k ohms; neck, 7.3k ohms
Pole pieces: six individually-adjustable threaded slot-head steel poles in one coil, six fixed steel slugs in the other
Sound: redesign of DiMarzio's original PAF, intended to capture vintage Gibson humbucker tone.

other guitar and pickup makers

● DiMarzio MiniBucker
Type: humbucker
Magnet: ceramic
Wire: N/A
Resistance: 12k ohms
Pole pieces: six fixed poles in each coil
Sound: Gibson Firebird-sized mini humbucker with airy, open tone and enhanced clarity (not a high-output pickup, despite resistance spec).

● DiMarzio Hot MiniBucker
Type: humbucker
Magnet: ceramic
Wire: N/A
Resistance: 13.4k ohms
Pole pieces: six fixed poles in each coil
Sound: as MiniBucker above, with added midrange punch and a little more sizzle for lead playing.

● DiMarzio Air Norton S
Type: hum-canceling 'single-coil' sized
Magnet: ceramic
Wire: N/A
Resistance: 11.2k ohms
Pole pieces: two fixed steel blade poles in side-by-side coils
Sound: a warm, round, rich sounding dual-coil Stratocaster style pickup, designed to minimize string pull.

● DiMarzio Area '58, '61 & '67
Type: hum-canceling 'single-coil' sized
Magnet: Alnico II
Wire: N/A
Resistance: 6.2k ohms, 6.5k ohms and 5.8k ohms respectively
Pole pieces: six fixed alnico rod magnet poles with beveled tops
Sound: update of Virtual Vintage technology (see text above) to reproduce an accurate, but low-hum, Fender Stratocaster pickup circa 1958, 1961 and 1967.

● DiMarzio Chopper
Type: hum-canceling 'single-coil' sized
Magnet: ceramic
Wire: N/A
Resistance: 9.2k ohms
Pole pieces: two fixed steel blade polls in side-by-side coils
Sound: thick, crunchy Strat-sized humbucker for rock.

● DiMarzio Cruiser
Type: hum-canceling 'single-coil' sized
Magnet: ceramic
Wire: N/A
Resistance: bridge, 5.8k ohms; neck, 3.2k ohms
Pole pieces: two fixed steel blade polls in side-by-side coils
Sound: harmonically rich, well defined, 'high-fidelity' style pickup for Stratocaster-sized routes; punchy and more powerful than vintage-style single coils, despite misleading resistance readings.

● DiMarzio Fast Track 2
Type: hum-canceling 'single-coil' sized
Magnet: ceramic
Wire: N/A
Resistance: 17.53k ohms
Pole pieces: two fixed steel blade polls in side-by-side coils
Sound: big lows, aggressive mids and mammoth output in a Strat-sized humbucker for rock players.

● DiMarzio HS2 & HS3
Type: hum-canceling 'single-coil' sized
Magnet: Alnico V
Wire: N/A
Resistance: 15k ohms, (HS-3 23k ohms)
Pole pieces: six fixed alnico rod magnet poles in stacked coils
Sound: the original stacked-coils Strat-sized humbucker; HS-2 is bright, rich and well defined; HS-3 is fatter and hotter.

● DiMarzio Pro Track
Type: hum-canceling 'single-coil' sized
Magnet: ceramic
Wire: N/A
Resistance: 8.2k ohms
Pole pieces: two fixed steel blade poles in side-by-side coils
Sound: a contemporary ceramic humbucker for a Strat-sized route, aims to capture PAF humbucker-like tones.

● DiMarzio Super Distortion S
Type: hum-canceling 'single-coil' sized
Magnet: ceramic
Wire: N/A
Resistance: 13.8k ohms
Pole pieces: two fixed steel blade poles in side-by-side coils
Sound: fat, crunchy, mid-heavy; aims to do the original Super Distortion humbucker vibe for the Stratocaster and similar guitars.

other guitar and pickup makers

● DiMarzio Tone Zone S
Type: hum-canceling 'single-coil' sized
Magnet: ceramic
Wire: N/A
Resistance: 12.4k ohms
Pole pieces: two fixed steel blade poles in side-by-side coils
Sound: punchy lows, balanced mids and lively harmonics; aims to do the original Tone Zone humbucker dance for the Stratocaster and similar guitars.

● DiMarzio Virtual Solo
Type: hum-canceling 'single-coil' sized
Magnet: Alnico V
Wire: N/A
Resistance: 11.2k ohms
Pole pieces: six fixed alnico rod magnet poles in top coil, steel 'dummy poles' in shallower bottom coil
Sound: an evolution of the Virtual Vintage technology (see text above, specs below), designed to sound fuller and smoother than the VV Solo and VV Solo Pro.

● DiMarzio Virtual Vintage '54 Pro
Type: hum-canceling 'single-coil' sized
Magnet: Alnico II
Wire: N/A
Resistance: 7.5k ohms
Pole pieces: six fixed alnico rod magnet poles in top coil, steel 'dummy poles' in shallower bottom coil
Sound: hum-canceling rendition of the original vintage Stratocaster single-coil tone.

● DiMarzio Virtual Vintage Blues
Type: hum-canceling 'single-coil' sized
Magnet: Alnico V
Wire: N/A
Resistance: 8.3k ohms
Pole pieces: six fixed alnico rod magnet poles in top coil, steel 'dummy poles' in shallower bottom coil
Sound: thicker mids and more punch than '54 Pro (above).

● DiMarzio Virtual Vintage Heavy Blues 2
Type: hum-canceling 'single-coil' sized
Magnet: Alnico II
Wire: N/A
Resistance: 8.6k ohms
Pole pieces: six fixed alnico rod magnet poles in top coil, steel 'dummy poles' in shallower bottom coil
Sound: designed as a hot blues bridge pickup with enhanced attack, but made with softer Alnico II magnets for a smooth performance in the neck position.

● DiMarzio Virtual Vintage Solo
Type: hum-canceling 'single-coil' sized
Magnet: Alnico V
Wire: N/A
Resistance: 10.8k ohms
Pole pieces: six fixed alnico rod magnet poles in top coil, steel 'dummy poles' in shallower bottom coil
Sound: enhanced highs and aggressive mids in a rockier Strat-sized pickup that approaches a P-90 tonality.

● DiMarzio YJM
Type: hum-canceling 'single-coil' sized
Magnet: Alnico V
Wire: N/A
Resistance: 23.5k ohms
Pole pieces: six fixed alnico rod magnet poles in stacked coils
Sound: designed for Yngwie Malmsteen and similar to HS-3, but with vintage-staggered pole pieces.

● DiMarzio FS-1
Type: single coil
Magnet: Alnico V
Wire: N/A
Resistance: 13k ohms
Pole pieces: six fixed alnico rod magnet poles
Sound: one of DiMarzio's earliest 'hotrod' models, an overwound Stratocaster-style pickup for more midrange muscle and higher output in the bridge position.

other guitar and pickup makers

● DiMarzio Red Velvet
Type: single coil
Magnet: Alnico V, with steel bottom plate
Wire: N/A
Resistance: 8.5k ohms
Pole pieces: six fixed alnico rod magnet poles
Sound: seeks to blend a hot-Strat sound with the midrange punch and attack of a Telecaster pickup.

● DiMarzio SDS-1
Type: single coil
Magnet: ceramic
Wire: N/A
Resistance: 8.7k ohms
Pole pieces: six adjustable threaded still Allen-head bolts
Sound: hot, fat and compressed; the original crunchy high-output Strat replacement pickup.

● DiMarzio True Velvet
Type: single coil
Magnet: Alnico V
Wire: N/A
Resistance: bridge, 6.5k ohms; neck and middle, 6.2k ohms
Pole pieces: six fixed alnico rod magnet poles
Sound: calibrated set of vintage-voiced Stratocaster replacement pickups.

● DiMarzio Air Norton T
Type: hum-canceling 'single-coil' sized
Magnet: ceramic
Wire: N/A
Resistance: 11.2k ohms
Pole pieces: two fixed steel blade poles in side-by-side coils
Sound: a warm, round, rich sounding dual-coil Telecaster-style bridge pickup, designed to minimize string pull.

● DiMarzio Area T
Type: hum-canceling 'single-coil' sized
Magnet: Alnico II
Wire: N/A
Resistance: bridge, 7.5k ohms; neck, 8.4k ohms
Pole pieces: six fixed alnico rod magnet poles with beveled tops
Sound: update of Virtual Vintage technology (see text above) to reproduce an accurate, but low-hum, vintage-voiced Telecaster-style pickup.

● DiMarzio Chopper T
Type: hum-canceling 'single-coil' sized
Magnet: ceramic
Wire: N/A
Resistance: 9.2k ohms
Pole pieces: two fixed steel blade polls in side-by-side coils
Sound: thick, crunchy Tele-sized humbucker for rock.

● DiMarzio Fast Track T
Type: hum-canceling 'single-coil' sized
Magnet: ceramic
Wire: N/A
Resistance: 5.7k ohms
Pole pieces: two fixed steel blade polls in side-by-side coils
Sound: a hot twin-rail Tele humbucker, but with more twang and definition than traditional humbuckers.

● DiMarzio Super Distortion S
Type: hum-canceling 'single-coil' sized
Magnet: ceramic
Wire: N/A
Resistance: 13.2k ohms
Pole pieces: two fixed steel blade poles in side-by-side coils
Sound: fat, crunchy, mid-heavy; aims to do the original Super Distortion humbucker vibe for the Telecaster.

● DiMarzio Tone Zone T
Type: hum-canceling 'single-coil' sized
Magnet: ceramic
Wire: N/A
Resistance: 12.4k ohms
Pole pieces: two fixed steel blade poles in side-by-side coils
Sound: punchy lows, balanced mids and lively harmonics; an approximation of the original Tone Zone humbucker in a Tele-compatible package.

● DiMarzio Virtual Hot T Bridge
Type: hum-canceling 'single-coil' sized
Magnet: Alnico V
Wire: N/A
Resistance: 9.3k ohms
Pole pieces: six fixed alnico rod magnet poles in top coil, steel 'dummy poles' in shallower bottom coil
Sound: an evolution of the Virtual Vintage technology (see text above, specs below), designed for twangy yet fat and aggressive sounds in the Telecaster bridge position.

other guitar and pickup makers

● DiMarzio Pre B-1
Type: single coil
Magnet: Alnico V
Wire: N/A
Resistance: 14.2k ohms
Pole pieces: six fixed alnico rod magnet poles
Sound: overwound Tele bridge-style pickup for with increased output and enhanced midrange crunch.

● DiMarzio Twang King
Type: single coil
Magnet: Alnico V
Wire: N/A
Resistance: bridge, 8k ohms; neck, 6.22k ohms
Pole pieces: six fixed alnico rod magnet poles
Sound: vintage-voiced Telecaster pickups, hotrodded for added attack and sizzle, but retaining some traditional twang.

● DiMarzio DLX 90
Type: humbucker
Magnet: ceramic
Wire: N/A
Resistance: 9.6k ohms
Pole pieces: six adjustable threaded steel slot-head poles in each coil
Sound: humbucker in a P-90 sized package, voiced for semi-hot vintage P-90 tone.

● DiMarzio DLX Plus
Type: humbucker
Magnet: ceramic
Wire: N/A
Resistance: bridge, 17.3k ohms; neck, 13.8k ohms
Pole pieces: six adjustable threaded steel slot-head poles in each coil
Sound: high-output humbucker in a P-90 sized package, voiced to sound more like a traditional hot 'bucker, namely the DiMarzio Steve's Special.

● DiMarzio P-90 Super Distortion
Type: humbucker
Magnet: ceramic
Wire: N/A
Resistance: 12.8k ohms
Pole pieces: six adjustable threaded steel Allen-head poles in each coil
Sound: super-high-output humbucker in a P-90 sized package, for major crunch and midrange aggression.

● DiMarzio Tone Zone P-90
Type: humbucker
Magnet: ceramic
Wire: N/A
Resistance: 16.8k ohms
Pole pieces: six adjustable threaded steel slot-head poles in each coil
Sound: high-output humbucker in a P-90 sized package, designed to sound like the full-sized Tone Zone humbucker (see above).

● DiMarzio Virtual P-90
Type: humbucker
Magnet: ceramic
Wire: N/A
Resistance: 9k ohms
Pole pieces: six adjustable threaded steel slot-head poles in each coil
Sound: a twist on Virtual Vintage technology in a pickup voiced to capture vintage P-90 tone.

● DiMarzio Soapbar
Type: single coil
Magnet: ceramic
Wire: N/A
Resistance: 9.6k ohms
Pole pieces: six adjustable threaded steel slot-head poles
Sound: intended as a ceramic update on the traditional Gibson P-90, with added midrange punch and tighter lows.

other guitar and pickup makers

Seymour Duncan

An early player in the replacement pickup market, if not the first on the scene, Seymour Duncan has grown from a one-man operation run by the company's namesake and his wife, Cathy Carter Duncan, to become one of the world's largest and most respected pickup manufacturers. The company now boasts more than 100 employees and currently offers more than 80 models for electric guitar line (not including the Antiquity and Antiquity II vintage reproduction lines), and is a major OEM supplier to a wide range of guitar manufacturers. Duncan, born in New Jersey, became obsessed with all things tone, and pickups in particular, while playing the East Coast clubs as a gigging guitarist in the 1960s. During these early years he took the opportunity to rub shoulders with many of his own heroes such as Les Paul and Roy Buchanan, rewound his first coil (on a 33⅓ rpm record player) after the bridge pickup of his own vintage Telecaster shorted out mid-set, and starting stacking in some the knowledge that would form the foundation of his craft.

At the urging of Les Paul, Duncan headed to London in the late 1960s, where he worked in repair at the Fender Soundhouse, and famously began his association with – and rewound pickups for – Jeff Beck, while also doing pickup and repair work for Jimi Hendrix, Pete Townshend, Eric Clapton, Jimmy Page, and other luminaries of the London scene. After returning to the USA, and eventually finding his way to California – where he continued to repair guitars and rewind pickups while, more and more often now, also making his own custom-designed units – Duncan and his wife Cathy established Seymour Duncan Pickups in 1978.

Like many other makers in the early days of the replacement pickup industry, Seymour Duncan (SD) forged their way in the market first by mainly offering hotrod designs for players who wanted to boost the output of their guitars. The Quarter Pounder for both Tele and Strat was an early favorite, and remains in the lineup today. Using fat quarter-inch Alnico V rod magnet polls and wound to around 17k and 14k ohms respectively, these provided an easy way of boosting potentially thin, over-bright sounding Fenders into thick crunch and saturated overdrive for rock and heavy-blues players. Other hot true single-coil designs have followed through the years, although – also in parallel with other manufacturers of the early 1980s – much of SD's hot-pickup models chased the occasionally illusive notion of single-coil tone in a hum-canceling package. He filed a patent in 1983 (granted 1985), shortly after the 1982 filing by Larry DiMarzio in line with a similar concept (granted to him in 1984), for a stacked-

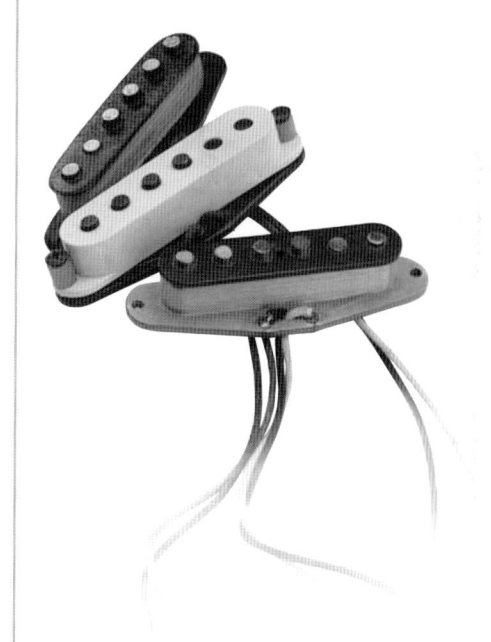

A selection of Seymour Duncan's Antiquity pickups

Fig 1

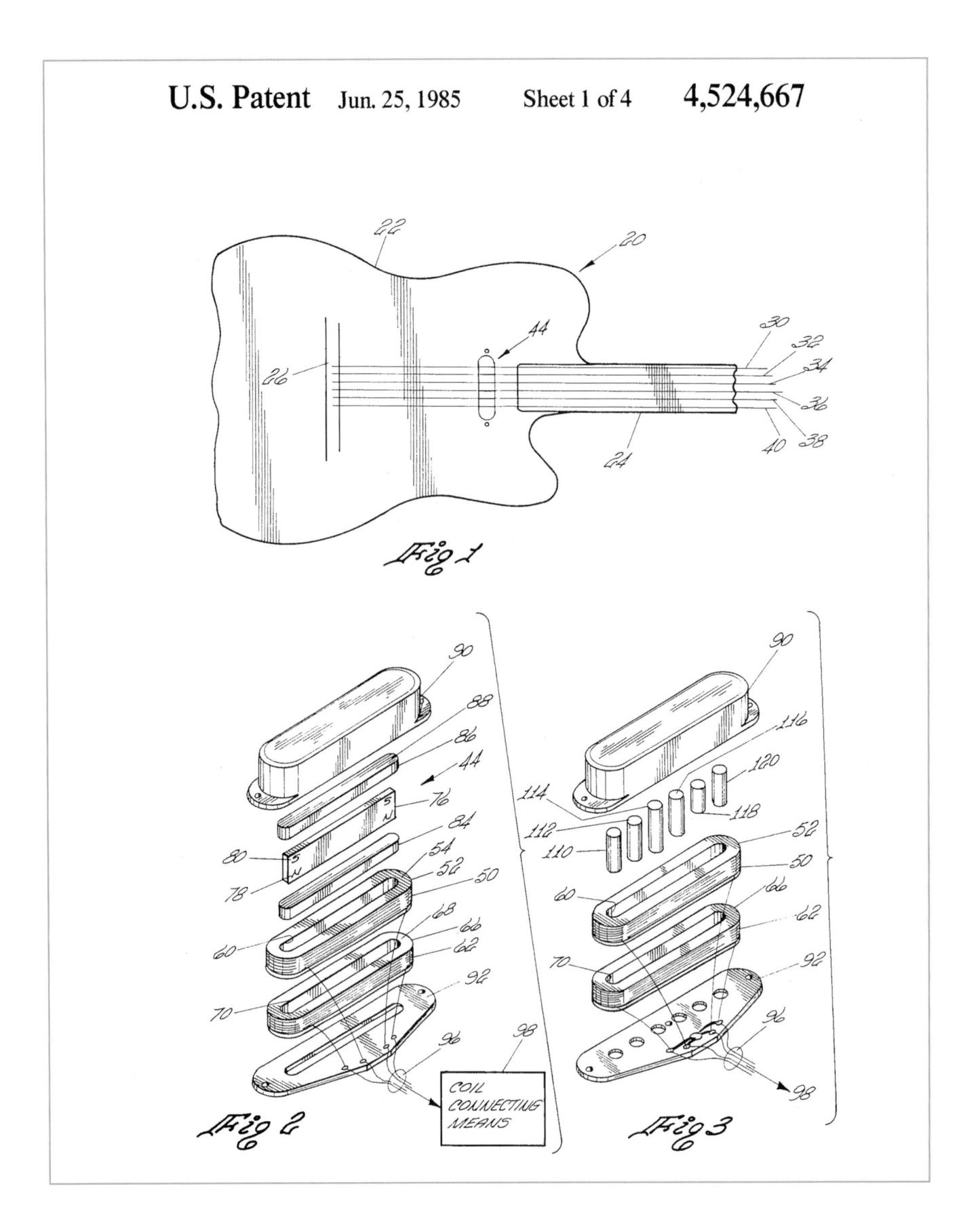

Fig 2

COIL CONNECTING MEANS

Fig 3

other guitar and pickup makers

coil humbucker designed to fit a single-coil Stratocaster routing. SD's application is differentiated from DiMarzio's slightly by the inclusion of alternatives in bar pole and blade pole form, in addition to the main drawing with two stacked coils surrounding six individual alnico bar magnet pole pieces.

The technology has hit the market in the form of the Stack Plus and Hot Stack, the latter with a ceramic bar magnet sandwiched beneath a steel bar pole piece. From about the mid 1980s on, however, SD concentrated more on developing single-coil-sized humbuckers with narrow, side-by-side coils. One seminal unit, the Hot Rails, followed the template established by Joe Barden, using thin steel blades in contact with a ceramic magnet mounted below, but was wound extremely hot at around 17k for a sizzling, crunch, midrange-forward performance. The Cool Rails that followed was a more moderate-output design. Using six individually adjustable threaded steel poles in each coil instead of the fixed blades of the 'Rail' designs, the Little '59, Li'l Screamin' Demon, and JB Jr. offered further moderate, hot and hotter options respectively for players of Strat-style guitars. The Little '59, also available for Tele bridge position, is voiced to sound like a PAF humbucker, although it uses a ceramic bar magnet rather than alnico, as do all of these designs. The Li'l Screamin' Demon is a compact version of the full-sized humbucker designed for George Lynch, the Screamin' Demon, and uses Allen-head poles in one coil and slot-head in the other. Similarly, the JB Jr. is the Strat-sized version of the full-sized humbucker designed for Jeff Beck; a high-output pickup, it is just a little less powerful than the Hot Rails – king of the hill in SD land – with sweeter highs and a more balanced tone.

Although he first made his mark with replacements for single-coil pickups, Seymour Duncan has a long history of providing a broad range of humbucker designs, too. While early users of single-coil replacement pickups were usually seeking more output, many humbucker players were inclined toward illusive, vintage-PAF-styled tones, given that the real thing was already very difficult to acquire by the late 1970s and early '80s. Cornerstone SD models such as the '59 Model SH-1 and Alnico II Pro address the needs for low and moderate-output 'buckers respectively. The Pearly Gates, designed to replicate the sound of the hot bridge pickup in Billy Gibbons's legendary '59 Les Paul Standard, cranks it up a notch further, with a hot-vintage output, while the Seth Lover SH-55, designed by Duncan in conjunction with Seth Lover, seeks an authentic, mid-50s, low-output humbucker voice, complete with unspotted coils and slightly microphonic cover.

Not that SD ignores the large market for high-output humbuckers, by any

Seymour Duncan Stack Plus (covered and uncovered)

FACING PAGE **Seymour Duncan's design for the stacked single-coil sized humbucking pickup, with variations for bar magnets and individual pole pieces, filed 1983, granted 1985.**

other guitar and pickup makers

means, and the range has expanded further in this direction than in any other. The JB Model (for Jeff Beck) laid the foundation for SD's hotrodded humbuckers some 30 years ago, and still offers the kicking mids and sizzling highs that were *de rigueur* in a hotrodded rock humbucker in the early 1980s. The more contemporary sounding Custom 5 tames the highs a bit, while remaining every bit as fierce, and the Invader, George Lynch Screamin' Demon, Full Shred and Duncan Distortion ... well, they pretty much speak for themselves. The passive range also includes the high-output, dual-rail Dimebucker, popular among devotees of the slammin' sound of the late Dimebag Darrell, while SD's active Livewire range has been giving specialists such as EMG a run for their money. SD's Trembucker range, which offers coils with pole pieces spaced to suit Fender bridge string spacing, has long been a favorite of players who use 'bucker-loaded Strat-style guitars. The innovative new P-Rails offers the unusual combination of P-90-style and blade-style single-coil pickups housed in the same package, and selectable together or independently.

While SD's standard line includes a great many models designed to provide accurate renditions of vintage-styled tone, the company made even greater strides toward offering aged, period-correct replacement pickups with the introduction of the Antiquity Series in the late 1990s. Now updated with many Antiquity II models, representing desirable 1960s-style pickups to complement the '50s-style models in the Antiquity line, the range includes impressive recreations of desirable, rare vintage Fender Telecaster, Stratocaster, Jazzmaster and Mustang pickups, along Gibson PAF and P-90 models, and an interesting range of more specialized units. Details include distressing of bobbins, magnets, covers and insulation to indicate 50-plus years of wear and tear, all of which is partnered by an exacting accuracy of materials and construction – so much as can be achieved from supplies available today.

The American-made SD line is rounded out by the products of the Custom Shop. These include a vast number of standard – if lesser seen – replacement pickups, such as a Gretsch DynaSonic, Gibson Alnico V ('Staple'), and Mosrite pickups, along with more unusual creations, like Strat-style pickups under P-90 covers, three variations of Charlie Christians, a P-90-styled pickup housed in a Gretsch Filter'Tron-style cover, and so on. Finally, the Duncan Designed series, begun in 1995, offers a wide range of pickups that are, well, designed by Seymour Duncan, but manufactured in Korea for use as OEM parts on lower and mid-priced guitars.

Although the full Seymour Duncan line up constitutes the greatest number

Seymour Duncan P-Rails

other guitar and pickup makers

of high-end pickup models currently manufactured in the USA, I won't list the specs of those that seek to be accurate replacements for vintage originals. This, of course, constitutes the entirety of the highly respected Antiquity and Antiquity II line (although models such as the Strat Texas Hot could be considered exceptions to this rule), so be aware that these and other SD units are very much worth checking out, if you're in the market for an accurate replacement pickups for a 1950s or '60s original.

● Seymour Duncan '59 Model
Type: humbucker
Magnet: Alnico V
Wire: 42-gauge plain enamel
Resistance: neck, 7.6k ohms; bridge, 8.1k ohms
Pole pieces: six adjustable threaded steel slot-head poles in one coil, six fixed steel slugs in the other
Sound: intended as an accurate low to moderate-output PAF-style humbucker.

● Seymour Duncan Alnico II Pro
Type: humbucker
Magnet: Alnico II
Wire: 42-gauge plain enamel
Resistance: neck, 7.6k ohms; bridge, 7.8k ohms
Pole pieces: six adjustable threaded steel slot-head poles in one coil, six fixed steel slugs in the other
Sound: intended as an accurate low to moderate-output PAF-style humbucker, but with the softer attack and added compression of Alnico II.

● Seymour Duncan Seth Lover Model
Type: humbucker
Magnet: Alnico II
Wire: 42-gauge plain enamel
Resistance: neck, 7.2k ohms; bridge, 8.1k ohms
Pole pieces: six adjustable threaded steel slot-head poles in one coil, six fixed steel slugs in the other
Sound: intended as an accurate low to moderate-output PAF-style humbucker, complete with unpotted coils and slightly microphonic cover 'honk'.

● Seymour Duncan Pearly Gates
Type: humbucker
Magnet: Alnico II
Wire: 42-gauge plain enamel
Resistance: neck, 7.3k ohms; bridge, 8.4k ohms
Pole pieces: six adjustable threaded steel slot-head poles in one coil, six fixed steel slugs in the other
Sound: intended as moderate-output PAF-style bridge pickup in particular, with hot-vintage voicing – thick, grunty midrange response.

● Seymour Duncan Stag Mag
Type: humbucker
Magnet: Alnico II
Wire: 43-gauge plain enamel
Resistance: neck, 16.2k ohms; bridge, 8.1k ohms
Pole pieces: six fixed alnico rod magnet poles in each coil
Sound: a thick, rich moderate-output humbucker, yet with the added definition and enhanced treble response of rod-magnet pole pieces.

● Seymour Duncan Jazz Model
Type: humbucker
Magnet: Alnico V
Wire: 42-gauge plain enamel
Resistance: neck, 7.7k ohms; bridge, 7.9k ohms
Pole pieces: six adjustable threaded steel slot-head poles in one coil, six fixed steel slugs in the other
Sound: round, warm, smooth jazz humbucker (intended for neck position in particular).

other guitar and pickup makers

● Seymour Duncan P-Rails
Type: humbucker
Magnet: Alnico V
Wire: 42-gauge plain enamel
Resistance: 7.25k ohms P-90 coil, 5.6k ohms bridge coil
Pole pieces: six adjustable threaded steel slot-head poles in one coil, single fixed steel blade in the other
Sound: a tri-sound pickup that offers full humbucker with both coils, or blade single coil or P-90 single coil with either/or selected independently.

● Seymour Duncan JB Model
Type: humbucker
Magnet: Alnico V
Wire: 42-gauge plain enamel
Resistance: bridge, 16.4k ohms
Pole pieces: six adjustable threaded steel slot-head poles in one coil, six fixed steel slugs in the other
Sound: a hot, punchy rock and fusion humbucker with sizzling highs.

● Seymour Duncan Duncan Distortion
Type: humbucker
Magnet: ceramic
Wire: 42-gauge plain enamel
Resistance: neck, 12.7k ohms; bridge, 16.6k ohms
Pole pieces: six adjustable threaded steel slot-head poles in one coil, six fixed steel slugs in the other
Sound: fat, scorching, high-output ceramic humbucker tones.

● Seymour Duncan Duncan Custom
Type: humbucker
Magnet: ceramic
Wire: 42-gauge plain enamel
Resistance: 14k ohms
Pole pieces: six adjustable threaded steel slot-head poles in one coil, six fixed steel slugs in the other
Sound: high-output PAF-style tone.

● Seymour Duncan Custom Custom
Type: humbucker
Magnet: ceramic
Wire: 42-gauge plain enamel
Resistance: 14.4k ohms
Pole pieces: six adjustable threaded steel slot-head poles in one coil, six fixed steel slugs in the other
Sound: high-output humbucker with enhanced warmth and richness for use in bright guitars.

● Seymour Duncan Full Shred
Type: humbucker
Magnet: Alnico V
Wire: 42-gauge plain enamel
Resistance: neck, 7.4k ohms; bridge, 14.6k ohms
Pole pieces: six adjustable threaded steel Allen-key poles in each coil
Sound: hot, super-sustaining pickup for shred styles, with added texture and smoothness from alnico magnet.

● Seymour Duncan George Lynch Screamin' Demon
Type: humbucker
Magnet: Alnico V
Wire: 42-gauge plain enamel
Resistance: 10k ohms
Pole pieces: six adjustable threaded steel slot-head poles in one coil, six adjustable threaded steel Allen-key poles in the other
Sound: medium-output humbucker with enhanced cut and high end.

● Seymour Duncan Invader
Type: ceramic
Magnet: ceramic
Wire: 42-gauge plain enamel
Resistance: neck, 7.2k ohms; bridge, 16.8k ohms
Pole pieces: six adjustable threaded steel Allen-key, dome-head bolts in each coil
Sound: super-hot humbucker for metal-style lead guitar tones.

other guitar and pickup makers

● Seymour Duncan Dimebucker
Type: humbucker
Magnet: ceramic
Wire: 42-gauge plain enamel
Resistance: 16.25k ohms
Pole pieces: single fixed steel blade pole in each coil
Sound: fat, aggressive, high-output humbucker for sizzling led tones and super-crunch rhythm playing.

● Seymour Duncan Custom 8
Type: humbucker
Magnet: Alnico VIII
Wire: N/A
Resistance: 17.68k ohms
Pole pieces: six adjustable threaded steel slot-head poles in one coil, six fixed steel slugs in the other
Sound: high-output humbucker with classic warmth but enhanced attack, using unusual Alnico VIII magnet.

● Seymour Duncan Original Parallel Axis Trembucker
Type: humbucker
Magnet: Alnico V
Wire: 42-gauge plain enamel
Resistance: neck, 7.5k ohms; bridge, 15.7k ohms
Pole pieces: twelve paired fixed steel bar poles in each coil
Sound: a high-output contemporary humbucker with a broad frequency response and excellent clarity.

● Seymour Duncan Distortion Parallel Axis Trembucker
Type: humbucker
Magnet: ceramic
Wire: N/A
Resistance: bridge, 21.3k ohms
Pole pieces: twelve paired fixed steel bar poles in each coil
Sound: a super-high-output contemporary humbucker with enhanced lows, screaming highs, but good clarity.

● Seymour Duncan Blues Saraceno Parallel Axis Trembucker
Type: humbucker
Magnet: Alnico V
Wire: 42-gauge plain enamel
Resistance: bridge, 9.8k ohms
Pole pieces: twelve paired fixed steel bar poles in each coil
Sound: a moderate-output contemporary humbucker intended to capture enhanced-PAF sound for vibrato-equipped guitars.

● Seymour Duncan Blackouts
Type: humbucker
Magnet: Alnico V neck, ceramic bridge
Wire: N/A
Resistance: N/A
Pole pieces: fixed steel poles
Sound: a high-output active humbucker for rock and nu-metal styles.

● Seymour Duncan Blackouts Metal
Type: humbucker
Magnet: Alnico V neck
Wire: N/A
Resistance: N/A
Pole pieces: fixed steel poles
Sound: increased attack and aggression when compared to original Blackouts.

● Seymour Duncan Livewire Classic II
Type: humbucker
Magnet: Alnico II
Wire: N/A
Resistance: N/A
Pole pieces: fixed steel poles
Sound: a well balanced, high-output active humbucker using Alnico II magnet for smooth, slightly compressed response.

● Seymour Duncan Dave Mustaine Livewires
Type: humbucker
Magnet: Alnico V
Wire: N/A
Resistance: N/A
Pole pieces: fixed steel poles
Sound: a full, rich, high-output active humbucker designed for shred-rocker Mustaine.

other guitar and pickup makers

● Seymour Duncan Livewire Metal
Type: humbucker
Magnet: Alnico V
Wire: N/A
Resistance: N/A
Pole pieces: fixed steel poles
Sound: active humbucker with increased output and grind when compared to original Livewire model.

● Seymour Duncan Alnico II Pro Strat (Flat or Staggered)
Type: single coil
Magnet: Alnico II
Wire: 42-gauge heavy Formvar
Resistance: 6.4k ohms
Pole pieces: six fixed alnico rod magnet poles with beveled tops
Sound: traditional bright, clear, bell-like Stratocaster tone, but with added smoothness from Alnico II.

● Seymour Duncan Hot Strat
Type: single coil
Magnet: Alnico V
Wire: N/A
Resistance: 16.4k ohms (8.8k ohms tapped)
Pole pieces: six fixed alnico rod magnet poles with beveled tops
Sound: a hot single-coil tone with increased midrange, plus clearer, brighter tapped tone.

● Seymour Duncan Quarter Pound Strat (Flat or Staggered)
Type: single coil
Magnet: Alnico V
Wire: N/A
Resistance: 14k ohms (7k ohms tapped)
Pole pieces: six fixed poles made from extra-thick quarter-inch alnico rod magnets
Sound: fat, mid-forward, high-output single-coil tone.

● Seymour Duncan Custom Strat (Flat or Staggered)
Type: single coil
Magnet: Alnico V
Wire: N/A
Resistance: 13k ohms (6.6k ohms tapped, Staggered only)
Pole pieces: six fixed alnico rod magnet poles
Sound: enhanced body and warmth to temper bright guitars.

● Seymour Duncan Vintage Strat (Flat or Staggered)
Type: single coil
Magnet: Alnico V
Wire: 42-gauge heavy Formvar
Resistance: 6.5k ohms
Pole pieces: six fixed alnico rod magnet poles with beveled tops
Sound: traditional bright, clear, bell-like Stratocaster tone with plenty of snap and bite.

● Seymour Duncan Five Two Strat
Type: single coil
Magnet: Alnico II & V
Wire: 42-gauge heavy Formvar
Resistance: 6.7k ohms (Custom Bridge version 6.9k ohms)
Pole pieces: six fixed, staggered alnico rod magnet poles with beveled tops, with Alnico II & V mixed three and three
Sound: enhanced-vintage Strat-style tones, with Alnico V on the three wound strings for added punch, and Alnico II on the plain strings for a softer, smoother response.

● Seymour Duncan Lipstick Tube for Strat
Type: single coil
Magnet: Alnico V
Wire: N/A
Resistance: 4.3k ohms
Pole pieces: alnico bar magnet within coil
Sound: bright, clear, trebly pickup styles like Danelectro Lipstick Tube, but to fit Stratocaster-style mounting and routing.

● Seymour Duncan Twang Banger
Type: single coil
Magnet: Alnico II
Wire: N/A
Resistance: 8.3k ohms
Pole pieces: six fixed, staggered alnico rod magnet poles
Sound: a hot single-coil Strat replacement with added steel base plate for Tele-like twang tones.

other guitar and pickup makers

● Seymour Duncan Parallel Axis Single Coil Stack
Type: hum-canceling 'single-coil' sized
Magnet: ceramic
Wire: 42-gauge plain enamel
Resistance: 6.8k ohms
Pole pieces: twelve paired fixed steel bar poles
Sound: a moderate-output contemporary stacked-humbucker with a broad frequency response and good clarity, intended for the neck position in particular.

● Seymour Duncan Hot Rails
Type: hum-canceling 'single-coil' sized
Magnet: ceramic
Wire: N/A
Resistance: neck, 10.8k ohms; bridge, 16.9k ohms
Pole pieces: single fixed steel blade in each coil
Sound: super-hot narrow-profile ceramic pickup for Strat-type guitars, with major output and sustain.

● Seymour Duncan Vintage Rails
Type: hum-canceling 'single-coil' sized
Magnet: ceramic
Wire: N/A
Resistance: neck, 9.4k ohms; bridge, 10.3k ohms
Pole pieces: single fixed steel blade in each coil
Sound: a moderate-output pickups, cleaner, bluesier version of the Hot Rails.

● Seymour Duncan Vintage Rails
Type: hum-canceling 'single-coil' sized
Magnet: ceramic
Wire: N/A
Resistance: neck, 2.3k ohms; bridge, 2.7k ohms
Pole pieces: two-part fixed steel blade in each coil
Sound: sweet, clean, vintage-voiced version of the Rails line.

● Seymour Duncan Duck Buckers
Type: hum-canceling 'single-coil' sized
Magnet: ceramic
Wire: N/A
Resistance: neck, 2.6k ohms; bridge, 3k ohms
Pole pieces: three adjustable threaded steel poles and single fixed (unseen) steel blade in each coil (staggered/offset design)
Sound: clean, vintage-voiced tones in a narrow-'bucker design.

● Seymour Duncan JB Jr.
Type: hum-canceling 'single-coil' sized
Magnet: ceramic
Wire: N/A
Resistance: neck, 9.6k ohms; bridge, 16k ohms
Pole pieces: six adjustable threaded steel poles in each coil
Sound: single-coil-sized version of the full-sized JB humbucker; hot, creamy, with sizzling highs.

● Seymour Duncan Li'l Screamin' Demon
Type: hum-canceling 'single-coil' sized
Magnet: ceramic
Wire: N/A
Resistance: neck, 9.7k ohms; bridge, 13.4k ohms
Pole pieces: six adjustable threaded steel poles in each coil
Sound: single-coil-sized version of the full-sized George Lynch Screamin' Demon humbucker; hot, aggressive, punchy, but with decent definition.

● Seymour Duncan Li'l '59
Type: hum-canceling 'single-coil' sized
Magnet: ceramic
Wire: N/A
Resistance: neck, 9.8k ohms; bridge, 11.8k ohms
Pole pieces: six adjustable threaded steel poles in each coil
Sound: single-coil-sized version of the '59 Model humbucker; smooth, hot-PAF-style tones, with extra punch and treble bite.

● Seymour Duncan Stack Plus
Type: hum-canceling 'single-coil' design
Magnet: Alnico V
Wire: N/A
Resistance: neck, 9.6k ohms; bridge, 10.4k ohms
Pole pieces: six fixed alnico rod magnet poles in upper string-sensing coil, with smaller noise-elimination coil beneath
Sound: medium-output single-coil style pickup with good hum rejection thanks to stacked-coil design.

● Seymour Duncan Hot Stack
Type: hum-canceling 'single-coil' design
Magnet: ceramic
Wire: N/A
Resistance: neck, 13.2k ohms; bridge, 20.6k ohms
Pole pieces: six fixed steel poles
Sound: super-high-output hum-rejecting replacement for single coil Strat pickups; thick, chunky and aggressive.

other guitar and pickup makers

● Seymour Duncan Livewire Classic II
Type: active single coil
Magnet: Alnico II
Wire: N/A
Resistance: N/A
Pole pieces: six fixed alnico rod magnet poles
Sound: active medium-output pickup for Strat; broad frequency response and enhanced attack for rock guitar.

● Seymour Duncan Blackouts Singles
Type: active single coil
Magnet: Alnico V
Wire: N/A
Resistance: N/A
Pole pieces: six fixed poles made from alnico rod magnets
Sound: high-output contemporary single-coil rock tone.

● Seymour Duncan Vintage Broadcaster Lead
Type: single coil
Magnet: Alnico V
Wire: 42-gauge plain enamel
Resistance: 7.6k ohms
Pole pieces: six fixed alnico rod magnet poles
Sound: twangy, somewhat 'nasal' Tele tone with snap, definition and good midrange body.

● Seymour Duncan Vintage '54 Tele
Type: single coil
Magnet: Alnico V
Wire: 43-gauge neck; 42-gauge plain enamel bridge
Resistance: neck, 7.3k ohms; bridge, 7.2k ohms
Pole pieces: six fixed alnico rod magnet poles
Sound: bright, punchy twang in bridge position; warm and round in neck.

● Seymour Duncan Vintage Hot Tele
Type: single coil
Magnet: Alnico V
Wire: N/A
Resistance: bridge, 15.6k ohms (7.4k tapped); neck, 9.7k ohms
Pole pieces: six fixed alnico rod magnet poles
Sound: fat, crunchy, mid-forward hot-Tele set.

● Seymour Duncan Quarter Pound Tele
Type: single coil
Magnet: Alnico V
Wire: N/A
Resistance: bridge, 17.4k ohms (8k ohms tapped); neck, 11.8k ohms (6.6k ohms tapped)
Pole pieces: six fixed poles made from extra-thick quarter-inch alnico rod magnets
Sound: thick, mid-forward, high-output single-coil tone with enhanced sustain.

● Seymour Duncan Alnico II Pro
Type: single coil
Magnet: Alnico V
Wire: 42-gauge plain enamel bridge, 43-gauge neck
Resistance: bridge, 6.2k ohms; neck, 8.1k ohms
Pole pieces: six fixed alnico rod magnet poles
Sound: traditional snappy, twangy Tele tone, but with softer attack thanks to Alnico II magnets.

● Seymour Duncan Five Two Tele
Type: single coil
Magnet: Alnico II & V
Wire: 42-gauge plain enamel bridge, 43-gauge neck
Resistance: bridge, 7.5k ohms; neck, 7.9k ohms
Pole pieces: six fixed, staggered alnico rod magnet poles with beveled tops, with Alnico II & V mixed three and three
Sound: enhanced-vintage Tele-style tones, with Alnico V on the three wound strings for added punch, and Alnico II on the plain strings for a softer, smoother response.

● Seymour Duncan Vintage Stack Tele
Type: hum-canceling 'single-coil' sized
Magnet: Alnico V
Wire: N/A
Resistance: bridge, 18k ohms; neck, 15.9k ohms
Pole pieces: six fixed, staggered alnico rod magnet poles
Sound: thick, mid-heavy, single-coil-styled tone with good hum rejection.

other guitar and pickup makers

● Seymour Duncan Hot Stack Tele
Type: hum-canceling 'single-coil' sized
Magnet: Alnico V
Wire: 42-gauge heavy Formvar
Resistance: 21.4k ohms
Pole pieces: fixed steel bar pole
Sound: super-hot, mega-sustain, rock-minded pickup for the Tele bridge position.

● Seymour Duncan Little '59 Tele
Type: hum-canceling 'single-coil' sized
Magnet: ceramic
Wire: N/A
Resistance: 17k ohms
Pole pieces: six adjustable threaded steel poles in each coil
Sound: single-coil-sized version of the '59 Model humbucker; smooth, hot-PAF-style tones, with extra punch and treble bite.

● Seymour Duncan Hot Rails Tele
Type: hum-canceling 'single-coil' sized
Magnet: ceramic
Wire: N/A
Resistance: 14.8k ohms
Pole pieces: single fixed steel blade in each coil
Sound: super-hot narrow-profile ceramic pickup for bridge position of Tele-type guitars, with major output and sustain.

● Seymour Duncan Vintage P-90 Soapbar
Type: single coil
Magnet: Alnico V
Wire: 42-gauge plain enamel
Resistance: neck, 8.2k ohms; bridge, 9.35k ohms
Pole pieces: six adjustable threaded steel slot-head poles
Sound: fat, gritty, snarly single-coil tone – toward the medium-hot side of the vintage-P-90 spectrum.

● Seymour Duncan Hot P-90 Soapbar
Type: single coil
Magnet: ceramic
Wire: N/A
Resistance: neck, 11.8k ohms; bridge, 15k ohms
Pole pieces: six adjustable threaded steel slot-head poles
Sound: two small ceramic bar magnets employed here for a thick, punchy, compressed, rock-minded P-90 tone.

● Seymour Duncan Custom P-90 Soapbar
Type: single coil
Magnet: ceramic
Wire: N/A
Resistance: neck, 12 ohms; bridge, 14.6k ohms
Pole pieces: six adjustable threaded steel slot-head poles
Sound: two large ceramic bar magnets employed here for a hotter, snarlier performance than the Hot P-90, above.

● Seymour Duncan P-90 Stack
Type: hum-canceling 'single-coil' sized
Magnet: Alnico V
Wire: N/A
Resistance: neck, 10.7k ohms; bridge, 15.8k ohms
Pole pieces: six adjustable threaded steel slot-head poles
Sound: contemporary P-90 voicings for rock, with good hum rejection.

● Seymour Duncan Phat Cat
Type: single coil
Magnet: Alnico II
Wire: 42-gauge plain enamel
Resistance: neck, 8k ohms; bridge, 8.5k ohms
Pole pieces: six adjustable threaded steel slot-head poles
Sound: rendition of a P-90 in a cover designed to fit standard humbucker mounting.

● Seymour Duncan Hot Jaguar
Type: single coil
Magnet: Alnico V
Wire: N/A
Resistance: neck, 11.5k ohms; bridge, 12.3k ohms
Pole pieces: six fixed alnico rod magnet poles
Sound: thick, snappy, aggressive single-coil tone for the underserved Fender 24-incher.

● Seymour Duncan Quarter Pound Jaguar
Type: single coil
Magnet: Alnico V
Wire: N/A
Resistance: neck, 11.7k ohms; bridge, 14k ohms
Pole pieces: six fixed poles made from extra-thick quarter-inch alnico rod magnets
Sound: thick, snappy, aggressive single-coil tone for the underserved Fender 24-incher, MkII.

other guitar and pickup makers

● Seymour Duncan Hot Jazzmaster
Type: single coil
Magnet: Alnico V
Wire: N/A
Resistance: neck, 11k ohms; bridge, 14k ohms
Pole pieces: six fixed alnico rod magnet poles
Sound: round, rich, punchy single-coil tone for the one with the wide pickups.

● Seymour Duncan Quarter Pound Jazzmaster
Type: single coil
Magnet: Alnico V
Wire: N/A
Resistance: neck, 11.8k ohms; bridge, 13k ohms
Pole pieces: six fixed poles made from extra-thick quarter-inch alnico rod magnets
Sound: round, rich, punchy single-coil tone for the one with the wide pickups, MkII.

EMG

Founder Rob Turner started EMG in the back of his parents' garage in 1974, having tinkered with pickups since 1969. His work in electronics originally included amplifier repairs and the building of other items of musical electronics, but focused on EMG pickups toward the end of the 1970s, via the company names Dirtywork Studios and (in 1978) Overlend, a name chosen because the venture was so badly over-extended on credit. The company name was finally changed to EMG, Inc. in 1983, although the three-letter acronym – short for Electro-Magnetic Generator – is the name Turner gave to his pickups from the very start.

Although EMG has also designed and manufactured passive pickups since 1984, the company is far and away best know for its active low-impedance pickups. This book doesn't deal with the technology behind active low-impedance pickups in any great detail, but EMG is worth a mention nevertheless, because it remains a significant player in the market, with the rock and heavy metal crowd in particular. Good, active low-impedance pickups display a broad, even frequency response, great character and detail, and a low-noise performance – and many EMG units offer those qualities in spades. Such units can also be used with extra-long cable runs without loss of highs and a generally dulling of overall tone, caused by the loading that cables of more than 20-feet long can put on your guitar's signal. Active pickups do require a preamp to give them enough oomph to pump that low-impedance signal on down the line, and EMG takes care of this necessity by mounting a miniature preamp circuit right inside each pickup, all of which is sealed in epoxy along with the pickup components themselves. Such a configuration allows for pickups that can be voiced as desired without compromises due to considerations regarding

EMG 81 top and bottom

other guitar and pickup makers

● EMG H1
Type: humbucker
Magnet: ceramic
Wire: N/A
Resistance: 13.65k ohms
Pole pieces: six adjustable threaded steel slot-head poles in one coil, six fixed steel slugs in the other
Sound: a hot humbucker with enhanced punch and attack, yet good clarity.

● EMG H1A
Type: humbucker
Magnet: alnico
Wire: N/A
Resistance: 13.65k ohms
Pole pieces: six adjustable threaded steel slot-head poles in one coil, six fixed steel slugs in the other
Sound: similar to that of the H1A, but with a warmer, smoother response with less high-end presence.

● EMG H2
Type: humbucker
Magnet: ceramic
Wire: N/A
Resistance: 8.4k ohms
Pole pieces: six adjustable threaded steel slot-head poles in one coil, six fixed steel slugs in the other
Sound: 'hotrod vintage' tone in a contemporary package.

● EMG H2A
Type: humbucker
Magnet: alnico
Wire: N/A
Resistance: 8.4k ohms
Pole pieces: six adjustable threaded steel slot-head poles in one coil, six fixed steel slugs in the other
Sound: smooth mids, punchy lows in a vintage-voiced contemporary humbucker.

● EMG H3
Type: humbucker
Magnet: ceramic
Wire: N/A
Resistance: 13.65k ohms
Pole pieces: six fixed steel slugs in each coil
Sound: much as the H1 above, but with improved hum rejection.

● EMG H3A
Type: humbucker
Magnet: alnico
Wire: N/A
Resistance: 13.65k ohms
Pole pieces: six fixed steel slugs in each coil
Sound: warmer, smoother response than H3 with less high-end presence.

● EMG H4
Type: humbucker
Magnet: ceramic
Wire: N/A
Resistance: 13.65k ohms
Pole pieces: steel bar pole within each coil
Sound: passive equivalent to active 81 humbucker, with hot, sizzling lead tone.

● EMG H4A
Type: humbucker
Magnet: alnico
Wire: N/A
Resistance: 13.65k ohms
Pole pieces: steel bar pole within each coil
Sound: a high-output humbucker that's a little warmer and smoother than the H4 thanks to an alnico bar magnet rather than ceramic.

● EMG S1
Type: hum-canceling 'single coil' size
Magnet: alnico
Wire: N/A
Resistance: 11k ohms
Pole pieces: six alnico bar magnet poles
Sound: a high-output Strat replacement pickup with prominent midrange and good noise rejection.

other guitar and pickup makers

● EMG S2
Type: hum-canceling 'single coil' size
Magnet: alnico
Wire: N/A
Resistance: 6.6k ohms
Pole pieces: six alnico bar magnet poles
Sound: bright, percussive, snappy vintage-voiced Strat replacement.

● EMG S1
Type: hum-canceling 'single coil' size
Magnet: alnico
Wire: N/A
Resistance: 11k ohms
Pole pieces: six alnico bar magnet poles
Sound: a high-output Strat replacement pickup with prominent midrange and good noise rejection.

output level, with any desirable output achievable (within reason) thanks to the internal preamp. Put more simply, creating a brighter pickup with better string definition doesn't necessarily require a sacrifice in output level, as it often does in the making of passive, high-impedance pickups.

Specs for individual pickups in EMG's active range would mean little alongside those for the majority of pickups in this book, but brief descriptions of the tone and intentions of some models tells you something about what the range offers. Turner's original EMG designs of 1974 are still available in the form of the H and the HA, both round, full-frequencied, more traditional sounding humbuckers with ceramic and alnico magnets respectively. The 81 is one of EMG's most popular humbuckers for high-gain rock lead guitar, and offers sizzling attack and impressive sustain, with good clarity amid saturated high-gain amplifier distortion. The 85 is still a high-output humbucker, but uses alnico in place of the 81's ceramic magnet, and is voiced for a smoother, more natural tone. Zakk Wylde, for one, uses an 81 in the bridge and an 85 in the neck of his Gibson Les Paul Bullseye signature model, and EMG recommends them in this configuration. The 60 is a ceramic humbucker with close-aperture coils for a bright, well-defined tone. It's still a high-output rocker, though, and is the choice of many crunch-rocking metal rhythm players, such as Metallica's James Hetfield. The 60A variant warms up the formula a little with help from an alnico magnet structure. The 89 is a genuine two-pickups-in-one design, offering humbucking and single-coil modes, while the 91 is a floating jazz pickup originally designed for guitarist Ron Eschete. P-90-sized variations on many of these themes are available as the P81, P85, P60 and P60A, while the active single-coil line caters for a range of output and voicing requirements – 'enhanced vintage Strat' tones from the alnico SA, for example, as used by David Gilmour and Steve Lukather; a brighter, more contemporary sound from the S, and so on. Two replacement sets for Telecaster are also available as the

other guitar and pickup makers

FT/RT and FTC/RTC pairs. EMG declares that the FT – the neck-position unit from the first of these Tele sets – is "undoubtedly the best pickup we make."

The passive high-Z pickups have never acquired quite the kudos of EMG's active pickups, but are well-constructed units nonetheless, and aim again at the rock market primarily, although they offer some more traditional tones too. Specs here bear comparison with other high-Z pickups, but a few particulars of construction are worth mentioning. All humbuckers feature EMG's 'Quik Connect' wiring system, with a five-pin connection at the pickup and specially made cables that provide for a number of switching options. Many of these models use the traditional, PAF-style format of one coil with adjustable threaded poles beside another with fixed steel slugs, although the H3 and H4 employ two identical coils with fixed slugs in order to maximize hum rejection. All passive EMG Stratocaster replacement pickups are low-noise types, the S1, S2 and S3 being 'stacked' humbuckers, while the S4 uses side-by-side coils with 'rail' poles. Both of the P-90-sized passives, the P91 and P92, are side-by-side humbuckers in a compact housing.

Lindy Fralin

Guitarist and coil-winder supreme Lindy Fralin has been one of the top names in the field since the early days of what we might call 'the latest boutique pickup boom'. Fralin began making his own pickups some 25 years ago, and rose to prominence as a small maker of note through the course of the 1990s, and now heads a small team of skilled pickup-makers in his facility in Richmond, VA. (You can read his views on coils, magnets and tone in the full interview in the *Meet the Makers* section of this book.)

The lion's share of Fralin's output involves contemporary renderings of vintage pickup designs from Fender and Gibson, but he gives the venture a twist by being extremely receptive to custom orders. To use his Telecaster bridge replacements as an example, the 'standard' line includes four variations: Stock (at 6.6k ohms standard with 42-gauge wire), Blues Specials (7.3k with 42-gauge wire), High Output (9.5k with 43-gauge wire), and Steel Poled (7.5k with 42-gauge wire and magnet beneath threaded steel poles; or 7k to 9k with 43-gauge wire). But each of these can also be wound to request at the customer's desired percentage over the standard wind – say, a further 2 percent above the Blues Special wind – made with three different magnet staggers, and made with either Alnico V or Alnico III magnets, or a half-and-half mix of the two (Steel Poles excepted on these final options). Similar options apply to the Stratocaster-style

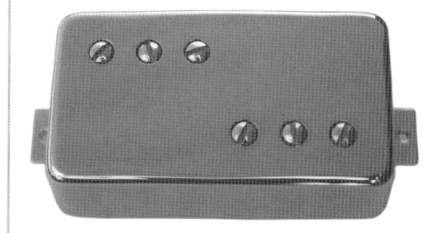

Lindy Fralin P-92

Fralin P-90 Alnico
Type: single-coil
Magnet: Alnico V
Wire: 42-gauge plain enamel
Resistance: 7k to 10k ohms, as desired
Pole pieces: six alnico bar magnet poles
Sound: an alnico-pole pickup housed in a traditional P-90 bobbin; thick, meaty, yet twangy – blend of P-90 and Jazzmaster tone.

Fralin P-92
Type: hum-canceling
Magnet: Alnico V
Wire: 42-gauge plain enamel
Resistance: 7k to 10k ohms, as desired
Pole pieces: six adjustable threaded steel poles
Sound: beefy yet well-defined single-coil tone with good noise rejection thanks to the staggered 3/3 split coil design.

Fralin Twangmaster
Type: hum-canceling
Magnet: Alnico V
Wire: 42-gauge plain enamel
Resistance: 7k to 10k ohms, as desired
Pole pieces: six fixed alnico rod magnet poles
Sound: similar to P-92, with more twang and bite, with good noise rejection thanks to the staggered 3/3 split coil design.

Fralin Unbucker
Type: humbucker
Magnet: Alnico V
Wire: 42-gauge plain enamel
Resistance: 7.5k to 10k ohms, as desired
Pole pieces: six adjustable threaded steel poles in one coil, six fixed steel slugs in the other (the latter with far fewer turns of wire)
Sound: a PAF-styled humbucker that has more edge, cut and definition than the traditional variation on the theme, and which splits coils very effectively for authentic single-coil sound.

Fralin High Output Humbucker
Type: humbucker
Magnet: Alnico IV
Wire: 43-gauge plain enamel
Resistance: 12.5k to 13.5k ohms
Pole pieces: six adjustable threaded steel poles in one coil, six fixed steel slugs in the other
Sound: a rocking high-output humbucker (duh!) with added midrange aggression and sizzling cut in high-gain amps, which retains good note definition.

Fralin High Steel Poled 42
Type: single coil
Magnet: Alnico V
Wire: 42-gauge plain enamel
Resistance: 6k to 7.5k ohms
Pole pieces: six adjustable threaded steel poles, with alnico bar magnets mounted beneath
Sound: variations for Stratocaster and Telecaster, all offering a grittier, thicker tone than the traditional alnico rod magnet variations

Fralin High Steel Poled 43
Type: single coil
Magnet: Alnico V
Wire: 43-gauge plain enamel
Resistance: 8.5k to 10k ohms
Pole pieces: six adjustable threaded steel poles, with alnico bar magnets mounted beneath
Sound: higher-output variation of the Steel Poled 42 above, wound with finer coil wire.

Fralin Steel Poled 42
Type: single coil
Magnet: Alnico V
Wire: 42-gauge plain enamel
Resistance: 6k to 7.5k ohms
Pole pieces: six adjustable threaded steel poles, with alnico bar magnets mounted beneath
Sound: variations for Stratocaster and Telecaster, all offering a grittier, thicker tone than the traditional alnico rod magnet variations.

other guitar and pickup makers

> **● Fralin Steel Poled 43**
> **Type:** single coil
> **Magnet:** Alnico V
> **Wire:** 43-gauge plain enamel
> **Resistance:** 8.5k to 10k ohms
> **Pole pieces:** six adjustable threaded steel poles, with alnico bar magnets mounted beneath
> **Sound:** higher-output variation of the Steel Poled 42 above, wound with finer coil wire.

> **● Fralin Steel Poled Jazzmaster**
> **Type:** single coil
> **Magnet:** Alnico V
> **Wire:** 42-gauge plain enamel
> **Resistance:** 6k to 10k ohms (wound to order)
> **Pole pieces:** six adjustable threaded steel poles, with alnico bar magnets mounted beneath
> **Sound:** a pickup to fit the Fender Jazzmaster that is built more like a Gibson P-90, offering a grittier, thicker tone than the traditional alnico rod magnet Jazzmaster pickups.

single coils, while PAF-style humbuckers come in six DC resistance ratings from 7.5k to 10k ohms, all wound with 42-gauge plain enamel wire, plus a High Output variant wound with 43-gauge wire to from 12.5k to 13.5k ohms. Fralin has long been known as a maker of superior P-90 replacement pickups, too, where his thoughts on *under*winding these wide single coils for a cleaner tone and better note definition has caught on with a lot of players, and his line up also now carries replacements for Fender Mustang and Jazzmaster models, and a floating jazz-style humbucker.

Beyond the extremely user-friendly catalog of direct replacement pickups, however, Fralin has also coined a few custom designs that have made waves in a market that's ever hot for new variations on beloved themes. His Unbucker could be described as a 'semi-humbucker', perhaps, and looks like a standard PAF-styled humbucker, but uses two coils with considerable mismatches in their number of winds, for example, a screw coil wound to 5k ohms with a slug coil wound to only 3.5k ohms, for a pickup that measures 8.5k ohms. The result is a humbucker that offers a little more cut and definition, but one that also splits into a far more authentic single-coil mode when the slug coil is grounded off using a push/pull pot or toggle switch; the compromise here is of course that hum rejection is weakened but the use of two such mismatched coils.

Taking the 'bucker-sized-single-coil thinking a step further, Fralin also offers two forms of 'Split Singles', single-coil-style pickups housed in humbucker sized covers and mounts. The first is the P-92, a pickup that is in fact a dual-coil hum-canceling design, but which carries one three-pole coil under the treble strings at the back of the housing, and another three-pole coil under the bass strings at the front of the housing, with these two staggered coils wound reverse phase/reverse polarity to reject unwanted noise. The second is the

other guitar and pickup makers

Twangmaster, which follows the P-92 formula but uses Alnico V rod magnet poles for a brighter, twangier tone. Fralin's P-90 range also includes an alnico-pole version that brings more cut and treble to players of guitars that were born with traditional P-90s. In addition to the manufactured line, Fralin also still offers pickup rewinding, repair and repotting services.

G&L

From the perspective of the history and development of electromagnetic guitar pickups, the story of G&L isn't so much the story of an arguably under-rated US guitar-maker, but the story of *what Leo did next*. Upon founding G&L (for George and Leo) with George Fullerton in 1979, Leo Fender proceeded to put into play many of the somewhat radical ideas with which he had experimented during his lame-duck consultancy with Fender under CBS in the late 1960s, and in the process created a new line of guitars that was at once both identifiably 'Fenderish' and clearly something other. While the use of his three-bolt neck joint and bullet-head truss-rod adjustment systems were part of this, the pickups he created for G&L took the guitar designs further forward than any other element of their make up. More impressively than this, they showed the drive and dynamic of a great inventor who could easily have rested on his laurels – such stellar laurels that he still would have been praised as innovative for the rest of his years – but chose to continue pushing the envelope, to improve on designs that were great but not *perfect*, until his dying day.

Fender's Magnetic Field Design (MFD) pickups for G&L are a radical departure from his traditional single-coil designs for Fender Electric Instruments in the 1950s and '60s, and it takes a brave man to depart from some of the most iconic pickup models of all time. Rather than the fixed alnico rod magnet poles that formed the six beating hearts of the Fender Telecaster, Stratocaster and Jazzmaster pickups, G&L MFD pickups employ ceramic bar magnets beneath soft iron pole pieces, each of which is a two-part construction with a threaded adjustable Allen-head 'bolt' within a fixed 'sleeve'. A patent filed in June 1979, and granted to Leo Fender in September 1980 (which includes drawings of the unit mounted in a guitar that looks strikingly like the early G&L models), describes a pickup that "creates a magnetic field that is significantly stronger and better defined than the magnetic fields created by prior pickups such that the output thereof is rich in harmonics and far more pleasing than the output of pickups of the prior art."

In performance, MFD pickups – which now extend to myriad formats – do

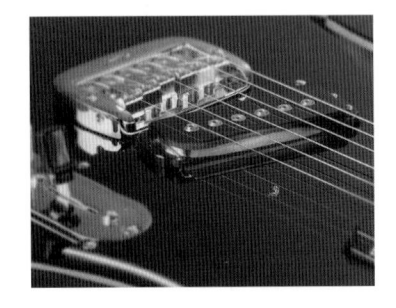

G&L MFD pickup on an ASAT Semi-Hollow, with cover partially cut away to show coil

FACING PAGE **Leo Fender/G&L MFD pickup.**

162 the guitar pickup handbook

other guitar and pickup makers

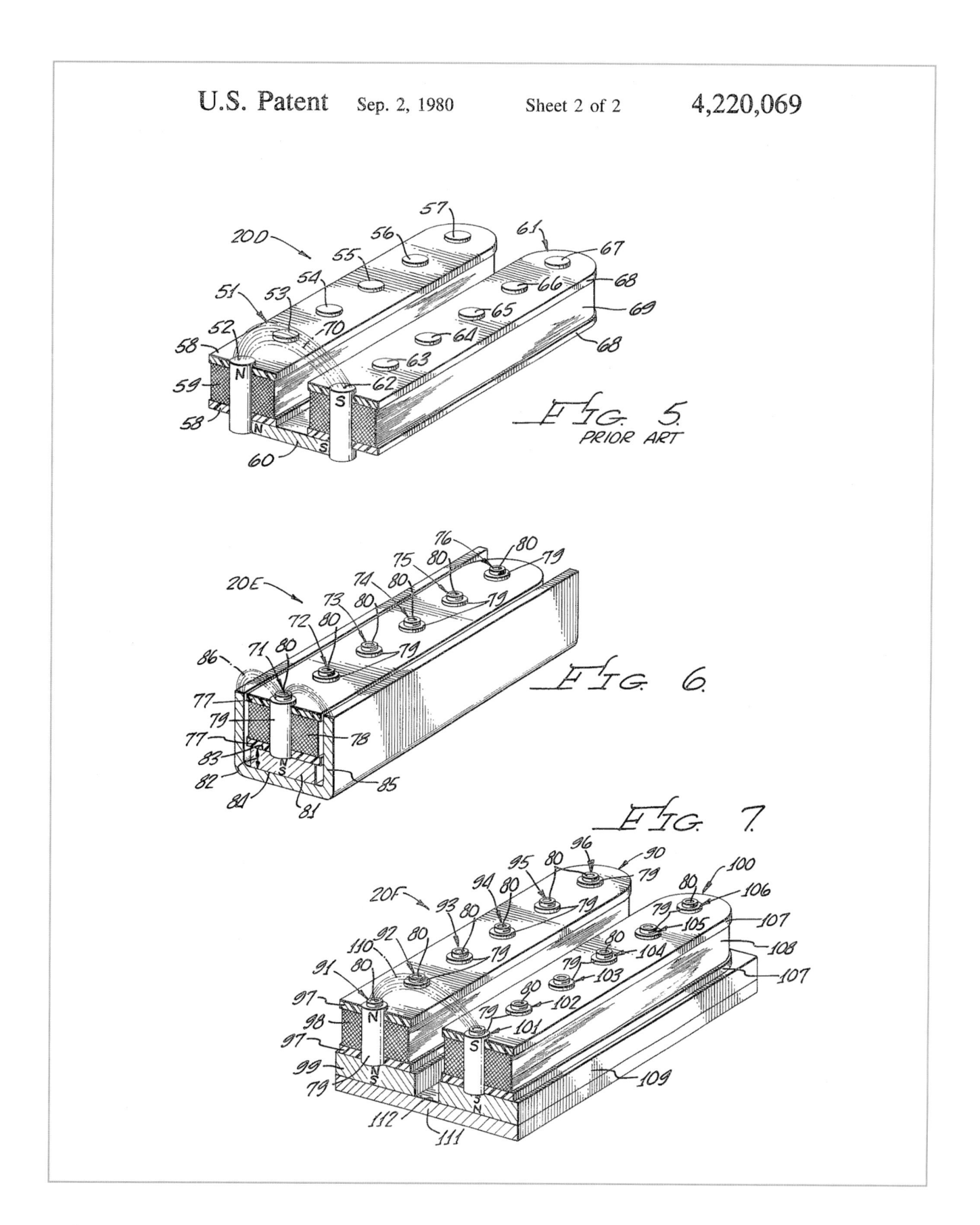

U.S. Patent   Sep. 2, 1980   Sheet 2 of 2   4,220,069

Fig. 5. PRIOR ART

Fig. 6.

Fig. 7.

other guitar and pickup makers

FACING PAGE **Leo Fender/G&L – angled humbucker**

bear out this claim. While their tone isn't necessarily 'un-vintage' in character, or at least can be bent toward vintage-like soundscapes, they yield enhanced definition, attack, and sparkle when compared to conventional alnico-rod pickups. They are also fairly powerful, without being muddy or midrange-humpy, a balancing act achieved by the combination of a ceramic bar magnet, said soft iron pole pieces, and a lower number of turns of coil wire than would be required to produce a similar output from an old-school Fender alnico pickup. This lower number of winds in the coil also contributes to a lower-noise single-coil pickup. MFD pickups aren't to everyone's taste, certainly (and if they were – if any pickup was – a book such of this would be pointless), and some players who have tried them to bemoan the absence of a certain 'softness' or 'smoothness' they experience with traditional alnico pickups, and sometimes the presence of a slightly harsh edge. *Viva la difference*. Plenty of players, on the other hand, find

● G&L MFD (original 'soapbar')
Type: single coil
Magnet: ceramic
Wire: N/A
Resistance: around 4.7k ohms pre-1992, 5k ohms post-1992
Pole pieces: six adjustable threaded soft iron poles
Sound: clear, rich and well defined, yet gutsy and powerful with good midrange grind; occasionally described as a blend of classic Tele bridge and P-90 tones.

● G&L MFD 'narrow cover'
Type: single coil
Magnet: ceramic
Wire: N/A
Resistance: around 4.5k ohms
Pole pieces: six adjustable threaded soft iron poles
Sound: bright and harmonically rich, yet with good body.

● G&L MFD ASAT Classic
Type: single coil
Magnet: ceramic
Wire: N/A
Resistance: bridge, 4.8k ohms pre-1993 (5.1k ohms post-1993); neck, around 4k ohms
Pole pieces: six adjustable threaded soft iron poles
Sound: MFD design for Tele-style mountings; plenty of twang and definition, with muscular midrange presence and good balance throughout the frequency range.

● G&L MFD Z-Coil
Type: hum-canceling
Magnet: ceramic
Wire: N/A
Resistance: 4.5k ohms
Pole pieces: three adjustable threaded soft iron poles in each of two staggered/offset coils
Sound: bright, clear and balanced, with good hum rejection.

● G&L MFD Humbucker
Type: humbucker
Magnet: ceramic
Wire: N/A
Resistance: around 7k ohms
Pole pieces: six adjustable threaded soft iron poles in each coil
Sound: thick and gutsy, yet with good clarity and definition; also splits well in single-coil mode.

other guitar and pickup makers

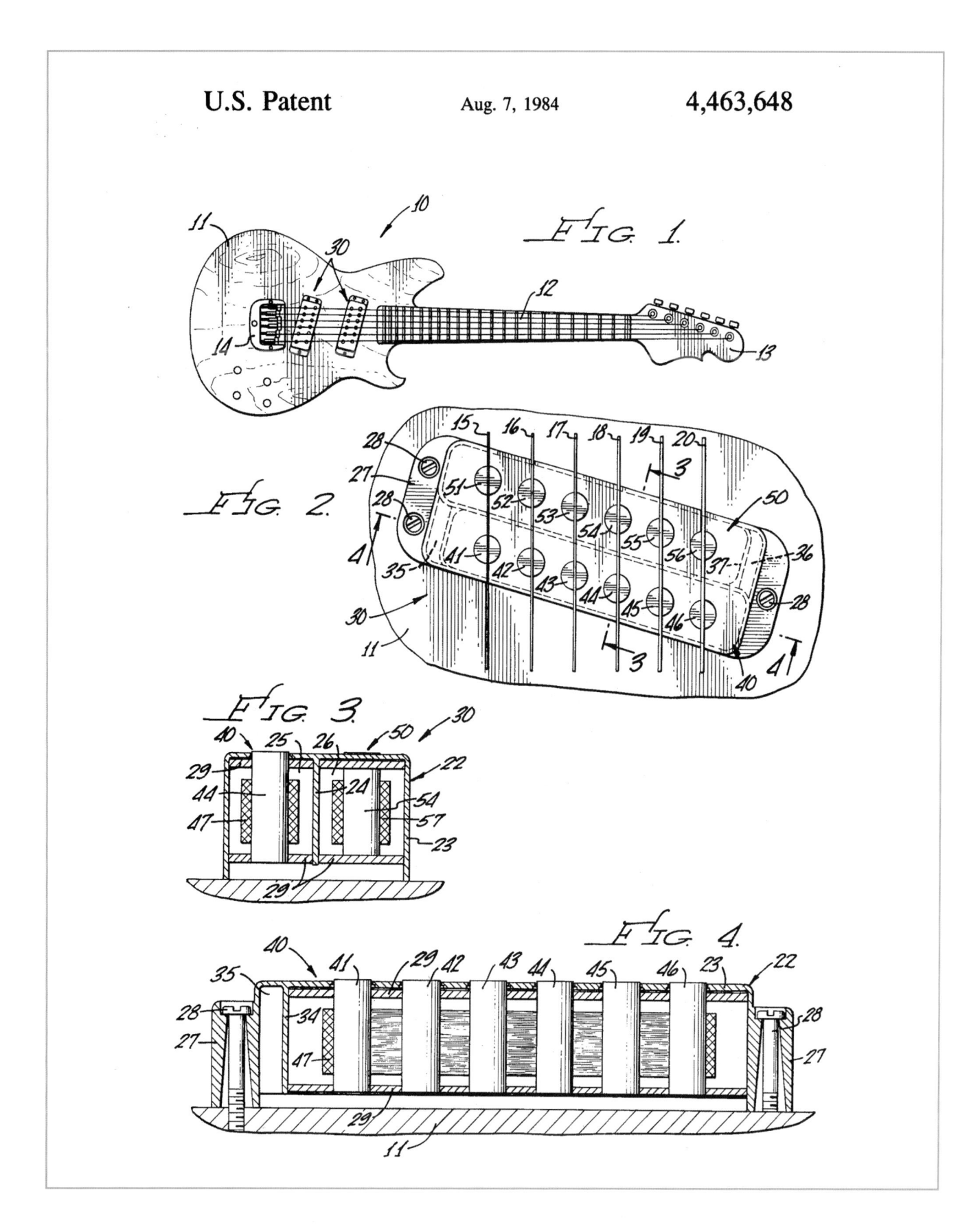

U.S. Patent   Aug. 7, 1984   4,463,648

other guitar and pickup makers

> **● G&L MFD GHB Humbucker**
> **Type:** humbucker
> **Magnet:** ceramic
> **Wire:** N/A
> **Resistance:** around 4.4k ohms
> **Pole pieces:** six adjustable threaded soft iron poles in each coil
> **Sound:** a narrow humbucker designed to fit ASAT guitar mounting; smooth and punchy, with more enhanced treble response when compared to traditional PAF-style humbucker, or full-sized MFD humbucker above.

> **● G&L MFD HG-2R Humbucker ('Angled/Offset')**
> **Type:** humbucker
> **Magnet:** ceramic
> **Wire:** N/A
> **Resistance:** around 4.4k ohms
> **Pole pieces:** six adjustable threaded soft iron poles in each coil
> **Sound:** warm, round, and rich, with good note definition.

them as warm, smooth, and pleasing as desired, among them Will Ray of the Hellecasters, Art Alexakis of Everclear, Jerry Cantrell of Alice in Chains, and Joe Gore with P.J. Harvey, as broad a church of tone crafters as you'd hope to find.

The MFD format has been applied to a wide range of pickups in the G&L line up, including the original units that are often referred to as 'soapbar' MFD, variations for the ASAT Classic and S500/SC-3 and related models (Stratocaster and Telecaster-style guitars respectively), a humbucker, a slant-mount angled/offset humbucker (the offspring of another Fender patent), and the Z-Coil pickup. The latter is a unique staggered-split-coil unit that remains single-coil in sound, but offers hum-canceling thanks to its use of two 3-pole coils that are reverse wound/reverse polarity.

While the MFD is the G&L pickup design of note, alnico-pole pickups have also had a place on this company's guitars. Legacy models from around 1992 to '94 used Seymour Duncan Vintage Series Strat-style pickups, and post-1995 G&L brought the manufacture of alnico pickups in-house for these guitars, as well as for the George Fullerton model. Certain models, such as the ASAT Bluesboy and ASAT Deluxe variations, have also used Seymour Duncan humbuckers in the neck position, a Seth Lover and '59 respectively.

Guild

Many early Guild guitars used DeArmond Model 200 pickups (with white top plates rather than the black of the 'Dynasonics' that DeArmond made for Gretsch), or narrower DeArmond makes with non-adjustable pole pieces, but a couple of Guild's own pickups are worthy of a brief mention here. The first of these, a single coil from the 1950s and early '60s, is often referred to as the Guild 'soapbar' pickup, sometimes in error as a 'P-90' (incorrectly so, since P-90 is a

other guitar and pickup makers

Gibson pickup model), and occasionally referred to in Guild 'Frequency Tested' pickup. It's a pickup that I always like, personally, but I never knew much about the inner workings of them other than that they were indeed slightly 'P-90-ish', but made slightly different, and were a little weaker than the Gibson single coil too. So I turned to the ever-helpful Evan Skopp at Seymour Duncan, who tells us: "The Guild soapbars were constructed like a P-90 but the bobbins were made of vulcanized fiber, not plastic. The bobbins were riveted together and they used slightly smaller magnets than a Gibson P-90." On the whole, these pickups were probably not made quite as well as actual P-90s, and are more prone to microphony, but a good one can also be packed with tonal splendor, with plenty of metallic clank and sizzle, sweet highs, and slightly gritty, meaty lows.

Evan also shed some light on the other notable Guild pickup, the HB-1 humbucker, by informing me that these were actually made by Seymour Duncan for a couple years after Fender Musical Instrument Corp. first bought Guild, after which they were brought in-house once Fender in California was tooled up to do the manufacturing themselves. "They were wound similar to our SH-1 '59 models," says Skopp, "but slightly weaker. We used NOS Guild bottom plates and covers supplied to us by FMIC. We used Seymour Duncan bobbins, but molded them out of a slightly different plastic with a different shrink rat that allowed them to fit the Guild hardware."

Original Guild HB-1 humbuckers from the mid 1960s to the late 1990s offer an interesting take on the PAF formula established by Gibson in the late 1950s. The Guilds are a little brighter and more percussive than the legendary Gibson 'bucker, with a somewhat clearer note-to-note response and a degree of cut and twang that some players really enjoy. They are also slightly weaker pickups than the average PAF, and occasionally more prone to microphonic squeal. In the wake of its ever-expanding Gretsch line up, FMIC has recently ceased production of Guild electrics, while it continues to manufacture a range of Guild acoustic guitars. I don't have any reliable specs for the Guild 'soapbar' and HB-1; suffice to say they are fairly standard constructions of alnico and steel, with occasionally rather loosely-wound coils, and offer an interesting, edgy alternative in low-output tone.

Harmonic Design

Since its founding by Scott Petersen in 1983, this small Bakersfield, CA manufacturer has made a name for itself by providing solutions to tonal puzzles for guitarists eager to go beyond the plethora of vintage-reproduction-style

other guitar and pickup makers

pickups on the market. Harmonic Design does make a couple of very well-respected, vintage-voiced replacement in the form of its '54 Special Tele and '54 Special Strat pickups (although even these use original twists such as off-spec glass-fiber bobbins), but the company has made its mark more with a handful of original designs that nevertheless drop right in as retrofit replacements for classic guitar models.

The Vintage Plus pickups for Telecaster and Stratocaster style guitars use a magnet mounted beneath fixed steel pole pieces to create a more powerful pickup that nevertheless retains the clarity and definition that Fender players require in their tone. The Super 90 for Tele and Strat kicks the formula more toward P-90 territory, with adjustable pole pieces and a somewhat crunchier sound. The Vintage Plus Humbuckers, designed from the ground up to suit the sonic requirements of either the bridge or the neck position, are designed to achieve more depth, breadth, and dynamic response than traditional humbuckers. Harmonic Design Z-90s, on the other hand, were one of the first successful pickups to address a recent fad: the attainment of single-coil tone in a humbucker-sized pickup. Looking outwardly like a rendition of the Gibson P-90 in a wider bobbin, they use fixed steel pole pieces with a magnet beneath to produce a fat, open, highly textured tone.

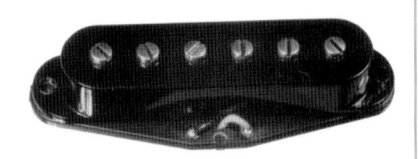

Harmonic Design Super 90 S

Harmonic Design Vintage Plus with tortoiseshell top plate

● Harmonic Design '54 Special Strat
Type: single coil
Magnet: Alnico V
Wire: 42 gauge
Resistance: 6.4k ohms
Pole pieces: six fixed alnico rod magnet poles
Sound: sweet, clear and bright – the smoother side of the 'classic Strat' tone.

● Harmonic Design '54 Special Tele
Type: single coil
Magnet: Alnico V
Wire: 43 gauge
Resistance: 9.6k ohms
Pole pieces: six fixed alnico rod magnet poles
Sound: girthy, bright and well defined, with plenty of twang.

● Harmonic Design Z-90
Type: single coil
Magnet: Alnico IV
Wire: 43 gauge
Resistance: 11k ohms
Pole pieces: six fixed steel poles
Sound: fat, thick, rich, with wide frequency response and medium output.

● Harmonic Design Classic Humbucker
Type: humbucker
Magnet: Alnico IV
Wire: 42 gauge
Resistance: 8.2k ohms
Pole pieces: six fixed alnico rod magnet poles
Sound: round, warm PAF-style tone but with broadened frequency response and enhanced high-end definition.

other guitar and pickup makers

TV Jones

While many players agree that the build quality of today's Gretsch guitars – now overseen by Fender, and mostly manufactured in Japan – is on a par, or arguably above, that of many guitars made by Gretsch in the USA in the 1950s and '60s, plenty of guitarists have still experienced some frustration in their efforts to attain 'that great Gretsch sound'. Enter TV Jones, the first pickup-maker to take up the task of out-Filter'Troning Gretsch itself. Having worked on Brian Setzer's guitars since 1993, Thomas V. Jones has had plenty of opportunity to contemplate the workings of the illusive, classic Gretsch humbucker and, moreover, to put in the hard graft required to make these pickups *right*. As much as the Filter'Trons on Gretsches of the 1990s looked somewhat like the real thing, many experienced Gretsch-o-philes remained disappointed with their sound. But Jones's reverse-engineering of the formula from the ground-up has resulted in a pickup, the TV Classic, that is broadly accepted as the closest thing to an original Filter'Tron currently available ... so much so, in fact, that Gretsch buys in TV Classics and variations on the theme from TV Jones as original parts for many of its upmarket models.

Like many contemporary manufacturers seeking to produce accurate renditions of classic pickups from some 50 years ago, Jones encountered the stumbling blocks that are thrown up by the unavailability of the original materials that Fender, Gibson, Gretsch and DeArmond used back in the day. Which is to say, it isn't just enough to reverse-engineer a particular design and order up parts that appear to be to spec on paper, but these materials often have to be further bent to your will before they will behave, musically, the way that magnets, coil wire, base-plate steel stocks and so forth did back in the 1950s and early '60s. Having gotten it so thoroughly right – as acknowledged by major Gretsch-playing artists such as Setzer, The Cult's Billy Duffy, Dave Alvin, Reverend Horton Heat and others – he's reluctant to reveal just what kind of alchemy as been performed under the hood, but suffice to say it works. If a set of original Filter'Trons is beyond your means, TV Classics are very likely to provide all the bite, spank, dynamics and clarity of 'the only humbucker with twang'.

Beyond recreating the 'standard' Filter'Tron, TV Jones has also adapted the template to many modified versions to suit the needs of some players that were never quite addressed by original 'Trons. The TV Classic Plus is wound with thinner wire than the standard Classic, to produce more midrange oomph and a slightly hotter output, making it a good bridge-position partner to a TV Classic in the neck. The Power'Tron further ups the ante by winding a taller bobbin with

other guitar and pickup makers

● TV Jones Classic
Type: humbucker
Magnet: Alnico V
Wire: 43-gauge plain enamel
Resistance: 4.2k ohms neck, 4.8k ohms bridge
Pole pieces: six adjustable threaded fillister-head steel poles in each coil
Sound: round, rich and dynamic, with plenty of definition, firm lows, and a percussive, twangy edge, though no harshness.

● TV Jones Classic Plus
Type: humbucker
Magnet: Alnico V
Wire: 44-gauge plain enamel
Resistance: 8k ohms
Pole pieces: six adjustable threaded fillister-head steel poles in each coil
Sound: still offers plenty of Gretschy definition, clarity and twang, but with thicker midrange.

● TV Jones Super'Tron
Type: humbucker
Magnet: Alnico V
Wire: 43-gauge plain enamel
Resistance: 4.2k ohms neck, 4.8k ohms bridge
Pole pieces: one fixed steel bar blade in each coil
Sound: similar to TV Classic, but change of pole structure increases the pickup's inductances and produces a fatter, slightly punchier voice.

● TV Jones Power'Tron
Type: humbucker
Magnet: Alnico V
Wire: 43-gauge plain enamel
Resistance: 5.2k ohms neck, 8k ohms bridge (Power'Tron plus)
Pole pieces: six adjustable threaded fillister-head steel poles in each coil
Sound: round, rich, and dynamic, with plenty of definition and a percussive, twangy edge, though no harshness.

● TV Jones Magna'Tron
Type: humbucker
Magnet: Alnico V
Wire: 43-gauge plain enamel
Resistance: neck, 4.2k ohms; bridge, 4.8k ohms
Pole pieces: six fixed alnico rod magnet poles in each coil
Sound: bright, snappy, and twangy, but with musical highs and good compression.

● TV Jones TV-HT
Type: single coil
Magnet: Alnico V
Wire: 43-gauge plain enamel
Resistance: 4k ohms
Pole pieces: six adjustable threaded steel slot-head grub screws
Sound: thin, bright, clean, and snappy, with good sensitivity and excellent note definition.

standard-gauge wire to produce a fatter, thicker sounding pickup with higher output, but one that retains a recognizable degree of Filter'Tron twang and clarity. To further expand the versatility of his line, Jones also offers these models in a range of housings and mounting styles, to bring a degree of vintage-Gretsch tone to player of other instruments. The TV'Tron puts a Filter'Tron-style pickup in a housing that fits a standard PAF-sized humbucker mounting (while the English Mount retains the look of the TV Classic/Filter'Tron but offers a mounting arrangement for 'bucker-loaded guitars), the P'Tron fits a P-90 route and mounting, and the Dyna'Tron fits to the footprint of a surface-mounted Gretsch Dynasonic/DeArmond single-coil pickup. The Magna'Tron humbucker is a blend of Filter'Tron and Dynasonic, with Alnico V rod magnet pole pieces. The

other guitar and pickup makers

TV-HT, on the other hand, is a true single-coil pickup designed in the sonic image of the Gretsch HiLo'Tron (with 'some improvements'), but engineered to fit in place of a Gretsch Filter'Tron humbucker.

In addition to selling as replacement pickups, TV Jones's creations are standard equipment on the current Gretsch Brian Setzer Hotrod, Power Jet, 6120RHH (Reverend Horton Heat signature model), and many others.

Kinman

Australian Chris Kinman has made a name for himself mainly thanks to his authentic sounding stacked noise-canceling 'single-coil sized' replacement pickups for Stratocasters and similar guitars. After experimenting with noise-reduction circuitry for electric guitars for years, a pursuit that resulted in the development of the Kinman Buzzbucker dummy coil system in the late 1980s and early '90s, popular with some players in Australia at the time, Kinman hit upon a new design for a stacked 'bucker that would cancel the noise but not the tone. Attesting that previous conventional designs for stacked humbuckers suffered sonically because the opposing coils canceled some tone and output voltage along with canceling the noise (and therefore had to be overwound to make up the loss of output, a move that took them even further from the sound of traditional single-coil pickups), Kinman developed a pickup with a string-sensing coil on top and a differently wound noise-sensing coil on the bottom, with the two separated by both an upper and a lower magnetic shield for further noise reduction. When summed, the two coils cancel unwanted noise but pass on a realistic single-coil style guitar signal. He applied for a US patent for this design in March 1996, and received it in March 1997.

Kinman's Stratocaster replacement range, dubbed the AVn series for 'Authentic Vintage noiseless', comes in a range of strengths and voices, the sources of which are tipped off by the model number (equate them with years that are associated with particular tones in Fender Stratocaster history and you're on your way). There's also a vintage-voiced set designed for British instrumental artist Hank Marvin, formerly of The Shadows, which consists of an AVn-63 in the neck and middle and an AVn-64 in the bridge. The Strat lineup is completed by the SCn, designed as a more contemporary Strat replacement pickup, and the Hx-85, a pickup intended to come close to the P-90 tone.

Two replacement sets for Telecasters now grace the Kinman range, too. The AVn-48n and AVn-48b are designed for punchy, thick early Broadcaster-style tones, while the AVn-60n and AVn-60b are for twangier '60s-era Tele voicings. All

other guitar and pickup makers

● Kinman AVn-56
Type: hum-canceling 'single coil' size
Magnet: alnico
Wire: N/A
Resistance: 5.6k ohms
Pole pieces: six alnico bar magnet poles
Sound: a vintage-voiced Strat replacement with sweet mids, musical highs, and more oomph than the low resistance rating might imply.

● Kinman AVn-59
Type: hum-canceling 'single coil' size
Magnet: alnico
Wire: N/A
Resistance: 6.4k ohms
Pole pieces: six alnico bar magnet poles
Sound: a Strat replacement with a fuller voice and punchier mids than the 56 above, but still voiced toward the vintage side of the spectrum.

● Kinman AVn-62
Type: hum-canceling 'single coil' size
Magnet: alnico
Wire: N/A
Resistance: 6k ohms
Pole pieces: six alnico bar magnet poles
Sound: a vintage-voiced Strat replacement with more of a Texas-blues leaning than the bright 56.

● Kinman AVn-69
Type: hum-canceling 'single coil' size
Magnet: alnico
Wire: N/A
Resistance: 7.5k ohms
Pole pieces: six alnico bar magnet poles
Sound: a snappy, meaty pickup voiced to reproduce Hendrix-like late-60s Stratocaster tones.

● Kinman SCn
Type: hum-canceling 'single coil' size
Magnet: alnico
Wire: N/A
Resistance: 6.8k ohms
Pole pieces: six alnico bar magnet poles
Sound: designed to produce more hotrod-vintage style tones in the bridge position, or contemporary tones in the middle or neck; smooth, yet with solid attack and good midrange presence.

● Kinman Hx-85
Type: hum-canceling 'single coil' size
Magnet: alnico
Wire: N/A
Resistance: 9.5k ohms
Pole pieces: six alnico bar magnet poles
Sound: high-output single-coil tone, approaching P-90-style midrange bark and aggression.

● Kinman AVn-48b & AVn-48n
Type: hum-canceling 'single coil' size
Magnet: alnico
Wire: N/A
Resistance: bridge, 7.35k ohms; neck, 7.8k ohms
Pole pieces: six alnico bar magnet poles
Sound: thick, creamy, percussive Broadcaster-style tone that still retains some snap and twang.

● Kinman AVn-60b & AVn60n
Type: hum-canceling 'single coil' size
Magnet: alnico
Wire: N/A
Resistance: bridge, 6.8k ohms; neck, 7.4k ohms
Pole pieces: six alnico bar magnet poles
Sound: more definition and bright Tele-like twang from the bridge pickup, with round, scooped Strat-like warmth and bite from the neck pickup.

are made somewhat differently from Kinman's AVn designs for Stratocasters. The lower, noise-canceling bobbin of the stacked Tele pickups is an unusual steel 'H-core' unit made from 150 H-shaped plates laminated together (with a super-thin 7-micron gap between each) and wound with coil wire. This unique coil picks up 60-cycle hum but no string vibration, while the more traditional top

other guitar and pickup makers

coil – which carries six alnico rod magnet poles – picks up both. When wired together, noise is rejected.

Lace

Available exclusively on Fender guitars from 1985 to 1996, Lace Sensor pickups, and other Lace designs, are now available in a full range of replacement pickups for use on other makes of guitars. (See the Fender entry in the previous chapter for further details of the design and construction of these unusual pickups, and their history as associated with Fender.) Lace Sensor low-noise single coils are available in an expanded range of models color-coded according to their output: Emerald, Gold, Silver, Light Blue, Burgundy, Purple, Blue, and Red (weakest to hottest), a line that includes a few more options than the Fender-Lace range. A similarly constructed set for Telecaster is also available, as are a number of Lace Dually pairings, sets that come as two joined Lace Sensor units in mix-and-matchable colors/strengths, that can be wired up for switching between double-coil 'humbucker' mode or single-coil performance from either of the two distinct coils.

Lace has also recently introduced a new Alumitone pickup, a modernistic unit described as a low-resistance, high-output 'current drive device' based on an aluminum structure rather than the copper coil of the traditional electromagnetic pickup (although there is some copper wire in a small secondary coil). In short, the space-aged laminated aluminum structure that makes up the bulk of the pickup's body performs as one fat turn of coil wire, while a second, small coil mounted beneath it – wound with only around five to ten percent of the length of wire used in a conventional pickup coil – helps to voice the unit. The result is a pickup that measures a piffling 2.5k ohms DC resistance, but clocks in a whopping 16.7 Henries of inductance (where a standard sigle-coil pickup might display an inductance of 2.5 or 3 Henries). The sonic results are described as having more bass and treble, with a smooth yet enhanced midrange and high output ... which, added together, sounds like a little more of everything.

A third Lace range of note, the Holy Grail, combines Lace Sensor coil technology with a central core that holds six alnico rod magnet poles in the Strat replacement model, and six threaded steel poles in the PS-900 and PS-905 Soap Bar (P-90-style) pickups. The intention is to produce a more vintage-voiced and traditional-looking pickup that nevertheless offers the low-noise performance and enhanced sensitivity of the original Lace Sensor.

Lace Alumitone

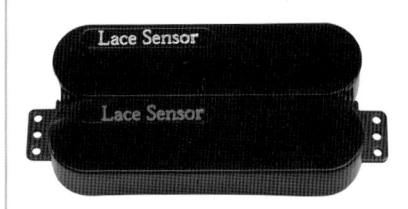

Lace Sensor Dually

● Lace Sensor
Type: low-noise unconventional single coil
Magnet: ceramic
Wire: N/A
Resistance: Emerald 5.7k ohms, Gold 5.8k ohms, Silver 7.1k ohms, Light Blue 8k ohms, Burgundy 8.9k ohms, Purple 10.5k ohms, Blue 12.8k ohms, Red 14.5k ohms
Pole pieces: 36 individual steel teeth in a 'comb' configuration
Sound: from bright, percussive 'vintage Strat' tones (Gold), to singing high-output tones (Red), all with extended frequency range and low-noise operation.

● Lace Alumintone
Type: low-noise unconventional single coil
Magnet: ceramic
Wire: N/A
Resistance: 2.5k ohms
Pole pieces: two offset ceramic bar magnets
Sound: enhanced lows and highs vs traditional single-coil pickups, with more output overall.

● Lace Sensor Holy Grail
Type: noise-canceling
Magnet: alnico
Wire: N/A
Resistance: neck and middle (HG-1000), 10.7k ohms; bridge (HG-1500), 11.5k ohms
Pole pieces: six alnico rod magnet poles
Sound: traditional 'bell like' Stratocaster tones with excellent hum rejection.

● Lace Sensor PS-900 & PS-905
Type: noise-canceling
Magnet: alnico
Wire: N/A
Resistance: neck (PS-900); 12.2k ohms; bridge (PS-905), 13.6k ohms
Pole pieces: six threaded steel slot-head screws
Sound: thick, gritty, mids-forward single-coil tone with excellent hum rejection.

Bill Lawrence (Wildeusa, Keystone)

Young Willi Lorenz Stich first took up the guitar in his boyhood home of Cologne, Germany, toward the end of World War II after injuries sustained in an experiment with a rocket-propelled bicycle left him unable to play the violin. An early career as a performer found him headlining shows on American military bases in Europe, and earned him an endorsement deal with Framus guitars, but Willi remained ever the tinkerer, and applied the same blend of curiosity and zeal that sent him hurtling along on a homemade rocket-bike to the winding of his first pickup, way back in 1948. In the early 1960s Lorenz, now using the professional name Bill Lawrence, formed the Lawrence Electro Sounds company in Germany, which supplied many of his early pickup designs to German guitar-makers, and in the late 1960s he brought the venture to the USA., where he found a home at Dan Armstrong's workshop in New York City. Having guided two notable young apprentices by the names of Kent Armstrong and Larry DiMarzio in the Armstrong shop, Lawrence moved to Kalamazoo, MI, to head Gibson's pickup department, then to Nashville, TN, where the first of his most recognizable designs took root.

Designs of the mid 1970s and early '80s such as the single-blade L-220 (the

other guitar and pickup makers

first hum-canceling, single-sized replacement pickup for Fender guitars), the L-90 humbucker, and the L-500 series put the Bill Lawrence name on the map with mod-hungry guitarists, and the brand became established as one of the first respected makes of after-market pickups. In 1982 Lawrence was awarded the first US patent for a double-blade pickup, the designs for which formed the foundations of these successful lines. In the early 1990s, Lawrence further expanded his line with the popular L-280 series of stacked single-coil-sized humbucker for Stratocaster and Telecaster.

A long-time proponent of ceramic magnets, Lawrence frequently dispels the parallel misconceptions that 'ceramic magnets sound cold' while 'alnico magnets sound musical'. His contention is that the magnet has no sound in and of itself, it merely provides the force that the pickup design employs to do its work. Quite rightly, he argues, the design and construction of the coil and of the entire unit itself determines the sonic quality of the pickup – a verdict backed up by the use of ceramic magnets by other notable, forward-thinking makers such as Joe Barden and Leo Fender with G&L, not to mention the use of ceramic magnets by both Seymour Duncan and Larry DiMarzio in much of their product range.

Bill Lawrence is currently based in Corona, CA, where he has worked as a consultant to Fender, and recently developed the new SCN (Samarium Cobalt Noiseless) pickup line that uses powerful Samarium Cobalt 'rare earth' magnets (see the Fender entry in the previous chapter for further details). Lawrence, his wife Becky, and a small staff of employees continue to manufacture many of his most popular pickups in Corona, along with some new variations, although the brand has recently reorganized under the WildeUSA brand.

Jason Lollar

As much some players are willing to accept entirely new advances in pickup technology, the lion's share of the boutique market still falls into what we can call the 'high-end vintage reproduction' category – and Jason Lollar is right up there with the handful of makers that are most highly regarded by guitarists seeking authentic golden-age tone, occasionally with a twist. Lollar, a 1979 graduate of the Roberto-Venn School of Luthiery in Phoenix, AZ, started his working life as a professional guitar-maker and repairman, and segued toward his specialization in pickup-making upon realizing he could achieve things himself with coil wire and magnets that just couldn't be found in available replacement pickups. (For more details on Jason Lollar's working history and his

Lollar Horseshoe
Type: single coil
Magnet: nickel-plated 'horseshoe' magnets
Wire: N/A
Resistance: N/A
Pole pieces: six fixed steel poles
Sound: bright and a little snarly, yet with good warmth and body.

Lollar Special T Series Bridge
Type: single coil
Magnet: Alnico V
Wire: 42-gauge plain enamel
Resistance: 8.2k ohms +/−
Pole pieces: six alnico rod magnet poles
Sound: the hotter, yet still vintage-voiced, variant of Lollar's most popular Tele replacement, the Vintage T, this one has more grunt and midrange punch, with smoother highs.

Lollar Vintage Tweed/Blonde/Blackface S Series
Type: single coil
Magnet: Alnico II in Tweed & Blonde, Alnico V in Blackface
Wire: 42-gauge heavy Formvar
Resistance: medians of approximately 5k, 5.8k, 6.2k ohms respectively (with each available in calibrated sets according to position)
Pole pieces: six alnico rod magnet poles
Sound: Lollar's vintage-voiced Strat replacement pickup range, in ouitput levels from super-clean to bluesy, all voiced to attain classic, authentic tone.

Lollar Special S Series
Type: single coil
Magnet: Alnico V
Wire: 42-gauge heavy Formvar
Resistance: N/A
Pole pieces: six alnico rod magnet poles
Sound: a hot, yet vintage-style, replacement pickup to achieve more cut and grind from the Strat bridge position.

Lollar Charlie Christian Archtop Pickup
Type: single coil
Magnet: Alnico V
Wire: 38 gauge
Resistance: N/A
Pole pieces: fixed steel blade
Sound: round, rich, warm tone with good high-end definition.

Lollar Chicago Steel
Type: single coil
Magnet: ceramic
Wire: N/A
Resistance: N/A
Pole pieces: six adjustable threaded steel poles
Sound: hot, spanky, high-definition sizzle for slide guitar.

thoughts on pickups and tone, read the full interview in the *Meet the Makers* section that follows.) As if to drum up some competition for his own efforts, Lollar's own book on pickup-making, *Basic Pickup Winding and Complete Guide to Making Your Own Pickup Winder* (1996, out of print), can be largely credited with launching the boom in cottage-industry pickup-makers of the late 1990s.

Lollar's recreations of desirable vintage pickups, all manufactured by hand in his workshop in Vashon, WA, are born out of intense and repeated examination of countless examples of the genuine article. Before majoring in pickup manufacture, Lollar was a busy pickup rewinder and repairman, and took the

other guitar and pickup makers

opportunity to note every possible tone-affecting facet of each of the many classic pickups he dissected in the course of his servicing work. When he began making pickups from scratch he initially did so on a custom-order basis, and the 'standard' line he offers now was born out of his recognition of the pickup types that were most frequently requested by these customers.

To that end, his most popular vintage-style single coils for Telecaster and Stratocaster aim to capture that magical twang or bell-like chime that players imagine to be the archetypal 'classic sound' of these guitars – and deduced by Lollar from many, many original examples of each – rather than meticulous copies of any individual 1954 Telecaster pickup, 1956 Stratocaster pickup, or the like. Along with these, he also tends to offer a few minor variations on the type (a little cleaner, a little hotter) without often straying into 'hotrod' or high-gain territory. The most popular pickup of Lollar's line, however, is a P-90 replacement – and one that has received consistently stellar reviews – that leans toward the hotter side of the range of readings one would get from examining a selection of original examples. Clocking in at around 8.2k ohms, these offer the thick, clanky, slightly gritty, mids-forward tone that many players have come to consider 'the classic P-90 sound'. Also available, however, is a set that Lollar says are closer to the specs he tends to find for genuine mid-50s P-90s, which yields a DC resistance more in the ballpark of 7.2k ohms and exhibits a cleaner, brighter, sweeter voice as a result (at the time of writing, this model is not yet listed in the Lollar catalog, although he tells us it's available upon request as the "56 P-90').

Humbuckers are a more recent addition to the Lollar range, and are the product of intensive R&D toward the end of reproducing an accurate PAF-style pickup. The result, the Imperial Humbucker, comes in three flavors: the standard, wound to around 7.6k ohms neck and 8.4k ohms bridge; the Low Wind Imperial, 7k ohms neck and 7.9k ohms bridge; and the High Wind Imperial, 8.5k ohms neck and 9.4k ohms bridge.

More specialist needs are catered for by the Charlie Christian Archtop Pickup, a big fella' using Alnico V bar magnets and wound with 38-gauge wire in the image of the iconic 1930s design from Gibson, and the Chicago Steel, a high-output, high-sensitivity single coil with ceramic magnet that's particularly suited to slide playing, designed along the lines of the Oahu/Valco/Supro lap-steel guitar pickups of the 1940s and early '50s, but adapted to fit a Stratocaster-style guitar (with minor modification to the instrument). Lollar's recreation of the horseshoe pickup has also found a home with many players seeking

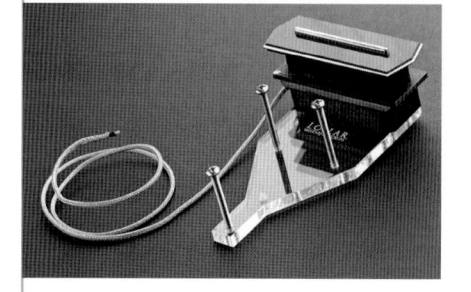

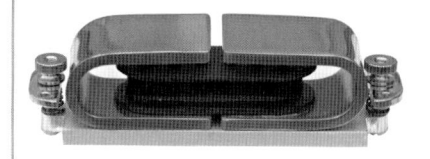

Jason Lollar's variations on the Charlie Christian pickup, top, and horseshoe pickup

replacements for their original Rickenbacker units, or looking to build original guitars using this unusual design. In fact, Lollar found himself getting a lot of business from the steel-guitar market in the early days of his pickup venture, and he continues to offer many replacement models for classic lap-steel instruments. (Since Lollars are mostly vintage-repro-style pickups, not all specs will be listed here.)

PRS

Paul Reed Smith built guitars for Peter Frampton, Al DiMeola, Ted Nugent, and Carlos Santana before clearing his mid 20s, and before the age of 30 had established the PRS company – soon to be one of the most successful and best respected high-end guitar manufacturers in the USA. And although, like many smaller (if growing) guitar-makers, Smith bought in pickups made by other companies in the fledgling years – from Seymour Duncan in particular – PRS set about winding their own designs surprisingly early in the process. Since 1985, other than for special requests or unusual requirements, PRS has made all its own pickups, and the range of styles available today is impressively broad.

The first PRS pickups, the Standard Treble and Standard Bass ('treble' and 'bass' being PRS nomenclature for bridge and neck), appeared outwardly to be standard, moderate-output humbuckers, but had a few keys differences from the classic PAF template. They used a bar magnet mounted beneath the coils to charge the six adjustable threaded steel pole pieces in one coil, but the fixed poles in the other coil were actually rod magnets themselves. The design was intended to yield a more authentic and 'Fender-ish' single-coil tone when the pickup was split, a factor that was often an important consideration in PRS pickup designs, given the five-way switching that many two-humbucker models employed. A few years later the fixed poles of the high E and B strings were changed to steel, to tame the overt brightness found here in the single-coil mode. The PRS pickup range had expanded from these two debutantes of 1985 to a full six models in 1987, with the addition of the Vintage Treble and Vintage Bass, HFS, and Single-Coil Bass. The latter was a Strat-styled pickup, best known for its appearance in the neck and middle positions of the PRS Studio that came out a year later. The HFS (for 'Hot, Fat, Screams') was an overwound humbucker with a ceramic magnet and a sound that … well, the name pretty much says it all. The Vintage pair, the Bass sibling from which was often used in the neck position with a different, hotter pickup in the bridge, was PRS's early shot at a more vintage, low-output PAF-style humbucker, although in fact they

other guitar and pickup makers

● **PRS Dragon II**
Type: humbucker
Magnet: alnico
Wire: N/A
Resistance: bridge, 12k ohms; neck, 8k ohms
Pole pieces: six adjustable threaded steel poles in one coil, six fixed steel slugs in the other
Sound: woody, rich, clear and powerful – an 'enhanced PAF' tone.

● **PRS HFS**
Type: humbucker
Magnet: ceramic
Wire: N/A
Resistance: 15k ohms
Pole pieces: six adjustable threaded steel poles in one coil, six fixed steel slugs in the other
Sound: A high-output contemporary rock humbucker. To quote Mr. Smith: "It's hot, it's fat, and it screams."

● **PRS McCarty**
Type: humbucker
Magnet: alnico
Wire: N/A
Resistance: bridge, 9k ohms; neck, 8k ohms
Pole pieces: six adjustable threaded steel poles in one coil, six fixed steel slugs in the other
Sound: styled after the PAF humbucker, with a little added definition and a broader frequency range.

● **PRS Santana III**
Type: humbucker
Magnet: alnico
Wire: N/A
Resistance: bridge, 12k ohms; neck, 7k ohms
Pole pieces: six adjustable threaded steel poles in one coil, six fixed steel slugs in the other
Sound: a high-output alnico humbucker in the bridge position for screaming lead tones and maximum sustain, paired with a smother, cleaner version in the neck.

● **PRS Swamp Ash**
Type: humbucker
Magnet: alnico
Wire: N/A
Resistance: bridge, 8.19k ohms; neck, 7.3k ohms
Pole pieces: six adjustable threaded steel poles in one coil, six fixed steel slugs in the other
Sound: a low-output humbucker set that's warm and full, but designed for added clarity, bite and twang.

● **PRS Tremonti Treble (bridge)**
Type: humbucker
Magnet: ceramic
Wire: N/A
Resistance: 15.42k
Pole pieces: six adjustable threaded steel poles in one coil, six fixed steel slugs in the other
Sound: a screaming, sizzling contemporary rocker with bags of punch and crunch.

● **PRS Vintage Bass**
Type: humbucker
Magnet: alnico
Wire: N/A
Resistance: 8.5k ohms
Pole pieces: six adjustable threaded steel poles in one coil, six fixed steel slugs in the other
Sound: full, round, warm PAF-voiced tone with enhanced high-end clarity.

● **PRS 7**
Type: humbucker
Magnet: alnico
Wire: N/A
Resistance: bridge, 8.44k ohms; neck, 7.3k ohms
Pole pieces: six adjustable threaded steel poles in one coil, six fixed steel slugs in the other
Sound: a woody, round, rich humbucker set in the image of the PAF, designed for the PRS Singlecut model.

are a little warmer and more mid-forward than most original Gibson PAFs.

Another high-output design, the short-lived (and aptly named) Chainsaw humbucker, joined the line for a brief time in the late 1980s. The warmer, sweeter Alnico V-mag Deep Dish humbucker that arrived around the same time, followed by the Deep Dish II with Alnico II magnet, has had more staying power, as have many popular PRS designs that followed, such as the Artist, Dragon, Hot Vintage Treble, and McCarty models. Along the way, PRS has also designed tailor-made pickups to suit the requirements of various signature guitars, such as the David Grissom (an adapted Standard), the Santana II (an adapted Dragon II), the Tremonti (with a high-output ceramic bridge pickup), and the Hiland (low-output humbuckers similar to the Swamp Ash pickups, designed to attain the twang required by country picker Johnny Hiland).

Rio Grande

Falling into a familiar category that we might call 'modified vintage', while offering plenty of original twists on classic themes in order to suit player's ever-whimsical tonal needs, the Rio Grande brand has been a popular choice in replacement pickups since its inception in 1993. Founded by guitar repairman John 'Bart' Wittroc, and based in Houston, TX, Rio Grande makes mucho mileage out of its associations with Texas-sized tone. Its pickup designs tend – more often than not – to offer output levels a little hotter than standard for blues and gnarly rock'n'roll players seeking a little more oomph out of their instruments.

Most popular of the Strat-style replacements is the Vintage Tallboy, a modified-vintage-voiced unit with a taller bobbin than standard, for slightly more winds but a magnetic focus that's still bright and well defined. The Muy Grande addresses the common need for a hotter bridge pickup for Strats, while the interesting Stelly design seeks to package a Tele bridge-like unit in a Strat-sized housing. The aptly named Half Breed blends the Tallboy's brightness and tight focus with a little of the Muy Grande's extra power. The newest Rio Grande design for Strats, the ceramic Dirty Harry, follows a recent trend for adjustable-steel-pole/magnet-beneath pickups made to fit Fender-sized single-coil mountings, and offers a gritty, P-90-ish sound (a high-output rendition, in this case). Tele players can choose from the same models.

The Bluesbar and Jazzbar offer high and medium-output options for P-90 players, and the Bastard and Fat Bastard were among the early designs in a wave that caters for humbucker players who want to achieve P-90-like single-coil

Rio Grande Dirty Harry Tele bridge

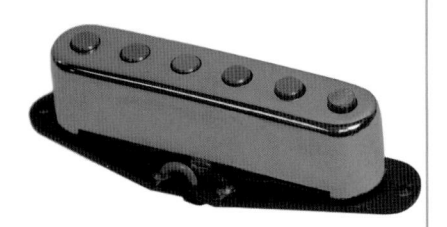

Rio Grande Tallboy Tele neck

other guitar and pickup makers

● **Rio Grande Vintage Tallboy Strat**
Type: single coil
Magnet: Alnico V
Wire: N/A
Resistance: 7.2k ohms
Pole pieces: fixed alnico rod magnet poles
Sound: bright, clear and well defined, yet richer than vintage Strat pickup.

● **Rio Grande Muy Grande Strat**
Type: single coil
Magnet: Alnico V
Wire: N/A
Resistance: 8k ohms
Pole pieces: fixed alnico rod magnet poles
Sound: gutsy, fat, and punchy.

● **Rio Grande Stelly**
Type: single coil
Magnet: Alnico V
Wire: N/A
Resistance: 8.6k ohms
Pole pieces: fixed alnico rod magnet poles
Sound: thick and round, yet with it's own mid-forward breed of twang.

● **Rio Grande Halfbreed Strat**
Type: single coil
Magnet: Alnico V
Wire: N/A
Resistance: 7.8k ohms
Pole pieces: fixed alnico rod magnet poles
Sound: halfway house between Tallboy and Muy Grande.

● **Rio Grande Dirty Harry Strat**
Type: single coil
Magnet: ceramic
Wire: N/A
Resistance: 13k ohms
Pole pieces: adjustable threaded steel pole pieces
Sound: fat, gritty, high-output tones.

● **Rio Grande Vintage Tallboy Tele**
Type: single coil
Magnet: Alnico V
Wire: N/A
Resistance: neck, 7k ohms; bridge, 8k ohms
Pole pieces: fixed alnico rod magnet poles
Sound: bright, snappy, and clear – archetypal twang.

● **Rio Grande Muy Grande Tele**
Type: single coil
Magnet: Alnico V
Wire: N/A
Resistance: neck, 7.8k ohms; bridge, 8.5k ohms
Pole pieces: fixed alnico rod magnet poles
Sound: gutsy, cutting and a little raunchy.

● **Rio Grande Dirty Harry Tele**
Type: single coil
Magnet: ceramic
Wire: N/A
Resistance: neck, 8k ohms; bridge, 12k ohms
Pole pieces: adjustable threaded steel pole pieces
Sound: fat, gritty, high-output tones.

● **Rio Grande Vintage Tallboy Twangbucker (Tele)**
Type: humbucker
Magnet: Alnico V
Wire: N/A
Resistance: 15k ohms
Pole pieces: six fixed alnico rod magnet poles in each coil
Sound: thick, round and fat in humbucker mode; splits to a bright, well-defined single-coil sound.

● **Rio Grande Bluesbar**
Type: single coil
Magnet: Alnico V
Wire: N/A
Resistance: 12.5k ohms
Pole pieces: adjustable threaded steel pole pieces
Sound: fat, gritty, high-output P-90-style tones.

● Rio Grande Jazzbar
Type: single coil
Magnet: Alnico V
Wire: N/A
Resistance: 10.5k ohms
Pole pieces: adjustable threaded steel pole pieces
Sound: fat, gritty, mid-forward, and more medium-high output P-90-style tones.

● Rio Grande Bastard
Type: single coil
Magnet: Alnico V
Wire: N/A
Resistance: 9.2k ohms
Pole pieces: adjustable threaded steel pole pieces
Sound: round, gritty P-90 aggression with sweetened highs, in a humbucker-sized package.

● Rio Grande Fat Bastard
Type: single coil
Magnet: Alnico V
Wire: N/A
Resistance: 12.5k ohms
Pole pieces: adjustable threaded steel pole pieces
Sound: higher-output version of the Bastard, above.

● Rio Grande Buffalo Humbucker
Type: humbucker
Magnet: Alnico V
Wire: N/A
Resistance: 8k ohms
Pole pieces: adjustable threaded steel pole pieces in one coil, fixed steel slugs in the other
Sound: warm, full and smooth, with decent high-end definition.

● Rio Grande Genuine Texas Humbucker
Type: humbucker
Magnet: Alnico V
Wire: N/A
Resistance: 9k ohms
Pole pieces: adjustable threaded steel pole pieces in one coil, fixed steel slugs in the other
Sound: thicker and more aggressive than the Genuine Texas, above, with more midrange emphasis.

● Rio Grande Barbeque Humbucker
Type: humbucker
Magnet: Alnico V
Wire: N/A
Resistance: 12.5k ohms
Pole pieces: adjustable threaded steel pole pieces in one coil, fixed steel slugs in the other
Sound: a medium-high output humbucker, for smooth yet sizzling lead tones and crunchy, aggressive rhythm.

● Rio Grande My Grande Humbucker
Type: humbucker
Magnet: Alnico V
Wire: N/A
Resistance: 16k ohms
Pole pieces: adjustable threaded steel pole pieces in one coil, fixed steel slugs in the other
Sound: hot humbucker for scorching lead work.

tone without modifying their humbucker routes. True humbucker options are found in the Buffalo, Genuine Texas, and Barbeque Humbuckers, with standard, hot, and hotter outputs respectively, while the Muy Grande tips the scales as Rio Grande's hottest humbucker, and the Tallboy Humbucker provides an option for players seeking a realistic 'single' style split-coil sound.

Rather than replicating the 'any color you want, as long as it's black (or

other guitar and pickup makers

white)' look of most vintage repro pickups, Rio Grande rather innovatively offers a wide range of creative covers and looks. Some bobbin-top colors available for a Strat-replacement pickup, for example, include White, Cream, and Black Pearl; Brown Tortoise; Blue, Gold, Green, Purple, Red, and Silver Sparkle, in addition to the more standard offerings. In another novel move, Rio Grande also makes two replacements for the 'narrow soapbar' shaped G&L ASAT MFD pickups, the Vintage Tallboy for ASAT and Muy Grande for ASAT.

J.M. Rolph

Kentuckian J.M. Rolph's small line of handmade pickups grew out of his highly respected rewinding business, which for some years had found him among the first-call repairmen when a vintage original Fender Stratocaster or Telecaster pickup was in need of urgent attention. Rolph's own productions go as far as possible toward replicating the look and vibe of original vintage examples to such an extent that it's pointless reproducing images of them here. Suffice to say his list of references is long, and he continues to find a place in today's booming market by, in many cases, addressing the specific, custom-order needs of myriad discerning players.

Van Zandt

A guitarist and trained machinist, W.L. Van Zandt started repairing and rewinding pickups in the Dallas/Ft. Worth area in the 1960s, and launched his own brand in the late '80s, following increased demand for his custom-made units. The limited Van Zandt range includes True Vintage, Vintage Plus, Blues, and Rock variants of Stratocaster (aka standard, enhanced standard, moderate, and high output winds); True Vintage and Vintage Plus for Telecasters; and the True Bucker Vintage Humbucker, designed to capture an authentic PAF sound with just a little extra output. All are made by hand, and capture the look of the original article. W.L. Van Zandt died in 1997, but his wife Gloria and nephew J.D. Prince have carried on the business.

MEET THE MAKERS: INTERVIEWS

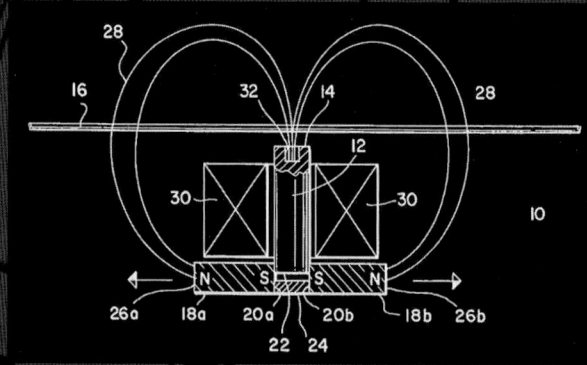

"Tweak an ingredient or two and you trigger a chaos-theory style fluttering of the butterfly wings that results in an entirely different sounding pickup and, therefore, guitar."
DAVE HUNTER, PORTSMOUTH, NH, MAY 2008

meet the makers: interviews

Kent Armstrong, Kent Armstrong Hand Made Pickups

Please tell us a little about how you found your way into the pickup business.
I started in my dad's [Dan Armstrong] music shop in 1969 in New York City. We moved down to Greenwich Village [NY] at the end of '69, and my brother and I lived down there above my dad. In about 1970 my dad decided he was going to go off to California to work for Neil Diamond. Bill Lawrence had taught him how to do fundamental rewinds, so I started doing all the rewinds while dad was away. Then in late '70 or early '71, the guys who were running dad's music shop went and set up their own repair shop, so I took over the repair shop there in dad's music store. After a month or two of doing it and doing a good job, my dad called up and said I had a new partner. I said, "Why?" And he said, "Well, because he needs a job!" So Bill Lawrence became my partner in the repair shop. He and I worked together for ten months.

At that point, dad closed the music shop and decided he was going to go and work in England with Orange Amplifiers. I was just finishing high school, and he said, "Here it is, guys: you can stay here and fend for yourselves in New York City, or come to England and I'll put you through college." So, of course, being the chicken, I went to England.

Understandable, I guess.
Well, had I stayed in New York I would have been doing great shit. I was making like $400 to $600 a week. It was *great* money in those days. I was working my ass off for it, six days a week. But still, it was good money and I was getting my high school education, because the music store didn't open until midday and closed at eight, because most musicians don't get up 'til midday. I was back from high school, in my senior year, by one in the afternoon, so I would work from one until eight in the repair shop. So that was how I got going in that sort of thing.

And it sounds like you got a boost in the pickup world from Bill Lawrence.
He showed me some of the finer points of rewinding, some of the things he never showed my father. In fact, just the other day I found the second pickup I ever made. Gibson would supply me with bobbins, covers and screws and everything, but they wouldn't supply me with any base plates, or any magnets. They figured that without base plates I couldn't make pickups. Of course, we were making pickups with ceramic magnets in those days. The first pickup I ever made from scratch was for a guy called Robbie Robertson of The Band. He wanted to put a humbucker in his Telecaster, but he didn't want to route out the pocket. So that day, out of fiberboard,

meet the makers: interviews

I made two base plates, glued magnets to them, used screws, and did everything. I made two pickups that day, and I still have the second one to this day, sitting in the shop here.

And it's the same type of pickup you made for Robbie Robertson?
Yep. I put it in his Tele, and that Tele itself now hangs in the Hard Rock Café in New York City.

These were the early days of people wanting to get a little more out of their guitars and pickups than what was stock. Plenty of guys had always messed around with their gear, but it seems like the late '60s and early '70s is when the notion really struck players that they could modify guitars, and even pickups.
Exactly. So at the end of '71 my dad closes up shop and goes off to England, and Bill Lawrence goes off and starts his own repair shop. He takes on a young apprentice to come in and clean up and do some bits and pieces around the place, and his young apprentice was a guy named Larry DiMarzio.

It's a very incestuous little group here, isn't it!
Yes, we all knew each other. That's how we all got started.

But I went to England, and I started doing rewinds for the music shops in London. I was doing more and more rewinds, and I realized the futility of the way pickups had such built-in obsolescence. I started experimenting with epoxies and different potting materials, and I designed my own way of manufacturing pickups with no bobbins. My handmade pickups … there's nothing holding the bobbins together but hot wax, because once it's embedded in the epoxy it can't go anywhere, you can't touch it, you can't break it. Of course, by getting rid of that extra plastic of the bobbins I can make pickups really small. There's not a lot in my pickups. So I was able to make all kinds of weird and wonderful things.

And of course, because of my technique of manufacture there's no molding required, other than the rubber molding of a pickup. So I was able to produce things for people very inexpensively, for prototyping. If you want a pickup made, people will say, "Give me a check with lots of zeros after the numbers and let's get going!"

Sure, if you've got to tool up for base plates and bobbins and all that …
Oh, punching tools, molding tools, don't get me talking. To put a pickup into production will probably cost you something close to $100,000. I can do it for less than $50 or $60, so that's how it came about.

So I stayed in England and took over doing all the rewinds in England. I wasn't making enough money at first, so I started up a motorcycle dispatch courier service. I would zoom in and out of London all day long and pick up the rewinds, bring them out to my shop. In my slack periods I'd do all the rewinds, and the next day I would take them back into the music shops. I could do literally a 24-hour turnaround service on rewinds, and that helped supplement my income.

Basically, things just started to grow. One of my first big customers was Burns Guitars. I made a lot of pickups for their reincarnation in the late '70s and '80s. I sold my dispatch company in '79, and went into full-time pickup-making.

You were in on the very early days of the first after-market pickup boom.
Sure. DiMarzio's the one that really cracked that market. Of course he learned all about ceramic magnets from Bill Lawrence.

Bill's always been into ceramic magnets, hasn't he.
Yeah, Bill thinks the sun shines on ceramic magnets. He's a big ceramic buff. But now he's into the rare earth stuff, like neodymiums and stuff like that. I'm afraid I don't see a lot of performance difference between them and alnico, so I'm not going to the added expense of rare earth, because rare earth is very expensive.

Early on you used a lot of ceramic magnets, I guess because of Bill's influence?
Yeah, in fact the only way I would use alnico is if I was stripping them out of old Gibsons and things.

It sounds like your own pickup designs, even early on, became original and unique pretty quickly, rather than being the usual copies of something already out there.
Yeah. Do you remember the Schecter Z+? That was my first pickup design, and my father pirated it to Schecter. After I'd heard that the whole project had collapsed for like a third of a million dollars, I called up Schecter and said, "Hey, listen guys, that pickup really wasn't my father's." And they said, "Yeah, we kind of got that after he ended up never being able to produce it correctly." So they sent their director over to me, and he watched me make them in my basement and said, "Yeah, you really do know what you're doing!" They took me out to California and tried to resurrect the project, but it only lasted a month or two, then the decided to call it quits on the whole project.

You eventually moved on, out of the necessity of maintaining a pickup business, to making replacement pickups for just about anything.
Well, that's only come about in the past 10 to 15 years. A guy came to me from [Dong Ho Electronics in] Korea and said, "I make $2 pickups – *crap* pickups. I'd really like to get into the big-time pickup world. Would you be able to help me?" I said, "Yeah, sure. Let's strike up a deal and get going." So that's how that came about; I helped him to be able to make better pickups. And it also enabled me to get better

components, because getting components has always been the biggest problem. Tooling costs are just huge.

Now a lot of the guys buy components from me. We've done good things like ... well, base plates on our humbuckers are stainless steel. Nobody [except us] makes stainless steel base plates. Even [another US maker] uses brass plates that are coated, and they crap out – forever I've been soldering nuts to the bottom of those humbuckers so they have an extended life, because the threads strip out. When you're using a steel screw in a brass plate, guess what gives up quicker? I refuse to build pickups with crap in them. We have never had one of our bass plates fail.

It's just one of the better ways to go. And we use alnico magnets, and we can do small productions even out of my Korean factory. [Another maker] would be saying, "How many thousand pickups do you want?" And you'd be saying, "Geez, I only want 20 pickups." So I cater to all the small guys, custom, basically. So we give them custom at Ford prices.

Of your Kent Armstrong Hand Made Pickups, which ones have been the most popular?
I seem to have captured the jazz market. My first big customer was Bob Benedetto. He was the first guy who came along and asked me to design him a sound. Of course, it wasn't too hard to do. He sent me a master and I made his shape for him, the way he wanted it, and it just kind of blossomed from there. He was selling his pickups separately, and more and more people heard about them, like John Buscarino. I just seem to have captured the jazz guitar world.

I do so many different models, but the one thing that I'm very proud of is the fact that all of my humbuckers are equal-balanced humbuckers. A Gibson humbucker's not equally balanced between the slugs and the screws. People used to say, "I took the cover off my humbucker and it sounded so much better." Well, duh. Everybody knows that – you take the cover off and the slugs get closer to the strings, hence generate more power. But even then, the screws are far more powerful than the slugs. So all my pickups have equal slugs, or equal screws, or equal bars, but both coils are always equal, and that helps to drive the sound. Especially my 12-pole humbuckers for jazz guitars, people can use phosphor-bronze strings, because they can balance the strings. By using longer screws or shorter screws you can actually compensate quite well for the string imbalance.

See, any metal object breaking a magnetic field will induce a current in the coil. It's just that iron happens to be the best. You can use aluminum strings and it will still generate some signal, it just wouldn't be as powerful as ferrous.

Interesting. You don't hear it described that way. Usually the talk is about pure-nickel-wrapped strings weakening the signal, as if the nickel doesn't interact with the magnetic field at all.

meet the makers: interviews

Right, but they're not putting out nothing. You can make a completely solid-nickel string, it's just not going to have as much magnetic oomph as an iron string. That's the only difference.

So that's how it works. With my 12 Pole, people have said it's the most balanced, even pickup they've ever used, and that's because both coils are generating equally, at equal strength.

And with the coils being closer to mirror images of each other, you're going to get a truer humbucker too, a better hum-rejection performance.
Exactly. That's exactly what it is. But I've come out with some other unique designs, too. One called the SS, and people have done something similar to it, but never gotten it quite right. In my Stratocaster model, for example, the two coils are actually lying on their sides – in one model I make – with magnets inside the coils, and a single blade source right up the middle. You have the hum-canceling properties, but you still have the single-coil sound.

And what contributes to that, is it the thinner single-coil shape?
Exactly. A humbucker looks, literally, magnetically, at twice as much width of string as a single coil. Okay, here's something interesting: a Gibson P-90 is a humbucker. Same gauge wire, same amount of wire, same DC resistance, but they sound totally different, because you've only got the one-blade source – that single row of pole pieces – looking at the strings. That's why they wound uniquely different.

Sure, and it often surprising to players to discover that if you measure DC resistance on a selection of vintage Gibson humbuckers and a selection of P-90s, they average out about the same.
Sure, but the humbucker is warmer, thicker, fuller. But you also have to remember that [in the humbucker] you've got about 5,000 turns around each bobbin, which is very close to the source and heart of the magnetic field. Whereas the P-90 is a very big, wide coil. It's like the old Fender Jazzmaster. The coils in those things were monsters. Well, the magnetic field doesn't even extend all the way out to the end. The outside, say, 5,000 turns of wire are there as a tone generator, not an electrical generator, because the magnetic field doesn't blossom out that far.

What I'm hearing from so many makers is that the shape and depth of the coil play a critical role in determining the sound of the pickup.
Oh yeah, there are definitely variables. First, I probably make the thinnest humbucker in the world that's a full humbucker, the coils are 8mm tall, a little over a quarter of an inch – it's the same coil I use in any of my Benedettos or any of my other styles of pickups. So say I build two jazz guitar pickups, the coils are absolutely identical, the only difference is, instead of having two steel blades in the middle of the coils

and then a magnet going across connecting them into a horseshoe [shaped] magnet, what I do is I take an alnico magnet and literally cut it in half so I have two alnicos, and shove them down inside the coils. So it's acting like two single coils put together. These two pickups, even though the coils are identical, the windings are identical, the gauge of wire's is identical, because the magnetic layout is different, they sound different. They say my little humbucker sounds more like a single coil than it does a full humbucker. So, you lose something, but it's ultra, ultra thin.

It seems like, despite all the work you've done, and all the pickup designs for WD Music and OEM jobs for various guitar-makers, you tend to stay somewhat under the radar. I even had some difficulty finding information on your Hand Made line.
That's because I don't advertise it. I have a client base of over 2,000 and I don't need to really expand that. I'm almost afraid to advertise. If I become too well known to the general public I'd spend most of my time on the phone. There's only so much I can do in a day. When I call them 'Hand Made', they're handmade by *me*. I don't have a staff, I have one assistant, and that's it. Usually there's just me, myself, and I – and we get on quite well, the three of us. We fight sometimes …

Like right now, I'm sitting here making coils. If you buy a Kent Armstrong Hand Made, believe me, it was handmade by Kent Armstrong. But my technique is so labor-intensive that it's got to be handmade. Right now I'm sitting here wrapping a coil in aluminum foil. This is my shield, I use heavy-duty Reynolds Wrap. That's what I use.

But you will still make models that will fit lots of traditional positions?
Oh, sure. Stratocaters, Telecasters, P-Bass, Jazz Bass, humbuckers, of course. In fact, I can remake any pickup I have made since day one, because I still have the mold. And I guarantee my Hand Made pickups for life. If somebody comes back to me with a broken pickup, I'll replace it, free of charge. But it only happens very rarely.

Here's a little story. Do you remember the Aria SB Bass, with the big, molded black pickup? Well, I had a guy contact me to ask if I could repair his, because it had died. It turns out I couldn't get into it to fix it because it was totally sealed in epoxy, so I totally rebuilt it. Now, word got around, and I ended up doing a lot of these Aria SB Bass pickups. Then, years later, I was at the NAMM show at the Sperzel booth, and this little Japanese gentleman walked up. He said, "Ah, you're Kent Armstrong?" I said, "Yes, I am." He said, "I'm Shiro Arai, I own Aria … ." And I thought, "Oh, shit, here comes the lawsuit. He's going to sue the nuts off me or something."

But instead, he said, "I want to thank you and shake your hand. You have made many of our customers very happy in England. We no longer make the SB pickup, and you are keeping our basses in the market!" Boy, I was sweating. I thought this was the end of my career in the pickup business. In fact, I think they do now make that pickup again, but he was very happy that I had helped out their customers.

meet the makers: interviews

In addition to the jazz pickups, it seems like you make a lot of humbucker pickups in single-coil size housings.
Yeah, I do a lot of those. What I also made for someone just this week, I make a humbucker-covered P-90, with six pole pieces down the middle. We make a few of those because people like that P-90 sound. I also made a couple of humbucker-sized Charlie Christian pickups this week, because people want that Charlie Christian sound, but they don't want that huge, honkin' monster pickup in there.

How do you get that sound in a smaller package, without that pair of big magnets hanging under there?
Well, it was just an alnico magnet, that's all it was. It was actually a very poor design. It didn't bring a lot of the magnetic force into the pickup. In fact most of that magnet was doing nothing, it was just used for the mountings. So by just using good alnicos you can replace it, and I also do my humbucking SS system in the Charlie Christian. Basically, I designed out all the original Charlie Christian's faults. They were microphonic as heck, hummed like something terrible, weren't very powerful. They had a great sound, but they weren't a very well-made pickup.

I recently encountered another of your pickup designs, the one that First Act Guitar Studio is putting in their USA-made Delia guitar, kind of a Filter'Tron styled humbucker.
Yeah, I handmake that here. I have rewound so many thousands of Gretsch pickups over the years. In fact, somewhere here I've got a letter from Chet Atkins, thanking me for rebuilding people's pickups and giving them that great Gretsch sound.

What do you see as some of the secrets in the sound of those old Gretsch pickups?
Basically, the Filter'Tron was just a de-wound Gibson humbucker. That's what gave it that brightness and toppiness, the fact that it only had about 4,000 turns instead of 5,000 turns. And that's all it really was. It's the same with Gibson Mini-Humbuckers. I don't know why, but they never sound very good. Well I guarantee you, you give me your Gibson Mini-Humbucker and by the time I'm finished with it, it'll sound like a big, fat Gibson. Same with the Johnny Smith pickups. Everybody always says they're thin and useless, but you let me rewind that thing and it'll be a ballsy pickup.

Speaking of Filter'Trons, it seems like a lot of players have discovered that hotter isn't always better, although of course the hot pickup was the real trend in the early days of the replacement pickup boom.
Sure, the sound suffers for that. To achieve the power, they either put loads of magnetic force in – and that just kills your strings dead – or they would make it into

meet the makers: interviews

a distortion-type pickup. The problem with that is, you have got to use an incredibly fine-gauge wire to get super distortion. These guys were using, like, 45-gauge wire, and that would be the equivalent of trying to put the Hoover Dam through a garden hose. You'll get a lot of pressure, but you ain't got no volume. Try and squeeze these great big frequencies through a teeny weeny pipe, it just gets garbled, it comes out all horrible.

Even with our [high-output distortion] pickup, we use bigger bobbins and 44-gauge wire, and that is a world of difference. It's incredibly clear; you can still hear the notes but they're beautiful notes. Whereas the typical distortion pickup sound is just grunge. You've hacked off the tops and bottoms of the notes, you've compressed it so bad.

And I guess that's where you lose your dynamics and sensitivity, too.
Oh, big time. It's dreadful. Everything suffers. There's the right combination, and the wrong combination. I mean, the early Charlie Christians used a gauge of wire that is hard to break with your hand. It's 38-gauge wire. Elephant leg wire. It's huge. And you'd be surprised how little you can get on that coil, because it's so big it takes up space very quickly. Those things only DC'd out at about 1,200 ohms.

What is your favorite pickup design of all time?
If I had to play a pickup that I like the most, it would be a P-90. I just love the sound of a P-90, I don't know why. I have a 1949 Gibson ES-125 – the big, jumbo one, not the thin-bodied one – and it just sounds so good. My very first ever guitar was a '54 Les Paul Junior, so that's another P-90 on there. I just loved it, it was so good. My dad had all the Les Pauls and the other guitars to compare with, a Byrdland, a D'Angelico New Yorker. He had all the greatest guitars in the world, and I just loved my little Junior.

The P-90 strikes me as another pickup that some makers can get very wrong, if they're not careful. Overwind them too much, and you're in danger of just getting mud out of them.
I even handmake a few variations on that theme. I do a coil-tapped P-90, so one minute it sounds like a Stratocaster, and the next minute it sounds like a P-90. I do another dual version, and instead of putting the original screws in there I put six alnico magnets.

Which gives it a little more brightness and clarity.
That's exactly what it is. See, the steel screws help to shape the magnetic sound. It doesn't let the flux flow the way it should, whereas if you've actually got a magnet pole like in a Stratocaster pickup, the magnetic field is able to flow its own way. That's the difference. The steel screws are shaping the magnetic field. The coils on

meet the makers: interviews

my two pickups are absolutely identical, the only difference is, one's got two magnets underneath going up through six screws, the other one's got six magnets.

And which of your own pickup designs are you most proud of?
I would say my 12-pole jazz pickup. It really seems to have hit the right spot for everybody. And a close second would be my Ultra-Slim Jazz. It's unique, and it's so small that it cures a lot of the old L-5 problems where you can't get a pickup underneath the strings because the neck's so close to the body. Those are the two that have hit the market and done very well.

Joe Barden, Barden Engineering

Tell us a bit about what first triggered your interest in guitar pickups.
The story's pretty simple, although it's been mangled quite a bit over the years. I met Danny [Gatton] on January 5 1975. It was a Sunday night. And it was one of the foremost moments in my life, that I know of, that I was completely transfixed. I mean, I walked in and saw this guy wearing Charlie Christian's belt buckle – and I certainly knew who Charlie Christian was – and the band happened to be playing 'Good Enough to Keep', which I knew intimately because my father was a four-mallet vibe player who happens to have had the same year and model of Leedy vibes that Hamp [Lionel Hampton] had when he joined Goodman's big band: 1935 Leedys.

I'm watching this short, stumpy little redneck, and he's covering everything, from the solos to the fills … It was The Fat Boys, which was a five-piece at the time, Dick Heintze was alive, playing B-3 [Hammond organ] and Ralph McDuffy's playing alto. Danny's playing everything, but he's not stepping on anybody. When he went to the solos, what really killed me was – and I'd studied conservatory classical guitar for about six and a half years, and I knew from my training that when one's playing an ascending run on the guitar, your little finger is the weakest and your first finger is the strongest and most agile. So I notices this guy playing ascending runs with his thumb on the skunk stripe of the Tele, instead of wrapped around B.B. King style, and his little finger and his ring finger are standing up with his knuckles as right angles, as if he was Julian Bream, his first finger laid over inside of it is fingering notes as if he's Julian Bream, and the Coupe DeVille is that while he's playing his left arm is basically in the same position, and he's moving the guitar basically by grabbing the bridge to accommodate his hand and arm, more than he's moving his hand and arm to accommodate the guitar. I nearly shit.

Where was this gig?
This was at a club called The Keg, in Georgetown, DC, on a snowy Sunday night. I was one of two paying customers, and there was a drunk passed out, leftover from the afternoon happy hour. So there was a grand total of three people in attendance. I just stood there absolutely transfixed. Of course he played a Charlie solo, then he played his own, then he did a Van Epps type thing, and then he started to trade in fours, then in eighths, with Heinze on the B-3, who was … I was going to say, "every bit his equal," but Dick was probably better than Danny, in reality. My controversial opinion is that the beginning of the end for Danny was when Dick died, because he was the last known person who could challenge him and push him, and put him in a place where he had to grapple to get out. Dick had that ability.

Then Ralph would take his solo … and they were playing the most bizarre mix of shit, from straight-up 'Mystery Train' rockabilly to ancient chestnuts like 'Matilda', to Benny Goodman, to slow blues. But none of it is 'normal' music at all. It's not

meet the makers: interviews

rock'n'roll, it's not regular jazz. I thought I'd walked into a timewarp, or an alternate universe or something. And the only reason I was there was to shut up one of my best friends – who turns out to have been a very good friend of Dan's, and one of the best guitar players I know, by the name of Steve Bishop, who lives in Nashville now – who had been coming into the record store where I worked with one of those Panasonic portable tape recorders, with the cheesy condenser mic, playing me these awful tapes [of Danny's shows]. So just to shut him up and finally get him out of my face, I went down there on a Sunday night, so I could say, "Okay, I've seen it. Thanks. Turn that off." Because you couldn't hear much through these tapes.

I immediately said, "If there's some sort of a way to have a part of this, I'm joining this army." And it wasn't as a groupie or a hanger-on, or a sycophant, or anything like that. I said, "I'm going to contribute to this. I'm joining this army. I'm enlisting now!" I introduced myself to Danny that night. The whole band went to a table to sit and drink; he was very cordial and we talked. At the time I drank alcohol, and I happened to notice that the band was drinking for free, so another key thing went off in my head. So I asked him where they were playing next and he told me where it was. Of course I stayed for the whole gig, I helped him load out, and I noted what kind of vehicle he had, you know, jotted down the tag number. And I'd asked him, "Do you normally get to these gigs real early?" And he'd said, "Noooo, I come at the *very* last minute." Which was characteristic of Dan. So I would get there 45 minutes early, with a tape recorder, and I would just wait until he'd pull past the club, and I'd hop in, we'd find a parking place, I'd help him load in, and thus get to drink for free, and also get a killer tape out of the deal.

How did you progress from carrying amps and drinking with the band to making pickups for one of the most acclaimed guitarists of all time?
I'll go through it in sequence. So now I'm his road crew, and I know how to set his stuff up, but I knew I wanted to do more – I wanted to be more a part of this. I mean, we had a lot of fun at this time, and at this time, before I started making pickups, Danny also played pedal-steel in the band. Very few people know this, but he was left handed. So he would tune the E9 side of the steel guitar and I would tune the C6 side, and we had a double contest whenever we did it: one was who could do it the fastest; two was who could get the most strings in tune by tension alone. And we would alternate winning, believe it or not, so we both were blessed with these ears from hell.

I had bought a DiMarzio Pre-B1 pickup as a retail customer, just as a guy looking out for something for his Telecaster. And I did not know Danny at the time, this pre-dated my knowledge of him. I put it on my guitar and it sounded real muddy and skanky. I had a '67 Tele at the time, and I didn't know enough to realize it was still wired in 'deep/soft', where when the switch is in the bridge position you've got the bridge with the volume and tone; in the middle position you've got the neck with the volume and tone; then in the neck position you've got the neck with the volume only and these horrendous capacitors. Which is why – and I'll clue you in on another secret that few people know – Roy [Buchanan] never rewired his guitars. If you listen, you'll never hear a middle-position sound on any of his recordings, because all he used was the bridge and the neck, because he never rewired the guitars.

In any event, this pickup sounded terrible. Danny had opened a repair shop, and I took my guitar to get refretted by him with big frets, and to have a brass nut added, and hopefully one of those cool round string trees like the older Teles had, and maybe get my pickup rewound if they had enough time. So while Danny was doing a bang-up fret job on my guitar – and I do mean bang-up, he was not a sophisticated worker, let's put it that way, and I'm sorry to say quite often the guitar reflected the amount of time he took to do the work, he was not a patient person – and while he did the fret job, the other guy in the shop rewound the pickup.

Their theme while winding the pickups was to put as much wire on the bobbin as possible. I thought, "I don't know Dick about any of this, but that does not strike me as a premise that is useful or rational." But I rode with it, and I'll never forget when they took it out of the wax – and they didn't have any temperature control on the wax, so the wax was like red hot and would take some of the insulation off the wire – and the pickup cooled down and everything, and it didn't look very good. The top was all curled up at the ends, and it was bulging with wire, but it was able to fit through the cavity and the plate. They measured the resistance with a needle meter, and I remember everybody going, "Wow, 11,000 ohms man, that thing really is going to put out!" And this was where I first encountered 'putting out' ohms, something which … contradictory doesn't even begin to describe it. 'Putting out' and 'ohms' have no relation to each other at all, none whatsoever. Ohms is simply an absolutely linear measurement of resistance along the length of a piece of wire, it's a yardstick. And 42-gauge wire is 1.66 ohms per foot. You can measure the ohms on your pickups, divide it by 1.66, and that's how many feet of wire are on it. As if that does anything for anybody. But to this day, people say "This pickup 'puts out' 6,000 ohms", which is a ridiculous statement, because the number of ohms doesn't tell you anything, except in slight conjunction with a bunch of other things, regarding what the pickup's actually putting out regarding frequency response, power, and other things.

So in any event, I put the pickup in my guitar and it sounded just as shitty as that DiMarzio Pre-B1. The DiMarzio was wound with 43 [gauge wire] to about 12,000 ohms or something.

I guess all that a lot of replacement pickup-makers were doing in the early days was just trying to make hot pickups – pickups that were noticeably more 'rock' than what guitars of the '70s were being made with.

Yeah. Are you familiar with the Alembic hotrod kits? They had longer Gibson humbucker base plate mounting screws, and what you would do was you would take two of your screws out, slide your magnet halfway out, then you would take this big, fat ceramic magnet and align it with the other one, then slide it in. Take the other two screws out, put the longer screws in, and now you had this monstrously powerful pickup. But one factor that they neglected was that alnico conducts electricity, and ceramic does not. Therefore there's no inductance bridge between the coils, so they're not unified as one inductive unit, it's two separate inductive units combined. And the magnet that they put in was so large that it over-saturated the metal that it came into contact with, which meant that the metal could not carry all the magnetic flux that it was being asked to. Both of these things, by the way, artificially lowered the inductance, and when you lower the inductance that's when the pickup becomes more spiky and trebly. All DiMarzio did [in the early days], with the Super Distortion, was to rewind a Gibson humbucker along the lines of an Alembic hotrod kit. And everyone bought one.

Is there a means of giving, in statistics, what a pickup's going to put out and sound like, or is it beyond putting on paper.
Oh, very definitely you can. But it's many factors that have to be taken into consideration, and all these factors have to be measured at various frequencies and so on. You can absolutely duplicate a PAF humbucker with my ceramic magnets, no problem. I can do that. And I can absolutely duplicate my pickup with alnico magnets. Essentially what it boils down to is, magnetism is magnetism. It doesn't matter where you get it, it's how you apply it. So when these guys took out the inductance bridge, which is the electrical connection between two coils – because the alnico magnet was touching the pole pieces on both sides, but the ceramic magnet wasn't making that electrical connection – now you've got these two separate inductance units operating independently. And if you do it to a Gibson pickup you'll really notice the hum, because the inductance of the coil with the slugs is considerably different than the one with the screws.

A buddy of mine just bought a reissue Les Paul, you know, spent a million bucks for it. He called me up and said, "Man, this thing hums like a bitch! What's the matter with it?" I went over and listened to it and said, "No, it hums like it should." I had brought a stock Strat with me and plugged it in and said, "Now, *this* is hum." He said, "Well, why does this thing hum at all, they're supposed to be 'humbuckers'?" I explained the inductance to him: my pickups are equal inductance on both sides – we work to a tolerance of a third of a percent – and in many cases, with a properly shielded guitar, you don't hear any perceptible hum at all. I used to sit in my living room with three of those torchier lamps and turn down half way to make sure that I was making the transformers go off, and turn my Twin up to six, and just take my hand off the strings gently, and all you'd hear was "*pffff*" [replicates amp white noise, without hum]. Nothing.

meet the makers: interviews

And of course those Gibson humbuckers are not completely bucking the hum. The coils are not equal, which is what the job requires in the first place.
No, and Seth Lover knew that. He and I had a long discussion about that, and he had complained about it. They said, "We want one side of it to be adjustable!" So he said "fine."

Apparently the sales people wanted something to talk about when they plugged the guitars, regarding the fancy new pickups.
Yeah. As opposed to the Charlie Christian. Essentially, by the time of the humbucker, a screw-adjustment had already been established with the P-90, so they couldn't go back from that. And he knew that, which is why he put that little helper, the rectangular thing with the six holes in it on the screw side, to try and help it out. But he knew it wasn't going to equalize it.

As he told me, "I learned early on in my career how to pick my fights. And my checks cashed, so if that's the way you want it … ."

When did you first start making pickups that looked like what we think of today as Joe Barden pickups?
I first started by rewinding pickups. I didn't want to tell Danny that I didn't like what had been done in his shop. I fibbed and told him that I wanted some other pickups to mess around with, and he told me to go and see this guy – who shall remain nameless – who repaired organs and TVs and also rewound pickups. By now I had taken apart a pickup that I'd found, and I knew how fragile these things were. So what I did was, I went down to Zavarella's Music – that's where Dan shopped, and Phil Zavarella was the patron saint of all of us trying to get started, they're no longer there now – and I went down there and bought four stock Tele bridge pickups for like $17 a piece or something. They were all repair parts, because there was no industry at this point. Seymour has just now come out with his trashcan ads, where he's got the trashcan with pickups stacked up in it. That's how low level they were at that point, and they weren't even doing humbuckers yet.

I took these four pickups down to this repairman, two for me and two for another guy, another mind-blowing guitar player named Steve Merritt – he was my other set of ears, unfortunately he died a year and a half after Dan did – and he and I went to high school together, and stayed tight after. So we had these pickups rewound, and came back the next week to pick them up and pay for them, and every one of them looked different. They all looked like they'd been run over by a truck. Instead of being wrapped in black string or even black tape they're wrapped in white adhesive tape, I mean … you know, flashing red flags, right? So we got them home, and we had a pretty good guitar – Steve had a '63 red sparkle Tele – and we put them in there, and one sounded good, but the other three didn't. I had no electrical knowledge, no

meet the makers: interviews

meters, no nothing. I had nothing except my uncommon sense, and I was like, "He's either got to redo these other three, or give us our money back."

When we went back the week after that, these three are *really* starting to look rough now – and keep in mind, I'd purchased brand new ones for him so he'd have the best shot at making good looking pickups. And he still managed to have these horrendously curled up ends, with wire loops hanging out under the tape, and just horrible stuff. They didn't sound any good either, so now we're a month into this thing. On week five, I went back and said, "I'm going to stand here and watch you do this." And he was like, "Oh no, you can't do that man. This wire is finer than your hair … " and so forth. And I was like, "Shut up. You're dealing with a disgruntled consumer, not someone trying to steel your trade secrets. I want to see what you're doing, because we're wasting a lot of time and money and gas here."

In any event, I watched him, and he had a spool of wire on the floor, and the pickup mounted on this cheesy rig, holding onto it with his thumb and forefinger – what we call 'the Armstrong method' – and I was smart enough about stuff in general that I didn't know what he was doing, but I also knew that *he* didn't either. So there's two dummies standing there, only one's got a coil of wire. It was at that point that I just said, "Stop. Just give us our money back on these two, you can have 'em. Where do you get this wire?" He said, "Oh, that's the most closely guarded secret in the business … ." Phew. Bad thing to say to me. I soon found out that you can order a tractor-trailer full of wire if you want to.

I found this transformer shop in Kensington, MD, and they had two and a half pound spools of wire, and they would sell me ones that had maybe three-quarters of a pound left on them, not enough for them to use for anything. So I went down to Zavarella's, bought a couple more stock Tele bridge pickups, took 'em apart, and I was pretty certain that there would be some electronics involved, and I was a little worried about that. I remember unspooling the pickups, layer by layer, and eventually I started to see something on the other side, and I'm seeing through the last layers, and it's my fingers I'm looking at. And I suddenly realized that there are no circuits or anything in there – all it is is wire, magnets and cardboard. I remember throwing the thing against the basement wall and going, "Hell with this, I'll be at the bottom of this thing in two weeks! Three factors? For Christ's sake!"

Arrogance is its own reward, as I've said many times, and of course it actually took me about two years to make any kind of pickup. I put together a winding rig and started to wind some pickups, and I simply kept empirical notes. I learned from a good friend of the family whose father lent me a meter and some tools – and I still use his father's tools on every amp that I work on – and his name was Don Hansen, and his son was Rod – he was dating my sister – and they turned me on to the basics of things like resistance and so forth like that. I finally made a pickup that sounded good, or that I thought sounded good.

Keep in mind I'm deeply into Roy [Buchanan] at this point. His pickups are like religion to me, although I hadn't seen him live yet. And was also listening to Poco, and Jim Mesina, and I wasn't into the hardcore guys like Buck Owens and Roy Nichols yet, but the modern guys were turning me onto the question, "why a Telecaster?" Teaching me what was compelling about this instrument that is so unforgiving, so crude, so unfinished.

It is a strange thing, isn't it? The Stratocaster must be the master of rock guitars, design-wise, but the Tele has its addicts, for whom nothing else will do.
Well, it is the most unforgiving of guitars, and if you master that, no one can take that away from you. It will fight you tooth and nail every step of the way, and with my pickups in it, for every misstep you might as well set off a canon. My pickups are as ruthless as the guitar is, and I get that from Danny being ruthlessly accurate. He comes from that Nashville school where you don't make a mistake. You just don't. And you don't read; if you need a chart, we don't need you, end of story. So I was brought up in that discipline.

Anyway, I took this pickup I had made down to a club Danny was playing in, and I'd only been doing about half as much roadie work for him as I had previously – I'd quit school at this point – and it didn't occur to me until years later that I'd quit school basically in about tenth grade to work with Dan. And I remember he came off the bandstand after the first set, and I said, "I've got something to show you." I took the pickup out of my pocket and told him I'd rewound it. And he said, "Get the f— out of here! Since when do you rewind pickups? You didn't say anything to me." I told him I'd been doing it for about three months, but I wasn't going to say anything to him until I had something to look at. I wasn't going to make a fool out of myself.

So we went back to this aisle on the way to the bathrooms to take a look at the thing, right where the cigarette machine was, and I remember Dan bending over under the sign for the Marlboro Lites to look at this pickup – and my balls were in my throat – but I had done a superb job of this thing. Had taken it apart completely, kept the magnets separate, had sanded the cardboard then epoxied the magnets to the cardboard so that there would be no curl ... I'd gone all out to make sure that this thing looked as puss as it possibly could. And I'll never forget Dan leaning over and looking at this thing, and turning it over and over in his hand, and of course his shirt-tail's hanging out and he's got the plumber's ass hanging out, the usual deal. And he stands up and goes, "This is amazing. This is better than any of us can do. From now on, you're the pickup guy."

Oh, I nearly fell over. It was like being made an Indian. Here I was, this suburban white boy, literally from the bland-o suburbs, and his family goes way back. There were Gattons on the third ship coming up behind Captain Smith and Pocahontas. He's the real deal from southern Maryland, and he's nine years older than I am – accomplished, adult, and I still didn't see myself in that way.

meet the makers: interviews

And this was just your standard rewind of a Tele pickup.
That's all it was. A rewind, just to see what I could do. Eventually we did get around to putting it in his guitar, and we came to the conclusion that it was a bit thick, but it certainly twanged better than anything they did, because I was open to the concept of restraint. You know, just because we *have* extra space we don't need to use it. I'd seen so many Fender pickups from different guitars, and they weren't full [of wire].

I started rewinding pickups, and the first time I rewound a pickup for public consumption was for the aforementioned Steve Bishop of Tennessee. He was playing in a real big rock band around here, and he knew Mike Stern who played in a Top 40 rock band around here, and he was the baddest f—in' rock player you ever saw in your life, except for maybe Bishop. I begged Steve Bishop to let me rewind a pickup for him for free, and if he liked it he could pay me something for it, and if not I'd put his old one in, and no harm, no foul. He was really reluctant, and he probably talked to Dan, but he eventually came over to my shop with a Strat pickup and said, "Okay, rewind this." I didn't have any thoughts about what we were trying to achieve until I got half-way through, then started to consider, "what are we trying to accomplish, what position is this going to go in?" And I was panicked huge. So I just kind of shot for the yellow line in the center of the highway.

He brought his guitar back, '54 Strat, all original – although I think the pickups had been changed, which is why he'd let me do it in the first place – and we soldered this pickup in, he played a little bit and it sounded okay. So he said, "All right, I've got a gig tonight. I'll try it out and see how it sounds."

The next morning I get a phone call and pick it up, and it's Steve, and he just goes, "It soars!" Those were the only two words I heard, and then a click. As far as I know, that pickup is still in that Strat.

When did you transition to your benchmark double-blade design?
In April of 1980 was when I did my first rewind, so we're talking August of '80 that I'd done this for Bishop, and I've already turned Dan on in July, trying that pickup in his Tele. I was going to make a lighter one for him to get more twang, because it finally dawned on him, too, that less may be more. We talked about it and figured that we don't know shit, but let's go this way.

So I guess around August or September of '80 I got a really, really good bridge pickup in Dan's guitar. Keep in mind, he's using the Charlie Christian pickups in the neck position, and one of the things that's knocking him out about my pickups is that they had more output. I was using the same wire – and I now know why they had more output, but we'll leave that out because it's kind of a trade secret – and they also had twang and presence and all this kind of stuff. That, I know, is because I was winding them so slowly and I was not stretching the wire on the ends. When you wind them so fast, when you're winding an elliptical shape like that, you get a yank, yank, yank every 180 degrees. So you've got 42 gauge along the long sides, and 44 gauge along the ends. I didn't have that because I was going so slowly, trying my best to lay the wire neatly alongside each turn and all that.

The Christian pickup was put in the guitar to overcome the problem of the Tele neck pickup, because as anyone will tell you, there's always an imbalance between Tele pickups. Dan just couldn't stand that, but once he put the Christian in he'd transferred the problem. Now he's got this Christian pickup that is *blowing* away the bridge pickup … Well, my bridge pickup is helping that. One day he said to me, "Why don't you make a Christian pickup with a blade and the magnet underneath?" Because at the time, Dan, and his mom and his brother and dad, were all making these things – Dan was selling Telecasters at the time for between $500 and $550 with a Christian, a fret job and a brass nut. He had a little business going. Steve Bishop actually owns one of those. In any event he said, "Find magnets you can put underneath, make a blade like a Christian only shape the plastic exactly like a Tele, then it will bolt right in." Because their method for installing these Christians in the neck position was the old technique of the repeated drill press holes one next to the other, then caving them all in … .

Hacking it out …

Yeah, with a spoon. Really nice. And I mean, they were really raping these guitars. I had enough to talk about with St. Peter already, without keeping this up. Anyway, I said, "How am I supposed to do that?" And he said, "I dunno!"

I'd always been good mechanically, even as a young kid, but still we're talking disciplines that I don't know a thing about. Eventually I put together a bridge pickup. I didn't know anything about tapping or threading, so I drilled holes and glued nuts underneath the holes. I traced everything from a grounding plate and all that. He brought his guitar over and we put it in, and he played a couple little things – flicking the switch – checking it out. He adjusted the pickup, played for about 15 minutes … and it just stopped time. We stared at each other for a while. It was every bit as loud, and could have been raised up to be even louder than the Christian pickup, had infinitely more articulation, twang. And we're talking a single-coil pickup, but it's got split blades, because the only thing I could conceive of doing was have a hole down the middle of the bobbin for a spindle to rotate on, so the blades were actually two different blades, and I'd carved them myself out of a street sign that I'd hacksawed.

So now he's got this bridge pickup that's the equivalent of the Christian pickups, and he was just gassed beyond belief, I was gassed – we were just shitting bricks. We couldn't believe it. Then a real tribute, the first of many from him, he said, "Make a neck version." And I thought, "Oh my god, he wants to abandon the Christian!" Which, if you've ever seen a picture of one of those Teles, they have got to be the coolest thing going. Wow. Nobody had ever treated me that way – given me that kind of latitude, or trust. I was blown away.

meet the makers: interviews

What kind of magnets did you use in that pickup?
I had found some ceramic magnets out of some toy or something. I can't remember. And one thing I did learn was that the same pole phase had to go on either side of the blade, otherwise the magnetism would simply pass through the blade. Whereas if you put the same magnetism on the pole face on each blade it had to go up the blade – it had to go somewhere – because it was repelling itself, right? So it repelled itself right up the blade. I'm keeping copious notes on all this stuff, but they're all empirical because I don't have any basis for anything.

I made a Tele neck pickup – and I still have those exact two pickups that Dan first used, which I thought I had lost. At the time Danny was working with Roger Miller, who also had Thumbs Carllile playing with him, and if you can imagine Danny on one side of the stage and Thumbs on the other. I mean, Jesus God, that's just not fair! So Thumbs starts calling me up, and I tell him how long it will take to make him some pickups. And just like Dan, he has the patience of a two year old. Dan came home with no pickups in his guitar, because Thumbs wouldn't let him leave California until he took the pickups out. And I thought that was set number one, but when we found set number one I had the vaguest snippet of a memory that Dan had suggested making a set or two extra at the start, when we got those first pickups right. Unfortunately the guitar was stolen from Thumbs a year or two before he died, but he used to call me up every so often and say, "Goddamn boy, do those pickups sound good!" And of course I couldn't believe it, I'm this white boy from the suburbs and I'm getting calls from Thumbs Carllile.

So you were using ceramic magnets right from the start?
Ceramics, yeah. I didn't have any idea where to get alnico.

And when is this?
Let's see – I did his first bridge pickup in September of '80, and I don't know when that *Austin City Limits* ran [with Gatton, Miller and Carllile], but that's when Danny came home with no pickups, so we're probably in the first quarter of 1981. I'm making these pickups with two halves of a blade per pickup, and they're sharp as hell on the inside – they're tearing the shit out of people, and ripping people's fingernails off. The problem was that, as much fidelity and all that other stuff that the pickups had, they had a corresponding increase in hum. I mean, these bastards, you got them at the right angle to a neon sign and they hummed like a bitch. To the point where Dan would reflexively just roll the guitar volume to nothing between songs. I'm selling these things as fast as I can make them, but everyone kept telling me, "You've got to find a way to get rid of the hum!"

By 1982, when I was living in Springfield, VA, in the house of a pilot who had been relocated to the west coast, and I was making my pickups in his basement, I realized that I needed to get to work on a Strat pickup, and also that we needed to

meet the makers: interviews

get the blades machined, because they were taking the greatest amount of time. I looked into the phone book, and there was a machinist close to me – and they were on Fullerton Road, so I said, "That's got to be the place!" – and Dan agreed, we both lived by associations like that. I went down there, and he made me a jig that fit on the spindle of a sewing machine motor, same thing Leo used, and I hooked up a rheostat, because I'd been an electrician, wiring up houses. I put that together, and he made an aluminum block with set screws that the pickups could sit on, and they would spin perfectly.

So now I've got nicely cut blades from him, and he turns me on to the concept of plating, because the blades were rusting and so forth. I started getting these blades nickel plated, and then electroless nickel plated, so you didn't get the buildup at the ends from standard plating. Once I got to electroless plating, my pickups were looking good. I was cranking out pieces of plastic that were absolutely identical in size and shape. Machine shop people had taught me about tolerances and so forth, and by now I was working to tolerances of three thousandths. But that was something I'd learned from Dan – this unspoken professionalism.

In his playing, more than his own guitar repair work I guess?
Uh-huh, yeah. But it was another world being around him. That's why I say "it was like being made an Indian." I got to go places that no kid from the suburbs would ever have gotten to go. Meet people like Buck Owens and Merle Haggard, all kinds of people, and every time Dan would introduce me and go, "This is the guy who makes my guitars sound the way they do!" He never once held back, he always gave it up for me. That was one of the benefits of him already being one of the best guitar players in the world; he already had that bird, and he didn't need to be best pickup-maker to. And we both came to understand what a burden 'best' can be. I'm surviving my realization; Dan didn't survive his.

But you finally cracked the noise thing, right?
The noise thing came this way. I had gone down to a Bonnie Raitt concert at Constitution Hall in Washington, DC, on Danny's suggestion. I took a Strat down to show her, and I didn't put any strings on it because I didn't know what kind she used – so they were going to have to give me a set of strings, that was rude in the first place! I remember dropping the guitar off with no strings on it, and they said, "Well *that* definitely is not going to make any noise!" And I went, "Ah, Joe ... " Where's the door, you know.

But anyway, they put strings on it and put it in tuning, because she's going to use it for slide. And I'll never forget sitting on the side of the stage next to the side fills during the sound check, shitting my pants, not even knowing what's real. She came out and had her guitar, the brown one, and kicked off 'Tumbling Dice', and I remember realizing this was the first time I'd ever heard professional musicians.

meet the makers: interviews

They just tore the shit out of it, and all this stuff came crashing down on me as I looked at the sound man, the monitors, all that stuff. 'Cos I was still caught in this mindset that rock'n'roll was dope-smoking hippies and all that.

And guys in the clubs, where Danny was playing, had it pretty basic.
Yeah, they were not playing super-great gear or anything. And all of a sudden I realized: this is beyond dead serious. This is real shit.

I know my eyes must have been like saucers. And all of a sudden she points at me, and goes, "Come here!" I go running over, and a couple of her aides come out. I didn't say a word, I didn't know what to say. I'm standing in Constitution Hall in the middle of the stage with Bonnie Raitt, and she's like, "What am I looking at?" All I could think to say was, "Pickups." So she plugged into a Jim Kelley [amplifier], and started playing. She hit a couple of chords, got a funny look on her face, adjusted a couple of knobs, got another wrinkled-up look on her face. Meanwhile, I'm looking at the side door, going, "Bail, Joe. Just get out of here before you make any more of a mess!"

And all of a sudden she's going, "This is f—in' unbelievable!" This is on the 'Greenlight' tour, and she went into 'Greenlight', and just tore it up. She was asking me, "How did you do it?" and I couldn't put two sentences together – blah, blah, blah. And all of these people are suddenly going around my saying, "Mr Barden, would you like something to eat? Something to drink? Where are you parked, can we put you in the compound?" And I'm just spinning.

She looked at me and asked, "Can I borrow this guitar and use it tonight?" And I was like, "Of course." I was stunned. It had never occurred to me that she would want to do that – to open the show with it. They asked me if I wanted to stay for dinner, and I didn't know enough then to know that you always get a meal ticket, always get a laminate. I was trying to be polite, so I drove home to my parent's house in DC. I remember riding up Pennsylvania Avenue, right around 9th or 10th, and I just broke into tears. It was just overwhelming.

I went to my parents' house and ate, and then went back there for the show. She used the guitar, absolutely loved the pickups, and wanted to keep it, so I sold her the pickguard with the pickups in it. And when they paid me, they sent me to the trailer in the back where the road manager was – all these women, these groupies hanging around, all kinds of shady characters, a really gross scene – and in the middle of the trailer was a steel pole bolted to the floor and the ceiling, with a briefcase full of money handcuffed to it … and that's how I got paid.

And the Bonnie Raitt experience led you toward the necessity of hum-rejecting pickups?
Yeah. Okay … during the course of all this Bonnie Raitt and I had a discussion about hum, and I realized that with all that professional gear, with the increase in power,

the guitar pickup handbook

the lights, and everything, that this would be a necessity. It was a week or two after that that I … I won't say 'invented', but that the good man upstairs hit me with the idea of how to do the double-blade pickups. I was infuriated that she had anything to complain about, although she wasn't complaining, she was simply commenting. But I didn't want to report back to Dan that there was any bummers. So it was as a direct result of that that I worked out the double blade.

And I guess the double blade worked best for Dan, too. Because somehow in working up the new design you still retained that clarity and that twang.
Yes indeed. There were many, many iterations. The first double blades were nothing to write home about. In fact, they were something that should have been destroyed. They were way too humbuckery. But again, using the 'less is more' theory, we eventually tailored it to the point where I got that sound right.

Probably the last part of the story was in '91 when Eric Johnson straightening me out on the output levels of the three different pickups, which was an issue that had come up by that time, and was a pretty sophisticated issue considering we were only a couple years into it by then. He straightened me out on that, and we haven't changed the recipe since.

As much fuss as people make about alnico magnets, it seems like you have proved as much as anyone that you can do whatever you want with ceramic magnets, it just depends how you use them.
Well, it's that same old story, magnetism is magnetism. You just can't go substituting, blindly, one for the other. It depends how you go about it. Like you can't go taking a tire off my car and putting it on yours and expecting it to work. "Hey, they're both round!" You've got to know if it's the right size, the right tread, blah-blah. Once you've learned how to work with the material, and learn your lessons on how to apply it in order to achieve and end result, then you can do what you want with it.

I learned all this empirically because it was very late that I got into the mathematics of coil winding and all that. Books for those are the kind that the first half of the first page has words, and the rest is all numbers – trigonometry. But I always had Dan, and I always had all these other people when I came up with something new. The Bonnie Raitts and the Mick Taylors, and they would try things out for me. All due to Dan … I just can't stress enough, it was like a guy that had come along and found a kid wandering and said, "Here kid, you don't have a life – have a life!" All of a sudden I've got all these people to consult with and all these situations to be in.

And how did you crack the design for the double-coil pickups?
Well, most people don't realize how much the word spreads in this business,

meet the makers: interviews

especially among road bands. It never really dawned on me that Bonnie Raitt was going home and telling umpteen zillion people about these pickups. At the time they were still single coils, I was getting a lot of attention for them, and the need for a hum-free version became entirely apparent. But the real big development came after Bonnie Raitt. By carefully measuring on either side of my single coil I found out I had exactly enough plastic hanging over my coil to equal the width of another blade. It was like getting hit in the head with a rock or something. I was like, "Oh my god, volume equals volume, no matter where you put it, so half the wire can go on one blade and half can go other the other … ."

I mean, literally, my world started to get very fuzzy and I went and sat on the basement steps, and as opposed to being elated, I was *scared*. I knew that, regardless of what this thing sounds like, I could wind it to sound right, because I knew that there were enough variables in winding that, although it would have its own character, you could definitely make a Strat pickup out of it, you could definitely make a Tele pickup out of it…

So this was like the lightning bolt for you? This was your revolution?
Oh, it was definitely the revolution. After the idea I made one in about an hour, and I put it in this white Strat that you can actually see Mick Taylor using on the *Blues Live* DVD with Coco Taylor and John Mayall and the Blues Breakers. Mick really liked the pickups, and wanted me to make him one just like the Strat that had them on for him to sample that night, but it didn't work out.

But anyway, what I had also found was – due to the fact that a ceramic magnet does not conduct electricity, and there's no conductive bridge between the two coils – I had to drastically alter the wind to compensate for that. Like, with my wind today, if I were to put in an identical alnico magnet, the inductance would skyrocket, the pickup would be extremely dark and muddy, and no one would get near it with a barge pole. What I found was that I needed to use a lot less wire [than conventional designs], so people are constantly calling me up and going, "My Lindy Fralins 'put out' 6,500 ohms, and yours only measure around 4,000 – so they must be broken!" But if they don't measure it when they get it and put it in the guitar first, and play it, then they're totally dumbfounded, because it's way louder, *way* louder, than any stock type pickup, it has fidelity like a Neumann mic compared to a Shure SM57. It has bandwidth that goes so low and so high – I mean, it reproduces things that you never heard out of your guitar.

It literally takes a while for people to get used to playing. Your knob settings are all going to change, because suddenly instead of this real narrow band width that's real peaky, this pickup that just concentrates on this one narrow little band of frequencies, you've got a full-frequency-response pickup. So then they're like, "It's more powerful, it's got more band width, more sustain, it attacks like a humbucker but sounds exactly like a Strat pickup, but it only measures 4,000 ohms. What's the deal?" So I then explain to people that that's what was necessary to utilize the magnet. It's just a matter of how you apply it.

And your pickups are not like, well, Seymour Duncan Hotrails pickups, or what people are used to seeing from single-coil-sized dual-rail pickups, which is the hot rock sound. Yours, on the other hand, are sweet and clean.
Oh, ours is a totally different pickup than that. My list of Telecaster players is ridiculous: Danny, Bill Kirchen, Johnny Hiland – these are guys that could play anything. What these pickups are is oddities in that they're extremely high-end merchandise, in a category of merchandise where there *is* no other high-end. Now, people think there's high-end, with the vintage replicas, and some of those are very good – I mean, Seymour's Antiquity line is damned impressive. For someone who's looking for a dead, bone-stock sound, I tell them, "Don't buy [my] pickups." And also, I tell people not to buy just one of them, because if you have two other pickups in there next to it they're going to sound like broken transistor radios next to this one. The cut that these pickups have, I mean even at low volume, they cut through the PA, through all the mush, through all the idiocy that's up on stage.

They're highly unforgiving, much like a Telecaster. They're like real high-camber short skis: if you're a great skier, you'll love 'em, but if you've never skied before you'll end up on your ass. Or like a Ferrari. I ask people, "Have you ever driven a Ferrari?" Most people say "no", but of the people who say "yes", when you talk to them for a little while they usually end up admitting that it was a pretty terrible experience. You touch the brake and you go through the windshield, you touch the gas and you're flying through intersections. You turn the wheel and you're making U-turns.

Those are good analogies, and I hear that from people who do like your pickups, that they took some getting used to because all of a sudden everything they were playing was right up there on display.
Oh, they illuminate every part of your playing and every part of your guitar and your rig. And if there's a lot of sloppiness in your playing you're going to hear that, and that's going to bug you. Danny had a great analogy, with his usual crudeness. He said, if you did a graph, with anybody else's pickups it would be like a guy taking a piss: it just comes out and goes straight down. Whereas with yours it's like a guy hitting a golf ball, it just takes off and soars. And I used to think, "If I could just find a way to put that in an ad!"

You have always maintained a fairly limited line, you just do what you do, but do you have any other developments that you want to tell us about?
Probably our Two Tone humbuckers, which I developed out of a design for pickups

meet the makers: interviews

I did for the Kubicki Factor Bass years ago. The pickups for him were active, low-impedance pickups and I wound them with very few turns of wire [because they fed into preamps], but with wires coming out from taps that gave you two completely different pickup sounds when you wanted them. Years later I realized that instead of that tiny little signal that I was giving him for his integrated circuit, why not adapt that to a Strat sound, and we did, very successfully. We sell more Two Tone humbuckers than we sell regular humbuckers. They're ideal for matching sounds with two single coils pickups in an H/S/S configuration. Or what's really neat is if you put two of them in a Les Paul and switch them to the alternate sound, the single-coil-type sound, and put the pickup selector switch in the middle, it sounds exactly like the Merle Travis *Yellow* album, which is a singular tone. So that, I thought, was innovative.

Has there been any other innovation out there, by another maker, that has caught your attention?
In pickups … hmm? Well, a guitar I thought was pretty cool, that I saw at the Frankfurt [Germany] show a few years ago, was the Teuffel Birdfish.

Sure, I know the one – completely modernistic design.
Exactly. It's totally different, it looks very cool, and it sounds good – not Fender, not Gibson, but the guy is making his own statement. I have to be honest, though, in pickups I haven't seen much of anything, other than the boom in vintage-reproduction pickups. And what strikes me about those, well, people used to say to me, "Does your pickup sound like a 1950 Broadcaster?" And I'd reply, "Which 1950 Broadcaster have you played recently that you want it to sound like?" And they'd just go, "Uhhh … ." So, with these vintage replica pickups, I don't know one person in 10,000 that has actually played a '59 burst. I had the great fortune of playing Keith's guitar – they took it right off the wall for me at the Hard Rock Café – and I can tell you I have never heard a sound like that ever, before or since. Like I said, my pickups are way high fidelity and the band width is way high, but this guitar had the beat old strings on it and everything, and I plugged it into my little amp and just stood there and played, and I was just *mesmerized*. To say "now I get it" – this was more like, "now I get it, *times a hundred*." Now I can understand why people want these guitars, and why they're willing to pay that kind of money for them.

Larry DiMarzio and Steve Blucher, DiMarzio

Tell me a little bit about how you got started in the pickup business.
Larry DiMarzio: My first pickup repair was in 1970, when I had a broken pickup from a 1959 rosewood Stratocaster. The middle pickup was not working and it had wires hanging from it, so I assumed that it could be repaired by cutting off all of the wire and rewinding it with new wire. I found an electronic supply house in Syosset, Long Island, that had magnet wire. I took samples of the wire that I removed from the original pickup. Since I was a student and had no money, I hitchhiked from Staten Island to Syosset, a round trip that took over nine hours. When I arrived at the shop I realized that the available wire was thicker than the original. I bought it anyway, assuming that it would probably work OK. Upon returning to my apartment, I made a cardboard holder, which I fitted to the top of my phonograph turntable, and then put the turntable on 78 rpm and began rewinding my first pickup. After about 38 hours of winding, with numerous breaks in the new wire, I finally finished the bobbin and was ready to plug it in. Much to my disappointment, the pickup sounded terrible, and I did not work on another guitar pickup for at least four months. After my failure, I decided not to try working on pickups again.

However, while I was working for Charlie LoBue at Guitar Lab, he gave me a large box of broken guitar pickups. He knew about my electronics background and he said, "See what you can do." I took them home and began to keep records on everything that I learned. I gained guitar knowledge from different people: Jimmy D'Aquisto taught me how he did frets, Charlie LoBue taught me about guitar building, and Bill Lawrence filled in my pickup knowledge. However, none of these people played rock'n'roll or a contemporary style of guitar. I brought something completely new to the mix that made all the ideas work together. I learned to make pickups by myself. Charlie didn't know anything about pickups. Eventually all the LoBue guitars had my handmade pickups.

When I first met Bill Lawrence, I already had rebuilt many pickups. Bill hired me after seeing my guitar work, and by this time I was also well known for doing fret jobs and setups. Bill had made his own coil-winding machine with a counter. He had also figured out how to control the wire flow and tension. It was like being in a dark room and having someone turn on the light. The first day I met Bill we talked for two hours about making pickups and I went home and started making new models. Please keep in mind that Bill's ideas about what sounded good were very different from mine. Bill was all about jazz, and I was about sustain and tone.

Without insulting anyone, what "went wrong" between the golden age of pickups – arguably the '50s and early '60s with both Fender and Gibson – and the mid-'70s or so?

meet the makers: interviews

Larry: In clarification, guitars being made during this time did not measure up to the older guitars. It wasn't just pickups. Everything went wrong. I knew this because I was a player and worked in the stores as a guitar repairman, at The Guitar Lab on 47th street and later at Alex Music on 48th Street. Decisions were made by Gibson to discontinue the Les Paul. The neck shapes were changed. When the thick-body Les Paul was re-issued, the fret work was so poor that people would buy their guitars at Manny's and then bring them to me at the Guitar Lab to have the frets fixed. The guitars were equipped with mini humbuckers – duh!

By 1964 Fender had been purchased by CBS, and the lack of knowledge displayed by the corporate bosses was frightening. Nitrocellulose lacquer was replaced by polyurethane. Truss rods didn't work. The pickups suffered from similar corporate decisions. My initial research led me to learn that I could compensate for a number of the shortcomings of the new guitars by altering the pickups, and as a result I invented the replacement pickup business. By 1976, DiMarzio pickups were well established as *the* aftermarket pickup and were on tour and in the studio with The Who, David Bowie, Al DiMeola, Edgar Winter, John Abercrombie, Wishbone Ash, Steppenwolf, Eddie Martinez, Aerosmith, Blackfoot, Blue Oyster Cult, Brownsville Station, Kiss and many others.

Steve Blucher: I think the golden age of pickups is now. There are far more models available than there have ever been in the past, with a very wide range of sonic choices. The guitars and pickups of the '50s and early '60s created the basis for all the gear that followed, but the actual range of choices for guitars, pickups, amplifiers and accessories was extremely limited by comparison.

Were you surprised at the demand for your products?
Larry: DiMarzio pickups were a success from the day they were introduced. Before there was even a DiMarzio corporation, I had opened my own guitar repair shop in Staten Island and we were increasing in sales every month. After incorporation in 1975, the following year business went up by seventeen times what we'd had the first year. It was a good idea, and we were the first.

Are there any myths or common misconceptions about pickups that you'd like to take the time to dispel?
Steve: Too many to fully describe, actually. The broadest misconception is that an electric guitar is simply a platform for pickups, and it should therefore be possible to completely transform the sound of any guitar with the proper pickup. This is a fallacy. The essential character of any guitar is determined by its construction, and no two guitars will sound or perform identically unless they are entirely composed of synthetic material. It's certainly possible to alter the sound of any electric guitar by replacing pickups, but it may not be possible to "fix" a guitar whose sound is very far from what you had in mind. This also partially explains why we offer many pickup

models; experienced players appreciate the ability to fine-tune individual guitars with specific pickups to hone in on their desired sound.

For a time, especially early on in the "high-gain era" (I'd say the late '70s and '80s in particular) it seemed like the thinking, with rock players in particular, was "the hotter the better" regarding replacement pickups. Sometimes, of course, that's true for certain styles, but tell us a little bit about how and why that might not always work for people.

Larry: Originally I felt that the pickup-to-amp relationship had to be one of high gain. By overwhelming the front end of the amplifier, the effect was increased sustain. Keep in mind that my first guitar heroes, Leslie West, Jeff Beck, Jimmy Page, relied on guitar-to-amp distortion, and I never liked the sound of distortion pedals. It allowed the guitarist to control everything based on the volume control of the guitar, since by lowering it, it would clean up and by raising it to 10 it would put the amp into a smooth, natural overdrive. This is a very different experience from stepping on a box. With the introduction of higher adjustable gain on the front end of the amplifier, you could have a lower output pickup still driving the amp into distortion. Basically, amplifier manufacturers were responding to the desire to sustain and distortion from their point of view, while I had already responded to it from the pickup-maker's point of view.

Steve: The original reason for the success of hotter pickups was the absence of high-gain amplifiers in the 1970s. The only ways to achieve a thicker sound with more sustain with the amplifiers of the era were with either a hotter pickup or a floor pedal. This was certainly the case when we entered the business, and is a major reason for the initial success of the Super Distortion, which was the first pickup to address the problem. Vintage tube amps are still widely available today, but high-gain and multi-channel amps have become an accepted standard. Today it is possible to achieve a good sound with hot pickups and high-gain amps if a player takes the time to dial in a sound, but it's now equally possible to get a heavy sound with a low-output pickup.

Other than the DC resistance, what else do we need to know to make a judgment of a pickup's power, short of hearing it, of course?

Steve: DC resistance by itself does not actually offer any indication of pickup power, since it takes no account of wire gauge or magnet strength. We have a test fixture that measures pickup power in millivolts, which provides a straightforward output comparison between our pickups. The fixture is unique to us, and the measuring procedure therefore can't be duplicated outside of our factory.

What are some of the tricks of achieving an accurate "vintage" single coil?

meet the makers: interviews

Steve: Vintage single-coils varied greatly in terms of both output and tone quality, so it is basically a matter of reproducing the qualities we found most appealing. We don't consider them to be "tricks" per se, but we pay a lot of attention to how the individual coils are wound, and we monitor the specs very closely to be certain every pickup falls within a very tight range in terms of DC resistance and inductance. We have discovered that small differences can produce noticeable changes in performance.

Is it possible to make a hum-free pickup that still sounds very much like a vintage single-coil? How is it done?
Steve: Yes, we believe we've done this with our most recent models such as the Area '67, Area '58, Area '61 and Area T models. It's taken 10 years of research to make pickups that both sound and feel like vintage single-coils. Previous "stacked" pickups have either sounded too sterile or lacked the presence and attack of vintage single-coils. We can't fully describe how it's done, as the technology falls under the Official DiMarzio Secrets Act.

Can you tell us a little about the characteristics of some of the different basic types of pickups please – I'm thinking, coils around magnet polepieces, vs. steel polepieces that contact magnets mounted below the pickups.
Steve: If both types of pickups in question use the same magnet material, I would expect the pickup with the steel poles to be at least a little warmer-sounding, as there is more iron in and around the coil. However, a P-90-style pickup could in fact be made to sound very similar to a Strat if the amount of iron were reduced. Likewise, a Strat-style pickup can be made to perform similarly to a P-90 if the amount of iron is increased and the coil is wound to a similar spec. My belief is that we've managed to blur the boundaries between different types of pickups as we've learned more about pickup design, so the basic distinctions between different types of pickups are no longer as clearly defined as they were when we started.

What's your favorite vintage/classic pickup type?
Larry: My favorite is the PAF humbucker from 1959.

Please talk us through a couple of your favorites of your own pickup designs, and what makes them special.
Steve: I have a soft spot in my heart (or possibly my brain) for the Bluesbucker, because it performs in a surprising fashion, inasmuch as it looks like a standard humbucker but sounds and "feels" like a single-coil pickup. This goes back to the boundary-blurring I referred to earlier. It's always been more interesting to try to do something different than to make spot-on reproductions of older pickups.

Seymour Duncan, Seymour Duncan Pickups

Tell us a little bit about how you got started in the pickup business.
I got my start in the pickup business basically from necessity and the need to get a tone I was looking for. In my early days, I was hanging out with players like James Burton, Roy Buchanan, Albert Lee, Albert Collins, Jeff Beck, The Ventures, and others. I was attracted to the unique and different tones they all had even though they were playing basically stock guitars. I would take my Fender and Gibson catalogs to school and study all the guitar models from each year and the types of pickups they had. I collected old catalogs from music stores and noticed some instruments had single coils and others had humbucking pickups. I looked for the various artists featured in the catalogs and listened to their music. Soon, I began to learn the tone of various instruments such as Telecasters, Stratocasters, Jazzmasters, Les Pauls with P-90s and PAF pickups. I started making and rewinding pickups in the early '60s after talking with Les Paul, who I met during a show at Steel Pier in Atlantic City. After school, I worked at a music store in Vineland, New Jersey, giving lessons, repairing guitars, and winding pickups. I began to have first-hand experience with the many guitars models and the pickups associated with them.

During the early '70s I moved to London and began working at the Fender Sound House with Ron Roka, doing repairs and mods for artists such as Jeff Beck, Eric Clapton, Pete Townshend, Robin Trower, Paul Kossoff, Jack Bruce, Jimmy Page, Paul McCartney, George Harrison, John Wetton, and many others. At the Fender Sound House, I was rewinding and building custom pickups and modifying the three-position Centralab 1452 Stratocaster 'knife' switches into five-position switches. During the '70s, you'd see very few custom pickup builders and only a handful of OEM builders. I started reading that the pickups being made were being sold as 'vintage', but when I looked at them, in no way did they even look or sound 'vintage'. There was so much miss-information about what 'vintage' was and I wanted to make a vintage pickup using the proper Alnico magnets and materials for the vintage appearance and tone.

Over the years, the major guitar companies were going through changes and you could easily see that the specifications changed on many of their pickups. My theory was to build them how the early ones were made, in order to make a pickup that would fit the time era and look of the vintage instrument. I made the Stratocaster pickups with calibrated specs, and I would reverse wind, reverse polarize the middle pickup so in the two- and four-positions, the pickups would be humbucking. I wasn't trying to do it better than other manufacturers but to make something that the players were looking for, and I enjoyed making them by hand one at a time. I learned that some pickup companies don't even own their own tooling for making pickups and end up buying parts from a few major suppliers. Some companies don't even

meet the makers: interviews

check the magnetic gauss, wire tension, number of turns, number of turns per layer, and number of layers of magnet wire when winding pickup. Many of the aftermarket pickup components are made using different measurements, some of which are SAE and some are metric. There needs to be a parts standard and specification that keeps everyone in the same boat!

Without insulting anyone, does it seem to you that something 'went wrong' between the 'Golden Age' of pickups – arguably the '50s and early '60s with both Fender and Gibson – and the mid '70s or so, when the replacement pickup industry really came into existence?
I think during the time of the 'Golden Age' of pickups, the electric guitar was quite new and wasn't as popular as today. You can look up the records of the major guitar companies and find their manufacturing records of guitars built during the month or year. The production was much lower compared to today's standards and more time was spent on making the pickups. Making pickups during the '50s and '60s was not quite the assembly line it is today in some of the huge guitar and pickup factories I've visited. I believe too that's why there are small companies that still build beautiful instruments one at a time and you can see the quality and talent of these builders. During the '50s and '60s, there wasn't the demand for after-market pickups or other guitar and bass accessories. There wasn't the need for after-market pickups since most large manufacturers offered a warranty and would repair your instrument; and if the pickups were faulty, they would replace them. Nowadays, all the after-market accessories for stringed instruments help the player build an instrument for better playability and a tone that inspires him or her.

What were some of your earliest pickup designs. Do any of these exist in the catalog today?
Many of my earlier custom pickup designs came about after working with players wanting something different or to have a custom wind in tune to what he or she hears. I wound the JB Model for my favorite player: Jeff Beck. The Duncan Custom was done for Carlos Santana. The Alnico II Pro Series humbuckers were done for Billy Gibbons. The Full Shred was made for Nancy Wilson of Heart. My Strat series was made for Robin Trower, Mark Knopfler, Eric Johnson, and of course Jeff Beck. Many of my Tele models came from working and listening to Roy Buchanan, Albert Collins, Steve Cropper, Albert Lee, James Burton, Jerry Donahue, Jesse Ed Davis, Jimmy Bryant and Gerry McGee, to name a few. Just about all my early pickups are still in the catalog today.

Your pickups found a place in the market pretty quickly, although it seems you also avoided expanding too quickly in the early days.
I always wanted to control the production and availability of our pickup in the market

place. I didn't want to grow too fast and didn't want to get overwhelmed with the number of products being made. Our brand and our place in the market are watched over very closely by Evan Skopp (Vice President, Marketing). I never wanted to flood the market by putting our pickups on every guitar sold. That's not what we're about.

For a time, especially early on in the 'high-gain era' (I'd say the late '70s and '80s in particular) it seemed like the thinking, with rock players in particular, was 'the hotter the better' regarding replacement pickups. Sometimes, of course, that's true for certain styles, but tell us a little bit about how and why that might not always work for people.

A pickup bobbin that uses more turns of a thinner gauge of wire can often increase the output of a pickup, but you sacrifice the tonal clarity. Using a stronger ceramic or other rare earth magnet can increase output, but again can add too much string pull and make the pickup sound harsh, overly distorted, and really play havoc with other effects such as foot pedals or rack mount equipment. You can have a high powered pickup, but in some cases, you do sacrifice tone. The inductance, capacitance and voltage of a pickup have limits to what sounds good or not. Hotter pickups will give you more sustain, attack, bite, and growl, and some players like the overdrive a pickup will give you, especially through Marshall. For my playing style, I prefer lower-gain pickups and the tone weaker magnets give for a smoother sustain and attack. I don't use guitar picks and really don't hit the strings the same way as you do with a pick, and certain model pickups work better for my playing style. I like the JB Model in the bridge position and the Jazz Model in the neck, and they both work well with my playing style. I used the JB on my recordings of 'King Tone Blues' and 'When a Man Loves a Woman". If I need more output or volume I turn the amp up.

When recording, you don't always need a 100 watt amplifier to make the guitar sound great. I love the tone of Steve Cropper when he recorded 'Green Onions' with Booker T & The MGs using a Fender Harvard amp. Jeff Beck recorded many times using small Fender Princeton Reverb amps and he has one of the best tones I've ever heard. Jeff's Strat pickups would average from 5.7k to 6.3k ohms. Slash uses the Alnico II Pro Series which have a DC resistance in the 8k range. You can increase the number of turns and increase the magnet strength, but having a higher DC resistance doesn't always mean the pickup will be hotter.

Gibson and Fender always set the standard by which many after-market products are compared. Many of the earlier instrumentals in the '50s and '60s used small amps that produced a great tone. Listen to Lonnie Mack who was one of Stevie Ray Vaughan's favorite players using his stock Gibson humbucking pickups designed by Seth Lover in his famous Flying V. Lonnie used a small Magnatone amplifier for his unique tone when he recorded 'Memphis', 'Wham!', and 'Down in the Dumps'. It's a player's personal choice of pickup that can inspire your playing, performance and personal tone.

meet the makers: interviews

Other than the DC resistance, what else do we need to know to make a judgment of a pickup's power, short of hearing it, of course?

Besides the DC resistance of a pickup, there are several variables that can determine the tone and output of a pickup, such as resonant frequency, choice of magnet, etc. Some of the basic elements are the player's choice of instrument and playing technique. The body and neck wood play an important role in the tone of a pickup. The same pickup can sound different in different types of instruments using different wood and manufacturing techniques. The finish material used is very important to the tone of an instrument. Earlier Gibson and Fender instruments used nitrocellulose lacquer and automotive enamels. There's much written about guitar and bass finishes on the internet. Some things that can effect the tone and output of a pickup are: string gauge, alloy and diameter and string-winding technique; pickup construction and materials; ferrous pole piece materials and shape; magnet material, shape and gauss; number of turns, winding pitch, winding tension, bobbin shape and dimensions; machine or hand wound coils; magnet wire (AWG) dimensions and tolerances; insulation material and thickness; hookup wire; potentiometers values and tolerances; guitar cord resistance and length; pickup height adjustment to strings; pickup placement to bridge and neck; and pickup mounting (surface of body, pickguard or mounting rings).

These are some examples and ideas that can change the tone and output of a pickup in your instrument. Playing on a hardwood floor or tiles can make your guitar sound louder and brighter. Playing on carpet or outdoors and make your instruments sound dark and duller. I don't like playing outside with no walls or curtain behind the amplifiers. I also keep my amp on the floor so I don't blow out my ears, and have the speakers facing the microphones. Often the sound can get lost when you put your faith in an audio engineer that might not be familiar with your set list or song arrangement. I like playing small clubs as you can hear the rest of the band and get a better mix and blend of the instruments.

Are there any myths or common misconceptions about pickups that you'd like to take the time to dispel?

This can be very subjective. We use the same old formula and molding technique in making our butyrate bobbins [for humbucking pickups]. I've done much research in finding the raw materials to make certain pickup models. It's important to use the proper materials for the cover and bottom plate, and again we have our own formula and materials. We have a specific magnet wire made to our specifications and ferrous alloy used for various mounting components. I don't give out my formula or any specifications in materials used in the Seymour Duncan line of pickups.

I know you put a lot of thought into recreating a PAF-style humbucker. What did you find to be some of the keys to the success of that effort?

I have Seth E. Lover's notes and specs on making the PAF pickup, or PU 490. We've talked a lot about the various specifications and they are not all alike. The materials available at the time were not always made to the same specifications or formula. The Gibson purchasing department had various vendors and suppliers for various components and hardware. Just because it has a 'Patent Applied For' sticker doesn't always make it a great-sounding pickup, and again much of it is the personal preference for the sound of a particular pickup. Again, not all PAF Gibson pickups sound the same when used in different instruments. The potentiometers play an important part of the tone, too. The plastic bobbins were originally made of black butyrate plastic mainly because it was used for other molded parts such as the mounting rings. In 1959, the molder for Gibson called Seth and said there was a shortage of the black material and could they run the bobbins in cream for a short time 'til the supply of black came in. Seth said, "Go ahead and mold the bobbins in cream because they'll be under the cover anyway," and the rest is history. Seth and I often heard that the cream PAF humbuckers sounded different than black bobbin ones. We both laughed!

What are some of the tricks of achieving an accurate 'vintage' single coil?
Again, I have my theories and much of it again is priority information. I don't call them tricks, but keeping the integrity of the product by using the right materials, manufacturing techniques, custom tooling and fabrication. We make all our own flatwork and have our own molds to make our vintage style pickups. I've been using vulcanized fiber for many years to make replicas of single coil Fender style pickups, and we make our own molds for making P-90 and humbucker bobbins. We stamp out all our own hardware such as bottom plates, spacers, studs, magnet specifications, along with grinding and calibration. I've done the research and kept notes on thousands of pickups I've rewound and restored over the past 40 years. I have file cabinets filled with notes and records of every pickup I've wound. There are many historic and vintage instruments guitars out there that I've restored. I try to restore a pickup so you can't tell it's been repaired, to keep the integrity of the instrument.

Over the many years of repairing and restoring pickups, I've seen many single coil pickups fail due to ICPC, or 'inner coil pole corrosion'. This can happen due to moisture getting trapped inside the coil, causing it to eventually fail. I've seen guitars that have been kept under a bed and all three pickups had ICPC due to high humidity and moisture being trapped inside the guitar case. I want to make a replica pickup with my specifications and tone and not make vintage duplicates to fool the player that my pickups were made in the '50s.

Is it possible to make a hum-free pickup that still sounds very much like a vintage single-coil?

meet the makers: interviews

Making a hum-free pickup that sounds like vintage single-coil can be very subjective, but we've devoted a lot of time and energy to it. Our early Stack designs used two symmetrical coils. We still use that for some of our pickups. But we've recently patented a new design that uses a top coil that has a geometry that's very close to a single-coil pickup. The bottom coil is very short and has just a few turns of wire. We also use a hum-transfer shield to inject hum into the bottom coil. The way I think of it is the top coil gives you the tone and the bottom coil cancels the hum. We also put a resistor in series with the bottom coil so we can perfectly match the noise figure to the top coil. That's key to optimizing hum cancellation.

In addition to the new Stack design, which we call the Stack Plus, we have some side-by-side humbucking designs that drop into a Strat or Tele. They use two very thin coils and a magnet that sits on the bottom of the pickup. We call them our Rails series, and they come in several voicings, including vintage voicings.

You make one of the most highly regarded DeArmond 200/Gretsch DynaSonic type pickups available today. That's an interesting pickup – what are some of the keys to the sound of that one?
I was excited to make our molded bobbin for the single coil Dynosonic Pickup, originally by Rowe-DeArmond. The important factors and interesting components are the bobbin shape and specifications, mounting ring/cover, the rod alnico magnets and materials used for height adjustment. I enjoy winding the bobbins and the magnet wire, the number of turns, winding pitch and hookup are quite different from most traditional pickups. The pickups have a stronger magnetic field than most traditional single coil pickups using alnico rod magnets. We do many time-consuming steps in making this pickup to keep the traditional look and tone of the originals. Again, we use many specific and custom components to make this pickup. I also enjoy making the traditional Gibson Staple single-coil pickup used on a few Gibson instruments during the mid '50s. It was the neck pickup on the Les Paul Custom (Fretless Wonder) and some top-of-the-line Gibson Acoustic-Electric instruments during that time period. The Duncan Staple pickup has many components and lots of hand work and fabrication to make this great replacement pickup.

What's your favorite vintage pickup type?
My favorite vintage style pickups are the Antiquity models, and are made in the Custom Shop. Maricela Juarez and I enjoy hand-making many styles of vintage replica pickups. My favorite production model is still the JB and Jazz Model Neck. I've used those two pickups on my favorite recording instrument I call the 'Tele-Gib'. I made two of them and gave the first one to Jeff Beck during the time he recorded *Blow by Blow*, especially on the recording 'Cause We've Ended as Lovers'. Many of our pickups became models in the Seymour Duncan line because of the many

clients I've had over the years. I enjoyed making the first Stack pickups for Michael Sembello who used it on his recording 'Maniac', and a custom model for George Lynch called the Screamin' Demon. I've enjoyed making pickups for artists such as Eddie Van Halen, Slash, David Gilmour, Mark Knopfler, and Hank Marvin on several signature model guitars.

Please talk us through a couple of your favorites of your own pickup designs, and what makes them special.
My favorite pickups are the Antiquity series, and I love making replicas of several old Gibson and DeArmond designs. I like aging the parts and hand winding to keep the authentic appearance and unique tone of the early pickups. Bobbins are aged, magnets hand-ground and calibrated after being magnetized and then aged to specific calibration. I love making the aged humbucking pickups and especially using the original materials and injection mold made from the same company that made the original Gibson molds. I have Seth E. Lover's notes and journals on various pickup models he's designed. I especially enjoy working in the custom shop with Maricela Juarez and my son Derek. I work at my studio and do experiments with new pickup models. We design our own bobbins and have our own tooling for our production and custom shop products.

Do you think there are still improvements and discoveries to be made in the field of magnetic pickups for electric guitars, or has it pretty much all been done by now?
You'll be surprised what new magnetic pickup designs we've come up with over the years. One obvious problem with so many different pickup models that are standard looking is when you change to a new design, everyone compares it to the old design. Many times a new model pickup doesn't fit the pre-existing cavity or route in a guitar or it really detracts from the look of an instrument, so the new models don't really catch on. We have every type of test equipment to test every pickup model out there, and see so many using the same winding specs or materials. Again I hope the guitar and bass industry tries to move away from mixing metric and SAE parts in the same instrument.

meet the makers: interviews

Mike Eldred, Fender Custom Shop

What's your official title with Fender?
The official title today is Director of Marketing for the Fender Custom Shop, but I've done everything, really. I started building guitars when I was 19 years old, I got hired by Grover Jackson at Charvel. It was right after Grover had bought the business from Wayne Charvel, and I was the first employee he ever hired. That was early 1979. I worked there for about eight or nine years, then left and went to work for Yamaha – via working at a small violin repair shop. I worked at Yamaha for eight or nine years, then after I left there for about a year I played full-time in a band with Lee Rocker called Big Blue. Then John Page called me up and asked if I wanted a job with Fender, and I've been at Fender now almost 12 years.

So from the perspective of the Fender Custom Shop, and Fender in general, you have seen pickup production from many sides. What is it, do you think, that has contributed to the pickup boom we're seeing now? Which, perhaps, started even with the replacement pickup industry of the '70s.
When I look at it, as far as pickup manufacturing, I think that people tend to romanticize certain eras, and certainly the '50s and '60s are part of that – and this is my personal opinion of it. I've taken apart lots of guitars, and lots of famous guitars, like the Woodstock Strat that Jimi Hendrix played, Stevie Ray Vaughan's Strat, Jeff Beck's Esquire, a bunch of different guitars...

And this is for examination in order to reproduce them to some extent?
Yeah, to do replicas of them. Also, over the years, just preparing famous players' guitars. I've personally seen a lot of guitars that had pickups that were from the mid '70s, or the early '70s, or the late '60s, and those are guitars that have a signature sound, and these artists have used these guitars to really make an impact on music. And they've done it, in some instances, with early-70s pickups and later. So I think, by and large, it's just the public's perception. They want to think, "In the '50s it was this, in the '60s it was that," and all this other stuff. The biggest thing that I could gauge was that in the '50s and '60s there was a lot of inconsistency. With the older guitars that we've seen, when you take them and spec out the pickups, it varies so much. If you had a Stratocaster, it varies so much from pickup to pickup – the front pickup is maybe the hottest pickup on the whole guitar.

The way that they wound them back then was definitely different, using smaller sewing-machine motors and hand-held wire, and more erratic winding techniques, so that maybe you'll have more windings at the bottom of the pickup and less windings at the top of the pickup. That influences the tone of the pickup. How tightly you hold that wire influences it, too.

meet the makers: interviews

It seems that there were a lot of happy accidents going on, but also, of course, some unhappy accidents.
Yeah, that's the thing. But that gets into the perception of what sounds great. I could sit down with a guitar and say, "Okay, this is exactly what I like." But that can be totally different for you, and totally different for the next guy. Do you like Coke, or do you like Pepsi? That's really what it gets into. There's no saying, "*These* are the best pickups," because it's a personal preference of tone. If it was a real easy formula, then everybody would play the same thing, and everybody would play the same amp and use the same cable.

Which is a very good point to make, because the search for the Holy Grail of gear is a big motivator these days.
I think the point about the search for the Holy Grail is that it's a very personal search. People have a perception of what they think is great for them, and they're going to continue on that search for themselves, and that's not a formula that fits for everybody.

Any myths or snake oil that you are personally fond of debunking?
I don't want to step on anybody's marketing plan, but I guess it just keeps coming back to the fact that it is a personal preference. If somebody has a certain thing that they say, "Hey, this is the mojo, this is what we do." If you're a player and you get one of those pickups and you really like it, then that works for you. Who am I to sit back and say, "Oh no, that doesn't work for you."?

What kinds of things is Fender doing to replicate some of the 'happy accidents', as I described them earlier, that made some of the best of the vintage pickups sound the way they did?
There are certain things that you can do. Searching out wire, particularly getting wire with a certain thickness of insulation. Hand-winding definitely has its own sound, and we definitely do that from time to time, and it's not just Abigail [Ybarra] who's doing that now. She has shown a lot of the other builders how to do it. Magnet structure – stagger in magnets – we messed around for a lot of time with a certain stagger on magnets, and it's not a traditional stagger, but it's something that works today. And it was a personal thing for me, because I sat down and said, "Hey, I want to hear more of this string," so I did a different stagger and gave it to Abi, and she wound some pickups, and they sound really, really great.

So some of it is searching out the components, some of it is esthetics. For Fender it's historical, such as sometimes they used light-gray fiber on the bottom and dark-gray fiber on the top part of the bobbin. It's all over the place.

I bet. And for Fender, there was a period of reclaiming a lot of the

original specs for all kinds of things. Body shapes for one model and another, and so forth. But for pickups, I guess a lot of that had to occur – beta testing and reverse engineering, tearing down originals to re-learn how it works. And once you do that, presumably it's hard to find sources for supplies that match what was originally used, like the correct grade of alnico and so forth.

No, actually there are a lot of guys out there messing with magnets, so we're pretty good from that standpoint. For example, when we did the 50th Anniversary 1954 Stratocaster, the magnets are of a larger diameter [than in later Strat pickups], so those pickups sound different just because of that. Now you get even further into some of the windings and the gauge of the wire, and it's a real different-sounding pickup.

How does the larger-diameter magnet affect the sound of those pickups?

My feeling was that it was a lot more responsive. It's like if you have a light on something – if I give you a small-diameter Maglite flashlight, then I give you a larger-diameter Maglite flashlight, you'd light up that area a lot better. That's exactly what it was like for me.

Which puts me in mind of the Gretsch DynaSonics, the DeArmonds that Gretsch used.

We own those winders.

Wow, interesting. But I'm thinking, those have much larger-diameter alnico pole pieces too, and those are some unique sounding pickups. But back to Fender for now – what are some of the major differences between Strat and Tele pickups?

They are so different. The bridge pickup on a Telecaster sounds like no other bridge pickup. You just look at the construction of that pickup. The bobbin is squatter, there's a larger area to put more wire on that thing, and then you add in that plate on the bottom. There are so many variables on that pickup, and they all add up. And you can wind that pickup so many different ways. Or you can put taller magnets on it, you can put more windings on it, and all those things make a huge difference.

Sure, and on top of that you've got all the considerations of the guitar itself – the through-body stringing, and the bridge and saddle design. But even within the pickup itself it seems like a very different design, and the result tends to be a slightly gnarlier, hotter sound.

Yeah, it's much bigger. Then with the plate on the bottom, and with the whole thing screwed into the bridge plate, you have put some major variables in there. But like with a Strat pickup, it's mounted on a plastic pickguard; if I change that plastic and I use phenolic or nitrocellulose or vinyl, it's not going to change that pickup much. But man, you take a Telecaster pickup with that plate that's already on the bottom of it, and now you have machine screws that screw into that through a bridge plate, and now say I go punch that bridge plate out of nickel silver, or I punch it out of brass … it's a totally different sound, completely different.

Yeah, and with that arrangement you usually get a little microphonics, which becomes part of the whole brew. All of which makes it frustrating for Strat players who are seeking to get a Tele sound from their bridge pickup.
Well, I think Lowell George had a great trick: put a Tele pickup in the bridge of a Strat. That was a real interesting guitar. And what we did also with the front pickup is, in the Custom Shop, the front pickup on the Telecaster was always so under-powered. There's such a big change between the traditional front pickup of a Telecaster and the back pickup, night and day really. We were in the Custom Shop, and we said – because I'm a Tele player – I grabbed four of the builders, and I said, "Here's what I'm gonna' do: I want each of you guys to come up with a Tele pickup that you like, and we're going to load it in a Tele, and mark it so you guys know what it is, but I don't know what it is. And we'll find the Tele front pickup that sounds the best to all of us." So we did that. Everybody made a pickup, and we went in this little room, and I remember sitting around and just passing Teles around. And everybody said, by far, that this one was the best sounding pickup. We grabbed it, and that's what we call the Twisted Tele now.

What's the key to that one?
There are a bunch of different variables. It's a nickel silver cover, taller magnets, different winding. There are three wires coming off it so you can use it to get series/parallel, out of phase, or whatever you want to get off of it. Real neat pickup, I love that pickup. I have it in every Tele I own, and we put it in the Telecaster Pro that's out now. A lot of the Master Builders use it when they set out to build a Tele for somebody.

What was it doing for you, sonically, that you just couldn't find in other Tele neck pickups?
You know, when I play a Stratocaster I usually use the bridge pickup and the middle pickup together, or the middle pickup alone, or the front pickup. A lot of blues players love that front pickup on a Stratocaster. It's real thumpy, and it's like "boom". It's a really cool sound. And because I was a Tele player, I wanted that out of a Tele's front pickup. And that's where this thing lands, it gives you a real front-pickup Strat sound out of a Tele, and it blends better with whatever you're using in the back.

meet the makers: interviews

Are there any other new developments that really excite you?
We're constantly trying new stuff. There's a pickguard sitting on my desk right now with a set of pickups that a couple of the sales guys came up with. A lot of the people at Fender play, so they say, "Hey, I'm thinking this might be kind of cool … " and they're just getting my opinion of it. A lot of the builders, if they're doing a particular Stratocaster, will say, "I want to design a whole set." So three or four of the builders have come up with a design for a set that really works well for them in the pickguard assembly of a Stratocaster, so we're thinking of offering those to the public.

And some of the artists have come to us and said, "Hey, I've got this idea for a pickup assembly." Robin Trower is one of them. He has this little recipe for a Strat set up that's great, it sounds really, really cool. It's the combination of two Custom Shop pickups and a TexMex pickup, which is a really cool little set up. And the SCN pickups, those sound amazing. My main Stratocaster, the one I use when I play out, has the SCN pickups in it. Those are the Samarium Cobalt Noiseless pickups that Bill Lawrence co-designed with us. It's a really neat pickup that I really like the sound of. I would run so far away from any kind of a noise-cancelling pickup in the past, but this one … I really like the sound of it. It has a real neat midrange.

Tell us a little bit about some of the unsung Fender pickups over the years. What are your thoughts on the Jazzmaster pickup?
The Jazzmaster pickup is an amazing pickup. We don't do a whole lot with the Jazzmaster in the Custom Shop. We have customers who come to us and will have us build Jazzmasters, but we really don't have a Jazzmaster in our Custom Shop line right now because you can still get [original vintage Jazzmasters] for pretty reasonable prices. But they are such great-sounding guitars – that pickup design: squatty, wide. Those pickups sound so good, and they fit great in the track for recording and things like that. The problem that we have is that you can still find a lot of them at a pretty reasonable price, and when we make something in the Custom it costs more money, just because of the amount of labor that we put into the thing.

The really neat thing about the Jazzmaster is we have drawings of one of the first prototypes that Freddie Tavares worked on, and the pickups that were in that guitar were pedal-steel pickups.

Let's talk about some of the Gretsch pickups, since those fall under the umbrella of the Fender Musical Instruments Corp. now.
We have been using TV Jones to make a lot of those pickups. I have a Gretsch here with TV Jones pickups on it that I use some, and they sound really great. Seymour [Duncan], in the past, has made some really great Filter'Tron pickups that I have put in other guitars. That's a real neat pickup design, too. You have two side-by-side

bobbins with a pretty heavy-duty magnet in there, but the bobbins aren't wound real hot.

Sure, and the result is a lot different than a Gibson PAF humbucker.
Yeah, you get a lot more clarity and brightness.

Is Fender making its own DynaSonics now?
We make some of them, and we'll have Seymour make some of them for us too. Sometimes people want us to make them for custom stuff, so we have the capability of making them at the shop, but some of them we buy from Seymour Duncan.

That's a quirky pickup.
Yeah, real interesting sounding pickup. When you look at the bottom of that pickup – mechanically, you look at it and you go, "Wow, that's really interesting." Sonically, you look at it and go, "There's machine screws, springs, brass holders that take those poles up and down … ." All of that affects the sound.

And there's nothing else in the world that sounds quite like that pickup.
No. To me, the one word that describes the sound of that pickup is 'clarity'. It's so big, clear, and transparent sounding. I had a Tele that I had made myself, and it had two P-90s on it, and I pulled the bridge P-90 out and put a DynaSonic on the bridge. And man, that was a real neat sound. But to me, it's a real clarity thing. There's nothing else out there that sounds like that pickup.

Any other Fender pickups you're particularly fond of?
I really like the Broadcaster pickup. It's the same pickup that's in those [late '40s, early '50s] snake-headed lap-steels. When we were doing the GE Smith guitar, I did the prototype for that guitar myself and I worked with GE on it, and GE and I both loved that pickup a lot. And if anybody knows tone, it's GE Smith. He has a great collection of guitars, and he still has this old Nocaster that his mom bought him when he was a kid. That was kind of the basis we were looking at for that pickup, and you can find them in those old snake-head lap steels. I have one, GE has many, so when we were coming up with that guitar, that was really the focus for that pickup, because it's a real hot, real beautiful sounding Tele pickup. Then on GE's guitar the pickup is mounted into the wood, it's not mounted on the plate, so it's a completely different thing.

Otherwise, we just keep doing what we're doing. It's funny, when people come to Corona and I take them around the shop, I say, "This is what I consider the heart of Fender," because it's all the original tools, and we're still using them every day. There's a guy over there and he's hand-grinding tremolo bridges, and there's a girl

meet the makers: interviews

over there who is hand-polishing bridge pieces, and on the same tools that Leo bought they're hand-punching all the fiber. When you get into how we're doing it, it hasn't changed, except that now we've got a lot more consistency. But I've seen a lot of old guitars, and I think anyone else who has seen a lot of old guitars will also tell you, you can find some good old guitars, but you can find a lot of really, really bad ones from the '50s and '60s, and the biggest thing was consistency. Because when you pin route a guitar, a neck slot, and you change the pin or something's out of alignment, it's all over the place. You get big gaps. So I think the biggest thing that I've seen, not just being a Fender employee, but from a builder's standpoint, in the Custom Shop you now have such a high level of consistency. Everything fits right, everything's in the right places. It's all taken off [the designs] of the original things, but there are no variances. That's the biggest thing for me – the high level of consistency with new Fender stuff. GE Smith even told me: "I think the stuff coming out of Fender now is the best guitars they've ever made."

meet the makers: interviews

Lindy Fralin, Fralin Pickups

Please give us a little bit of an overview of how a magnetic pickup works.
A magnetic pickup needs a steel string to react, because it is typically a coil around a magnet. It can be six poles or one bar magnet, or it can also be a steel blade or a set of screws that are charged up by a magnet. But the point is, you've got a coil around a core, which is either charged-up steel or an actual magnet. And when steel moves above it, or of course below it, it makes this field move, and the coil senses the movement of the field, and that's where your signal is created.

The field moves exactly corresponding to the string, which in the long run corresponds to the movement of a speaker cone. It doesn't produce a lot of voltage, and that's why amps are two and three-stage amps. But that is the simplest pickup, a coil around a magnet.

It seems like the more you learn about pickups, the more you discover there are an awful lot of variables between them, even if they all work on the same principles.
Of course there are huge differences between magnet material, types of wire, the shape of the magnetic field, how many turns (of wire) you've put on there … . There are all kinds of things you can vary for different effect. And of course the biggest difference is, if the magnet material is in the coil it's one school of pickup, and if it's steel (inside the coil) it's the other school.

That's the biggest division, because you can just picture how a P-90 sounds so different from a Jazzmaster pickup, and yet they have the same coil around them: 10,000 turns of 42-gauge plain enamel-coated wire. And they are drastically different pickups, because anything with a magnet in it tends to give you a cleaner, clearer, but thinner signal; anything with steel in it tends to give you the bigger, beefier, more rounded but more distorted signal.

I know we're generally talking here about Fender-style pickups with magnetic pole pieces, or Gibson types with the magnets mounted beneath the coil charging steel poles that run through the coil …
Well that is the big difference. All pickups kind of fit in one of those two categories, whether it's a blade or a screw, that's that kind of pickup, and if it's alnico, whether it's a bar magnet or six pole pieces, as in the Fender kind of pickup. So the similarities between Rickenbacker, Danelectro and Fender to your ear, is that they're all pickups with the magnet in the coil. Or old DeArmonds, they're clean and clear. And then the beefy pickups are anything with a blade, from a Charlie Christian, or P-90s with screws, or humbuckers, Mosrite pickups, a lot of Nationals, anything with adjustable steel pole pieces makes it a beefier, louder, more distorted kind of pickup.

meet the makers: interviews

What is it that makes the steel-in-the-coil pickup fatter sounding?
That gets us into some really heavy duty physics, but it's partly that it's a more complicated magnetic field, because your bar magnets are sideways under everything. It also leads to a higher inductance, which just means more output for whatever movement of the string. Because, you see, a magnet is only 50 percent iron; it's got other things in it: aluminum, nickel, cobalt. And a 100 percent iron core is more efficient, but by the same token it's more distorted. Why is it more distorted? I don't know – maybe for no other reason than that it gets more voltage and that distorts the tubes.

So even if the weight of the bar magnet and the weight of the six individual magnet pole pieces are about the same, there's still going to be a difference in the output of that pickup?
There's a big difference, because there's a difference in inductance. And what you're creating here is a type of inductance, but any pickup's sound is an incredibly complex relationship of capacitance, inductance, impedance, and reluctance. This is why not just anyone can wind a pickup … or, anyone can make a pickup that makes noise, but it's actually much harder than people think to make good pickups that sound good consistently.

We have to go to a great deal of trouble to keep our pickups consistent. For example, instead of just making mass-produced pickups that might be stacked six-deep on a machine and machine wound all at once, we have to stop each coil six times to check how it's winding, because the biggest thing that shapes tone is the distance between each layer of copper. Some of that's insulation, some of that's air. You hear about 'scatter wound' or 'randomly layered' pickups, and that's nothing but adding more air to the mix. If you get a batch of wire where the insulation's thicker then it needs less air, or if you get a batch of wire where the copper core is bigger now you've got lower ohm readings.

You have to compensate constantly for whatever the wire's doing, because 42 gauge, by definition, means the copper core is between 2.1 thousandths and 2.4 thousandths of an inch in diameter. That's a big range, and there's a huge difference between the sound of those two extremes. So you learn that big-core wire winds good P-Basses, and small-core wire winds overwound pickups better than big-core wire. You just know what to do with it. We always wind a pickup or two off of each spool of wire, then decide, "All right, this is going to do *that* type of pickup." We'll write on it, "this is Strat bridges" or "this is Jazz Basses" or whatever. You know, Fender didn't do this, so that's why their pickups are so much less consistent. Any of your mass-produced pickups, they don't have time to do this. They stack 'em six-deep and crank 'em out. But a lot of the custom builders like me take a lot more time and a lot more care. So a ten-year-old Vintage Hot should sound like next year's Vintage Hot.

meet the makers: interviews

Of course people like Fender set the templates for these designs, but everyone who has played more than one Strat or Tele knows there are good Strat pickups, and there are less good Strat pickups.
Of course. And they didn't count the turns, they just filled up the coils with wire. But Leo did know – and I've heard this from a good source, so I'm confident in quoting it – that hand-winding was important. Because, you know, he had machinery and patents on every other kind of machinery, and he still hand-wound coils until he was not involved in the company any more. All the way up until 1964 they still hand-wound coils.

And when you say "hand-wound," you mean they hand-guided the wire onto the coil?
Yeah, it was spun by a machine just like I'm doing, but I'm guiding – right now – the back-and-forth movement of the wire, and I'm in complete control of the tension. So while Fender didn't care about making a hotter bridge then, or a reverse middle, they did know that it sounded better to have a hand-wound coil. All of the sloppiness that a human adds was important. Certainly you can get too sloppy and sound bad, or you can get too tight and too neat and sound bad. But Leo Fender knew this, just like he knew lighter wood sounded better than heavier wood.

Being a pickup-maker, I'm very aware – because I've put together dozens of guitars – that the wood is every bit as important as the pickups. You can never discount the importance of how a particular piece of wood vibrates. If it either soaks up a certain frequency or resonates at a certain frequency, *of course* it comes out of the amplified instrument. I say this to people all the time, even on my website: in Fenders, what you really don't want is a guitar that soaks up anywhere from 150 Hz to 450 Hz, that's essentially your treble strings. You've got to have a lot of resonance in the treble in particular, because the pickup itself doesn't boost that frequency or you see it as a ton of high end, but you don't want thin treble strings on your guitar. People love Fenders that are bright, so it's essentially a very hollow-midrange pickup. You can't have the guitar soaking up your midrange. You've heard bad Fenders that sound thin and clanky, and others with a set of 6k Strat pickups on them sound huge. And that's the wood just as much on the pickups.

It seems like there was a school of thinking for a time – maybe the late 1970s and '80s, if I recall – that held that pickups mattered more than anything else. That you could pretty much bolt a good pickup to a plank of wood, and that would do the trick.
Yeah, and even Fender in the late 1960s and '70s thought that heavier wood was better because it would get longer sustatain. Everybody was starting to use hotter pickups and fuzz boxes. But after a while everybody came back to liking the traditional sound, and I sell far more stock-output pickups than hotter stuff. There are

meet the makers: interviews

pedals and amps and all these great ways to get easy hot tones. And Fender as a company has gotten very good at picking their wood correctly again; considering how many guitars they ship a day, they're doing an amazing job at keeping their quality high and their company well run. I don't know how they do it.

It is pretty impressive, given the prices they sell things at today, which make decent guitars cheaper in real terms than they were back in the 1950s and '60s.
Sure, even the Mexican stuff is really pretty good, and I own some Korean stuff from other makers that I'm really very happy with. I've got a couple of Korean Danelectros and a Korean PRS, and I can't believe how good that is. A $500 guitar, and it's awesome.

You mentioned a minute a go that many players had come back around to liking more traditional sounds, and it seems to me that part of that involves a realization that the most powerful pickup available isn't always the best choice for your sound.
It totally depends on your style. One of the rules of pickups that I mention to people all the time it, hotter pickups are less dynamic, less articulate, but longer sustaining. What you tend to hear is, you can hit a note soft or hard, but it comes out of the amp about the same. Which is fabulous for really fast playing, hammer-ons with the double-handed thing on the fingerboard stuff, because you need to be less delicate on your tough. But if you want a real expressive, bluesy pickup, a weaker pickup – with your amp up louder – does a better job. Because now, when you hit it hard it gets louder, when you hit it soft it gets quieter, when you hit it near the bridge it sounds twangy, when you hit it near the neck it sounds mellow. You have much more control with a weak pickup, and that's another reason why people are coming back to the original, weaker outputs of these things, and just trying to get really good instruments and good amps and good pedals, and whatever makes them happy.

It's interesting to follow what a learning curve it has been for a lot of players. And when you talk about the expressiveness and dynamics available from weaker pickups, consider what a player like Jimi Hendrix was using most of the time ...
Yeah, they didn't have hot pickups yet.

And even Eddie Van Halen was playing a standard PAF-style pickup.
Somebody told me it was only 8.2k, but that's not something I can say reliably.

Sure, I've heard it quoted as being something in the 8.5k region.
Yeah, and that's not all that hot for a humbucker. Just an average PAF. You heard him

getting all his tweaks and whistles and wild stuff in the early days, and you don't get that stuff out of a really hot pickup.

And with a good distortion pedal into a Marshall, you're going to get a pretty heavy sound anyway.
Of course. Unless your amp's on ten all the time and you're still wishing for more power, you don't always need a hotter pickup. But then again, it depends on the guy's style, and his amp. I tended for years to play blackface Fender Princetons and other amps of that size, and they don't like a whole lot of input from a hot pickup. But a Twin Reverb maybe, or a Marshall, responds better to a much louder pickup. It overwhelms the Princeton, it just doesn't need it.

For years, the main way people judged pickups was by their DC resistance readings, but it seems there is actually a lot more to it than that.
Well, that's actually one of the least important numbers. The crucial things for tone are the number of turns – that directly relates to your voltage – and the strength of the magnetic field, then capacitance and inductance shape treble and bass. So balancing all of those things is important, as also reluctance, the term for the magnetic field's resistance to change. You're getting way complex here, and none of this is stuff that someone listening to a guitar needs to know. They need to know if the sound pleases them.

I used to have all this fancy test equipment: inductance bridges and frequency analyzers, and I learned to use it all, and then I would go listen to the pickups. So I know now, by just listening, what kind of Q and resonant peak I've got going. I don't use any of that equipment any more. I have a test guitar and a little amp in the shop, and I can listen to anything I want – and we do all day long.

Another thing that's talked about a lot is the difference between different types of alnico.
That stuff does matter, particularly when they magnet is in the coil. Then it really matters which magnet material you're using, because of something called 'hysteresis.' Hysteresis is a graph of the resistance to change of any magnetic material. You can have the exact same coil on a pickup that you can slide rod magnets in and out of like the plastic Fender pickups, and you can totally change the sound of it by switching magnets.

Just between an Alnico II and an Alnico V, for example?
Oh yeah. We even mix them in some pickups, although I don't know that that helps a whole lot. It (a could, with mixed magnet types) doesn't always treat strings differently, it kind of averages out the sound of the whole sound of the pickup. I think

meet the makers: interviews

hysteresis affects the coil, and not just the sound of that one string, but we still do it when people insist. To me, the biggest reason to mix magnets is not to achieve some tone, but if you put a weaker magnet under that E string, you tend to get rid of some of that detuning trouble from the magnetic pull. When we mix the magnets, we tend to put them under E, A, and G. They're always the ones that respond worst to that lack of sustain that you hear from a real strong magnet pulling on the strings. The weak-magnet pickups do have a longer sustain on the guitar, or backing your pickups off.

Which is interesting to note. I think that fact is confusing to some players when they first discover it: that lowering your pickups can actually increase the sustain of your guitar, even though it lessens the output a little too.
Sure. Personally, I have always like brighter sounding guitars, too – I have always liked to twang. That's why I could never play the old-fashioned humbuckers. We developed this new humbucker recently that sounds like a single coil all the way. It's the Split Single, it's on my website. One is just a two-coil P-90, and the other is a two-coil pickup that's somewhere between a Strat and a Jazzmaster. It's got shorter magnets than a Strat, but longer magnets than a Jazzmaster, and I have room for anywhere from 8,000 to 11,000 turns (of wire around the coil). Jazzmasters had 10,000 and Strats had 8,000 so we can really get any Fender sound you want, but out of a humbucker.

They're quiet, they're drop-in humbucker replacements, and they're for people who just want cleaner wound string sounds, like me.

Is there anything in this talk of magnets aging?
Yeah, there's something in it, but there's a lot of bunk, too, a lot of misinformation. Alnico in itself has a 300,000 year half-life, but you see, anything can demagnetize it. A strong field nearby it will demag it. The transformers on your amp, or speaker magnets, or who knows what else. Banging on the pole piece with the string repeatedly will gradually weaken it. So magnets do degauss (weaken), but it's all to do with their environment, what they have experienced over the years, that determines how much they have degaussed. I'm not convinced that they sound better degaussed, though, because I like my high-end. Also, I've degaussed them on purpose, and they don't really get much different. You can feel a little bit of a weaker magnet, but it doesn't seem much duller or much quieter. The magnet is incredibly forgiving.

So that's another pretty complex issue.
Yeah, and I certainly wouldn't recommend people trying to demag (degauss) their own pickups, because it's hard to mag 'em again.

And if the change is so subtle, you're going to find a desired change by tweaking something else in your guitar or rig.
I feel it's much more important to get the right number of turns on there, and get the right piece of wood. What we offer with our exchange policy, is that you can try something else to get the sound you're looking for if the first one you order isn't right. If you get a Vintage Hot and you still go, "Man, I was looking for something darker and warmer … ." Well, what you need is more turns, because you can't change the wood. I can't make a pickup that's perfect for everyone's guitar and taste, so we offer an exchange policy.

I have always been interested to see that you offer both over-wound and under-wound pickups, which is something you don't often hear about.
It's my job to wind a pickup correctly so that it has its full output. If you wind it too tight or too loose or choose the wrong magnets or wire, it's going to sound bad, even though it has X number of turns on it. But picking the right number of turns for each person … that's a very personal thing, and I can't be the guy that tells them, "Oh, you need this … ." Unless a guy says, "I've had four different sets of Tele pickups and my Tele is still really bright. But if he's only tried the set his guitar came with, we really don't know anything.

Speaking of which, I know you have put a lot of thought into Telecaster pickups, and in particular the function of the plate under it.
A Tele pickup really is a Strat pickup, except you've added a steel plate under it. Also, the bridge is a piece of steel on old Teles, and that becomes part of the pickup. So a Telecaster is a different animal, and the body being different, too, is why they sound so different from Strats. You don't have the routing for a whammy bar or a middle pickup, and the strings go into the wood instead of a huge steel block. But the bridge is the main difference: you've got a piece of steel under the pickup, and a piece of steel around the pickup. Both of those focus the magnetic field in a positive way, to get the most output out of that coil. So they really seem louder than the same number of turns on a Strat pickup.

Is the magnetic field otherwise a little different, because it's a slightly different coil shape?
It's really not much different, and the way Leo designed them they both would have had the same turns on the same magnets. The Tele is a tiny bit taller and wider, but those are insignificant factors.

I know you also use a Tele-style bottom plate on some Strat pickups.
Yeah. That gets you 20 percent closer to sounding like a Telecaster, but it doesn't get you all the way.

meet the makers: interviews

Which, I guess, might be just enough for someone who wants their bridge pickup to be just a little hotter.
Part of our success is because I still play bars, and I still know what a good guitar sounds like verses a bad one. We work really hard to make our sets for Strats. The neck and middle are essentially the same pickup, but the bridge is totally different. It's wound with a different type of wire for a little bit bigger midrange, and it has more turns, and we recommend that steel plate, because the biggest thing you hear with that steel under it is the pickup's louder and bassier even without having anymore turns. So hopefully between those things we get a bridge pickup that is useable on the same amp setting as the neck and middle. That's why I got into coil winding in the first place, because all my Strats had an unusable bridge pickup.

Do you have any unsung heroes of older undiscovered pickups?
I've always been a huge Danelectro fan. Of all my instruments, my Danelectros have always been the ones I've never modified. I've monkeyed with everything I've ever bought, but with my Danelectros I've never even replaced the cheap toggle switch that always breaks. Danelectros are just so cheap and so functional. I've bought a lot of cheap guitars over the years, because I usually bought guitars that had something wrong with them so I could monkey with them and modify them.

My favorite guitar right now is a Gibson ES-225 that a friend of mine found for me in a music store for $350 that was painted black and stripped of all its hardware. So he stripped it for me and I put new everything on it, and it plays like a dream. But I never would have bought a $2,000 or $3,000 guitar and put my pickups on it.

You wouldn't want to devalue the thing.
I just couldn't afford it. It was much easier to buy a $350 guitar and fix it up.

What do you think of the pickups on the reissue Danelectros?
I have two of those, and I think they're fine. I own a lot of old ones, too, several U-2s and a couple of old basses. But they're pretty sweet-sounding little pickups.

One pickup that gets a bum rap from a lot of people is the Gretsch HiLo'Tron. What's your opinion on those?
They're very weak and clean, and if that's not what you want, don't play them. I think they're great, because I am a fan of clarity. I owned an Anniversary over the years, and the reason I sold it was not the sound, it was just because I couldn't keep it in tune.

Certainly the Dynasonics – the DeArmond 200 model – was a punchier pickup, despite being single coil.
Oh, they're great.

the guitar pickup handbook

I know you have also put a lot of thought into P-90s.
I love P-90s, but I didn't like them for years. It took a lot of experimenting with them to realize that I could under-wind them, and they were still loud as hell. Gibson intended that pickup to have 10,000 turns, but in that blond ES-225 I mentioned it has 8,000 on the neck and 9,500 on the bridge, so they're cleaner. They still break an amp up like crazy if you push an amp, but you can now twang your low E string and play Duane Eddy and rockabilly on them too.

It comes back to one of the first things we talked about: you have more control over a weaker pickup. You can dig in and make it nasty, you can twang it close to the bridge to get brighter, and in every way – with that P-90 for example – you have more control than a 10,000-turn pickup, which tends to be just muddy all the time. I sell them over-wound too, but I think more people buy 10 percent under and stock bridge than any other set we sell. I mention to people that I'm using 20 percent under neck and 5 percent under bridge as a set, and people try that, and they always like it. If you get brave enough to try a weaker pickup, you'll find that you can turn your amp up, and you've got pedals, so you've got plenty of control over your sound.

Any final tips?
Match your pickup to your guitar, because the pickup can only pick up what the guitar is doing.

meet the makers: interviews

Jason Lollar, Lollar Guitars

How did you get started in the pickup business?
Well, I never planned to start a pickup-making business. A lot of people don't know that. Unlike the normal business where you come up with an idea, then you advertise it, this all came out the back door … .

Back around 1971 I found this book called *Classical Guitar Making*, by Arthur Overholtzer, and that was the one that got a lot of guys started. I thought, "Man, that's what I want to do. I want to build guitars, and I want to play guitars." I built some stuff when I was in junior high and high school that were just lousy, horrible electric guitars. I went to school at Roberto-Venn [School of Luthiery] in 1979, and they taught us how to wind pickups back then, which I guess they don't teach any more. It was Semi Mosely and Bob Venn, showing us how to do what people call 'hand winding' now, which is actually guiding the wire by hand with a machine that spins the bobbin around.

So we made some rudimentary pickups where we actually cut parts out with tin snips, and then cut some wood out on the bandsaw for the core of it and then glued these pieces together and then drilled holes for the poles, and that was your bobbin. They were kind of like Semi Mosely's version of P-90s, and we had a choice of alnico magnets just like Semi used, which were these segmented bar magnets that looked like a radiator, we also used ceramic magnets. That was your choice: "You use ceramic if it's going to be hot, and you use alnico if it's not," and there really wasn't anything explained about exactly what you can do to change the sound. It was really rudimentary, kind of what a lot of the pickups in the '50s and '60s on Japanese guitars were like: they were funky, and they didn't hold together very well. The humbucker pickups that we made were wound without bobbins, just a coil that we wound on a form, and you would pull the coil off this form and wrap tape around it. They were microphonic as hell.

I bet, wow.
Then Bob Venn – I called him 'Bondo Bob', because he would use Bondo on all his guitars as a wood filler – would mix Bondo and casting resin and then pour it into wood pickup covers we had made with the whole pickup inside the cover, you flipped it upside down, and poured that mixture inside to seal it together. Now people are making wood pickup covers, but we did that back in the '70s and found that unless you use a really dark wood, if you use maple or something, it's going to get scratched up real quick.

And end up looking like a maple neck.
Yeah, it does that. So, I went through that school and got out and thought, "Oh, I thought I was going to be a guitar-maker, but I don't really have any idea what I'm

doing, at least as much as I thought I would!" But I made guitars through the '80s on a limited basis, and I got into a blues band and ended up playing two to five nights a week – so doing that, working a full-time job, and making the guitars as a third job, and that's how I got by. After about ten years of playing clubs like that, which taught me to show up on time, and do a good job, and perform at 150 percent, and be responsible, I had learned how to get the job done. Also hanging around on the club scene, with all those different types of guitarists, helped me form a valuable perspective on the needs of musicians that I use daily.

I have a collection of vintage amps that I use to design my pickups on. I have a vintage Vox AC30, a vintage Marshall, and around ten different vintage Fenders too, and those are also invaluable to the process. So the experience of knowing what you're up against in a live situation and a recording situation helped me a lot in this business.

When did you decide that winding pickup was the thing to do?
I got to the point where I didn't want to play clubs anymore, so I started this guitar business and got serious about it, and spent a few years making guitars and getting the jigs ready and putting the shop together – this is in 1992 or '93. And I started thinking, well, I live on an island and there's a limited market here, and I didn't know how people were going to buy my stuff, unless I went to Seattle to push it. As I was kicking ideas around, I decided to write a book as a way of getting my name out, and then to sell guitars.

I looked around to see what ideas there were that no one had written about and it happened that there was no material on the actual hands-on procedures involved in making pickups. About the same time I found that when I would go to a show and have an archtop with my pickups on it, when people found out I made the pickups they became really focused on it – "Wow, you wound your own pickups?" I would have this beautiful archtop, and I suppose the ultimate guitar-making achievement is to build a good archtop, and people would just be like, "Oh, you made the pickups!"

So I thought, "Well, I'll write a book about making pickups." So I do that, and then all of a sudden everybody wants me to wind pickups for them. People saw that book and thought, "This guy can make pickups." They'd either come to me with an unusual problem for something that needed to be made special, or they just couldn't get what they wanted from what was available. Also, just after the book came out I started hanging out on the Steel Forum on the internet, because I played steel, and I found there was a lot of demand for new pickups there. This was around 1996, '97. They started sending me all these old pickups, and I was learning a lot more than I already knew by taking them apart and fixing or adapting them. I found if there was something I needed to know or didn't have access to, I could go on the Steel Guitar site and say, "Can anyone lend me a 1937 EH-150?" and they would do it – they'd send it to me.

meet the makers: interviews

So that whole thing snowballed from there ...
Yeah, and I started doing a lot of custom stuff. People would call me and say, "Most of the pickups I've tried are too bright, or they don't have enough output, or they have too much output," or some kind of specific thing they were looking for. So I'd custom-make stuff for them, and after hundreds of people I'd start seeing patterns in what they wanted in specific kinds of pickups. For instance, with Strat pickups one of the things that comes up a lot is that the top end is so bright that it sounds brittle to people. You can break it down into several groups of different qualifications of what people want. Once in a while you'll get someone who wants something that's just out of left field, but there are specific things that people follow.

My whole stock pickup line came from doing custom pickups and determining what people wanted most, from the requests that I would get over and over again. And then, the other thing that is really cool about how this all happened is that I "let it" grow really slow, I actually held back growth, as much as I could, so that I could get all my ducks in a row with my inventory and my R&D. If I'd let it go balls out and gotten as many dealers as I could from the get-go, I wouldn't have had as solid a foundation.

It's interesting that the market was there, given that by '95 or '96 there were some major replacement pickup-makers around already, and they were making some vintage stuff, but a lot of it was more in the pumped up, high-gain, hot rock realm.
I think Seymour [Duncan] had just started doing the Antiquity line, right in there somewhere. So the real boom in vintage-repro pickups was still more in its infancy. Of course companies like Seymour Duncan, Dimarzio and Bill Lawrence opened the door for after market pickup demand 10 and 20 years previous to that time.

These days, it seems like one of the biggest sectors of the market involves players' efforts to get the best vintage tones out of their replacement pickup. Whether they are authentic vintage tones, or slightly modified – idealized – vintage tones.
Yeah, a *lot* of people want that today, its what most of my business revolves around.

And it's interesting that, with all the pickups that were available even then – and there are so many more today ...
Yeah, a lot of new people ... I watched it grow from a handful of people to more than you would probably be able to find if you started keeping count of it.

... There was still enough demand to make it a viable business model.
Yeah, and the drive was and is not so much for a completely accurate vintage sound, but often players have that sound in mind, with some other specific requirement in mind to modify it slightly. But man, yes, it grew way beyond what I ever expected.

The business doubled every year for a time there. I see lots of makers that are pretty well known now who say, "I bought that book and started out of that." Oh, my god…! Now, every week I see [some new pickup maker] on the internet. My book has been out of print for about four or five years, and they're going for $250 on the internet.

Some of these guys claim that they custom-make a different pickup for everybody, but they must be working out of some kind of specification even if they don't acknowledge it.

Sure, and after a while they probably have certain variations, but many fall into the same camp.
Yeah you have to work off prior experience if you want a predictable outcome, and you have to look at it like, these pickups are going to be around longer than I am; people are going to resell them, and they're going to want to know what it is when they resell them, so it's better if you have some defined models to offer.

There's a lot of misinformation out there about pickups. Do you have any pet peeves that you like to dispel?
For one thing, somebody came out with some specs at some point – some of it, I think, goes back to that Donald Brosnac book (*Guitar Electronics for Musicians*, Beekman Books, 1995) – and it has just been reprinted and reprinted, over and over, and nobody has ever bothered to check it out.

What kinds of specs are these?
Oh, like windings, turn counts, specific resistances, the types of magnets used, and blah blah blah, and I've found that a lot of it doesn't match up. Somebody will write, "Vintage Fender Pickup Specifications," and then they'll list models with different specs, and a lot of it is just not right.

Also, one of my pet peeves is that there's so much information out there, but there are a lot of guys who are just kind of like hobbyists, but they'll post on the internet and everybody reads it and assumes it's correct, even though these guys don't necessarily know what they're talking about. Every once in a while I'll get somebody calling me up and they'll go, "I want you to make me a pickup with Alnico III magnets and 7,000 turns of heavy-build Formvar." And I'll ask, "Well, why do you want that?" And they'll say, "Because it'll do this and that and that … ." I'll tell them I can do it for them, but I'm not going to guarantee what it's going to sound like. Most of the time when somebody comes and tells me how to build the pickup, they wind up not getting what they want. Any more, I won't do it without a compelling reason, and I'll tell them that.

The internet is great for putting everything at your fingertips, but at the same time a lot of that 'everything' is misinformation, in all walks

of life. You've got professional news journalists covering important events, but you have all kinds of bloggers covering the same 'news'.
Once in a while a magazine will call me and actually fact check, and that's a great thing. The good thing about the internet is how it equalizes everyone's chances to be seen – you used to have to take out ads in magazines at great expense – it took a lot of money and dedication to get something going but now anyone can reach out and contact the whole world. The good thing about the old way was it would weed out a lot of people that didn't have a good business plan. When it comes down to it, it really doesn't matter if you can do good work if you can't do it consistently or in a timely manner. You also need to be responsive to receiving questions about your product, or when it's going to be delivered.

There are all kinds of crazy claims out there about the way the great pickups were originally made, but what are some of the keys to 'the vintage tone'?
This'll tie into your last question about pet peeves, and that is the fact that just because it's 'hand wound' doesn't mean it's *good*. There are a lot of people claiming, "Oh, I can take your Epiphone pickups and rewind it, and it's going to sound great." But the coil is just one factor in the thing. The pickup materials affect the outcome as much as the turns and type of wire and how you wind it.

So on a Fender, with its type of coil, it's really important that the magnets you use have a good sound to them. These magnets, alnico magnets, are a combination of different metals mixed together, and there are impurities in that mix, and the actual recipe for the metal has a huge impact on the tone. You can get an Alnico V from one factory that makes magnets and an Alnico V from another factory, and there can be a huge difference in the sound. So you've got to go through and find the magnet source that you can work with. Then, old Fender pickups – for instance, a '62 or '63 Strat coil – you're going to find that the power of the magnet is about 20 percent less than if you took that magnet and put it on the magnetizer and charged it back up. That's important too. It's a lot easier to put the pickup together with the magnets unmagnetized, because you don't have to worry about getting metal shavings on them and they're easier to handle, they don't bounce together, and there's no chance of getting a magnet put in upside down, if you charge it after it's all put together. So most makers charge magnets after they put them together, but it results in a different strength in the magnet.

Do you put them in already charged?
I put some of them in already charged, and some I charge after assembly. Most of my Fender pickups with Alnico V, I put them together already charged, and there's a specific range of level that's about 20 percent less than if you fully charged it. So that has a lot to do with the treble quality.

In what way?

It makes it a little sweeter, a little bit less brash. That's one aspect of it, and like I said, the material itself – you'll hear subtle differences from one batch of Alnico V to another batch, and you can sometimes get overtones that are inappropriate to the rest of the tones.

And just the shape of the coil. Take a Strat coil; you can get quite a different tone out of a Strat pickup by making the coil a little bit shorter or a little bit taller. It makes a measurable difference. You can hear the difference in as little as a 32nd of an inch. If you make the pickup taller it'll make the pickup a little more focused sounding, slightly brighter, a little clearer sounding.

It sounds like it almost corresponds a bit with the way the string-sensing area, the magnetic window, is working anyway.

Yeah. Of course, with a Fender Strat pickup your magnetic sensing is going to be a pretty typical shape because of the design. That's the way it is.

Does this have anything to do with the differences between Strat and Tele bridge pickups (although I'm aware the Tele bridge structure and the base plate affect that pickups performance, too)?

The coil shape isn't all that different. It's pretty similar. The big difference is that metal ashtray bridge.

The bottom plate of the pickup being metal makes a very subtle difference, but that bridge, that's where you get a 15 or 20 percent boost in volume, midrange, and bass. You take that plate away and just use a Strat bridge, or put a Telecaster bridge pickup in a Strat, and it doesn't sound like a Tele.

And there are some makers of Tele-style guitars that dispense with the old stamped steel bridge plate, and just sink a Telecaster type pickup into a route in the body and screw it into the wood …

Yeah, and you've heard those guitars – what's your experience with them?

Well … they don't really sound like a Tele, to me.

No. That ashtray bridge is a huge part of it.

It's a fascinating structure, because that tone is the result of a combination of so many factors.

And the bridge pieces themselves, what they're made out of – the saddles, and all that, contributes to the tone.

But to pick up where we were before, the height of the coil, the tension on the coil – how lose or tight it is, makes a difference – how microphonic the coil is, makes a big difference.

meet the makers: interviews

You mean not microphonic to the point where it's actually honking and detracting from the performance of the pickup, but microphonic in more imperceptible ways?

Right. When we make stuff, there's a specific length of time that we will pot it for. On Fender-style pickups, the waxing actually helps hold the pickups together, that's one of the things that binds the whole assembly together. If you don't wax the coil at all, if it gets bumped or the guitar gets dropped, it can knock the coil loose and it will become more microphonic. That's really common with old, vintage pickups.

So when I pot stuff, I have a vacuum potter, and I throw the pickups in there and I only pot for between ten seconds to a minute and 45 seconds, depending on the application is unless somebody specifically asks for something that's waxed really heavily. Generally it's just a light potting, because microphonics are part of the sound. You don't want them so microphonic that they're going to be unusable, but if you have them completely dead, most people will hear that if there's no microphonics at all. How much difference that makes if you're playing with a big band in a crowded room… probably doesn't make a whole lot of difference.

Well, like a lot of these things. People hone their tone at home, then they know what they've got, and they feel good about themselves.

Yeah exactly. At least it gives you a place to start from.

P-90s are such a different kettle of fish. What are some of the nuances with that design?

That's the same thing, regarding coil shape, and of course it's a much wider coil. You've got people that are selling a "P-90" that fits in a humbucker. Well, if you notice on a humbucker there's only actually a quarter-inch space between the end of the pole piece and the end of the pickup. It actually needs to be about a half-inch [on a P-90], so they take the coil and they make it taller, like a Strat pickup, so it'll fit in there, and it changes the whole nature of the pickup.

And those P-90s are long pickups, coil wise.

Way longer. You can take any pickups and make it shorter, or wider, and you'll hear a big difference in tone. That's one thing about the P-90, the shape of the coil. Then another is the shape of the magnetic field, because it's using two magnets underneath. Two magnets also make a different magnetism in the pole pieces than one magnet; two magnets are a little stronger. But you get less magnetism at the top of the pole piece with a pickup like that than you do with a Fender, so you can raise that pickup up really close to the strings and it's not going to pull the strings out of tune.

Yeah, I've heard people talk about not cranking the P-90 pole pieces up,

but raising up the whole pickup – the entire coil – when you want to increase the power.
Yeah, it works better. One thing I make is a shim for a dog-ear P-90 to raise it up, and it's exactly the same size as the dog-ear cover so you don't see it so much. That's important, to adjust the pickup right.

The other qualities of the P-90 are what the pole piece material is made of, the size and the shape of the pole piece – whether it's got a round-head or a flat-head screw – and the type of material on the plate underneath, whether it's nickel silver or brass. Anything that's close to the coil, or the magnet, if it's, metal it's going to have some effect.

Your P-90 replacements are highly regarded.
I have been making P-90's since I started making pickups 30 years ago and I watched them go from a pickup no one really wanted to one of the more popular designs around. I've probably made more P-90s than anything else. I make a variety of them. I make an exact copy of a set of P-90s out of a '56 [Gibson Les Paul] Goldtop, and they don't sound like what people expect from P-90s.

In what way are they different?
They're lower output, they're a real soft attack, they're brighter, they don't have as much midrange, and they're not gritty. They're sweeter, brighter, with less attack.

Interesting. When I've played vintage guitars from that era that I have really liked, that's the sound that has appealed to me. But very often people, when they think P-90, think of the gritty, aggressive sound with the midrange hump.
That's what they think '50s P-90s sound like, but it's not really the case. Same thing with humbuckers. The old humbuckers in dot neck ES-335s in particular, I've had quite a few of those in and most of them are around 7.2k [ohms, resistance].

What kind of readings are you expecting for genuine '50s P-90s?
I've seen them anywhere from 6.5k to 8.2k. It depends, they vary a lot. If I had to pick a number I'd put them around 7.2k. The one that I sell the most of is around 8.2k, it's a little grittier, a little snarlier. It's the one on my website. The more authentic '50s-style version isn't actually listed, but I make it.

A lot of it depends on the amp, too. If you're playing a Fender Twin, you wouldn't want a bright pickups. But if you're playing a Fender tweed champ, you wouldn't want my stock P-90 pickup, it would just be too much for it.

Tell us a little about some of the less-considered factors regarding humbuckers.

One thing worth considering is the pickup cover. People are always asking, "How much difference does that make?" And it can make anywhere from a huge difference to very little. What matters are exactly what the mix of metal that the cover is, and how thick it is. We went through this whole R&D thing that took months, to get these pickups covers made, and we wound up having covers made that are quite a bit thinner than what is generally available. It's easier to make them shriek, microphonically, so I put them upside down and pot them for 30 seconds so that it dampens the cover. But it doesn't really get into the coils very much. It's still microphonic, but the cover doesn't ping.

I have read Seth Lover saying that, sure, the covers on humbuckers reduce the highs somewhat, but he designed the pickup with that in mind, so he has accounted for that fact.
Yeah, and it smoothes the sound out too. I designed mine with the same considerations.

I stayed out of making humbuckers for many years. The big deal about doing them was getting consistent parts. We're one of the few companies that can actually make parts in-house, but to do humbucker parts, like the covers, it was going to be $20,000 to make a stamp. Then you've got to make a run of them. For the base plate, it was going to be $15,000 to make a stamp. So if you can find parts off the shelf, that's the way to go with them. But we won't use just anybody's parts, and that makes it difficult too, because if there's any problem with the supply chain, there's only one place you can go to. And my company is all about consistency. Consistency, service, and expertise.

Are you finding there are any different tricks with getting humbuckers right, in order to please the players who want them, compared with getting your single coil styles right?
With humbuckers it's more difficult to gauge people, because it's almost like a different type of guitar player than the single-coil guy. A lot of the humbucker guys are used to having all that padding around the note, but with a single coil it's almost like you're naked and in the spotlight. With a humbucker it's like you've got all your pals with you. So a lot of the public are looking for something that's a little bit softer and not quite so clear, with a humbucker. You've got to balance that, and we really don't cater to people who just want their humbucker to be loud and just rock out all the time. Most of the people who buy our stuff want dynamics out of it.

I make three different models of humbuckers. One's an over-wound one, which is more like what a lot of people want who are a certain level of player; they're softer and creamier, and you lose a little bit of that definition, but they really do sound nice and sweet. Then my stock one, which is called the Imperial, is a step down from that in output, and the bottom end is a little bit tighter. You've still got some roundness to it, but you've got better definition. If you took a late-60s, early-70s Les Paul, my neck pickup is going to be clearer than that. Les Pauls tend to make every note just like the last one you played, so my pickup should be able to go any direction you take it. It shouldn't color the tone too much, and if you want a harmonic out of it or a partial harmonic, or want to be able to clean it up by just playing it a tiny bit softer – all those things that the player puts in should come back out the other side.

Again, I think your pickups – whether single coils or humbuckers – have found a market mostly with players that might be termed 'touch' players or 'feel' players, and dynamics is always a big part of that style of playing.
Right. And also, my humbucker should have a little more treble than a lot of guys would think, so that it comes through and reaches the audience. You don't want too much treble, but you need a little more clarity than a lot of people expect from a humbucker. When I go play with guys that I usually don't play with, a lot of them put too much distortion on their amp, so that it gets muddy, and I'll kill 'em, because I don't have quite as much distortion, and I turn the reverb down, because there's already reverb in the room, and turn the treble up a little bit louder than you think you want it on stage, because the sound's got to get out there.

As they knew back in the day – the goal was always for more treble. Whereas you discover many players who craft their gorgeous, warm tone in the comfort of their own homes find it just gets lost once they get it up on stage with a band.
Yeah. What sounds good in your bedroom doesn't necessarily sound good in a club.

Which must make it a little hard for someone like you to please people all the time, because some guys are mainly looking for something that will sound great to them at home alone in the bedroom.
Oh, you know, that happens a lot. They get it home and go, "I don't know if I like it?" Then they take it to the band, and the band's going, "Man, that sounds better than ever!"

Are you finding that guitarists, by and large, are revising their thinking on what they want from replacement pickups? The early market was mostly in hotter pickups for players who wanted a little more oomph out of their setup, but in recent years guitarists seem to have learned that pickups like that didn't always result in the best overall tone.
Absolutely, over time the quest has become more about more clarity and dynamics over brute output.

Sometimes a weaker pickup will beat the crap out of a hotter pickup. I think originally players were going to hotter pickups because it was probably very obvious that the

meet the makers: interviews

new pickup they put in sounded very different from the old one. There was no subtlety about it. When you first had that whole industry getting going, it was probably very important to make it clear that this product was doing something different.

That's a good point. And also I'm sure it was a product of its time, and guys were largely replacing those late-70s Fender Strat and Tele pickups that weren't very good in the first place, and playing them through silverface Twin Reverbs that they couldn't make break up to save their lives.
Right. Those amps really can make use of more bottom end and more output from a pickup.

And it was a rock age, more than anything else.
Sure. And sometimes a pickup that doesn't have as much output as another will actually sound louder than a higher-wind pickup. The higher-wind pickup will be distorting the amp, but the one that is clearer has more treble, so it just rides right over the top of that and you hear everything you're doing. It's like playing a Tele; if you're playing a Tele in a band, you don't have to rely on volume to be heard.

Sure, and the other guy is sitting in with a Les Paul thinking, "How come this guy is cutting through so much better?"
Yeah, "How come he's all over the top of me?" And that's what I was saying earlier: a lot of guys use a little bit too much distortion, and they just don't get a good sound out of it to begin with. So the whole thing has to all work together. If somebody call me up and says, "I want my Les Paul to sound like "ABC … ." I had ten Les Pauls in my shop, and I put the same pickups in every Les Paul. Three of them sounded really dark and woody, three of them sounded really bright and snappy, and the other ones had very subtle differences. And then there's the player. How does he play? Does he play with a really thin pick, or a hard pick, or does he play with a pick at all? Does he even know how to play? And what's the guitar amp, and the speaker?

I've got so many amps, and if the pickup doesn't sound good in one amp I'll just go to another, and it'll sound great. And I often wonder, "Why do people even want hot pickups?" How much more distortion do you need?

One thing I have started to notice about some really good Les Paul or ES-335 players, is that they'll often plug into the number 2 input of any amp, just as a matter of course, before tweaking the rest of the controls. If they want a little more clarity and dynamics, they'll use that low-gain input so they're not slamming the front end of the amp with those humbuckers, then they can get the action happening later in the amp, at the output stage.

And a lot of guys will never turn the tone controls on their amp at all – that's ridiculous. And the big guys, I hear it on records all the time, they won't have their [guitar] volume on ten all the time, they'll roll it down about 20 percent, and you can hear that, it's a little bit sweeter.

There are a lot of little things like this that were the standard tricks in the 'golden years' of tone, when they didn't have all sorts of gizmos to craft their sound, and a lot of good players are rediscovering these simple things, which are really all a part of how guitars and amps were designed to work in the first place. And the notions of slightly weaker, more dynamic pickups, and of non-master-volume amps ... they seemed to come back into the general awareness around the same time, and they seem tied together in this thinking.
Yeah, people often think of the same thing at the same time. I am a big believer in using the pickup selector switch and the volume and tone controls. I watched a lot of top notch older blues players in the early '80s and copped that whole thing about rolling the volume and tone controls up and down, that's when I really learned to use my gear along with more basic things like having the whole band use dynamics. I have this pickup called the Chicago Steel pickup, and it's fun – you plug it into a little amp and it sounds like a big Marshall, and you can still play somewhat dynamically, but you wouldn't want that sound all the time. But that's a ceramic pickup, and it works well for that application when you want it.

What's your thinking on the use of ceramic magnets verses alnico in pickup-making?
Ceramic won't conduct electricity, so if you put a meter on a ceramic magnet it won't show any conductivity, so it doesn't affect the inductance of the coil like a metal would. When you put a piece of ceramic magnet in there, it's not loading the coil and putting more bass in there. Ceramic is really cheap, and [in the early days] they used it without tweaking the design at all, and that's probably why it got a bad name. The pickups were designed with alnico for the frequency response, and somebody substituted ceramic in there without any consideration to altering the design, so it just sounded hot, bright and nasty. But that Chicago Steel pickup of mine is ceramic, and it's also got a big hunk of metal in it. It's designed to work right with a ceramic magnet.

And of course guys like Bill Lawrence or Joe Barden have put a lot of thought into making pickups with ceramic magnets, and they'll confirm that you work from a completely different starting point, rather than just swapping in a ceramic magnet where an alnico magnet used to be.
Eexactly. It's more about the design than about how some guy's winding the coil.

PICKUP TONE CHART

Player	Song	Tone	Pickup
Charlie Christian	'Air Mail Special'	Jazz: crisp, thick, round	Gibson 'Charlie Christian'
Grant Green	'No. 1 Green Street'	Jazz: rich, warm, yet bright	Gibson P-90
Luther Perkins	Johnny Cash's 'Folsom Prison Blues'	Country: bright, dynamic, twangy	Fender Telecaster (bridge)
Cliff Gallup	Gene Vincent's 'Race With The Devil'	Rock'n'roll: chewy, gritty twang	Gretsch/DeArmond DynaSonic
George Harrison	The Beatles' 'She Loves You'	Rock'n'roll: driving, yet clear	Gretsch Filter'Tron
Eric Clapton	The Blues Breakers' 'Hideaway'	Blues rock: hot, juicy	Gibson PAF humbucker
Roger McGuinn	The Byrds' 'Eight Miles High'	Jangle: bright, clear, shimmering	Rickenbacker 'Toaster Top'
Jimi Hendrix	'Voodoo Chile'	Rock: lithe, clear, dynamic	Fender Stratocaster
Pete Townshend	The Who's 'Substitute' (*Live At Leeds* take)	Rock: punchy, crunchy, powerful	Gibson P-90
Paul Kossoff	Free's 'All Right Now'	Rock: singing, juicy, saturated	Gibson PAF humbucker
Bruce Springsteen	'Candy's Room'	Rock: stinging, cutting, sharp	Fender Esquire (bridge)
Paul Weller	The Jam's 'In The City'	Punk-Pop: punchy, sharp, dynamic	Rickenbacker 'Button Top'
Elvis Costello	'(What's So Funny 'Bout) Peace, Love, and Understanding'	Pop-Punk: bright, gritty, compressed	Fender Jazzmaster
Billy Zoom	X's 'Johnny Hit And Run Paulene'	Punk: grinding, crunchy, dynamic	Gretsch/DeArmond DynaSonic
James Hetfield	Metallica's 'Master of Puppets'	Metal: huge, eviscerating crunch	EMG-60
Kim Thayil	Soundgarden's 'My Wave'	Grunge: gutsy, dynamic crunch	Guild HB-1 humbucker
Carlos Santana	'Smooth'	Latin rock: juicy, sweet, sustaining	PRS Dragon II humbucker

CD NOTES AND TRACK LISTING

Listening Notes

The audio CD included with *The Guitar Pickup Handbook* contains 36 tracks with samples of a wide range of noteworthy pickups. The intention is to provide a little 'ear study', some sensory triggers to go along with the text in this book. Any 'sound samples' presentation requires a caveat, mainly to point out that any of these pickups (and guitars, for that matter) would very likely sound different once you got them into your own home, used them with your own gear, and played them with your own hands. To that end, I would be the first person to advise against purchasing pickups, new or used, based on what you hear in such sound samples, or on similar samples provided on the web sites of many pickup manufacturers. Use these to familiarize yourself with the general sounds of some classic pickups, and as an opportunity to hear some designs you might not have encountered 'in the flesh', and take from them what you will by way of tonal research.

I played these samples myself, with the intention of showing off the pickups more than the performances. The first three series of samples are done with similar musical passages played through the same amp settings for each series, to provide an easy means of comparison. For these, and the three extended samples that follow them (tracks 1-27 all together) I played through a Matchless DC-30 amplifier with the Celestion G12H-30 speaker miked by a Coles 4038 ribbon microphone placed approximately 12 inches from the speaker cone. The microphone was plugged into a Hamptone tube microphone preamp, and the pieces were recorded directly to disk, via a Motu 828 MkII, using Motu Digital Performer on a MacPro. No EQ or compression was used in the signal chain. All tracks include voice commentary to 'set the scene', to simplify the listening process, without need of referring back to the notes here in the book with each new track. Tracks 28 to 36 were taken from other sources, and were borrowed variously from the DVD or CDs accompanying Interactive *Gibson Bible, Guitar Effects Pedals: The Practical Handbook, Guitar Rigs: Classic Guitar & Amp Combinations,* and *Electric Guitar Sourcebook: How to Find the Sounds You Like.*

Sound Samples CD

1. Fender Stratocaster 57/62 Pickup bridge
2. '57 Esquire bridge
3. Gretsch Duo Jet, DeArmond/Dynasonic bridge
4. '53 Gibson Les Paul P-90 bridge
5. Fralin P-90 bridge, in Grosh ElectraJet
6. Fender Jazzmaster bridge
7. Joe Barden S-Deluxe bridge
8. Single Coil Bridge Medly, cleaner
9. Gibson '57 Les Paul VOS Burstbucker bridge
10. Gibson Custom ES-335 '57 Classic bridge
11. Gibson '61 Les Paul Standard/SG PAF bridge
12. Fralin Humbucker bridge, in Grosh ElectraJet
13. Humbucker Bridge Medly, cleaner
14. Fender Stratocaster 57/62 Pickup neck
15. Fender Twisted Tele neck
16. Gretsch Duo Jet, DeArmond/Dynosonic neck
17. '53 Gibson Les Paul P-90 neck
18. Fralin P-90 neck, in Don Grosh ElectraJet
19. Joe Barden S-Deluxe neck
20. Gibson Custom ES-335 '57 Classic neck
21. Gibson '57 Les Paul VOS Burstbucker neck
22. Gibson '57 Les Paul VOS Orig. w/'62 Patent # pickup neck
23. Gibson '61 Les Paul Standard/SG PAF neck
24. Fralin Humbucker neck, in Grosh ElectraJet
25. Orig. Gibson Patent # Humbucker Blowout
26. Orig. Gibson Patent # Humbucker Blowout2: Hotter
27. Joe Barden S-Deluxe neck pickup Blowout
28. PAF Heaven: Carl Verheyen & Six Vintage Gibsons
29. '64 Fender Stratocaster neck pickup into '60 tweed Tremolux
30. G&L ASAT Z-Coil bridge pickup
31. Danelectro Lipstick Tube pickups
32. Rickenbacker 360/12 Toaster-Top pickup
33. Mid-'40s Gibson ES-125 with pre-P-90
34. Gibson L-5 CES w/Alnico V pickup
35. Guild X-50 archtop with Guild 'Soapbar' pickup
36. Kay N-50 archtop with DeArmond 'Gold Foil' pickup

All music © Dave Hunter 2008. *Reproducing or sampling without expressed written permission is forbidden.*

INDEX

Page numbers in **bold** indicate illustrations.

A

AC impedance, 46
Acousti-Lectric company, 12
active pickups, 112, 156
Actodyne General company, 96
Alembic pickups, 111–113
alnico magnet, 31, 32, 33, 66–67
Anderson, Tom, 113, *see also* Tom Anderson Guitarworks
Armstrong, Kent, 117, 185–193, *see also* Kent Armstrong Pickups
Atkins, Chet, 103

B

Baldwin company, 19
Barden, Joe, 119, 194–209, *see also* Joe Barden Engineering
Bare Knuckle Pickups, 121–123
    Cold Sweat, 122
    Geoff Whitehorn Crawler, 122
    Holydiver, 122
    Miracle Man, 122
    Mississippi Queen HBP90, 123
    Nailbomb, 122
    Painkiller, 122
    Steve Stevens Rebel Yell, 122
    The Sinner, 123
    Trilogy Suite, 123
    Warpig, 122
Barth, Paul, 15, 16, 50
Beauchamp, George, 11, 13, 15, 16, 18, 50
Bill Lawrence, 34, 174–175
    L-90, 175
    L-220, 174
    L-280, 175
    L-500, 175
'blade' pickup, 33, 34, 46, 55, 107, 119, 120, 175
Blucher, Steve, 137, 210–213
bobbin, 35, 38, 70
Burns, 117, 119, 123–124
    Tri-Sonic, 123, 124
Burns, James, 123
Butts, Ray, 103, 105, 106

C

Carvin, 33, 124–126
    AP6, 124
    AP11, 125
    AP13, 125
    C22, 125
    H22, 125
    M22 Hex-Pole, 124, 125
    S60T/N, 125
    TBH60, 125
CD details 250–251
ceramic magnets, 22, 31, 33, 134, 175
Chandler, 127
Charvel, 127
coil types, 37–42
cover removal, 69–70

D

Danelectro, 126–127
    'Lipstick Tube', 33, 126, 127
D'Angelico, 128
Daniel, Nat, 126
DC resistance, 38, 43–45, 84
DeArmond, 127–133
    FH/FHC, 127, 128
    'gold foil', 130
    Model 1000 Rhythm Chief, 128, 133
    Model 1100 Adjustable Rhythm Chief, 128, 133
    RH/RHC, 127, 133
    'silver foil', 130
    2K, 131, 133
    200 model, 21, 39, 102–103, 105, 128, 130, 131, 133, 166
DeArmond, Harry, 127, 129, 130
DiMarzio, 134–144, 210–213
    Air Classic, **134**, 140
    Air Norton, 137, 139
    Air Norton S, 141
    Air Norton T, 143
    Air Zone, 139
    Area T, 143
    Area 58/61/67, 141
    Bluesbucker, 140
    Breed, 138
    Chopper, 141
    Chopper T, **134**, 143
    Cruiser, 141
    D Activator, 137, 138
    D Activator X, 138
    D Sonic, 138
    DLX Plus, 144
    DLX 90, 144
    Dual Sound, 138
    EJ Custom, 140
    Evo 2, 138
    Evolution, 138
    Fast Track, **35**, 137
    Fast Track T, 143
    Fast Track 2, 141
    FRED, 134, 139
    FS-1, 134, 142
    Hot Minibucker, 141
    HS2/HS3, 141
    Humbucker From Hell, 140
    Minibucker, 141
    Mo'Joe, 139
    Norton, 140
    PAF Joe, 140
    PAF Pro, 134, 140
    PAF 36th Anniversary, 140
    Pre B-1, 134, 144
    Pro Track, 141
    P-90 Super Distortion, 144
    Red Velvet, 143
    SDS-1, 134, 143
    Soapbar, 144
    Steve's Special, 139
    Super Distortion, **33**, 134, 139
    Super Distortion S, 141
    Super Distortion T, 143
    Tone Zone, 139
    Tone Zone P-90, 144
    Tone Zone S, 142
    Tone Zone T, 143
    True Velvet, 143
    Twang King, 144
    Virtual Hot T Bridge, 143
    Virtual P-90, 144

index

Virtual Solo, 142
Virtual Vintage, **35**, 136
Virtual Vintage Blues, 142
Virtual Vintage Heavy Blues 2, 142
Virtual Vintage Solo, 142
Virtual Vintage 54 Pro, 137, 142
X2N, 134, 139
YJM, 142
DiMarzio, Larry, 134, 210–213, *see also* DiMarzio
'dog-ear', *see* Gibson P-90
dual rail pickup, 46, **46**, 119, 120
Duncan, Seymour, 145, 214–220, *see also* Seymour Duncan

E

Eldred, Mike, 221–227
Electro String, 15–16
EMG Pickups, 23, 156–159
    F models, 159
    H models, 157, 159
    P models, 158, 159
    S models, 157, 158, 159
    60 model, 158
    60A model, 158
    81 model, **156**, 158
    85 model, 158
    89 model, 158
    91 model, 158
Epiphone, 18, 57, 72, 128
Ernie Ball, *see* Music Man

F

Fender, 80–101, 108, 221–227
    Atomic Humbucker, 99, 101
    Broadcaster, 81, 84, 95, 99
    Custom Shop, 93, 95, 100, 221–227
    Custom Shop Fat 50s, 93, 100
    Custom Shop Nocaster, 95, 100
    Custom 54 Strat, 93, 100
    Custom 69 Strat, 93, 100
    Duo-Sonic, 99
    Esquire, 85
    Hot Noiseless Strat, 96, 101
    humbucker, *see* Wide Range Humbucking
    Jaguar, 87, 90, 100
    Jazzmaster, 32, 37, 87, 99
    Lace Sensor, 96–99, 101
    lap-steel/early, 80–81, 82, 88
    Musicmaster, 99
    Mustang, 87
    Original Vintage Telecaster, 96
    Original 57/62 Stratocaster, 95, 100
    Precision Bass, 89, 94
    SCN, 95–96, 101
    seven-pole, 89, 92
    Stratocaster, 32, **32**, 40, 44, **44**, 60, 85–87, 93, 95, 96, 99
    Telecaster, 21, 32, **32**, 38, 40, 43, **43**, 81, 83–85, 95, 96, 99
    Tex Mex Stratocaster, 95, 101
    Texas Special, 93, 100
    Twisted Tele, 95
    Vintage Noiseless, 96, 101
    Vintage Telecaster, 101
    Wide Range Humbucking, 91, 99, 100
Fender, Leo, 80, 89, 91, 162
Fralin, Lindy, 159, 228–236, *see also* Lindy Fralin Pickups
'Frying Pan' guitar, 15, 51
Fuller, Walter, 20, 56, 60

G

Gibson, 55–80
    Alnico V, 21, 59–60, 78
    Angus Young Signature, 77, 80
    'bar', *see* Charlie Christian
    BurstBucker, 75, 76, 79
    Charlie Christian, 20, 33, 55, 57, 58, 78
    Dirty Fingers, 75, 77, 79
    'dog-ear', *see* P-90 (description, 57)
    Firebird, 33, 72–73, 78
    Hot Ceramics, 77
    humbucker, 22, 32, **33**, 36, 40, 42, 45, **45**, 60, 62, 63, 64, 65, 66–67, 69, 70–73, 74, 75–77, 78, 79
    low-impedance, 73
    Melody Maker, 74, 78
    Mini-humbucker, 72, 73, 78
    Modern Classic, 77
    PAF, *see* humbucker
    P-90, 20, 21, 32, **32**, 37, 40, 41, **41**, 42, 57, 59, 61, 78, 87
    P-94, 76–77, 79, 80
    'soapbar', *see* P-90 (description, 57, 59)
    'staple', *see* Alnico V
    Tom DeLonge Signature, 77
    Tony Iommi Signature, 77, 80
    'T-top', *see* humbucker
    57 Classic, 75, 76, 79
    490 series, 77, 79
    500T, 77, 79
G&L, 33, 34, 91, 162–166
    ASAT Classic, 164
    GHB Humbucker, 166
    HG-2R Humbucker, 166
    Humbucker, 164
    Magnetic Field Design (MFD), 162, **162**, 163, 164, 166
    Z-Coil, 164, 166
Gretsch, 102–109, 169–171
    Dynasonic, 21, 37, 39, 102–103, 104, 108, 109, 128, 131, 133
    Filter'Tron, 22, **38**, 102, 103, 105, 106, 107, 108, 109, 169
    High Sensitive Filter'Tron, 108, 109
    HiLo'Tron, 107, 108, 109
    Hot Rod Filter'Tron, 108, 109
    Super'Tron, 107–108, 109
Guild, 103, 130, 166–167
    'Frequency Tested', 167
    HB-1, 167
    'soapbar', 166

H

Hamel, Alan, 95
Harmonic Design Custom Pickups, 167–168
    Classic Humbucker, 168
    Super 90, , 168
    Vintage Plus, 168
    Z-90, 168
    54 Special Strat, 168
    54 Special Tele, 168
Hart, Guy, 55, 58
horseshoe pickup, *see* Lollar, Rickenbacker

index

I
Ibanez, 137
impedance, *see* AC impedance, DC impedance

J
Jackson, 127
Jerry Jones, 127
J.M. Rolph Pickups, 183
Joe Barden Engineering, 119–121, 194–209
    Danny Gatton T-Style, **34**, 120
    HB/HB Two Tone, 120
    S-Deluxe, 120
Jones, Thomas V., 108, *see also* T.V. Jones

K
Kent Armstrong Pickups, 117–119, 185–193
    Burns Tri-Sonic V, 118
    High Output Humbucker, 118
    Jazz Humbucker, 118
    Jazz Slimbucker, 118
    Kentron N, 118
    Mini Split Tube, 118
    Split Tube, **34**, 118
    Split Tube Hot, 118
Keystone, *see* Bill Lawrence
K&F, 80
Kiesel, Lowell C., 124
Kinman, 171–173
    AVn models, 171, 172
    Buzzbucker, 171
    Hx-85, 171, 172
    SCn, 171, 172
Kinman, Chris, 171
Knoblaugh, Armand F., 17, 19
Kustom, 130

L
Lace Music Products, 96–99, 101, 173–174
    Alumitone, 174
    Holy Grail, 173, 173
    PS 900/905, 173, 174
    Sensor, 96–99, 101, 174
Lace, Don, 96, *see also* Lace Music Products
Lawrence, Bill, 95, 174, *see also* Bill Lawrence
Levin guitars, 103, 130
Lindy Fralin Pickups, 159–162, 228–236
    Blues Special, 159
    High Output models, 160, 161
    P-90 Alnico, 160
    P-92, **159**, 160, 161
    Steel Poled models, 159, 160, 161
    Stock, 159
    Twangmaster, 160, 162
    Unbucker, 160, 161
Loar, Lloyd, 12
Lollar Guitars, 175–178, 237–248
    Charlie Christian Archtop, 176, 177, **177**
    Chicago Steel, 176, 177
    High Wind Imperial, 177
    Horseshoe, 176, **177**, 177–178
    Imperial Humbucker, 177
    Low Wind Imperial, 177
    P-90 replacement, 177
    Special S Series, 176
    Special T Series Bridge, 176
    Vintage Series, 176
    56 P-90, 177
Lollar, Jason, 175, 176, 237–248, *see also* Lollar Guitars
Lover, Seth, 21, 59, 60, 62, 91
low-impedance pickups, 73, 111, 156

M
magnet types, 30–35
Martin, 103, 130
microphony, 39, 42, 69
Mills, Tim, 121
Mosrite, 124
Music Man, 137

N
National, 11, 15

P
Petersen, Scott, 167
potting, *see* wax potting
PRS, 178–180
    Chainsaw, 180
    David Grissom, 180
    Deep Dish, 180
    Dragon II, 179
    HFS, 178, 179
    Hiland, 180
    McCarty, 179
    Santana II/III, 179, 180
    Single-Coil Bass, 178
    Standard Bass, 178
    Standard Treble, 178
    Swamp Ash, 179
    Tremonti, 179, 180
    Vintage Bass, 178, 179
    Vintage Treble, 178
    7 model, 179

R
Rickenbacker, Adolph, 11, 16, 50
Rickenbacker, 15, 16, 18, 49–54
    'button top', *see* High Gain
    High Gain, 53, 54
    horseshoe, 14, 15, 16, 18, 19, 20, 50, 51, 52, 54, 177
    'toaster top', 22, 53, 54
Rio Grande Pickups, 180–183
    Barbeque, 182
    Bastard, 180, 182
    Bluesbar, 180, 181
    Buffalo, 182
    Dirty Harry, 180, 181
    Fat Bastard, 180, 182
    Genuine Texas, 182
    G&L-style, 183
    Half Breed, 180, 181
    Jazzbar, 180, 182
    Muy Grande, 180, 181, 182
    Stelly, 180, 181
    Tallboy, 182
    Vintage Tallboy, 180, 181
Rolph, J.M., 183, *see also* J.M. Rolph Pickups

index

S

Seymour Duncan, 145–156, 214–220
   Alnico Pro II, 147, 149, 152, 154
   Antiquity/Antiquity II, **145**, 148
   Blackouts, 151
   Blackouts Metal, 151
   Blackouts Singles, 154
   Cool Rails, 147
   Custom, 150
   Custom Shop, 148
   Custom Strat, 152
   Custom 5, 148
   Custom 8, 151
   Dimebucker, 148, 151
   Duck Buckers, 153
   Duncan Custom, 150
   Duncan Designed, 148
   Duncan Distortion, 150
   Dyno-Sonic, 108
   Five Two Strat, 152
   Five Two Tele, 154
   Full Shred, 150
   Hot Jaguar, 155
   Hot Jazzmaster, 156
   Hot P-90 Soapbar, 155
   Hot Rails, 147, 153
   Hot Rails Tele, 155
   Hot Stack, 147, 153
   Hot Stack Tele, 155
   Hot Strat, 152
   Invader, 150
   Jazz, 149
   JB, 148, 150
   JB Jr., 147, 153
   L'il Screamin' Demon, 147, 153
   Li'l 59, **33**, 147, 153
   L'il 59 Tele, 155
   Lipstick Tube, 152
   Livewire, 148, 151
   Livewire Classic II, 154
   Livewire Metal, 152
   Pearly Gates, 147, 149
   Phat Cat, 155
   P-Rails, 148, 150
   P-90 Stack, 155
   Quarter Pound, 145, 152
   Quarter Pound Jaguar, 155
   Quarter Pound Jazzmaster, 156
   Quarter Pound Tele, 154
   Screamin' Demon, 147, 150
   Seth Lover SH-55, 147, 149
   Single Coil Stack, 153
   Stack Plus, 147, **147**, 153
   Stag Mag, 149
   Trembucker, 148, 151
   Twang Banger, 152
   Vintage Broadcaster Lead, 154
   Vintage Hot Tele, 154
   Vintage P-90 Soapbar, 155
   Vintage Rails, 153
   Vintage Stack Tele, 154
   Vintage Strat, 152
   Vintage 54 Tele, 154
   59 Model SH-1, 147, 149
Shaw, Tim, 74
Silvertone, see Danelectro
Smith, Paul Reed, 178, see also PRS
soapbar, see Gibson P-90
stacked(-coil) humbucker, 19, 47, 96, 135, 145, 146, 147, 171
Stromberg, 12

T

Tom Anderson Guitarworks, 34, 113–116
   Classic/Classic T, 113, 114
   H models, 114, 115
   M, 115
   P, 115
   S models, 114, 115, 116
   T models, **113**, 114, 115, 116
   VA, 114, 116
tone chart, 249
Turner, Rick (Alembic), 112
Turner, Rick (EMG), 156
TV Jones, 169–171
   Classic, 169, 170
   Classic Plus, 169, 170
   Dyna'Tron, 170
   English Mount, 170
   Magna'Tron, 170
   Power'Tron, 169, 170
   P'Tron, 170
   Super'Tron, 170
   TV-HT, 170, 171
   TV'Tron, 170

V

Van Zandt Pickups, 183
Van Zandt, W.L., 183, see also Van Zandt Pickups
Vivitone, 12

W

wax potting, 26, 41–42, 91
Wickersham, Ron, 111
WildeUSA, see Bill Lawrence
wire coating/insulation, 40–41, 71
wire gauge, 38, 40
wire wrap/wind/turns, 37–40, 44
Wittrock, John 'Bart', 180

Y

Ybarra, Abigail, 93

Acknowledgements

The author wishes to thank Joe Barden and Frank Troccoli at Joe Barden Engineering; Nate Riverhorse Nakadate; Jason Farrell and Mike Eldred at Fender Musical Instruments; Ari Surdoval and Ellen Mallernee at Gibson; Dana Lommen for his extensive research on pickup patent applications; Jason Lollar for both his interview and his added contributions to the knowledge; Michael Altilio, Larry DiMarzio and Steve Blucher at DiMarzio; Evan Skopp and Seymour Duncan at Seymour Duncan; David McLaren at BBE Sound/G&L Guitars and the administrators of guitarsbyleo.com; Scott Ferrara and James Kearney at EMG; Kent Armstrong; Rod Kelley at WD Music; and Scott Petersen at Harmonic Design. He would also like to thank his publishers, Nigel Osborne and Tony Bacon, Robert Webb for the meticulous copy-editing, Kevin Becketti and Mark Brend for promotions, and the entire team at Jawbone Press.